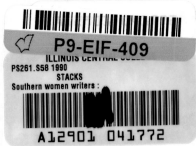

Southern Women Writers

**Illinois Central College
Learning Resources Center**

Southern Women Writers

The New Generation

*

EDITED BY

TONETTE BOND INGE

THE UNIVERSITY OF ALABAMA PRESS

TUSCALOOSA & LONDON

Copyright © 1990 by
The University of Alabama Press
Tuscaloosa, Alabama 35487

Manufactured in the United States of America

∞

The paper on which this book is printed meets the minimum
requirements of American National Standard for Information
Science-Permanence of Paper for Printed Library Materials,
ANSI A39.48-1984.

Library of Congress Cataloging-in-Publication Data

Southern women writers : the new generation / edited by Tonette Bond
Inge.
   p. cm.
  Bibliography: p.
  Includes index.
  ISBN 0-8173-0470-3 (alk. paper)
  1. American literature—Southern States—History and criticism.
2. Women and literature—Southern States—History—20th century.
3. American literature—Women authors—History and criticism
4. American literature—20th century—History and criticism.
5. Southern States—Intellectual life—1865– 6. Southern States in
literature. 7. Women in literature. I. Inge, Tonette Bond.
PS261.S58 1990
810.9′975—dc20   89-33863

British Library Cataloguing-in-Publication Data available

Designed by Laury A. Egan

Contents

*

Contents

Preface

*

THIS COLLECTION of fifteen essays constitutes an assessment of a new generation of Southern writers who are women. The Southern Literary Renaissance was initiated by a generation of principally male writers—William Faulkner, Thomas Wolfe, Robert Penn Warren, Allen Tate, John Crowe Ransom, Richard Wright—though Ellen Glasgow, Caroline Gordon, and Katherine Anne Porter can surely be numbered among this group. The next generation included some highly talented women—in particular, Eudora Welty, Flannery O'Connor, and Carson McCullers, all of whom have received extensive critical attention.

Since World War II, another generation of Southern writers to come to maturity has been dominated by women, a fact substantiated by the table of contents to this volume. The writers discussed here are not exhaustive of those who could, or even should, be included in such a collection. All the writers included here have published their significant works since World War II; all were selected as among those likely to achieve recognition beyond any immediate popularity. But all continue to write; their oeuvre is not complete. Thus, the principle for selection cannot be canonical. The collection makes no pretense at being anything more than a collection of essays about important Southern women writers who have been writing in the last half of this century. Even the selection criterion of Southernness is a tricky one: the women writers here treated live or have lived for some significant period in the South, and the South figures as place in their works. Doris Betts's introduction to the collection treats the reader to a writer's view of the whole question of Southernness and of the significance of contemporary Southern women writers whose careers are still unfolding.

The contributors to the collection, themselves representatives of a new generation of women critics, have included in each of their essays a survey of the writer's career, a critical assessment of her work, and some treatment of her relation to the Southern literary tradition. Beyond these general guidelines, the organization of the essay was left to the contributor, as was the treatment of feminist themes within the context of the Southern tradition. A bibliography of primary and selected secondary sources for each writer is included at the end of the essay. The book is but a beginning toward the evaluation of a number of important contemporary women writers who promise to maintain and contribute to the continuing tradition of Southern letters.

All the essays in the collection are original. Some had their origins in the 1982 and 1983 South Atlantic Modern Language Association Special Sessions on Southern Literature by Women. All the essays have been updated to include new works and important critical pieces published through February 1988.

ACKNOWLEDGMENTS

M. Thomas Inge had a lot to do with the origins of this book: in 1982, he recognized that a collection of critical essays on the work of these significant Southern writers was overdue. I owe a special debt as well to several others for their help, suggestions, or encouragement: Judith Knight, Judith Wittenberg, Elsa Nettels, and Dorothy Scura.

Southern Women Writers

Introduction

*

DORIS BETTS

A SECRET MOTIVE behind sending us senior professors to evaluate the classroom performance of young teachers may be the hope that some stimulating error or new idea will reawaken the buried student within those of us who have suffered brain damage from prolonged faculty meetings.

Observing such a class recently, I was admiring a young colleague's morning energy when discussion turned to Walt Whitman and Emily Dickinson. The buried student in me woke up and sat forward, as I had just read Adrienne Rich's essay that calls these the two mid-nineteenth-century American geniuses, noting that Miss Dickinson had heard Mr. Whitman's poems were "disgraceful."

The freshmen began examining diction in two poems, Whitman's "Noiseless Patient Spider" and Dickinson's "The Spider as Artist." Soon their discussion began contrasting Whitman's expansive (and male) development outward into the universal and abstract ("catch somewhere, O my soul!") with Dickinson's verbal contraction to concrete (and female) brooms and Bridgets at home.

The buried student in me could hardly keep her right, teacher's-pet hand from flapping wildly overhead. Later I simmered with associations and should-have-saids: Pope's and Dryden's spiders and Simone Weil's soul—or Dickinson's, for that matter, as it closed her "Valves of attention like Stone." Don Marquis's Archy. Arachne. How about those convenient spiders that inspired Robert Bruce, warned Frederick the Great, and saved Mohamet in the cave? (With the possible exceptions of Arachne and Weil, none of these ever swept down a web from that ceiling corner where, wrote Dickinson, it would eventually swing "fearless" when the housewife had become a corpse.) But if Shakespeare's wanton boy-gods kill us like flies for their sport, does Katherine Mansfield's "The Fly" merely shrink that same theme to domestic and concrete? Is Dickinson's "I Heard a Fly Buzz When I Died" further female shrinkage?

What Norman Mailer called "the profound materiality of women" is sometimes expressed as abstract versus concrete, large versus small thinking, sometimes as personal versus impersonal reaction. Mary Ellman, told that women, when disagreed with, always react by getting personal, responded, "If I were willing to play that game, which I certainly am not, I'd say men get *im*personal. If you hurt their feelings, they make Boyle's Law out of it."

As to Whitman's journalism and carpentry versus the brooms and Bridgets of Amherst, Eudora Welty ends *One Writer's Beginnings* by saying, " . . . I am a writer who came of a sheltered life. A sheltered life can be a daring life as well. For all serious daring starts from within."

It might seem that Welty and other established Southern women writers who have dared from within, such as Ellen Glasgow, Elizabeth Madox Roberts, Caroline Gordon, Katherine Anne Porter, Carson McCullers, and Flannery O'Connor, were not only of the right gender but were also born into the right geography; that generalizations about how Southern female writers emphasize the concrete in family and household might parallel certain generalizations about all Southern writing; and that below the Mason-Dixon, Ms. Brer Rabbit could be doubly at home in her true briar patch as last.

Sample generalizations about Southern writing are that it: distrusts the abstract; cares about time and place; is affected by religion; deals with the elemental; associates language with magic and incantation; explores the past, often within families; renders the natural world; and develops, among other themes, a sense of human limitation—not just housebound limitation but that philosophical limitation within which Glasgow's characters "may learn to live, may even learn to live gallantly, without delight."

Unfortunately, as there has been no common literary style or even content for these Southern women writers in these essays to practice, neither was there a monolithic South for them to be born into. C. Hugh Holman has called the South a union of opposites, of "calm grace and raw hatred, polished manners and violence," a region breeding both Thomas Jefferson and John C. Calhoun. In this Bible Belt lately turned Sun Belt, despite broad regional patterns, he always notes three subdivisions. The almost tropical Deep South (low country, Gulf Coast) is not quite the same South as the smoky blue hills of Appalachia; tidewater Virginia is not the industrial piedmont; Savannah and Charleston resemble each other more than metropolitan Atlanta; and

the Mississippi Delta, pine barrens, and rugged hills have not historically melded into a unit that locates Barry Hannah comfortably across
the same literary backyard as Walker Percy, anymore than gender alone
puts Doris Lessing down the sorority hall from Judith Krantz.

After allowing for three sub-Souths—the coastal/plantation South
with its claims to aristocracy; the piedmont red-clay South full of yeo-
man farmers and blue-collar workers; and the mountainous South, always less Confederate, its industry and mining mixed now with tourist
trade—literary critics since the sixties have needed to allow further for
reinterpretations of all three Souths by black and female natives who
have no taste for watermelon and no balance atop pedestals.

This long second look at the South by descendants of slaves, belles,
Snopeses, etc., sometimes produces fictions in which the grandchildren
of earlier fictional characters seem resurrected to star in transformed
books of their own—the way Alice Walker's Celie endures directly, for
herself, far worse experiences than Dilsey Gibson observed on the
fringes of Faulkner's Compson family. Updates occur in both regional
and gender-based novels. Mary McCarthy's reticent Lakey returns to
inhabit a full and unabashedly celebratory novel of her own in *Ruby-
fruit Jungle* by Rita Mae Brown (who grew up in Florida) or to live
more candidly in novels by North Carolina native Bertha Harris. Hes-
ter Prynne could not run away, but Anne Tyler's and Elizabeth Spencer's and Gail Godwin's women flee hometowns for less cause, though
their marks of home are not entirely erased. Margaret Mitchell (who
once called herself a "dynamo going to waste") provided in her white
myth *Gone with the Wind* a paradigm for the later black myth of *Roots*.
And, given longer wings across longer time, might Moll Flanders clap
them to applaud the airborne Isadora Wing?

Black and female writers are also reexamining biography. If the real
Nat Turner would have complained of his portrait by William Styron,
the real Zora Neale Hurston would like the way Alice Walker drew her.
As Faulkner used his great-grandfather as model for Colonel Sartoris,
and as the real W. O. Wolfe and brother Ben haunt Eugene Gant, remembered mothers and grandmothers get a second life in the fiction of
Wilkinson, Douglas, Godwin, Angelou, and Alice and Margaret
Walker. A boy who grew up to be Truman Capote appears as Dill in the
novel by his cousin Harper Lee. And biography acquires nuance and
warrants reconsidering when Joan Williams, in *The Wintering*, uses the
late William Faulkner as fictional character, much as Aline Bernstein
gave us a second look at Thomas Wolfe; Zelda Fitzgerald, at Scott;
Jean Rhys, at Ford Madox Ford; and Simone de Beauvoir, at Sartre.

"If one woman told the truth about her life," wrote Muriel Rukeyser in 1968, "the world would split open," but it hasn't yet, perhaps because whole truths are still in process.

While these re-visions show American literature and history through fresh eyes, poetry and fiction by Southern women and Southern men also see some subjects with equal clarity. Both, for instance, look keenly at "place," although Welty's place is now parked full of mobile homes, which are crammed full of televisions and plastic utensils, and although in modern Dixieland some of the "old times there" are being selectively forgotten by those writers benefiting less from total recall than from civil rights and the pill. Even so, well after Flannery O'Connor noted that the KKK was beginning to light its crosses with GE light bulbs, recognizable sub-Souths are still being rendered by these women writers: the Memphis of Giovanni and Williams; Welty's Jackson and Yazoo City, Mississippi; the southern Appalachia of Lee Smith, Wilma Dykeman, Harriet Arnow, Mary Lee Settle; Maya Angelou's Stamps, Arkansas (she lives now in Winston-Salem, North Carolina); the Mississippi Delta of Ellen Douglas and Ellen Gilchrist; and Sylvia Wilkinson's Durham County, North Carolina.

Some specific Southern places are viewed from the smaller "women's place" still located within them. Adrienne Rich's poem says to Emily Dickinson: "You chose to have it out at last / on your own premises." So have many Southern women writers: in the symbolic houses of Eleanor Ross Taylor and Nikki Giovanni; among the female-dominated families of Gail Godwin or Anne Tyler; through survivors in succeeding generations in Mary Lee Settle's Beulah Valley (Charleston, West Virginia); or inside the shaded houses of Harper Lee's small Alabama town, so much like Monroeville, where she still lives. Larger social issues of race, poverty, politics, violence, and religion are often viewed from parlor windows by such women as Abigail Tolliver, one of Grau's *Keepers of the House,* or in the end brought home to her Howland plantation by a mob that invades home property.

The training of these writers in how human conflict may be mirrored in family settings has been acquired firsthand. Many have married, borne, and reared children. For some, work and motherhood have produced periods of Tillie Olsen "silences," but these have delayed rather than prevented writing and publication; Ellen Douglas was forty when she published her first novel—about a family. Sometimes their house images stand for the female body itself. Even their single women protagonists, unlike Hemingway's male counterparts, have kinfolks. Like other Southern writers, these women are said to go back into the past for the stories of family members long since dead. However, inherited guilt more often frustrates those grandsons of slave owners and rebel soldiers than it seems to haunt these women writers or characters whose foremothers were field hands, farm wives, or beauty shop operators. Though Southern women writers are not blind to evil or irrationality, they are also less preoccupied by them than Robert Penn Warren or William Styron. Regional guilt over a morally unjustified war has become, since Vietnam, no longer regional. If anything, Southern women writers, as well as their female characters, keep tallying new guilts acquired near home since 1865, to distribute among those same guilty white Southern males who headed households. But there is growing emphasis, too, on what will result when all the old name-calling in these new accents is over. Black women writers, especially, want to move from yesterday to present opportunity. They also differ in a stronger sense of community than their Southern white counterparts, with a steady linkage of home truths and individual freedoms to their social and political consequences.

While place and the homeplace are still strong, each year female characters and their creators want, not rooms of their own, but even larger spaces. A number have escaped the house into careers: many of these writers, in fact, teach; and Gail Godwin, in *The Odd Woman,* has mixed her family microcosm with academia. Many other native daughters have, like Richard Wright, fled the South: Alice Walker, Katherine Anne Porter, Sonia Sanchez, Elizabeth Spencer, Maya Angelou, Lillian Hellman, Joan Williams. Some, like Angelou, who sees the South as a metaphor for racial bigotry but still a life-affirming force, have come back often to visit families or even to stay.

A few other patterns should be noted. Several of the older women writers were encouraged by literary prizes and publicity from *Mademoiselle* magazine, whose fiction editor used to be Georgia expatriate Margarita Smith, the sister of Carson McCullers. In later bibliographies, *Ms.* magazine more frequently appears.

Twain's gifts for storytelling and ironic humor plus a true ear for contemporary Southern speech are heard in the talents of Lee Smith. Other women who catch that daily cadence of ordinary conversation are Bobbie Ann Mason (Kentucky) and, especially for black youth, Toni Cade Bambara, who lives in Atlanta.

Religion seems less influential in the writing of these women than critics might predict, though its modifications (for example, the natural religion of Shug Avery in *The Color Purple*) contribute to a recurring thematic assertion that love, though it may not conquer all, is probably the best anodyne we have.

Three writers, Alice Walker, Shirley Ann Grau, and Anne Tyler have won Pulitzers. Walker's *The Color Purple* and Tyler's *The Accidental Tourist* have become highly successful films.

In addition to Southern patterns, can we test typical criticisms of women's writing against this group?

In *American Fictions 1940–80,* Frederick Karl criticizes contemporary female novelists' use of Edwardian models with little experimentation in structure or style. Other critics cite conservative poetic structures as well. Weak male characters are noted in both genres, though critics now admit that the American novel of the 1960s, reread, seems aggressively antiwoman. Specific books by women are said to rely on sensibility over plot, or to smother both in the narcissism of yet one more female's pilgrimage to self-identity. The critical version of that original Whitman/Dickinson contrast that began this essay is: that by reflecting accurately the daily restrictions of their actual lives, women write novels and poems that are insufficiently outwardly directed or socially conscious, and they conclude their stories with such tiny private victories of self-esteem for their heroines that plots diminish to trivial pursuits.

Possibly when more of us have gone on safari, we will set novels in the jungle, though even Isak Dinesen wrote of both Kenya and her house, emptied in the end "like a skull, a cool and roomy place to dwell in, with an echo to it." More important than instant defensiveness may be the commonality of "home" to both sexes in all latitudes. I also have great confidence in the lively change and growth already clear in the individual careers of the women in this collection and in new writers living in the region, such as Angela Davis-Gardner, Louise Shivers, Emily Ellison, Elizabeth Cox, Jill McCorkle, Mary Hood, Susan Ludvigson, and many others.

But in some ways Karl is right—we women novelists do not seem especially modern or postmodern. Like immigrants pushing wide-eyed off Ellis Island, some are still hollering, "Hey! We just got here!" But our depiction of male characters is improving faster for us than in reverse for today's male novelists. Marilyn French is not our sole model. Among others, Ellen Douglas, Elizabeth Spencer, Berry Morgan, and Sylvia Wilkinson have used males as narrators.

One can also point to examples of breadth and similarity. Settle populated her particular Yoknapatawpha across three centuries. Epistolary novels preceded both Alice Walker and John Barth.

If we are not as Whitmanesque as some might prefer, neither are we as restricted as clichés would have it. We have not all waited for Mr. Goodbar with our heads laid heavily in the oven alongside Plath's. Most of these women writers know very well who they are, thank you, and consider their imagined houses more as daily manifestations of reality than as refuges from reality. The advice in one Eleanor Ross Taylor poem is to "Stay here where the suffering's homemade, sure to fit."

Perhaps when our great-granddaughters are fabricating tales or spinning lyrics from their experiences, we may seem to them as quaint and constricted as Anne Bradstreet and Phillis Wheatley sometimes seem to us now.

But the root-bound are rising. Most have already exceeded the stage of self-identity. Frederick Karl also notes that "the novel of female experience, as we can already see in Didion, Oates and Morrison, will no longer be the separate body of material it was in the late 1960's and early 1970's." Distinctions of both gender and region are blurring, and Leslie Fiedler has already noted that, in the United States, geography is mythological, that all our novels could be classified as Northerns, Southerns, Easterns, and Westerns.

What other territory, then, will these "Southern" and "women" writers enter next?

In April 1984, novelist Daphne Athas (Chapel Hill, North Carolina) told a college conference on "Southern Writers and Feminism" that although "since Betty Friedan women have been speeding through the green light," nowadays most serious women writers, when asked if their work is feminist, will hedge. It is not de rigueur to nurture your sisterhood with Ti-Grace Atkinson or—on the other edge—with Phyllis Schlafly. The militancy is gone. She also has found Southernness to be out of vogue, lest any emphasis there might maintain a de facto minor league of letters. A second sex in a sub-South has troubles enough already.

What is essentially Southern among the younger women, Athas thinks, is not content or theme but the music of language still drawled in rhythm, still arranged in a particular way. That arrangement is becoming cooler and more underdone in a form of disguise known to all women, since the prose says one thing and means four, by implying dense, invisible secrets beneath the signs and allusions in the sentences. She calls Welty one of the experts of this method. Such indirection behind a mask of politeness has always functioned in the South; Athas cites Lisa Alther's distinction: "Northerners ignore you until they get to know you and then they ostracize you. Southerners bring casseroles until they get to know you and then they kill you." In Southern women's fiction, she thinks, any killing blows will arrive disguised, from ambush.

The women's "Southern" may offer one shift in theme—that thread of optimism previously mentioned. One sweet irony in Southern high school libraries, for instance, is that those white parents, who used to fear integrated schools might put their children in thrall to the rage of Eldridge Cleaver, now hope their children are reading such "positive" novelists as Ernest Gaines and Toni Morrison, who value family, duty, and love.

Though not uniform, such a positive streak in white and black Southern women writers is visible; it is also hard-earned, increasingly unsentimental, and rendered via Dickinson's concrete particulars. Some pragmatic affirmation of life even in the midst of death is implied—just as, in the South, women neighbors of all classes and skin colors still provide an avalanche of fried chicken and a flood of iced tea to those households where someone has died. In the future, when one and ten and many and, at last, nearly all women have told the truth about their lives, it may be that while part of that truth will indeed split open the world, another part may heal or at least try to do so.

Such insistence on the value of a love that keeps making an effort is already audible above our post–World War II battles between the sexes and races. Poet Josephine Jacobsen (Baltimore, Maryland) in "Breaking and Entering" presents a Catholic woman who feels simultaneously potent and humble when she breaks and eats the Host at Mass. She is mindful that every day God is also slowly eating her life substance away. Not only does the Eucharist enter her body with divine love, but human love has entered her flesh as well. Sometimes one or both of these loves have been able to show her the "green in the desert":

> She counts her life by such
> breaking and entering:
> understanding touch
> as central to God, man, woman.

Margaret Walker:
Black Woman Writer
of the South

*

JOYCE PETTIS

Margaret Walker is a writer who has never been separated for very long from her Southern roots. She is Southern not only because of her birth in Alabama but also because of her attitude toward the region and its people, particularly black people. She cherishes the beauty of the physical landscape but she decries the endemic violence, bigotry, and destruction there. Walker is a black Southerner whose ear for the distinctive rhythm of spoken words developed precociously. Her historical conscience was awakened early; its potential, coaxed and nurtured. Thus when she began to write professionally, the South and black Southerners were integral to her vision and were expressed through themes, imagery, and metaphor. The cadences of Southern speech, sermons, and Negro spirituals were already encoded in her mind, awaiting their transformation into art. Her work, therefore, is overtly Southern through her focus, attitude, voice, and sense of the past. To classify Walker as Southern, however, is not to suggest limiting her vision or her work, but to recognize what essentially propels them. Such recognition must extend to her family, for without their nurturing of her young talent and creative imagination, the poet, novelist, teacher, and essayist that Margaret Walker became might never have developed.

Walker's father, originally from the British West Indies, and her mother, a teacher of music, created a home environment that emphasized the rich heritage of black culture and inspired Walker's subsequent scholarship and creativity. She inherited her father's love of books and the spoken word, as she grew up listening to his sermons, as well as to narratives of slave life in Georgia, told by her maternal great-grandmother, who lived with the family. Walker finished high school in New Orleans, where the family had moved, and completed college studies in 1934 at Northwestern in Evanston, Illinois.

The thirties and the depression found Walker in Chicago, working on the WPA Writer's Project. She lived outside the South for almost ten years (except for visits) before reestablishing her life there. By this time, however, Walker carried the South within her. Her identity with the ways of her people—with their mannerisms, jokes, songs, tales, loves, and fears—had been well formed through both her home environment and living in Southern culture, and these ways constituted a richly complex reservoir from which she would draw the substance of both the poetry and the novel she wanted to write. The poems that she would write censuring the consequences of years of servitude, the notes of realistic protest that would distinguish her voice among other prominent voices of the 1930s were lying dormant, waiting to be activated. The nucleus of the award-winning novel that she would complete lay preserved in her memory to be nurtured over some thirty years, secured there by a grandmother who had wanted her granddaughter's spiritual growth to be informed by history.

Working with the WPA project in company with other writers, including Richard Wright, provided invaluable experience for Walker. "It was a wonderful time, and I was a very young writer then," Walker has said of those years, "but I remember the comradeship of the people on the project. It seems to me that was the wonderful thing."[1] During the thirties, Walker secured the poetic form she had been working to develop, began seriously trying to place poems in national publications, and wrote most of the poems that comprise *For My People* (1942), the book that established her literary reputation. The volume, including an introduction by Stephen Benét, won the prestigious Yale Younger Poets Prize when the poet was only twenty-seven years of age. Moreover, she became the first black woman so honored in national literary competition.[2] Clearly, then, Walker is classified among earlier Southern literary voices, such as Richard Wright, Arna Bontemps, Sterling Brown, Zora Neale Hurston, Eudora Welty, and Katherine Anne Porter.

Walker's inclusion as a member of the new generation of Southern women writers, therefore, may be questionable to some scholars. However, her rapport with younger writers, the appearance of a novel focusing on the survival and growth of a Southern black woman, her continual productivity, and the foresight that keeps her work reactive to emerging social conditions are substantial factors in her classification among a newer generation of Southern women writers. Her responsiveness to younger writers is symbolized by *Poetic Equation* (1974), a spirited and animated colloquy between Nikki Giovanni and Walker, two gregarious poets of different temperaments and ages. Indeed, the book originated from Walker's obvious rapport and bonding with younger and different writers.

The Civil War novel, *Jubilee* (1966), and two books of poetry, *Prophets for a New Day* (1970) and *October Journey* (1973), may be seen as the beginning of a second phase of Walker's career, for these publications locate her amidst a younger generation of writers, including Maya Angelou, Alice Walker, Sonia Sanchez, Shirley Ann Grau, and Elizabeth Spencer. Recently, the long-anticipated biocritical work *Richard Wright: Daemonic Genius* has been published, and a collected edition of Walker's poetry, *This Is My Century: Black Synthesis of Time,* including a previously unpublished group, is forthcoming. This continued literary activity is indicative of Walker's pace among the newer generation. Additionally, *Jubilee,* with its focus on a Southern black woman, secures Walker's position on the cutting edge of literary interest generated about black women characters. The poetry of the 1970s, although manifesting kinship with her earlier volume, is also responsive to emergent social conditions brought about by civil rights activities. Thus the tenor of Walker's poetry is consistent with the work of other poets of the decade, who are clearly of a different generation.

In considering her relationship to a younger generation of writers, Walker thinks first of age difference: "I recognize that I am a generation apart from them. Their boldness is not exactly what would have been boldness for me. I am sure people thought of me, when I was their age, as a bold new poet, but I am not at all certain that I had their kind of courage or even their kind of boldness."[3] Younger writers, however, have judiciously recognized the value of Walker's work to their own. Sonia Sanchez, for example, credits Walker, along with other writers, for helping to establish the tradition in which she has written: "Before me there was Brown, Walker and Brooks among others. Before them, there were others. Otherwise Sterling would not have been. You don't come out of a vacuum."[4]

Walker contributed to the earlier tradition of protest, realism, and rebellion, out of which *Prophets for a New Day* comes. In writing *Jubilee,* however, she becomes a primary forger of another tradition, out of which later black historical novels with women at their centers have come, such as Ernest Gaines's *The Autobiography of Miss Jane Pittman,* Shirley Ann Williams's *Dessa Rose,* and Toni Morrison's *Beloved.* Historical fiction structured in the same manner as *Jubilee* is also a vital precursor to complex, nonchronological approaches to Afro-American history, such as David Bradley's *The Chaneysville Incident,* John A. Williams's *Captain Blackman,* and Ishmael Reed's parody of the genre, *Flight to Canada. Jubilee* is precedent-setting black historical fiction.

Walker's tasks in the novel are to depict slave culture and Vyry, the protagonist, within a narrative that encompasses slavery, the war years, and Reconstruction. For Walker, the re-creation of slave culture with its folk beliefs and practices is the essence of the novel. Therefore, she enhances the folk concept by prefacing each of the fifty-eight chapters with proverbial folk sayings or lines excerpted from spirituals. Moreover, the narrative includes verses of songs sung by Vyry, her guardian, or other slaves; a portion of a sermon and the text of one of Vyry's prayers is printed. Slave children's rhymes, a conjure episode, and a catalog of herbs and their medicinal and cooking purposes are also included. More than physical setting and chronological time anchor this novel in the Southern experience of black Americans.

Black historical fiction was a sparsely used genre until the 1960s; only a few black writers had undertaken depicting the Southern black population during the slavery era and its immediate aftermath.[5] *Jubilee* is the first novel by a black author to depict extensively the slave culture from a daily perspective and to expose the havoc of the Civil War and Reconstruction on the black population. The novel, "a synthesis of folk tradition, imagination, and moral vision,"[6] focuses on the practical daily lives and survival of plain men and women instead of chronicling heroic feats of achievers such as Gabriel Prosser or Harriet Tubman. Thus it participates in revisionist social history. Moreover, it has the effect of reinterpreting a crucial period in the black experience, too frequently viewed with ignominy and humiliation. Exposing the realities of enslavement, Walker depicts its bitter cruelties for all the groups it touched, but particularly for black women. She reaches beyond enslavement and finds individualistic characters united by their desire for autonomy. Although the outlines of some stereotypes are visible (the extensive cast of characters necessitates that many of them must be types), they are personalized, rather than repugnant buffoons. Walker reaffirms the nature of the human spirit—even when the body is enslaved—to reject oppression and to effect change. Her confirmation that enslavement did not defeat the human spirit of her heroine, Vyry, is Walker's legacy to later female protagonists of historic fiction, including Miss Jane Pittman, Dessa Rose, and Sethe (*Beloved*).

Vyry's depiction within the daily working of slave culture is a necessary prerequisite to later fictional representations of enslaved women whose behavior, goals, or activities may be perceived as atypical or exceptional to enslaved women in general. Her characterization essentially balances that of other types of enslaved women and provides the fundamental model upon which they may be structured. She experiences all the pain, degradation, and loss common to slavery—orphaned at age two, victimized by a cruel mistress, denied the privilege of legal marriage to her children's father, offered for public sale, and flogged for attempted escape—but she endures and morally transcends. She is not destroyed by an environment with the capability for absolute destruction of morality and self-esteem. In short, Vyry's endurance, survival, and transcendence signals the potential of these realities for forthcoming portraits of slave women. Walker's depiction of Vyry offers a viable means for reinterpretation of the slave experience through gender.

When Walker committed herself to writing *Jubilee,* she also determined that the book would be realist rather than romantic. Therefore, she became a historian as well as a novelist, saturating herself in the antebellum, Civil War, and Reconstruction periods through history classes, reading, and research, including Southern historical collections and slave narratives. The research eventually extended to over twenty years, sandwiched between other obligations.

Walker has written of the ordeal of researching, writing, and living with *Jubilee* in a booklet titled *How I Wrote Jubilee* (1972); it is a narrative of perspiration and pertinacity in keeping a promise and attaining a goal. Moreover, it exposes the complications common to a woman writer because of gender, employment, marriage, and motherhood. In the years following her master's degree in 1940 from the University of Iowa, Walker accepted a college teaching position in North Carolina, married, and became a mother. In 1949, she and her family moved to Jackson, Mississippi, where she accepted at Jackson State University the teaching position that she retained until retirement. She continued her research through both the Rosenwald (1944) and Ford (1953) fellowships. Meanwhile, her family grew to include four children. Beset by illness and persistent financial pressures, for a seven-year period (1955–62), Walker wrote and published almost nothing, although she continued research for the novel. In 1961, she returned to the Writers Workshop at the University of Iowa and the next year began work toward completion of a doctorate degree, with *Jubilee* planned as her dissertation. She met degree requirements with the completion of the *Jubilee* manuscript in the spring of 1965.

The publication of *Jubilee* is evidence that Walker survived the "silences"[7] that often plague, limit, or terminate the literary careers of women writers. She has eloquently expressed her awareness of the trials that beset a woman writer in general and of black women writers and her own work in particular:

> To choose the life of a writer, a black female must arm herself with a fool's courage, foolhardiness, and serious purpose and dedication to the art of writing, strength of will and integrity, because the odds are always against her. . . . Sometimes the only quiet and private place where I could write a sonnet was in the bathroom, because that was the only room where the door could be locked and no one would intrude. I have written mostly at night in my adult life and especially since I have been married, because I was determined not to neglect any member of my family; so I cooked every meal daily, washed dishes and dirty clothes, and nursed sick babies.[8]

Even while Walker worked on the doctorate degree and *Jubilee*, she responded to the momentous social upheaval of the 1960s and wrote *Prophets for a New Day* (1970), her first book of poems since *For My People*. In structure and style, the poems of the second book are not remarkably different from those of the first. She retains what Blyden Jackson has called the "Whitmanesque"[9] method in stanza formation, and stylistically, the rhythmic cadence of the black Southern minister is apparent. More sonnets are evident in the first volume, however, than in the second. The second book, like the first, derives in large part from Walker's ethnic consciousness and her responsiveness to political changes directly affecting black Americans. The tonal difference between the two volumes primarily reflects the difference of political climate between the 1930s and the 1960s. Black people were passive in the 1930s rather than retaliatory, as in the 1960s. "We were apathetic, we were not militant, we were not altogether articulate," Walker has said of her perception of black people in the 1930s, but "in the Sixties Black people became very conscious, very articulate, very militant, very vocal. And all of the consciousness grew, and it has grown and continues to grow in the Seventies."[10]

Walker's voice, however, was loud among those articulating their dissatisfaction with the economic and political life of black Americans in the 1930s. Therefore, several of the poems in *For My People* protest the debilitating stagnancy in the political, social, and economic mobility of black Americans. She observes little in black life about which to write genteel or romantic poetry; thus the poems are characterized by direct, strong language, and realistic, accessible images and symbols. Some poems express raw rage at immobility ("How long since 1619 have I been singing spirituals?"), disgust with Southern living conditions ("moonlight hovered over ripe haystacks / or stumps of trees, and croppers' rotting shacks / with famine, terror, flood, and plague near by"), and enormity at the struggle still necessary to overcome ("The struggle staggers us / for bread, for pride, for simple dignity"). "We Have Been Believers" sardonically attacks blind faith as a contributor to nonproductivity and stasis. A different attitude, however, is recognized in the final stanza: "Now the needy no longer weep / and pray; the long-suffering arise, and our fists bleed / against the bars with a strange insistency."

"For My People," widely regarded as Walker's signature poem, contains the strongest demands for absolute change for oppressed black Americans. The nine stanzas or strophes of free verse—marked by parallelism, repetition of phrases, and paradox—are dependent upon the preemptory sentences of the tenth stanza for their completion and meaning. Meaning and form merge perfectly as Walker expertly sets out a panorama of the history of her people. As the speaker in each stanza telescopes a succinct vision of the black experience, the lenses freeze scenes that are representative of the multitextured collage of that experience:

> For my people thronging 47th Street in Chicago and Lenox
>   Avenue in New York and Rampart Street in New
>   Orleans, lost disinherited dispossessed and happy
>   people, filling the cabarets and taverns and other
>   people's pockets needing bread and shoes and milk. . . . (14)

Underlying the diction, absence of punctuation in word series, and the breathless tumbling of verbs and gerunds is the explicit meaning that, from a historical perspective, the frenetic efforts aimed at race "improvement" for the majority of the population have been futile and have resulted in appalling despair and disappointment. Disturbed by the plight of black Americans, the poet urgently speaks to them in this poem, graphically demonstrating that, historically, conditions remain largely unchanged. In eight short, strong, imperative sentences, the last stanza commands change that may have to be wrought through a "bloody peace." Knowing history, Walker also knows its resistance to change. Nothing less than another world and a bloody peace will effect the sweeping changes necessary.

In addition to the poems of protest, several poems communicate the poet's Southern ties. "Southern Song," "Sorrow Home," and "Delta" recall "For My People" in stanza format and use of parallel structure. In content, they recognize the South as home region. "Southern Song" and "Sorrow Home" are arresting in the poet's delicate balance of tension and lyricism. "I want my body bathed again by southern suns . . . / I want to rest / again in southern fields, in grass and hay and clover / bloom" (18) offers an example of the lush imagery of "Southern Song" and suggests the speaker's love of the Southern landscape. "Sorrow Home," too, communicates the speaker's reminiscence of things distinctly Southern—"I want the cotton fields, tobacco and the cane"—and rejects other places:

> I am no hothouse bulb to be reared in steamheated flats
> with the music of "L" and subway in my ears, walled
> in by steel and wood and brick far from the sky. (19)

Unfortunately, the beauty of the lyricism and pleasant memories is broken by the intrusiveness of stark reality in each poem:

> I want no mobs to wrench me from my southern rest; no
> forms to take me in the night and burn my shack and
> make for me a nightmare full of oil and flame. (18)

Eugenia Collier identifies "Delta" as the poem "that most completely exploits the motif of the South."[11] In this long poem, less lyrical but more assertive than the preceding Southern poems, the poet's message is precise: black Americans have lived miserably and labored for others in the Southland but reaped few rewards. However, "there is a new way to be worn and a path to be broken / from the past" (22). The realization crystallizes that the land belongs to its tillers, who "with [their] blood have watered these fields" and have earned their rights to it.

Although Walker emphasizes the spiritual links between black Americans and the South, she balances these ambivalent poems with others, such as "Dark Blood" and "How Many Silent Centuries Sleep in My Sultry Veins" (in *Prophets for a New Day*), that recognize Africa and the Caribbean as additional ancestral homes.

The ten poems of the middle section of *For My People* reflect the oral and folk traditions of Southern black culture. Writing in the tradition of James Weldon Johnson, Sterling Brown, and Zora Neale Hurston in drawing characters and speech from the Southern folk tradition, Walker offers ten folk heroes, among them, "Bad-Man Stagolee" and "Big John Henry," who had actually lived. Written in the "swinging ballad rhyme and meter" that "reveal a finely controlled and well-disciplined narrative technique,"[12] these poems offer broadly drawn portraits of men and women from the folk community, whose extraordinary lives or abilities incite awe and pride. One of the most engaging portraits in the series is "Molly Means," a ballad in which a conjure woman turns a young bride into a dog. The husband has the spell reversed on Molly, who subsequently dies. Her meanness, however, survives with her ghost; the ballad tells of the terror that Molly's ghost continues to inspire. These portraits confirm Walker's interest in and affection for her Southern roots and her affinity with the folklore of the region.

Only one poem, "Today," suggests that the poet's vision is not totally engaged by the black American experience. Here Walker foresees the imminence of World War II and decries the complacency with which the threat is received. Her fear is that Middle America, "complacently smug in a smug somnolescence" and occupied with petty concerns, is oblivious to the warnings rumbling in Europe. Beginning each stanza with "I sing," she effectively employs irony, for such images as "slum scabs on city faces / scrawny children scarred by bombs and dying of hunger," "wretched human scarecrows strung against lynching stakes," and "cankerous mutiny eating through the nipples of our breasts," images that offer no incitation to the beauty of song. The poet's hope is that the population will become aware of the imminently destructive situation.

Walker's second volume of poems, obviously kin to her first one in structure and tone, is also conceived with similar unity of design. The poems of *Prophets for a New Day* recognize, applaud, and eulogize those dedicating blood, sweat, and sometimes life to the destruction of racial inequity and injustice. Written during 1963 and called by the author her "civil rights poems," they record the history-making events and attitudes of that period. Only "Elegy" and "Ballad of the Hoppy Toad" are not inspired by the movement.

The unity of design—with the exception of "Elegy" and "Ballad of the Hoppy Toad"—is achieved by the development of the title, for the poems extol courageous leadership and the promise of a prophecy fulfilled. Employing her knowledge of the Bible, as she has done throughout her career, Walker constructs analogies between prophets of biblical times and old and new leaders in the history of the black experience. Moreover, the analogies are strengthened by her use of diction and imagery reminiscent of the language of the King James version of the Bible, as well as the undisguised rhetoric of a black minister in a Southern pulpit. "Ballad of the Free" pays homage to earlier advocates of freedom already preserved in history—Nat Turner, Gabriel Prosser, Denmark Vesey, and others like them—while "Street Demonstration" and "Sit-Ins" recognize the countless numbers of jailed civil rights advocates and the unnamed participants of the sit-ins. Martin Luther King, Jr., unidentified by name, is surely analogous to Moses leading

17

his people to the promised land in "At the Lincoln Monument in Washington August 28, 1963." "For Andy Goodman-Michael Schwerner-and James Chaney" recognizes the sacrifice and eulogizes the lives of the three young civil rights workers murdered in Mississippi. Many leaders/prophets are linked with specific Southern cities marked by racial unrest; "Micah," for example, evokes the memory of Medgar Evers of Mississippi.

The ambivalence that characterizes the poet's response to the South as one of the ancestral homes of black Americans in *For My People* is consistent in *Prophets*. In "Jackson, Mississippi," for example, the tension and violence in the city occasioned by racial unrest, its ugly and seamy side are juxtaposed with its physical beauty. However, since this city and others like it are repositories of black Southern history, black Americans can neither wholly leave it, ignore it, nor love it. Therein lies the ambivalence.

The vital elements of Walker's work—its identity with the South, its historical perspective, folk tradition, and racial themes—remain consistent in *Prophets for a New Day* as well as in the poems of *October Journey* (1973), a brief book (thirty-five pages) of mostly previously published poems. The title poem of the volume is notable for its thematic consistency with earlier ambivalent poems about the South. "October Journey," however, excels those earlier poems in its extravagant imagery of the physical appearance of the Southland in the fall, when the land is awash with warm autumnal colors. As in the earlier poems, landscape and memory change when reality intervenes and displaces the visual scene in the mind of the traveler.

The rigorous depiction of realism in the South and the demand for social, political, and economic changes for black Americans have been consistent characteristics of Walker's work. Her knowledge of tradition and history has constituted fecund sources from which she has extracted material for its transformation into art. Additionally, she has located her themes and insistence for change within a humanistic framework and within a tradition accessible to nonacademic as well as academic readers. But more than anything else, Walker has anchored her work in the love and experiences of her people.

Margaret Walker, Southern black woman poet and novelist, occupies a unique position in American literary history through her inclusion with two generations of writers. It is a well-earned position, however. Walker's work since the 1930s illustrates and confirms an unquestionable dedication to art, determination to survive as a writer, and refusal to be defeated by the "silences" that often have shut off women writer's voices. The second phase of her career, beginning with the appearance of *Jubilee,* affirms her commitment and perseverance. Since many of the pressures that have the potential for silencing have lessened during Walker's lifetime, readers can anticipate that her voice will continue to be raised strong and vibrantly among the current generation of Southern women writers.

MARGARET WALKER BIBLIOGRAPHY

NOVEL

Jubilee. Boston: Houghton Mifflin, 1966.

POETRY

For My People. New Haven, Conn.: Yale University Press, 1942.
Prophets for a New Day. Detroit: Broadside, 1970.
October Journey. Detroit: Broadside, 1973.

CRITICISM

"New Poets." *Phylon* 11 (1950): 345–54. Reprinted in *Black Expression,* ed. Addison Gayle, 89–100. New York: Weybright and Talley, 1969.
"Black Writer's Views on Literary Lions and Values." *Negro Digest* 17 (1968): 23.
"The Humanistic Tradition of Afro-American Literature." *American Libraries* 1 (October 1970): 849–54.
"Richard Wright." In *Impressions and Perspectives,* ed. David Ray and Robert M. Farnsworth, 47–67. Ann Arbor: University of Michigan Press, 1973.
"Some Aspects of the Black Aesthetic." *Freedomways* 16, no. 2 (1976): 95–102.

NONFICTION

"Willing to Pay the Price." In *Many Shades of Black,* ed. Stanton L. Wormley and Lewis H. Senderson. New York: Morrow, 1969.
Poetic Equation: Conversations between Nikki Giovanni and Margaret Walker, ed. Paula Giddings. Washington: Howard University Press, 1974.
"On Being Female, Black, and Free." In *The Writer on Her Work,* ed. Janet Sternburg, 95–106. New York: Norton, 1980.
Richard Wright: Daemonic Genius. New York: Dodd, Warner Books, 1988.

Montani Semper Liberi:
Mary Lee Settle and
the Myths
of Appalachia

*

JEAN HASKELL SPEER

WHEN I told a colleague of mine I was writing a study of Mary Lee Settle, an Appalachian novelist, he smiled sardonically and asked, "Is she one of those writers who depicts the quaint folks and curious customs of Appalachia?" Knowing he was a native of the eastern Tennessee mountains, I smiled back, aware of the sources of his sarcastic undertone and cynical attitude. He had seen too much of the mythology about his Appalachian homeland created and perpetuated by writers. Happily, I was able to tell him Settle was "not one of *those* writers about Appalachia."

For the most part, Appalachian literature has not fared well in critical esteem, often regarded as "a poor but eccentric relation of the rest of the South and in anthologies passed off with a tall tale or two and a story illustrative of local color."[1] To label a writer "Appalachian" may yet carry stigma. But in recent years, the body of good Appalachian writing has grown, interest in Appalachian literature has increased, and literary critics have sought new approaches for assessing the place and value of this frequently ignored regional literature in the spectrum of American literature.[2]

From the earliest American literature to the present, Appalachia and her people have generally been overromanticized or much maligned (frequently both at the same time) by hosts of novelists, poets, historians, and journalists. Turn-of-the-century literature about Appalachia, mostly written by nonnatives, portrayed the mountains and mountain people as simple and romantic, a "strange land inhabited by peculiar people," the stuff of myth. And the myths grew. Mountaineers were pure Anglo-Saxon stock. Mountaineers were "our contemporary ancestors," isolated from the rest of the world and living a pioneer life-style, while the rest of America moved forward progressively. Mountaineers were, in fact, resistant to progress, a resistance arising from ignorance, tradition, stubborn pride, a zeal for individual liberty bordering on anarchy and certainly leading to violence. In the inconsistency of myth, mountaineers were not only resistant to change but were passive in the face of any change foisted upon them, a passivity born of ignorance, indolence, and bizarre religious beliefs based on superstition and fatalism.[3]

Over time, the media for public consumption of Appalachia changed; the myths remained. Newspaper accounts, cartoon characters, films (from D. W. Griffith's *The Mountaineer's Honor* in 1909 to *Deliverance* in 1972), and television shows (from the "Beverly Hillbillies" to the "Dukes of Hazzard" to "Night Court") perpetuate the myths that Appalachia is either the home of an idyllic folk culture or a deviant subculture or both, neither able to cope with the modern, industrial world.

A current crop of native-born writers of fiction and nonfiction, among them Wilma Dykeman, David Whisnant, Jim Wayne Miller, Fred Chappell, Lee Smith, Gurney Norman, Denise Giardina, and Mary Lee Settle, say, "Enough is enough!" They are producing a body of writing in which they examine the complexity and causes of Appalachia's perceived "otherness." Cultural analyst David Whisnant observes that

> to this day there are a thousand people who "know" that mountaineers weave coverlets and sing ballads for every one who knows that millions of them have been industrial workers for a hundred years, have organized unions and picketed state and national capitals in pursuit of their constitutional rights, and have laid their bodies in front of strip-mine bull-dozers and overloaded coal trucks. Or that, today, they shop at the K-mart and Radio Shack, drive Camaros, and watch as much television as people anywhere.[4]

Mary Lee Settle is an Appalachian writer who knows and writes about both the mythology and the reality of Appalachian life.

Mary Lee Settle is an Appalachian writer by accident and by choice. By accident of birth, she is a native of West Virginia, where the heart of Appalachia beats. West Virginia is the only state whose boundaries fall entirely within the Appalachian region. It is rightly called "the mountain state," with an average elevation of fifteen hundred feet, higher than any other state east of the Mississippi. West Virginia supplies half the nation's coal (and Settle's family has longtime mining interests) and yearly hosts more folk festivals than any other Appalachian state. The state motto—*Montani Semper Liberi* (Mountaineers are always free)—expresses a belief, inherited from West Virginia's earliest settlers, that freedom is a state of mind. But it is a mental landscape inexorably linked to the physical landscape of the Appalachian mountains.

By choice, Settle explores the Appalachian geography of land and mind in the writing she has produced over the past thirty years. Critical responses to Settle's work place her within the "canon and character" of Appalachian literature described by W. H. Ward as "writing about the Southern mountains or writing which can plainly be shown to bear the impress of those mountains and the kinds of life they have nurtured."[5] Critics praise Settle for her "fine feeling for the geography of these hillsides," "for knowing her land and its people well and using this knowledge effectively," for "exploring the psychology of the mountain man."

But beyond these general statements, most critics have not assessed Settle's real achievement in capturing and finally understanding the elusive and complex saga of Appalachia. Settle knows that the history of Appalachia has been a history of economic and political struggle and of contested cultural space. A major stumbling block in the rest of America's relationship to Appalachia has been that perceptions of the region have rarely matched the economic and cultural realities of the region. The exploration of perceptions is Settle's central interest.

Although Settle's chosen genre is the historical novel, she is less interested in getting historical facts straight (though she does this with precision) than she is in discovering perceptions of historical events and the effects of these perceptions on the present. As T. S. Eliot, one of Settle's literary mentors, would say, she writes "not only of the pastness of the past, but of its presence."[6]

Settle herself consistently echoes this description of her purposes in interviews spanning more than twenty years. "In my historical writing," Settle told one interviewer, "I am concerned with what people thought was happening during the times they lived in, rather than what historians tell us was really happening."[7] She believes these perceptions of historical happenings enter family and national tradition through the inherited opinions, colorings, prejudices, and habits that censor history and become a shared mythology about the past. In a 1980 interview, Roger Shattuck asked Settle, as a West Virginia writer writing about West Virginia, how much of her material came out of family lore, grandparents' stories, and oral history. She replied: " 'Some of it naturally. But I knew that I'd been told myths, and I've distrusted them since I was tiny.' "[8]

This skepticism in her writing helps us understand mythology in and about Appalachia by explaining the dendritic patterns of its taproots and growth. Granville Hicks concludes that Settle is seeking the truth behind the myths, "writing not out of nostalgia but out of a passion to understand how things happen to be the way they are."[9] Settle does not romanticize the Appalachian past nor its cultural life, as so many writers have done over the years. She explores the past with the cold clear eyes of a seeker of wisdom and truth, believing this is the hope for the future of Appalachian America.

This passion to understand the past as prologue infuses all of Settle's major work, from her nonfictional account of the 1925 Scopes "monkey trial" in Dayton, Tennessee, to her exploration of the condition of exile in contemporary Turkey in *Blood Tie*, for which she won the 1978 National Book Award, to her most recent novel, *Celebration* (1986), called "something of a *tour de force*" by one reviewer.[10] But nowhere is her passion to understand so powerful as in her Appalachian opus, "The Beulah Quintet."

Critics have been slow to pay attention to Settle's individual novels or to her major body of work over the last thirty years. George Garrett notes that even fairly recently Settle was called an "unknown," an obscurity he blames on lack of support by her publishers rather than any deficiency in her accomplishments.[11] As recently as 1980, Garrett wrote that Settle's work "waits to be properly studied and appreciated."[12]

This critical void has begun to disappear, however, with a flurry of studies beginning in 1982. In that year, William J. Schafer wrote a sharply critical review of the Beulah Quintet, and in 1984, Jane Gentry Vance wrote an essay in which she explored Settle's theme of public issues emerging from private minds throughout the quintet.[13] In 1983, Nancy Joyner published an interesting essay on the connections between class and clothes in the five novels.[14] The most consistent critical voice has been Joyce Coyne Dyer, who has written about Settle's *Prisons,* the first book in the quintet; *The Clam Shell,* an early novel; and the influences of Settle's World War II experiences on her writing.[15] But Settle's significant contribution to our understanding of that complex place and intellectual construct called Appalachia has yet to receive appropriate attention. This is the subject of my essay.

In this essay, I review the five novels of the Beulah Quintet, summarizing the salient plot and character elements that help us understand the Appalachian past and present. I review critical reactions to Settle's work and provide an assessment of the place of her work in the literature of Appalachia. I hope to convey what I believe is Settle's major artistic achievement.

Through the Beulah Quintet

When I read the first book of Settle's Beulah Quintet, I embarked on a journey that took me from seventeenth-century England to the frontier of Virginia before the American Revolution; from West Virginia on the eve of the Civil War to the mine wars of the Appalachian coalfields in the 1920s; and, finally, to contemporary, suburban West Virginia. As one who has spent much of my life trying to understand and teach and write about the complexities of the Appalachian region, I realized how evocative and provocative a guide Settle had been on the journey, how much more I understood of Appalachian experience, and how much I enjoyed the circuitous routes to our destination.

Circuitous indeed! The conclusion of the last of the five novels is really the beginning of the entire quintet. The final section of *The Killing Ground* (1982) is entitled "The Beginning, 1960–1980" and carries this quotation from Joseph Conrad's *Lord Jim:* "Once some potent event evokes before your eyes the invisible thing, there is no way to make yourself blind again." An admirer of Conrad, Settle confesses that her books "have always begun with questions, appearing as images, as visions."[16] Once she has seen the compelling image, the potent event, she becomes obsessed with knowing "why things happen to be the way they are."

The vision that spawned the Beulah Quintet was one stranger hitting another in a drunk tank on a Saturday night. In the final novel, this vision becomes the killing of a Canona (presumably Charleston), West Virginia, playboy elite by a "hillbilly" as the result of "fight night on a sweet Saturday" (the original title of the novel). Hannah McKarkle, Settle's alter ego in the novel, is the dead man's sister and a celebrated writer living in New York. Not satisfied with any easy explanations, she has written the Beulah novels, spanning three centuries, to find out why her brother Johnny died and what forces led to a seemingly casual act of violence in an Appalachian jail.

When Hannah returns to West Virginia on a final quest, her childhood friend chides her: " 'What are you trying to find out, Hannah? Same old things? Just what is it you're trying to do? Still chasing

Johnny while the world goes to hell in a handcart? You think we're disintegrating? What did you call it once, the senility of the century?' "[17]

Furiously, Hannah replies: " 'To hell with the century. I'm trying to find out what lay behind one act of violence, the fist of one man hitting a man he didn't know. You say it doesn't have anything to do with what's going on. It's the goddamn center of it, one fist, one man, one act' " (53).

Going to the jail to confront Johnny's killer, Hannah knows what she will find—"a shirttail hill boy, slim and mean as a rattlesnake, a Saturday-night hell-raiser, car-roller, nigger-hater, tire-stealer . . . my feral twin from the underbelly of the Republic, White Anglo-Saxon Protestant, Quantrill raider, Indian killer, a Dalton Boy, a bushwhacker, agate-eyed wildcat" (235). Hannah knows the mythology of Appalachia well. Physically, Jake Catlett does not disappoint her. But as Hannah questions him about her brother's death, she unleashes a hatred steeped in beliefs as deeply held and keenly felt as her own.

When Hannah accuses Jake of striking out blind at an anonymous enemy, Jake corrects her with clarity and force. " 'I seen him standin' before he fell and he looked kind of surprised. Then he said, "Thank you." He said a real quiet thank you, and just sighed down on the floor and hit that iron rack. Jeez Christ, I hated him when he said that, that thank you, lording it over a goddamn drunk tank. I never hit him hard. Just blowed off the last of my steam. I figured he was makin' fun of the rest of us' " (237). The floodgate opened, Jake spills out for Hannah a tragic, personal history of land, health, jobs, pride, and dignity lost over the years to those of her class in West Virginia. Hannah mutters, " 'We didn't know' " (241).

Jake reassures himself that " 'we're good people . . . come from upriver, up around Lacey Creek' " (239), reminding Hannah of their distant kinship and their shared heritage of the Beulah homeplace. Shared heritage, shared family, shared land—all the ties that should bind have not been able to heal the wounds of shared misunderstandings that have sundered them. They shout at each other the epithets of class division. Jake accuses Hannah of " 'layin' under a tree like hawgs eatin' chestnuts and never look up to see whar they come from' " (241): " 'They ain't a damn thing, ain't even that dress on your back didn't come off the coal-face and don't forgit it. You people puttin' on to act high and mighty . . .' " (239). Hannah yells back, " 'You talk about us not giving a damn. You people won't walk across the hollow. Let people ride roughshod over you and you just back a little further up your hills and whine because you haven't real guts enough . . .' " (244).

Hannah stops, finally seeing herself and Jake and her brother Johnny not as strangers but inextricably and paradoxically bound to each other: "We faced each other, the razorback bone of the country, me stripped from the topsoil of training down to rock pride. If it was kinship that held me there, stark-stiff with the whole mess, the crisscross hatreds, if it was brothers, I had more of them than a dog had fleas, a whole hard valley of brothers" (244). Hannah begins to see, though darkly, that Jake and her brother Johnny and all of her other brothers in that hard valley had been willing to pay a dear price for freedom. Getting drunk for one sweet Saturday night of freedom from his troubles, Jake strikes a killing blow, also for a kind of freedom, that puts him in the prison cell where Hannah now faces him. Her brother Johnny thanks Jake quietly for a final freedom from some prisons inescapable in his life.

Writer Hannah McKarkle and writer Mary Lee Settle passionately need to know: What is the meaning and price of freedom? Must freedoms so desperately sought in acts of rebellion inevitably lead to imprisonment of one kind or other? What surged into the accumulated power of a single blow on a Saturday night in the mountains of West Virginia? How did it all go so wrong?

To find the answers, Settle originally wrote a trilogy, supported in her work by a Guggenheim Fellowship. Like Aeschylus and Sophocles, she seemed to believe that questions of individual freedom versus the collectivity of civilization, whether in Greece or Appalachia, demand a complex, cyclical treatment. Settle knew she could not answer her questions in a single, contemporary novel: "I had to go all the way back, as it turned out, to one lone woman lost in a wilderness in 1755."[18] Even her trilogy, *O Beulah Land* (1956), *Know Nothing* (1960), and *The Killing Ground* (as *Fight Night on a Sweet Saturday,* 1964) proved insufficient: "A whole part of our being as Americans was missing: our revolutionary sense."[19] In her archaeology of rebellion, Settle went digging in seventeenth-century England.

Prisons: The Prologue (1645–49)

In a manner that is typical of the intricate tapestry of her work, Settle found the clues for *Prisons* (1973), the first book of the quintet, while writing her nonfictional account of the Scopes evolution trial. Researching the involvement of the American Civil Liberties Union in the trial, Settle learned that the ACLU had taken its motto from the words of John Lilburne, a seventeenth-century Puritan martyr who kept on preaching individual freedom even as he was being flogged through the streets of London. "Freeborn John" Lilburne, initially an officer in Cromwell's parliamentary army opposing Charles I, resigned in 1645 rather than subscribe to a covenant with Scotland to reform the Church of England along Presbyterian lines. From then on, Lilburne became a leader and master propagandist of the Leveler party, demanding religious liberty, the extension of suffrage to craftsmen and small property owners, and complete equality before the law. Lilburne championed natural rights over common law, insisting that

> what is done to any one may be done to everyone; besides, being all members of one body, that is, of the English Commonwealth, one man should not suffer wrongfully, but all should be sensible, and endeavour his preservation; otherwise they give way to an inlet of the sea of will and power, upon their laws and liberties, which are the boundaries to keep out tyranny and oppression; and who assists not in such cases, betrays his own rights, and is overrun, and of a free man made a slave when he thinks not of it, or regards it not, and so shunning the censure of turbulency, incurs the guilt of treachery to the present and future generations.[20]

Because of his passion for freedom, Lilburne spent most of his life in prison.

Led by Lilburne's words, Settle found the potent event necessary for the beginning of her roman-fleuve:

> Lilburne led me to a churchyard in Burford, near Oxford. I noticed that there were pockmarks on the stone wall of the church, in two lines, one at head level and the other above it. I knew at once that men had been shot against the wall and that some of the firing squad had shot over their heads. I had literally walked into my story—the story of two rebels, Johnny and Thankful, and of Oliver Cromwell, whom I use as a major character. That book was *Prisons,* the first volume of the quintet, written and published [1973] after the trilogy.[21]

In *Prisons* (published in England in 1974 as *The Long Road to Paradise*), young Johnny Church, a rather ordinary son of a commoner-become-gentry, makes a choice for freedom. His choice leads him, like Antigone, to inevitable doom. During his childhood, Johnny lived in awe of his wealthy cousins at Lacey House, where he often heard political arguments charged with a force he did not fully understand. Bitter words about Scots, commoners, protecting investments in the New World, the Parliament, even King Charles.

At Oxford, young Johnny is introduced to the "democratical notions" of Lilburne and others—" 'Twas not only newfangled notions, but words too, words that rolled and tumbled through us in a new way, as we took to the heady speech of the new dangerous men."[22] As the Civil War between Parliament and the king intensifies, Johnny is called home from Oxford by a protective father worried that the "wild-worded rabblerousers" will "turn everyone against all the nobility and clergy and gentry in the land and destroy the monarchy itself" (48).

On the morning of Johnny's sixteenth birthday in 1645, Johnny's growing democratical notions force his hand. Charity and Lazarus, the peasant servants who had taught Johnny to see strength in the land and dignity in toil, face the dreaded "enclosure," the loss of their homes and the commonly shared land on which the crofters had lived for generations. It was these enclosures in England and Scotland that started the migration of many families who would ultimately become Appalachian settlers. Johnny says incredulously: "My father had decided to flood their village to make a lake and enclose the common up to Henlow Wood to run his deer. He had looked out one morning and found the village an offense to his eyes. There were only five squat houses in the way of his plans for a fine vista in the Italian manner" (49). In succeeding generations, the plain folk of Appalachia would continue to be "in the way of . . . plans" of others.

Shattered by his father's indifference to the common people who worked his land, Johnny chooses his first act of conscience—he refuses to show deference to his father, refuses to "doff his hat"—and in that gesture sparks a rebellious spirit that will span the generations through five novels. As Joyce Coyne Dyer observes, a central principle in Settle's historical theory is that "civil wars arise not from isolated events or decisions of kings and great men, but, rather, from anger, outrage, and tension within individuals and families."[23]

Disinherited, Johnny joins Cromwell's parliamentary army in its march aginst the king. He is befriended by Thankful Perkins, of the clear eyes and clear vision, and Gideon McKarkle, a Scot, enclosed off his Highland croft and now a pawn among the clashing armies of the night. Free to believe, to speak, to act, most for the first time, the ragtag army sees their hopes for freedom raised, only to be betrayed by Cromwell. As Johnny sadly observes, "The danger of the democratic way is that men are courted, instead of being honored, one by another" (155). But Gideon and Thankful and Johnny have come too far, have lost too much, to turn back. Gideon and Thankful and Johnny must die or betray conscience.

Cromwell offers Johnny his freedom if he will but speak his dissent and become contrite. Like Antigone confronting Creon, Johnny's silence speaks: "There are no more words, only the turning of the wrist, the dropping of the dirt on the dead, obscene face; I did not know before how inevitable the choice, how perpetual is the taking place of the thing, the ever asking of the question, the ever turning answer" (195).

Imprisoned in Burford church, awaiting execution, the condemned men argue and sob and talk of escape to freedom in Virginia. Johnny dreams and tells Gideon McKarkle, " 'I dreamed that all that sets men apart from the beasts is the act without hope of reward' " (206). As Johnny prepares to die, sustained by his dream, he nevertheless longs for someone to "speak a word. Hast forgot how to say no? Will no one cry cease?" (235). No one does. Johnny Church dies at twenty in the Burford churchyard where Mary Lee Settle found him three centuries later.

In Johnny Church's search for freedom, he comes to the conclusion that "freedom's no fine thing; it is as simple as the opening of a door, or a ceasing of persuasions upon you, or a blessing. . . . To bless and grant freedom are the same. We are in prisons of other men's beliefs" (204). For the descendants of Johnny Church (through his son by the mistress of Lacey House) and Gideon McKarkle, these words will reverberate from England to Appalachia. In her statement that "we are in prisons of other men's beliefs," Settle has encapsulated a dominant issue in understanding both the past and present in Appalachia.

O Beulah Land: The Promise (1754–74)

Although Johnny Church and Gideon McKarkle dreamed of freedom in Virginia, it would be left to their heirs to reach the promised land. Settle re-creates the trials and tribulations of the early settlement of Appalachia in *O Beulah Land,* a book critics have called "extraordinary," "head and shoulders above most of its contemporaries" that have "misinterpreted American history in recent years."

In the mid-1750s, the Virginia territory in America held the promise of freedom for some, imprisoning fear for others. Some, like Jonathan Lacey, came as planters or surveyors or officers in Braddock's army to tame the wild territory. Some, like the McKarkles, enclosed off their land in the Scottish Highlands, forced into Ulster to subdue the Irish, came lusting for land to call their own. For many others, the sea crossing to America was not a matter of duty or choice or desire:

> The convicts could not imagine the hot sun, never having felt it in their London hutches of cobble and damp. They knew only that picking tobacco leaves in the fields, after the uneasy pleasures of

the London streets, was in their world one of the familiar ways of dying. Virginia. The name was enough to shoot horror into the backbone of every convict aboard. Virginia, transportation to the plantations—next to death, the final punishment.[24]

Hannah Bridewell (named for St. Bride's Well prison in England) is one such "transportee," sent to America for whoring in London. Hannah, Johnny Lacey, Solomon McKarkle, and the whole polyglot of Europe and Africa pouring into America push their way into the Virginia wilderness to form improbable alliances.

The frontier has always been a liminal space, a place betwixt and between order and chaos, a threshold of expectations. The Virginia frontier, a land of wild beasts, wild savages, and endless mountains, fascinated and repulsed the early settlers. Those who still yearned for the "hairdressing, wig-combing, wit, heart, the fashion, the ton" (70) of England clung to the coast and were contemptuous of those who were compelled to go westward over the mountains. Beyond the Blue Ridge was bad enough; beyond the Alleghenies was unthinkable.

But for some, mostly those already fleeing one kind of contempt or another, the transmontane world held the promise of freedom and dignity derived from land and a chance for "democratical notions" to flourish. They were drawn to the mountains as if to paradise. The land was cheap; the price of freedom would be high.

This first Hannah (for whom Hannah McKarkle will be named in novel five) travels as servant to Braddock's army into the disastrous Battle of the Wilderness. As the army goes down to defeat, Hannah is taken captive by the Shawnee. Escaping her captors, Hannah makes her way, alone and terrified, through the mountain wilderness to the Virginia territory. *O Beulah Land* opens with the dramatic account of her flight. Near death, she is found by Jeremiah Catlett, the epitome of an early mountain man—a transportee who now lays claim to vast acres of land, an Indianized white man clad in buckskins and silence, alone in an endless wilderness sustained only by the bounty of the land and his belief in a fundamentalist New Light religion. Hannah, who seems to him a gift from God, joins Jeremiah in his solitary but sanguine existence. Jeremiah earnestly believes that " 'Gawd led me to this hyar valley. He meant it for me. Not that I deserve it. . . . But Gawd seed fitten to watch over me. He give me this hyar green pretty valley. I call it Goshen—the Land O'Goshen' " (186).

Too soon their solitude is broken by others led to the mountains by inspiration less divine. Jonathan Lacey, for his service in the French and Indian Wars, claims his bounty acreage of land and prepares to move his fashionable Tidewater family into the unknown. Aware that only a working community could stave off Indians, border ruffians, and "the war with the Elements," Lacey chooses his companions from the raggle-taggle Scots, Irish, Dutch (German or "Deutsch"), Dunkards and Quakers, American provincials and British, poised anxiously to move westward from such teeming river outposts as Brandon's Landing and Kregg's Crossing.

Lacey sizes up the possibilities with historical insight but with the consciousness of his class: the lowland Dutch and the highland Scots seem to make the best settlers, "bringing with them the self-reliance of people who are used to fending for themselves"; the Irish, poverty-ridden and too much ordered or "bossed," are useless, "like hound-dogs kept leashed too long, who turn to brainless cavorting beasts when they slip their lead"; the Protestant Irish "(they call themselves the Scotch-Irish) from the north of that island . . . are tough and self-reliant to the point of blind stubbornness" (256), carrying chips on their shoulders from religious persecution and the persecution of English law.

Lacey worries about the religious persuasions of the Scots—Presbyterianism—and of the northernmost and westerly English, "who are fine settlers, being used to small farms until forced out by so much enclosure" but who "tend to the new enthusiastic religions . . . that grow like weeds here among them" (257). Wisely, Lacey concludes that the interests of common problems "will outway religion [sic] scruple," that the great industry of these settlers "we had better to have with us than against us," and that, "in their favour, too great a class sensibility as among the English has not sapped their pride and turned it to Jealousy and Pretention" and "unbounded extravagance" (258).

Lacey populates his wilderness settlement with Carvers, Cutwrights, Catletts, Solomon McKarkle, Jarcey Pentacost (a printer), and the Lacey black slaves. (Their entwined descendants populate the remaining three novels of the quintet.) All believe the promise of Isaiah has been fulfilled: "Thou shalt no more be termed forsaken; neither shall thy land any more be termed desolate; but thou shalt be called Hepzibah, and thy land Beulah, for the Lord delighteth in thee, and thy land shall be married." So they call the Lacey settlement Beulah, and they are wedded to the land. Jarcey Pentacost tells Johnny Lacey prophetically, " 'Johnny, y'ought to be a proud man. . . . Ye've begun a dynasty in Beulah' " (303).

But Settle reminds us of the brewing troubles in paradise. Even at their far remove, the residents of Beulah hear of the growing unrest between the colonies and the English, who treat the Virginians "with

31

polite contempt." Closer to home, Johnny Lacey fears "some tumult," as wealthy land speculators purchase legal title to good bottomlands already claimed by sweat and toil and death, forcing "the poorer classes of settlers" into the hills. We hear in Johnny's assessment of the hill folk as "the poorer classes" grist for the mill of an already developing mythology about Appalachia in early America. But Johnny is one of the few of his class who feels sympathy for the mountaineer. " 'I am sorry for the people here,' " Johnny says, " 'to see the new land go in such large tracts. Some of them have waited long and patiently . . . and they seem to be poorly paid for their patience' " (255). The dispossession of the centuries continues.

Even closer to home, Johnny watches with growing concern the widening gulf between the stable and "civilized" Tidewater inhabitants, the Tuckahoes of Old Virginia, and the settlers of the Appalachian frontier, the Cohees of New Virginia, seen nowhere more clearly than in his own wife, Sally Brandon. A Tidewater Tuckahoe, she chafes under the lack of decorum and deference at Beulah and insults her husband and their small wilderness community. When it becomes clear that her daughter will marry the son of Hannah and Jeremiah Catlett, Sally Brandon is defeated: " 'That common lanky boy with them mountain eyes. . . . All them Cohees, common as dirt. . . . To think a daughter of mine should fetch up with such dirt as that' " (299). In Sally's words, the hillbilly stereotype is taking shape—the gaunt, unrefined mountaineer who is the symbolic dirt on which the ladder of social status rests but rises above.

As Jonathan Lacey prepares to leave Beulah for the House of Burgesses, his neighbors remind him to " 'stand bluff for New Virginia agin the damned Tidewater' " (328). Troubled, Lacey reflects on the promise and potential of the land called Beulah: " 'What can we become out here? We may have brought the virtues, but we've brought a cancer, too' " (233). Will "the skillful and industrious people we need . . . come to be looked down on and spurned because their ways are not ours? Back a man to a wall, with arrogance and contempt, and he strikes out blind in his roused pride" (232). Nearly two hundred years later, in the shadow of Beulah, two descendants of the whole panoply of Beulah settlers will play out Lacey's worst fears.

Know Nothing: The Kingdom of Kin (1837–61)

The cancer that Jonathan Lacey foretold has invaded the body of Beulah by 1837. The heirs have left the original homesite (now a much-mythologized "fort" in their minds) and established a river plantation

on the opposite side of the Kanawha River. They keep slaves for farm-
ing and Irish immigrants for operating the saltworks. The second
Gideon McKarkle of this quintet, unmindful of his family's sacrifices
for freedom at Burford and in taming the West Virginia wilderness,
runs a small inn on the plantation, cursing the "niggers" and foreigners
alike for the breath of disaster beginning to low over Beulah Land on
the eve of civil war.

Young Johnny Catlett, the third Johnny of the series and heir apparent to Beulah, is drawn like his predecessors to inevitable doom by the
gathering storm of irreconcilable political, social, and moral forces. As
he grows up in the novel, he struggles to understand his changing relationships with the black slaves he has loved and often admired, with
the upstart Irish immigrants, particularly the O'Neill clan, and with
the members of his own, now vastly extended kingdom of kin.

Beulah has become an asylum. "Cousins" of all the root-bound parts
of the family tree feed on Beulah like parasites—Catletts, Laceys, Bran-
dons, Cutwrights, Crawfords, and Kreggs. Even the high and mighty
Tidewater "connections," facing ruin in the economic panic of Andrew
Jackson's government, grudgingly look to their Cohee cousins at Beulah for help. Sally Crawford Lacey tells her husband as they travel west
to the endless mountains: " 'They won't let it happen . . . of course,
they're plainer people than we are, and haven't had our advantages, but
they're very kind . . . they are Virginians even if they are transmontane
and they're your kin, too.' "[25]

The Beulah kin try hard not to be transmontane, but to be genteel
Virginians with "connections" in an eastern Virginia contemptuous of
them. Cousin Annie, a Beulah parasite, points to the source of their defensive postures: " 'I always say as Papa did, the farther west you get,
the more people *care*. They're more Virginia than we are. . . . They
have to be. That's what Papa said. Though he never dreamed his own
daughter would end her days in Western Virginia. In Richmond we
never knew the western counties existed' " (306).

So the women of Beulah ape the fashion and the attitudes of the east
of Richmond civility. They "take the waters" at Egeria Springs resort
(the smelly sulfur springs of old Jeremiah Catlett's first wilderness
homestead), where they gossip and play brag, a ritual recital of family
genealogy, so " 'we can keep up the standard at least. Remember who
we are' " (307). The gentlemen of Beulah Land look on benevolently,
loose their passions on black slave women, and tell their sons, " 'Be
good to them. Poor innocent things. I've always taught you that, ain't
I . . . ? Women and niggers. They ain't fitten to look after themselves' "
(275).

The sons worry and marvel at the kinship and new politics that have brought together, by the 1850s, the interests of the Irish O'Neills, the eastern Kreggs, and the Beulah Catletts. Defending the platform of the Know-Nothing party,[26] Crawford Kregg argues with unrealized irony, " 'The foreign menace surrounds true Americans. . . . If your ancestors and mine, Johnny, could see the hungry evil-talking scum that inherit this fair land. Our forebears came here for freedom, not because they couldn't make a living, or were the spawn of foreign jails' " (272). And Dan O'Neill prophesies, " 'Folks here abouts are damn sick of talkin rum and niggers. They don't want no foreigners . . . we carried the western counties: they stuck together. Our turn's acomin. West Virginia' " (272). Both Johnny and Dan wonder if the railroad can be brought into Beulah Valley to reverse their crumbling fortunes.

Johnny Catlett is troubled by alarming new attitudes he does not fully understand, attitudes suggesting that slaves enslave their masters, that one man may rule over another to his own hurt. The McKarkles, "after all these years" at Beulah, move up into the mountains for " 'good land and not no niggers' " (184). They warn, Johnny says incredulously, " 'keep free of ownin niggers'—as if 'twas the whites that got freed after all' " (184). The McKarkles become "strange mountaineers." Tig, Johnny's slave and boyhood friend, pities Johnny: " 'I feel sorry for you. It's you got the burden—women and slaves . . . you ain't got no more freedom than we got. Tears, and people leanin on you— free, white, and twenty-one!' " (242).

"Backwoods" Beulah will not be spared the agony, ruin, or changing values that pit friends and brothers against each other in the cataclysm of civil war. The Catlett brothers themselves divide. Lewis Catlett cloaks himself in a stern religion, emulating his Beulah ancestor Jeremiah, and defies his family by ministering to the black slaves and ultimately joining the Union army. Johnny, escaping to the Kansas territory only to discover there is no escape from the country's turmoil, loyally returns to Beulah and family and the Confederacy for which he feels little commitment, only duty. He realizes he is among those men "fated to be the know nothings, to question, to see beyond their attitudes, but not to speak" (343). Impotent, all that remains is what might have been the prayer of Eteocles and Polyneices, "Oh, God . . . forgive us our sins and don't let me have to kill my brother" (344). Johnny Catlett leaves no heir.

The Scapegoat: Blood Sacrifice (1912)

As Johnny Catlett and Dan O'Neill had hoped in *Know Nothing*, the railroad came to Beulah. So did the foreigners they feared. So did the economy of the world. Beulah had been sitting on a coal seam waiting to unleash its terrible energy on the land and people. Mary Lee Settle has said, "In my series, the key scene is the discovery of coal in West Virginia. That changed the entire lives of everyone living there; it became a feudal coal culture, as it were."[27]

In June of 1912, Beulah is an armed camp, a Gatling gun on the porch of the family home and Baldwin-Felts detectives lurking in the shadows. The Lacey family's mine, Seven Stars, and most other southern West Virginia mines, are closed, the miners on strike. Miners are being evicted from their homes, the "transportation" (new immigrant miners) are railroaded in as hated strikebreakers, and threats of violence increase.

The Lacey branch of the family has reinherited Beulah, but Beverley Lacey is weak and dying in both body and spirit (the "cancer" his ancestor predicted). Lacey tries to protect "his miners," since they have been part of the family-owned mine operation for years (and some of them are, in fact, distant family kin). Beverley understands the miners, having worked the coal face himself on his father's orders—" 'no boy of mine is going to lay like a hog under a chestnut tree eating chestnuts and never looking up to see where they come from.' "[28] Beverley wants to negotiate, especially with his old friend and distant kinsman, Jake Catlett, a leader of the union miners. But Beverley and Beulah and the old verities prove too weak to withstand the violent changes about to occur, that will, quite literally, move mountains.

Divergent forces arrive at Beulah to escalate the strike and disintegrate the Lacey family fortunes. Mother Jones, eighty years old in black bombazine, frilly black hat, and lacy jabot, arrives to organize "her boys" and dramatize their resistance. Corporate giants, the likes of Pratt and Pierpont and Peabody and Rockefeller, arrive to buy up the land and the mines for development. The battle lines are drawn.

Beverley Lacey and his family function more as observers than actors in the drama unfolding all around them. Lacey says to himself, "When a man's fate has already been decided for fifty million years because his land happens to be over a seam of coal, he's licked before he starts. Coal and ideals. Goddamn both of them" (42). His wife, waiting for her husband to die, has headaches and retreats to her "sanctum sanctorum," the cupola room of the Beulah mansion. The Lacey daughters, Mary Rose, Althea, and Lily are in love—Mary Rose with herself, Althea with all the eligible young men, such as Dan Neill and Anderson Carver, and Lily with her liberal "movements"—women's suffrage, socialism, and improving the lot of the miners, particularly Eduardo Pagano, a young Italian miner.

In the end, it is only Lily who is able to act. When detective Captain

Dan Neill, humiliated by past political and financial scandal and now by Mother Jones, seeks revenge on Eddie Pagano, Lily spirits Eddie away on a freedom train to New York. Eddie escapes to a new life; Lily escapes the confinement of social convention in West Virginia, only to die in the war in Europe. For them both, for them all, an unknown, newly arrived Italian-born miner becomes the blood sacrifice, the scapegoat.

At the novel's close, Essie Catlett, Jake's wife, miner's wife, kin to the Beulah clan, moans: "They had killed a man and nothing was ever going to be the same. She could hear the change like a creek swell, flooding nearer and nearer, and all the former things were passed away. It wouldn't never be the same, not in her lifetime, never the same, never the same, she kept saying it over and over like a prayer . . ." (298).

Essie's unfortunate prayer is answered. Settle foreshadows the coal-field violence and destruction, both human and environmental, of suc-ceeding decades, particularly the mine wars of the 1920s. The coalfield struggles have become a popular subject in writing and media about Appalachia only recently, but Settle realized early the significance of and the need to understand the radical transformation taking place in Appalachia in the early days of this century. In *The Scapegoat,* she force-fully counters the view of local colorists that Appalachia has been an unchanging, nonindustrialized, quaint culture. It has been, instead, a place of blood sacrifice.

The Killing Ground: The End and the Beginning (1960–80)

Hannah McKarkle believes she is more like her dead Aunt Lily than her Aunt Althea or her mother, the social climbing Ann Eldridge. She, like Lily, left home for New York, left Canona, West Virginia, which has grown up and over Beulah Land. Like Lily, she has worked for causes, defending the UMW at New York dinner parties, campaigning for John F. Kennedy among the "hillbillies" of her home. Like Lily, she sees herself as Antigone, making a choice for freedom rather than se-curity.

Like Antigone, Hannah is obsessed with a duty to her dead brother, killed in a city jail. She must find out why his life meant so little; her quest gives meaning to her own life. She has written *Prisons, O Beulah Land,* and *Know Nothing* and is working on *The Scapegoat* when she comes back to West Virginia to tie up the loose threads of the story she has so carefully pieced together. The return to West Virginia reminds her of the night of Johnny's death, of her confrontation with Jake Catlett, the mountain boy who has killed him, and of her own decision for freedom—her refusal to replace her brother in the family's neatly ordered scheme. But hers is a bittersweet victory.

" 'Do you want to leave?' " Hannah's father asks when she refuses "to be needed at home." Hannah replies: " 'Whoever wants to leave home?' " (312). She wants to tell him that "we were made of people who for three-hundred years had left home because they had to, and who had to carry with them that sense of loss, all the way to the American soul, a black, tentative place in the spirit" (312). She now knows this is why her brother Johnny accepted death with a "thank you"—he had no place else left to go. Imprisoned by his mother's values—her foolish pride in a family heritage that, if the truth be known, had started with a London whore, included cruel oppressors of Indians and miners, "white trash," and exploiters of land and people—Johnny tried reckless living to break his dependency. But, as Hannah observes after his death, "impotent rebellion is a form of slavery" (159).

Although Johnny McKarkle never could act for freedom in his own behalf, he urged Hannah to " 'run for it, get in a little convertible prairie schooner and go West' " (159). His legacy to her, his desperate urging to rebel, to act, to search for the free frontier was a legacy of the centuries that epitomizes Settle's focus in the Beulah Quintet: "The model is Antigone, for all the principal characters. The oscillation between Antigone and Creon, between the settled and the wanderer, dreams and reality, gives the movement to all the volumes. It's the essence of democracy that Antigone and Creon are locked in endless conflict. They need each other. We need them both."[29]

Hannah's story comes to an end at the funeral of her Aunt Althea. There she encounters Jake Catlett, her brother's killer twenty years ago, now a successful strip mine operator, with a new Buick, a daughter running for the legislature, and a concern for reclaiming the despoiled mountain land. Hannah thinks, "It was so strange to be there with that dressed-up well-upholstered hillbilly in his Buick, who I had last seen caged behind bars in the county jail, desperate and skinny, that I could only take it all for granted" (326).

But Jake, "mountain conjure man, teller of tales," as Hannah calls him, tells her how it came to be that he was reclaimed from prison and from despair. At the time of Johnny's killing and Jake's arrest, Aunt Althea, an unlikely heroine, finally acknowledges the mutual dependence and long intertwined kinship between the once low but now socially elite McKarkles and the "trashy" Catletts, once one of the most aristocratic of the Beulah families.

Althea does not romanticize the Appalachian past, nor does she denigrate the culture that has produced Jake. She understands the past and the culture. This frees Althea for the potent revolutionary act of the quintet. She has the charges against Jake dismissed, she takes him from the prison herself, and she puts him to work running her mining operation. Centuries after Johnny Church, about to die in the Burford churchyard, pleaded for someone "to speak a word . . . say no . . . cry cease," Althea says, " 'This has gone far enough' " (327). The act without hope of reward. Johnny Church's definition of our humanity.

Hannah felt she was more like Lily than Althea until this moment of epiphany. Hannah now sees that Althea refused to mythologize the past, either of family or of place, transcended the stultifying effects of class conflict, and accepted her mountain brethren as equal sharehold-ers in Appalachia's future. This clear vision of shared humanity is Al-thea's legacy to Hannah, and Settle's literary legacy to Appalachia.

As Hannah flies away from West Virginia, from Beulah, the once promised land now exploited ground, she looks down on the landscape and ponders the turbulent history of Appalachia: "Arrogance and lack of care toward its riches had grown into arrogance and lack of care for each other" (335). Remembering the new generation she has just seen—the melting pot children of her uncle, one clearly McKarkle, one pure Pagano, and the upwardly mobile children of Jake Catlett—Han-nah hopes, "We had forgotten our frontier, the same frontier that we had always found, a frontier of indifference, whether of trees or men" (335). Hannah believes that in these children she has witnessed the only lasting result of revolution: the dream of one generation becom-ing the right of the next.

Moving from the external landscape below her to an interior one, Hannah reflects on what she has unearthed in her searching, "a thing deeper than land." It was

> stratum on stratum of connection, neither by blood nor by convic-tion, but by one minute, sometime of refusal, whether it was Johnny Church's to doff his hat, or even Jake's fist that had struck out and carried with it all the pent-up fury against "the way things are". . . . It was the choice to choose, to be singular, burn bridges, begin again, whether in a new country or a new way of seeing or a new question, which was as ancient as the wandering itself. (336)

Hannah joins the endless wanderers—Johnny Church, the first Han-nah, Jonathan Lacey, Johnny Catlett, Eduardo Pagano, Lily—all those filled with discontent, demanding the fulfillment of promises, destined to "always fail and always to win," burdened with eternal vigilance and sense of loss, unblessed—the price of freedom. But those early wanderers shared the sentiment of Johnny Church in *Prisons:* "Mostly my vision is through a glass darkly" (33); Hannah is imbued with the wisdom of her own search through the past and Althea's uncompromising humanity.

Reflecting on the work that has dominated her life, Settle once said, "I had a true obsession about the subject I was dealing with in 'The Beulah Quintet.' A writer with an obsession is very lucky—like Jacob with the Angel. You don't let it go until it blesses you, until you've finished."[30]

DEBUNKING THE MYTHS AND DOING IT WELL

What has Mary Lee Settle accomplished in her "quintessence" of Appalachia, as she once called her series of five novels? Has she stripped away the contours of mythology about Appalachia to discover the reality of its rich ore? To such questions Settle might likely remark, as David Whisnant once did, that "to ask me (or in fact anyone) to say what Appalachia is really like is roughly equivalent to asking Faulkner or Wolfe what the South was really like: It is both beside the point and impossible to answer."[31]

Settle has sought only to discover the causes of a single act. But in doing so, through her painstaking research and her careful attention to what E. L. Doctorow has called "vast historic forces in social conflict . . . the sense of the individual as a member of a family and as a political being in history,"[32] Settle brings us closer to the experience of Appalachia. She pinpoints the tension, so strong in the region, between rootedness to place and tradition, and the need for change, for freedom from the tyranny of tradition and misperception.

In her nonfictional study of the Scopes trial in Tennessee, written in the middle of her work on the Beulah Quintet, Settle reveals a major theme about Appalachia that she painstakingly represents in all her fiction: "Much misunderstanding . . . was caused by the outsiders' ignorance of and indifference to cultural habit."[33] She notes that people who would respect the customs of foreign cultures "were blind to different cultural habits in their own country."[34]

Settle amply demonstrates that Appalachia has never been a homogeneous culture nor a particularly isolated one. She examines the historical circumstances and human motives behind the mountaineers' supposed proclivities to fierce independence, resistance to change, and violent acts. She bursts the romantic bubble of belief that Appalachian people are innocent rustics who are therefore more virtuous than the rest of us. She explores the dimensions of truth in her state's motto: *Montani Semper Liberi*/Mountaineers are always free. Most importantly, Settle's Beulah Quintet counters historian Ron Eller's description of the results of Appalachian mythmaking:

> Cast in the static role, mountain people have . . . rarely appeared as conscious actors on the stage of American history, and almost never on center stage. They are acknowledged to exist somewhere in the background, as subjects to be acted upon, but not as people participating in the historical drama itself. As a result, our efforts to explain and deal with the social problems of the region have focused not on economic and political realities in the area as they evolved over time, but on the supposed inadequacies of a pathological culture that is seen to have equipped mountain people poorly for life in the modern industrial world. Having overlooked elements of movement and change that have tied the mountains to the rest of American experience, we have blamed the mountaineers for their own distress, rather than the forces which have caused it.[35]

Settle, in contrast, has put mountain people center stage in the historical drama, as conscious actors. She has focused most particularly on the economic and political realities, the elements of movement and change over centuries that have brought successes and failures to Appalachian people. She has not sought the easy answer of blaming the victims; she seeks the more difficult answers that come from understanding.

In the Beulah Quintet, Settle captures the important features of the Appalachian saga—the impulses that led people to the New World and democracy, the complexity of forging a new culture in the mountains, the rending choices of the Civil War era in Appalachia, the revolutionary changes that were a consequence of industrialization, the slow emergence of a new society in contemporary Appalachia. Schafer has charged that Settle obscures the whys and hows of a given era by concentrating on individuals as agents rather than on the main currents of history. He concludes her work is "very pretty, but it is not history."[36] Such a view, I believe, misses the mark. Settle's quintet, though certainly fictionalized, is the history of Appalachia. Appalachia's history has for too long been obscured by the "main currents" of historical thought.

Has Settle's attention to Appalachia diminished her stature as a novelist? Not in the estimation of Doctorow, who praises her "grand passion for what she's doing."[37] He describes Settle as "an author who relishes the precise moment and point of social conflict" and who is interested not in plot "so much as the irremediable longing of the human mind." William Peden acknowledges Settle's work "is of epic, even heroic, proportions" and that she brings to her work "literary integrity and admirable seriousness of purpose."[38]

Robert Houston believes Settle did not gain widespread recognition in her early years because she steadfastly refused the fads of experimentalism in fiction, choosing instead "to write about such things as justice, the human heart, right and wrong—things it has become fashionable to forget . . . she still writes about those things, and does it excellently."[39] Shattuck agrees with Houston's assessment that Settle does not play literary games or become "an antinovelist." In fact, Shattuck concludes, "The Beulah Quintet represents an act of faith in the novel, less as vicarious experience than as a source of energies we can carry back to life itself, to our lives. Literature in it highest form does not distract us. It puts us on our mettle."[40]

Praise for Settle's work rightly centers on her attention to detail, her impressive powers of description, her ability to evoke places and eras of the past. Peden, in his review of *Know Nothing,* says Settle effectively projects "certain phases of the social history of the period, such as the charming recreations of resort life at Egeria Springs."[41] Houston, reviewing *The Scapegoat,* writes: "When you finish *The Scapegoat,* you know how it felt to be alive in 1912 during a coal miners' strike in West Virginia. The rest is quibbling."[42] Houston called *The Scapegoat* "as good a novel as anyone writing in this country today could have written."

Settle makes us not only see the worlds she creates, but hear them as well. Throughout her writing, there is extraordinary attention to the qualities and meaning of sound, especially in human voices. Settle likely follows the dictum of her mentor, Eliot, that "the literature of a people takes its life from the people's speech and in turn gives life to it; and represents its highest point of consciousness, its greatest power and its most delicate sensibility."[43]

A major theme throughout the five novels is the tension between speaking and silence and the consequences of both, a tension that makes Settle's narrators acutely aware of the myriad ways of human speaking. Particularly important in *Prisons* (with countless references to speech), Johnny Church notes "the theeing and thouing of simple country speech," the voice of religion that can "grow loud and wild on waves of feeling," the voice of politics that "is low and has direction," and as he goes to his death he realizes "there are no words. I am empty." Johnny Church's emptiness is echoed in Hannah's long wilderness silence that marks the beginning of the next book, *O Beulah*

Land. In *O Beulah Land,* where Jeremiah's equally long wilderness silence is broken by Hannah's arrival, he begins "the time of his great
talk," his "perpetual hungry talk." Egeria Springs in *Know Nothing* is a
babble of voices, where the Northern ladies, who have brought books,
"as though they had no relatives to talk about," become a source of
even more gossipy talk.

To capture the appropriate voices for *The Scapegoat,* Settle recorded
fourteen hours of tape, reading aloud library records of a Senate investigation into the mine wars. Thinking there would be no record of
Mother Jones's speeches, since she always spoke extemporaneously,
Settle was excited to discover stenographic transcripts of three speeches
to the miners. "They left me clues to Mother Jones's rhythm, her
phrases. From that I could build both her character and her speech."[44]
In *The Killing Ground,* Hannah draws our attention to the speech of a
waitress—" 'Y'all take your time . . . we ain't got no turkey left. Hit
wadn't no good nohow' "—who "made the national anonymity of
Howard Johnson's restaurant as local as the town drugstore. . . ."

One critic says it is the interplay of voices that gives Settle's work its
rich texture, "it is those voices, in fact, that are most likely Settle's best
achievement. Settle makes . . . a symphony of her characters' voices,
captured with an unfailingly attuned ear."[45] Shattuck remarks on Settle's own distinctive voice, noting that "she can speak Tidewater or
mountain talk at will."[46]

Early in her career, Settle wrote plays, and that craft influences the
shape of her novels. She admits that Sophocles has been her model for
the quintet. In classical Greek tragedies, working out questions of justice always took more than one play; Settle's search for justice takes five
novels. Appreciation for the complexities of meaning and design in
Greek tragedies is enhanced when an audience sees or reads all the plays
in a trilogy or cycle and knows something of the mythology surround-
ing the plays. Likewise, Settle's achievements will be most clear to the
reader of all five of her novels (and her other work) in sequence; the
reader familiar with Appalachia will be rewarded all the more.

Recurring names, places, spoken phrases, ritual symbols, and bits of
song grow in resonance as they reverberate from novel to novel of the
quintet. As Shattuck points out in his introduction to the quintet,
"Everything is significant . . . we may not be able to notice everything . . . but Miss Settle patiently and convincingly . . . reveals that
nothing has to be lost for good."[47] Two of the most striking examples
of such *significa* are the family heirlooms and biblical allusions, particularly in hymns, that frame the quintet. When reading across the five

novels, it is fascinating to notice the humble origins of such family possessions as a ruby ring, a silver riding crop, and a tomahawk and to
watch their passage through intertwined family lines and their increasing embellishment in family memory. (Features of the landscape
around Beulah also become familiar territory by the end of the quintet,
though they constantly change in appearance and in legend over the
years.)

Biblical references to Beulah Land appear and reappear in each of the
five novels, either as verse (Isaiah 62: "Thou shalt be called Hepzibah,
and thy land Beulah") or as words of the gospel hymn "O Beulah
Land," usually in striking tableaux: the scripture quoted by common
soldier and great Cromwell in *Prisons* and by Jeremiah Catlett in his
Beulah wilderness; the hymn sung at Lewis Catlett's camp meeting
conversion in *Know Nothing,* by miners' wives at Mother Jones's resistance prayer meeting in *The Scapegoat,* and on the radio in *The Killing
Ground,* where it also appears on a tombstone.

Most striking, however, is Settle's subtle handling of the central tension of her long story through contrasting references to "O Beulah
Land" and one other hymn. The words of "O Beulah Land" offer the
hope, the promise her wanderers sought to fulfill:

O Beulah Land, sweet Beulah Land,
As on thy highest mount I stand,
I look away across the sea
Where mansions are prepared for me,
And view the shining Glory Shore,
My Heaven, my Home, forevermore.

In the final novel, Hannah looks for her brother's memory at the Wayfaring Stranger, Johnny's blue-collar, "escape hatch" bar, where he
took his troubles and his "common" girlfriend. The name of the bar recalls a counterpoint hymn, sadly evocative of Johnny McKarkle and
Settle's other impotent rebels:

I am a poor wayfaring stranger
While traveling through this world of woe
Yet there's no sickness, toil or danger
In that bright world to which I go.

I'm going there to meet my mother
She said she'd meet me when I come
I'm only going over Jordan
I'm only going over home.

The women in Settle's novels, like Johnny McKarkle's mother, are of particular interest, since they are survivors in one way or another. Her novels are peopled with households of grasping, domineering women who prove "women are more righteous but they have less mercy than men" (*Know Nothing*) and strong, lone women like the first Hannah, Mother Jones, Lily, and Hannah McKarkle who, like Antigone, choose independence. Asked if there was a feminist theme in her shift from male to female principal characters in the last two novels, Settle responded:

> Yes, but I didn't realize it until I had finished the whole series. These are deep waters. In many Southern men the inherited sense of responsibility to their families is too big for them. The loss of the Civil War did something to them, as if for 50 years, more even, they remained in a posture of apology to their wives. They lost the sense of escape. The women either got out or made demands on the men, dominated them. . . . In my last two books Lily and Hannah get out.[48]

Her heroines are reminiscent of Settle herself, who left West Virginia, became a member of the women's air force in England during the war (recounted in her *All the Brave Promises*), and walked out of a plush job at *Harper's Bazaar* one day when the "reality that crouches behind daily compromise" overcame her. In that moment, she became a writer.

Now, some thirty years later, Settle is an established and recognized writer, a winner of literary awards, and favorably reviewed in such places as The *New York Times Book Review,* The *Nation,* and *Saturday Review.* Although Settle is sometimes criticized for crowding her novels with too many characters, for giving some of them too much attention and others too little, for troublesome narrative structures and confusing, floating points of view, most reviewers agree with Doctorow that "if she sometimes fails to write along the nerve of her story, we don't lose faith in the enterprise nor the wish to read."[49]

Appalachian poet and literary critic Jim Wayne Miller says people in southern Appalachia, like rising groups everywhere, "have been searching for a usable past, attempting to understand who they are by knowing who they were." And he adds, "Literature is always central to such collective efforts."[50] Mary Lee Settle's commitment to this collective effort may be her most potent literary contribution. Through her careful construction of a fully researched and richly evoked past, through her passion for understanding the presentness of the past, Mary Lee

Settle helps us know more clearly, and less mythically, the human enterprise and the human condition in Appalachian America.

MARY LEE SETTLE BIBLIOGRAPHY

NOVELS

The Love Eaters. London: Heinemann, 1954; New York; Viking, 1956.

The Kiss of Kin. New York: Harper, 1955; London: Heinemann, 1955.

O Beulah Land. New York: Viking, 1956; London: Heinemann, 1956; New York: Ballantine, 1981.

Know Nothing. New York: Viking, 1960; London: Heinemann, 1981; New York: Ballantine, 1981.

Fight Night on a Sweet Saturday. New York: Viking, 1964; London: Heinemann, 1965.

The Clam Shell. New York: Delacorte, 1971; London: Bodley Head, 1975.

Prisons. New York: Putnam, 1973; Ballantine, 1981 (published in England as *The Long Road to Paradise*, Constable, 1974).

Blood Tie. Boston: Houghton Mifflin, 1977.

The Scapegoat. New York: Random House, 1980; Ballantine, 1982.

The Killing Ground. New York: Farrar, Straus, Giroux, 1982 (rewrite of *Fight Night on a Sweet Saturday*, 1964); Bantam Windstone, 1983.

Celebration. New York: Farrar, Straus, Giroux, 1986.

NONFICTION

All the Brave Promises: Memories of Aircraft Woman 2nd Class 2146391. New York: Delacorte, 1966; London: Heinemann, 1966.

The Story of Flight (juvenile nonfiction). New York: Random House, 1967.

The Scopes Trial: The State of Tennessee v. John Thomas Scopes. New York: Franklin Watts, 1972.

Water World (juvenile nonfiction). New York: Lodestar, 1984.

ARTICLES

"Old Wives' Tales" (fiction). *Harper's* 211 (September 1955): 73–78. Reprinted in *Prize Stories 1957: The O. Henry Awards,* ed. Paul Eagle (Garden City, N.Y.: Doubleday, 1957), 241–61.

"The Story of a Company Man." *Nation,* 3 December 1983, 559–62.

"Recapturing the Past in Fiction." *New York Times Book Review,* 12 February 1984, 1, 36–37.

Ellen Douglas

*

PANTHEA REID BROUGHTON

SUSAN MILLAR WILLIAMS

FOR SOME twenty-five years, Ellen Douglas has been recognized as a writer who deals poignantly, comically, and expertly with major crises facing Southerners and women: racial injustice, the heritage of the past, the demands of an extended family, the need for personal autonomy. In broader terms, she designates her focus as "human feelings in crisis." As a comic novelist, she concerns herself with the "predicament of people in society," rather than with "the fate of the lonely hero."[1] An ongoing source of comedy (and pathos) is her characters' inabilities to face the circumstances in which they are caught. An ongoing strength is her close observation of the details of everyday life.

Ellen Douglas has won both a Houghton Mifflin Esquire Fellowship and a grant from the National Endowment for the Arts. She has twice been awarded the Mississippi Institute of Arts and Literature prize. The *New York Times* in 1962 named her first novel and in 1963 her first story collection as among the years' best fiction titles. Her story "On the Lake" was one of the O. Henry prizewinning stories for 1963.

She was born Josephine Ayres on July 12, 1921, in Natchez, Mississippi, to Laura Davis Ayres and Richardson Ayres. Her father was a civil engineer, and from 1921 to 1931, the family lived in Hope, Arkansas, where he worked for the state highway department. In 1931, the family moved to Alexandria, Louisiana, where Ayres became an independent road and bridge builder. Ostensibly a product of Louisiana, Josephine Ayres always felt like an outsider in that state. Her heart and her imagination belonged to Mississippi, especially to Natchez, where both sets of grandparents lived and where Josephine spent her summers.

She attended Randolph-Macon Woman's College in Virginia and

then graduated from the University of Mississippi in 1942. She moved to New York, where she worked in the Gotham Book Mart, a center for New York literary life. There she enjoyed meeting the literati (including Allen Tate and Henry Miller),[2] but her real reason for moving to New York was not to escape the South or to find artistic freedom but rather to be near her future husband, who was in the navy and stationed in New York.[3] In 1945, she married Kenneth Haxton, and they moved to Greenville, Mississippi, his hometown, where she has spent much of her life. They had three sons, Richard, Ayres, and Brooks. In Greenville, Josephine and Kenneth Haxton had several notable literary friends, among them Shelby Foote, Walker Percy, Ben Wasson, and Hodding Carter. Carter, author and editor of the *Delta Democrat-Times*, a paper reputed to be the most liberal and the most activist in the South, hired Josephine for a time as researcher.

Though these associations were important in developing her literary sensibilities, Ellen Douglas denies that she was a part of any literary group. A more formidable influence upon her writing was her grandmother, who wrote children's stories and encouraged her granddaughter to write.[4] During World War II, Josephine worked as a disc jockey for radio station KALB in Alexandria. In the intervals while the records played, she began to write short stories. After her marriage and the birth of her children, she wrote in moments stolen from other, more pressing tasks. And when her youngest child started nursery school and her house was, for the first time in years, empty and silent for the mornings, Josephine Haxton became a dedicated, tireless writer of fiction. In twenty-five years, she has published six novels, one collection of original short fiction, and one collection of retold fairy tales. She has been writer-in-residence at Northeast Louisiana University in Monroe, at the University of Mississippi in Oxford, and at the University of Virginia in Charlottesville, and she has held the Eudora Welty Chair at Millsaps College in Jackson, Mississippi, where she now makes her home.

When Josephine Haxton began writing, she used stories and people from her past. Over the years, she integrated the stories into a several-hundred-page manuscript, which she lent to a novelist friend. The friend showed the typescript to an editor at Houghton Mifflin. Then, though she had not sent her novel to a publisher, one called her. A Houghton Mifflin editor asked if she would submit her novel for their twenty-fifth anniversary fellowship competition. Josephine Haxton was not sure the novel was ready for publication. As she tells the story, the editor called back to say, "If you want me to help you make up your mind, Mrs. Haxton, if you will enter the competition, your novel has won."[5] And so, as she turned forty, Josephine Haxton chose the pseudonym of Ellen Douglas and saw her first novel win the Houghton Mifflin Esquire Fellowship and be named by the *New York Times* as one of the year's five best books of fiction.

The novel—*A Family's Affairs*—is composed of eight stories chronologically arranged. They narrate tales of childhood, courtship, marriage, and death involving a widow, Kate Anderson, and her children and grandchildren. As the book progresses, one granddaughter, Anna McGovern, emerges as the narrative consciousness. Anna appears to be an autobiographical figure. However true the novel may be to Haxton's own family's affairs, its strength lies in its artistry of characterization, sensitive evocation of time and place, skillful interrelation of multiple narratives, and poignant rendering of eternal themes of love and death. Anna describes a visit to her grandmother's in terms that suggest the subject and method of the novel:

> Gathering, separating, gathering again, they came together with glad cries of recognition; and almost without pausing to say hello, to touch cheeks in the accepted gesture of reserved affection, began anew old conversations, old quarrels, the settling of old problems, the retelling or finishing of jokes and stories that had patiently awaited these occasions through months of separation. And all of it, every word they said to one another, rested lightly on the mysterious base of shared experience, layers and layers, hundreds and thousands of years of shared experience, changing imperceptibly from generation to generation like the mysterious changes in a living, growing language, the ambiguous liveliness of words that hold in their roots and affixes, in their very concrete appearance, in their shifts of position and meaning, the whole mysterious, trembling, changing life of a nation. (254)[6]

These imperceptible changes shed different and sometimes ironic light on the hymn sung at Kate's funeral: "Bles't be the tie that binds." Kate Anderson is a strong, active lover of her own family, but such strong love has its drawbacks. Her only son plays out a desperate game of running away from her, but finally he cannot let Kate leave him even to die. Two of Kate's three grown daughters live at home. One marries but does not leave her mother. The other, known as "Sis," late in life marries a man of whom her mother disapproves; Sis returns home a few years later as an abandoned woman. The story of Sis's marriage and divorce is one narrative element that links together the sections of *A Family's Affairs*. One section ends with her rebellious marriage, the next begins with a reference to her divorce. As Anna becomes increasingly the center of consciousness, her growing understanding of her favorite aunt's behavior exemplifies her initiation into womanhood and love. Some details of this initiation are handled in Douglas's superbly comic manner:

> It's like the Lysol bottle, she thought to herself. There's something about the label on the Lysol bottle that I don't understand. Now what is it?
>
> "Feminine hygiene," the advertisements said, and there was the worried lady in the picture, holding the Lysol bottle and frowning unhappily. What was she worried about? And how would Lysol solve her problems?
>
> Mama thinks she's told me all about it, Anna said to herself, and I understand what she said about babies and menstruating and all that, but where does the Lysol come in? (165)

Douglas handles other details of Anna's initiation—the high school teacher who tries to seduce her, the teenage romance—with a light and candid touch. Douglas uses an omniscient and relatively unobtrusive narrator to explain Anna's behavior and her ignorance. But dramatic instances, presented without comment, are more effective. After her teenage romance breaks up, Anna concludes: " 'It'll be a cold day in August when I fall in love again. . . . Loving is like getting born,' she said. 'Once it starts, there's no stopping it, and when it's over, you find you're alone in a new world' " (229). Here Douglas does not need to explain how wrong and how right Anna is.

Anna's knowledge of love is based on listening and observing as well as on experiencing. She considers "so many memories brought to bear on the same events" and asks, "Who even among the principals, was to say what really happened?" (235). Yet she knows that her aunt's assumption that "the end had been inevitable from the beginning" (235) is incorrect. Years later, the divorced aunt tells her to "marry her own kind," and Anna concludes that *there must be more to it than that it was a mistake, a social blunder*" (328). An uncle offers his explanation of the aunt's broken marriage: " 'living with a woman like Sis and a woman to boot, who adores the ground you walk on, could get to be—tiring. And . . . Miss Kate can be mighty ornery, if she takes a notion. I sometimes wonder . . . wonder if he didn't realize . . . if he didn't get to knowing for the first time that he was nothing but po' white trash' " (264). That same uncle gives Anna a glimpse of her own parents' rigidity and of the formula or "recipe" that made the breakup inevitable: " 'Take a little failing status, add a pineapple-post tester bed and a couple of authentic family portraits, fold in the Ten Commandments, and place in a casserole alternating with layers of *Ivanhoe, Kenilworth,* and *The Bride of Lammermoor.* Bake at 500 for fifteen years, and what do you get? Explosion!' " (285).

The final section of *A Family's Affairs* deals with Kate Anderson's death. At the same time that Anna's thoughtful presence at the funeral reaffirms family ties, her loyalty to her husband breaks those ties. Anna has married an outsider, a Jew, in a determination not to be "baked" by the family recipe. At the funeral, she considers the limitations of the Anderson family's love: "*I know, you open your doors, you make room for each other, for me, even for Richard* [her husband] *since he's mine, and* [the servants], *since they're yours. But suppose we weren't yours? What about all the poor bastards who are only human-beings, predestined—yes, to joy and death; and justified only in their own humanity. Isn't God, can't you be for us all?*" (440). This passage closely aligns Kate's love with Presbyterian election. The absence of faith in the mature Anna, here and in other Douglas fiction, seems to be a reaction against that alignment. While exposing her limits, *A Family's Affairs* also makes Kate Anderson a lovable and generally admirable woman. Kate

stubbornly refused to recognize the toll that time had taken of her agility and cataracts of her vision, and persisted in attempting what a woman of sixty might have hesitated to undertake. The strength and vitality that had been her family's bulwark in the years after Mr. Anderson's death, when they were still children, was their burden in her old age, when she was no longer able to put it to any practical use. She wanted to do everything for herself and most things for other people. Opposition was a challenge to which she had never failed to rise, and as she grew older, her unreasonableness took the exasperating forms that senility thrust upon it. (350)

Lizzie (the maid, now nurse) finally cannot control the aged Kate's "devilish contrariness" (350). Determined to hang bathroom curtains by herself, the old lady sneaks out to the storeroom for a ladder, sets it up in the bathtub, and climbs the ladder. Yelling at Lizzie, who comes to stop her, " 'I was hanging curtains before you were born' " (387), Kate falls from the ladder, breaks her pelvis, and goes into a coma.

The reader experiences the same conflicting emotions Anna feels. Kate is brave, complicated, lovable, but also rigid and sometimes destructive. At her funeral, Anna thinks about the disadvantages of such inflexible love as Kate's:

The very rigidity that galls so bitterly, the hanging on with locked jaws like Rikki-Tikki, even if the life is battered out of you, is what makes

*their life together possible, makes it possible to survive in the middle of
the whirlwind. . . . And then at last,* she thought, *you have to think
about love, about the terrible burden of love, about being created every
day in the image of every human being who loves you, about the impossibility of ever seeing yourself, the fate of always being caught, even in
your life's most secret moments in the rays of someone else's light.* (438)

But behind that passage and (one senses) behind the writing of *A
Family's Affairs* is also the refrain "Bles't be the tie that binds."

While Douglas's first novel deals with family ties, her second book—
Black Cloud, White Cloud—deals with social ties. This volume includes
two novellas told from the point of view of an omniscient narrator with
access to the mind of a woman named Anna. (She is Anna McGovern
in one, Anna Glover after her marriage in the other.) *Black Cloud,
White Cloud* also includes two stories narrated in the first person, one
by Anna, one by a Southern woman named Emma, who exhibits good
intentions and flawed sensibilities. These four narratives have in common the attempts of various white women to befriend blacks. The Anna
stories are, at least in part, initiation stories.

The first novella, "The House on the Bluff," moves from Anna's
childhood to her maturity. Its subject is the Baird family, who live in an
antebellum house on a bluff overlooking the Mississippi River. The
friendship between Anna and Caroline Baird is renewed each summer
when Anna visits her grandparents in Homochitto. The odd thing
about Caroline's family is that her widowed, glamorous, and wealthy
mother, Margaret Baird, has left the care of her children, Keith and
Caroline, in the hands of the family nurse, Tété, who lives with the
Bairds and is treated, Margaret insists, as one of the family. But Anna
hears her own family speak with "mild disapproval of Tété's position in
the [Baird] family. They would never have permitted a servant—a 'colored person'—no matter how devoted, how competent, to raise their
children" (8). Anna also overhears "gossip that Tété used a horsewhip
on Keith Baird when he misbehaved" (9). Anna accepts that gossip
though "she had never heard Tété raise her voice to the children, much
less seen her take a whip to them. It was no feat for her to accept everything she heard a grown person say as true, and at the same time to accept the evidence of her own senses that it was not true" (10–11).

Though puzzling, the Baird household remains glamorous to Anna
until she begins to see how much the Baird children really need love
and authority. Margaret loves Keith and Caroline chiefly as they promise to fit into her picture for them; she has relinquished her parental authority to Tété. But however much Margaret talks of treating her as a

member of the family, Tété remains a servant. Both her love of and authority over the children are limited by her status. That limit bears tragic consequences for Keith, while Caroline reacts to her upbringing by rejecting it. Unlike her mother, she is maternal; unlike Tété, she believes in self-disciplined children.

Douglas deftly narrates the various sequences from some twenty years of family history and offers little authorial comment. But the novella's thematic force is undermined by a sentimental ending in which Caroline and her family return to live with Margaret and Tété in the "house on the bluff."

In "Jesse," the second selection in *Black Cloud, White Cloud,* Anna tries to befriend a black man hired to give her son guitar lessons, but she comes to recognize that even when she is most anxious to abolish the color line, she actually is affirming its existence. She offers Jesse a beer when he first comes for the lessons. Her husband comments on her motives: " 'You never should have offered him the first can of beer,' Richard said. 'After all, he's supposed to be working for you, not paying a call. You only gave it to him because he's a Negro' " (105). Anna defends herself by saying that she was trying to be nice to Jesse. " 'And get a little free credit for high principles' " (105), her husband replies.

Douglas asks how decent, sensitive Southern whites can reach out to blacks without pride ("free credit") or patronizing. Anna has had a nightmare about Jesse after he has told her his grim life story, and she has, nevertheless, had to fire him. She remembers half waking from the dream and scribbling important sentences on a magazine: " 'There are those of us who are willing to say, "I am guilty," but who is to absolve us? And do we expect by our confession miraculously to relieve the suffering of the innocent?' I had written first, 'Do we expect to *escape* the suffering of the innocent?' but I had scratched through *escape* and written *relieve*" (115–16). All the stories in *Black Cloud, White Cloud* explore the related but contradictory impulses that lead white liberal Southerners to want both to relieve the blacks' suffering and to escape it.

Emma, who narrates "I Just Love Carrie Lee," prides herself upon relieving suffering. She knows that, unlike Northerners, she treats blacks, especially Carrie Lee, with humanity. She concludes that "Carrie Lee is all I have left of my own" (141). Nevertheless, we see Emma's condescension and social blindness. Apparently, Emma is trying less to relieve injustice than to escape it. "I Just Love Carrie Lee" is Douglas's first experiment with an unreliable narrator. The experiment is successful (and comic) but lacks the poignancy that typifies Douglas's more introspective tales.

"Hold On," the final novella in this volume, is a classic dramatic exploration of moral issues. The central story within the novella was published separately in the *New Yorker* under the title "On the Lake." This story tells of a near-drowning. Anna takes her two sons and their friend fishing. As she and the boys are loading their boat, they see Estella, the black woman who used to work for Anna. Estella has not been able to catch any fish, so Anna and the boys invite her to come with them to the other side of the lake. Estella does not like boats but agrees to come along in hopes of better fishing. Also, she and Anna relish the chance to share their experiences as women. On an isolated lake shore, they can most easily lose all sense of social taboo. Douglas describes Estella's physical control with delight:

> She stood over the pool like a priestess at her altar, all expectation and willingness, holding the pole lightly, as if her fingers could read the intentions of the fish vibrating through line and pole. Her bare arms were tense and she gazed down into the still water. A puff of wind made the leafy shadows waver and tremble on the pool, and the float rocked deceptively. Estella's arms quivered with a jerk begun and suppressed. Her flowery dress flapped around her legs, and her skin shone with sweat and oil where the sunlight struck through the leaves, across her forehead and down one cheek.
>   "Not yet," she muttered. (171)

Estella is not only the better fisherwoman, she is also the better crisis preventer. When a snake catches himself in the stringer with one of their fish half-swallowed, Anna can only suggest that they throw away the stringer and all their catch along with the snake. Estella takes charge and, with the help of Anna's son, kills and discards the snake, saving their fine catch of fish. But if Estella can do some things Anna cannot, Anna can think in ways that Estella cannot. Anna lives in a secular, rationalistic world, which Estella refuses to enter. Anna "had often thought, with pride both in herself and in Estella, what an accomplishment their friendship was, knowing how much delicacy of feeling, how much consideration and understanding they had both brought to it" (182). But Estella's superstition threatens their friendship:

> Anna was filled with a horror and confusion incommensurate with the commonplace superstitions that Estella had stated in confident expectation of understanding and acceptance. It was as if a chasm had opened between them from which there rose, like fog off the

nightmare waters of a dream, the wisps and trails of misted feelings: hates she had thought exorcised, contempt she had believed
rendered contemptible, the power that corrupts and the submission that envenoms. (183)

The difference between the two women emerges more dramatically on
the return boat trip before a gathering storm. Terrified, Estella overturns the boat. She has no life preserver and cannot swim. Anna struggles to save Estella, while the huge woman pulls Anna down with her.
Anna realizes: "Nothing she had ever learned in a lifesaving class
seemed to have any bearing on this reasonless two hundred pounds of
flesh with which she had to deal" (193). Douglas presents Anna's attempts to save Estella with compelling dramatic particularity. Not letting the body go, Anna assumes that Estella has drowned and that it is
"my fault" (197). At issue is not only Estella's life or death, but Anna's
guilt, for she took Estella in the boat without a preserver and without
even asking if Estella knew how to swim.

In the shorter "On the Lake," the issue of guilt is mostly implied.
The story focuses upon the issue of Estella's survival. Suspense builds,
and Douglas withholds until the end the news that Estella lives. The
novella "Hold On" begins after the accident and focuses upon Anna's
obsessive need to relive, explain, and expiate what was, as Douglas
soon makes clear, not a drowning but a near-drowning. The knowledge
that Estella will live does not diminish the suspense of the action
scenes. And Douglas's framing of those scenes with Anna's need to relive and understand the accident and to forgive herself makes this novella a serious moral investigation.

The novella ends as Anna and the man who actually did save Estella
find the black woman fishing some months after the accident and invite
her to " 'come on down and join us' " (232). But their invitation to
"join" them actually means only giving her a ride home. Here and elsewhere in *Black Cloud, White Cloud,* Douglas investigates the issue of
how caring white Southerners and blacks can join together. Her answers are partially limited to easy solutions (like giving Estella a ride)
and by her use of stereotypical characters. Anna recognizes the un-
bridgeable gap between her rationalism and Estella's primitivism, but
Douglas does not take herself or her characters beyond that gap.

Estella's tipping over the boat as she stands and screams " 'Miss
Anna! I can't swim!' " (191) is believable but clichéd. Douglas might
have brought together Estella's and Anna's children to suggest that the
gap between the next generation of blacks and whites need not persist.
Instead, like her characters, who are caught between relieving and es-

caping suffering, Douglas in *Black Cloud, White Cloud* depicts a problem without suggesting a solution. Her depiction is, nevertheless, provocative and wonderfully engaging.

After the first two books, Douglas abandoned the autobiographical Anna figure and began writing fiction about other men and women in the contemporary South. *Where the Dreams Cross* tells the story of Nat Stonebridge's return to her home in Philippi, Mississippi, to stay with her Aunt Louise and Uncle Aubrey while she waits for back alimony payments. Outspoken, thin, suntanned, sexy Nat fits into the patterns of genteel Mississippi living no better than she fit into a conventional, sentimental, but brutal marriage. She lets Floyd Shotwell, the owner of a sky blue Cadillac convertible, court her to relieve her boredom. The courtship ends when Floyd rapes her.

The plot of *Where the Dreams Cross* is an old-fashioned melodrama: Uncle Aubrey invents a washing machine that is almost too good because it will not wear out, and he turns to the Shotwells for financing; the machine is stolen, first by a gambler and then by Floyd Shotwell; Nat trades sexual favors to get the machine back and to rescue her uncle's ailing finances; both Nat and the machine are saved by her cousin Wilburn and some loyal black people. Beyond all that contrivance, *Where the Dreams Cross* offers a telling and comic exposé of middle-class Southern values in the late 1950s, when few people other than Aunt Louise still "cherish the old-fashioned notion that it is vulgar to have one's parties written up in the local newspaper" (2). But Aunt Louise has her own vulgarities. She believes a woman "needs a man around the house. . . . to open jars and—reach things on the top shelf" (76). She cannot think of another use. Aunt Louise is fond of china setting hens, of a "collection of fragile and uncomfortable chairs and sofas and graceless marble topped tables" (73), and of grits soufflé and caramel cake. She lives in a world in which men learn Sunday school pieties while shooting ducks and women define tragedy as having a daughter not pledge Tri Omega. In this world, Sputnik and integration are only vague threats.

Where the Dreams Cross offers some insight into the sexuality of these people. Nat's cousin Wilburn, whose wife refuses to have an operation for gallbladder stones, wonders about the relationship between gallbladder trouble and frigidity in women past thirty-five:

He stared gloomily at Sunny [his wife] standing on the other side of the room talking to a woman he had never seen. Her fat freckled arms bulged out below the cap sleeves of her dress, and her belly, in spite of being severely girdled, swelled against the tight silk shirt. Belly full of rocks, he thought. And she doesn't want to get rid of them. She'd rather carry them around the rest of her life, if she can use them against me. He had a moment's horrifying vision of those slimy stones built into a moss-covered wall against which he spent and bruised and ruined himself in a frantic effort to consummate the act of love. But maybe I want her that way, he thought. Is it possible that I married her just because she *is* that kind of woman? (175)

Wilburn, who is more introspective than the other characters, offers insights that enlarge the book's implications. Nevertheless, his thoughtful meditating on sexuality seems dead-ended because it is not consistently integrated into the book's thematic structure. Wilburn can explain his own sexuality and his wife's, but the novel explains neither Floyd's nor Nat's. Douglas offers details from his childhood, intended to make plausible the womanless Floyd (suspected of impotence), who tells Nat he does not care about sex but then rapes her and later bargains for a regular sexual relationship. But Floyd remains barely creditable. Even more improbable is the sexy but frigid Nat, who trades on her body's appeal but wants to attract a man who "never pesters me to jump in the sack" (86). She explains to Floyd:

> "You see, that was one reason I didn't do so well with being married. It's kind of hard to make anybody believe it, because of this. . . . " She ran her hands over her bosom down to the slim waist and patted her hips. "But I don't really like going to bed with anybody. . . . "
> "I would never marry," he said. And then, "If you don't want a man to think you're sexy, why do you get yourself up like you do?"
> "I didn't mean I didn't like myself," she said. (148)

Taken out of context, these lines suggest that Nat may not be erotic but certainly is autoerotic. That implication is not, however, pursued in *Where the Dreams Cross,* for Nat's self-love seems to be only a matter of image-maintaining (she claims that she would "disappear" (148) without makeup).

In an interview with Susan Williams, Ellen Douglas explains that Nat was destroyed by the pressures of the society in which she grew up. Douglas says: "Early in life she began to perceive herself as an object, as a work of art, as a creation of the world around her because of her strong sexuality, her striking appearance. That perception of herself kept her from seeing that if she used her intelligence, she might be something else."[7]

But Nat does not object to the typecasting that has victimized her; instead, she exploits it. She values her sex appeal but not her sexuality. Perhaps she fit in best when she lived with homosexuals, who dressed her glamorously in hopes that she would attract men for them. The intriguing but unanswered question in *Where the Dreams Cross* is "Why is Nat asexual?" Douglas waited another decade to write more explicit and explicable investigations of sexuality.

In these diverse works, the context remains the family, a collective consciousness that both drains and nurtures its members. Douglas explores relationships between the sexes, the inevitability of self-deception, and the difficulties of including blacks in the Southern white community. She frames her fiction in terms of the complex social and emotional bonds that link people even as they force them apart. Her characters find that attempts to escape the family lead directly to an even greater degree of entanglement: Sis's marriage to a laborer of whom her family disapproves ends in a disastrous divorce, and she becomes totally devoted to her aging and difficult mother; Anna's attempts to integrate blacks into a white collective unconscious fail; and Nat, the adventurous rebel against her family, sells her body to save the family's finances.

But while the family may be excessive in imposing "the terrible burden of love," Douglas's fiction suggests that only disaster can result from trying to evade familial responsibility. *Apostles of Light* focuses on the traditional extended family and its confrontation with aging and death in the modern world. Martha's sister dies, and the family concludes that the aged Martha should no longer live alone in the old house, since she is nearly blind. Howie Snyder, a cousin, intervenes with an apparently perfect solution. He is a widower; he needs a place to live; he will move in, pay board, and keep an eye on Martha. The family accepts this proposal as kinder than uprooting her (as well as potentially more profitable), and Howie becomes a boarder, oozing a combination of Rotary good fellowship and pop psychology. At first he seems to be simply a busybody with poor taste, but Howie's sphere of influence soon expands. He appeals to the greed and political aspirations of Martha's relatives in order to convince them to turn the old house into a "home" for the well-to-do elderly.

Martha's only stipulation is that her lover, an aging activist doctor named Lucas Alexander, be allowed to live in the home at a low rent. The old couple enjoy birding and walking in the woods together as they had in their youth, and the recollection of their earlier meetings provides a poignant pastoral counterpoint to the increasing impersonality of Martha's home. Howie has stripped the house of antiques—

they gather dust and do not appeal to everyone—and brings in vinyl and steel furniture and all the assembly line accoutrements of institutions. He hires the brusque Mrs. Crawley, whom Lucas recognizes as a woman who lost her nursing license for having performed a fatal illegal abortion. With her disheveled red hair, glass eye, and predatory mentality, Mrs. Crawley seems to have stepped right out of melodrama. But Howie's other employee, equally predatory, is a product of the civil rights movement. Lucy flaunts both her blackness and her lack of deference in a way that her grandfather, Martha's butler, never would because he recognizes its danger. She has no real affection for anyone, black or white, but she agrees to sleep with Howie in return for the promise that he will help her find a lucrative career.

At first Howie's intentions seem good, if misguided and vulgar. But when, inevitably, the residents begin to fall ill and become restless or disoriented, cracks appear in Howie's armor of piety. Abetted by Mrs. Crawley and Lucy, he uses crude cages and drugs to keep the residents quiet, and the house becomes a private hell for those unable to resist him. One old lady even attempts to commit suicide by hitting herself repeatedly in the head with her cane. Only two people can perceive the extent of the horror: Lucas Alexander and the black butler, Harper, Lucy's grandfather, a self-taught scholar who sees history as a bloody tide and believes that the way to survive is to go underground, becoming invisible and self-sufficient. Given Lucas's age and radicalism and Harper's race, both men know that the family will not take their accusations seriously.

The novel is plotted traditionally and dramatically, pitting powerful evil forces against weak good ones. Yet it resists oversimplification of this conflict, for Douglas focuses on the difficulty of identifying false apostles, agents of evil disguised as angels, when one has been taught that one's own perceptions are likely to be flawed and that one should not judge lest he or she be judged. As in all of Douglas's novels, the intelligent and sensitive can sense the irony of any situation and tend to doubt the veracity of their own perceptions, while opposing forces seem untroubled by ambiguity. The novel ends with an apocalyptic fire set by Lucas, in which he, Martha, and several of the old residents die. They are released from bondage, but Howie and his cohorts live on. Douglas subverts the patterns of melodrama; she refuses to allow Lucas and Martha to escape to a better life, refuses to simplify the problem. In both *Apostles of Light* and in her next novel, *The Rock Cried Out,* Douglas's plots involve the problems of contemporary life that make headlines; however, she always focuses on the personal, human, and eternal aspects of character. She does not write tracts or attempt to resolve social problems; she is content with suggesting the ways in which people react to such problems.

In *The Rock Cried Out,* Douglas uses a male narrator named Alan McLaurin, who wants to be a poet and who returns in the early 1970s to his family's Mississippi farm, now largely given over to a naval space surveillance station. Alan wants to return to a simple and elemental existence, but he can escape neither the past nor the present. Chickasaw Ridge for him holds memories of public and private disasters, both having occurred on the same day. Seven years before, the Ku Klux Klan had burned a black church, and his cousin/girlfriend, Phoebe, had been killed in an automobile accident. These two events and the gradual revelation to Alan of the web of circumstances and passions that caused their conjunction form the structure of *The Rock Cried Out.* Alan returns to Chickasaw Ridge with the confidence of youth, but he soon discovers that reality is neither simple nor pleasant. His Aunt Leila, a strong and creative woman, confesses to a long and passionate affair with Sam Daniels, the black overseer. Alan becomes entangled with the Boykin brothers, a pair who have reacted to their father's earlier association with the Klan in divergent ways: Lee is an opportunistic hippie who wants to make money off local history and who soon seduces Alan's girlfriend; Dallas, a redneck who longs to be saved, is married to an ethereal fundamentalist called Lorene. In talking to all of these people, Alan begins to realize the complexity of events, a realization climactically confirmed by Dallas's lengthy confession—over a CB radio—to responsibility for Phoebe's apparently accidental death.

Alan has lived through the bitterest of the civil rights battles, and Chickasaw Ridge is, in the words of a black youth, "the worst. . . . Worse than Yazoo City. Or Jackson" (6). Alan is defensive about his lack of participation: "I was only fifteen. I didn't know what was going on" (6). Yet he is not entirely able to shake off the sense that his passivity was really complicity. The ambivalence of racial relations, central to the novel, is portrayed in the first scene, when Alan is almost hit by a Coke bottle thrown from a carload of young blacks and is then picked up by them and warned that his long hair will make him suspect to the local white population. As he leaves the car, one of the girls tells him, " 'I *meant* to hit you' " (8). Alan responds to himself, "That's the way things are and I already know it. . . . Forget it" (8). But he does not really understand the way things are. An older Alan, seven years later, fourteen years after Phoebe's death, writes this story, explaining, "It was 'being right' (or blindness, or self-absorption—take your choice) that made me fail that winter to try to fit what was going on around me into the pattern it cried out for—a pattern I hadn't put my attention on" (12).

The Rock Cried Out is an initiation story that points up the artificialities of the genre. Traditionally enough, Alan returns to the homeplace, to his roots, in search of a pastoral ideal, an escape from industrialization, sexual entanglement, and complicated social issues. He expects to live simply, work with his hands, and forge the experience into poetry. But his romantic vision is assaulted from the moment he sets foot in Homochitto County. Now he must cope with ever more personal and painful manifestations of the very problems he had intended to flee.

Encouraging confessions from the people of Homochitto County, Alan does not anticipate the pain what he learns gives him. He and Lee set out to compile an oral history of the county, soliciting the memories of elderly black residents. Both young men, for different reasons, hope to produce an engaging, mildly provocative, and salable product. But once they decide to talk, their sources are determined to reveal the truth. And the truth has devastating personal implications for their interviewers.

Just as Alan failed to expect the consequences of his historical inquiries, so does he fail to see the implications of his sexual assumptions. When he tires of celibacy, he invites his girlfriend, Miriam, to visit, carefully providing a cover of respectability by also inviting his liberated aunt. Miriam happily accepts Alan's pronouncements about sexual freedom. She and Lee become lovers, and honoring Alan's commitment to total honesty, she tells him all about it. Too late, Alan realizes that he has wanted free love only for himself. He also realizes that honesty can become a weapon.

His Aunt Leila, who had seemed so convenient as a nonjudgmental pseudo-chaperon, is moved to explain her sexuality and her anger to Alan. And Alan, who at first wanted to *understand,* now wants only to stop this tide of confession. But the troubles of women and old black men are not so painful to Alan as the pathos of his uncle Lester—white, male, middle-class—who holds out a vision of J. C. Penney as the ultimate haven, a secure polyester fortress that offers protection from loss and want. Yet Alan cannot feel contempt for that pathetic vision, for he remembers watching Lester helplessly cradle the bloody body of his only daughter, killed in a car wreck.

Alan does confront pain and loss and evil during his winter on the farm. But Douglas emphasizes that his initiation is incomplete, that ego and immaturity seal him off from true vision. As narrator, an older Alan meditates on his youthful inability to see beyond himself, to respond to his girlfriend, his aunt, his acquaintances. His initiation and maturation have taken years, not months, and even now remain incomplete.

The narrative voice in *The Rock Cried Out* rings remarkably true; only once or twice does one detect a slight false note of language or perception. Alan is a sensitive young man, troubled by the injustices he sees, by the apparent contradictions between being a poet and being a participant in the political and social sphere. Douglas says that Alan was inspired by one of her own sons, a poet and a welder, who really did go back to live on the old family homeplace and who restored a house there. Some of Douglas's most beautiful paragraphs are detailed and loving descriptions of the work Alan does, including welding: "Cut off from the outside world by the roar of the engine, the enclosing blindness of the helmet, [I] start up the machine and lose [myself] in the work, watching the miniature sun at the tip of the rod send tiny planets of glowing metal ricocheting in every direction through the vaporizing slag, the cosmic dust cloud" (296).

In order to write about Alan's work, Douglas learned to weld;[8] this passage is typical of the kind of careful observation combined with poetic sensibility that characterizes all of her work. And the welding has broader implications as well—*The Rock Cried Out* is permeated with the awareness that the South, even the rural South, is an industrialized society. Military technology, Exxon, and International Paper provide a higher standard of living; whether one approves or not, one accepts the advantages. The image of the space station hovers over the novel, a silent but threatening parallel to the violence and passions of the past, symbolized by the burning of Mercy Seat Church. *The Rock Cried Out* is a complicated and ambitious work; it succeeds because Douglas is able to unify the shifting narrative, the contrivances that allow confessions and revelations, with her use of such evocative motifs.

Though only in *The Rock Cried Out* does Douglas adopt an exclusively male perspective, she often examines the male point of view. She writes about typical male professions and domains, such as machines and factories, with ease. To authenticate her engineers, lawyers, politicians, medical doctors, sugar mill workers, and welders, Douglas usually spends a substantial amount of time talking with practitioners, and even, as we have seen, learning to practice a trade such as welding. She explains, "I want the voice to be right for the profession. . . . I want to know the details, how it's done, how things work."[9]

If Douglas researches her male characters, she knows her female characters. To Susan Williams she said, "What I know about is how women live, because that's the way I've lived. I've cooked and made preserves and raised children and lived with children and kept house and that's no less absorbing and vital than practicing law or being a doctor."[10] Douglas has been happy combining domesticity and, later, university teaching (usually for only half a year) with writing. She has had no desire for another career: "Temperamentally speaking, from the point of view of a writer, what could be worse than to be 'liberated' from one's household and to have to go to work at eight in the morning and to have to stay until five in the afternoon?"[11]

A Lifetime Burning, Douglas's fifth novel, is a radically different exploration of "how women live." It employs an unreliable narrator who takes pains to prove her own duplicity, and the action moves in and out of authenticated experience. Corinne, the narrator, is a professor of literature married to a doctor, George, who has recently given up surgery for emergency medicine. Their three grown children are the primary audience for whom Corinne weaves this disturbing tale, written in diary form. Corinne is intimately aware of the autobiographer's dilemma: "I want to explain everything truthfully and at the same time to be always right, always charming, always lovable, always beautiful" (5). But her subject is sexual obsession, and obsession by its nature precludes equilibrium. She relates a series of episodes in the history of her marriage, constructed both to evade and to explain the course of events.

Corinne first tells about her discovery of her husband's affair with a neighbor, a very short woman whom she calls "The Toad." Her pursuit leads her to a small church, where she crouches on the floor of a nursery closet to overhear George and The Toad making love. The episode is both comic and pathetic—Corinne is painfully aware that she forfeits her own dignity and self-respect in her obsessive need to know. But the need is almost physical, strong enough to override decency and honor. The episode is skillfully timed and is so filled with eccentric detail and psychological revelation that it is entirely convincing. But at this point, Corinne pulls back, announces that she has fabricated it all. She has intended it, she says, as a "true lie." The truth, as she tells it, is that George really had a homosexual affair with a twenty-nine-year-old, but that she, after years of familiarity, has fallen obsessively in love with him again.

A Lifetime Burning was written before the threat of AIDS became a part of our collective imagination; the events of the late 1980s lend unintended ironic overtones to George's affair and Corinne's reaction. A present-day Corinne would perceive the threat not of potential blackmail but of potential death. Her considerable rage would be increased by the knowledge that she too had been put at risk. And chances are that she would never decide to share George with his male lover. These problems, however, lie beyond the text itself. Within the text, there are other stumbling blocks, put there intentionally.

Given the original setup, the reader is disinclined to trust Corinne completely, and indeed she fabricates other episodes, including the discovery of a bitter diary supposedly kept by a great-grandmother, a suicide. The diary presents a grim picture of male brutality and female subjection; its primary connection with Corinne's life, however, is in its introduction of a lesbian relationship. Corinne's final revelation is that she has had a love affair with another woman when her children were young. Is she lying about this as well? The use of such an entirely untrustworthy narrator is disturbing, yet it ultimately serves to emphasize Douglas's theme. While the apparent structure of *A Lifetime Burning* is chronological and linear in the most obvious way—the daily diary—the real unity is thematic. The novel explores the ways in which love and sexual passion can blind us, enrage us, change reasonable people into compulsives. And it explores the ways in which fiction explains us to ourselves—by indirection, metaphor, and the "true lie." Corinne emphasizes that what she relates is her inner life, that at the same time that she and George were acting out their secret passions they were going to work, entertaining friends, and functioning normally. The life she describes, however, is full of quiet devastation below the surface. Though Corinne struggles against the chaos of her passions, this is a tale not of depravity but of essentially decent, kind people, a mother, a father, a teacher, and a physician, who manage to comfort, protect, and get along with each other. Corinne is a possible mature version of Anna McGovern, still carrying bravely the terrible burden of love. Part of Corinne's distress is that she feels herself ridiculously old, and approaching death adds poignance to her dilemma. For her, age "brings passion, more passion, obsession, fury, frustration, as if one lived again through an adolescence that would open out not into maturity, but into oblivion. There was no need for the foolish whiskey-sodden poet to address his ancient passion-battered father: 'Do not go gentle into that good night.' No need at all" (80).

A Lifetime Burning continues the themes of all Ellen Douglas's fiction: how to preserve a community without being smothered or obsessed by it, how to break away without being impoverished. But it takes more risks than Douglas's earlier novels. In stripping away the layers of Corinne's dishonesty, it is a painfully honest narrative. Corinne so effectively exposes her own tendency to fabricate, she comments on it so accurately, that the reader is left with admiration, hatred, and total mistrust. Reading this novel is like making friends with a pathological liar.

As in none of her earlier novels, Douglas kills the Angel in the House, Virginia Woolf's metaphor for female repression and domestic self-sacrifice. A middle-aged, middle-class woman possessed by lust and rage is not, even now, a popular subject for fiction, and Corinne imagines that her "pent-up lust must have been as evident as the scarlet buttocks of a mandrill" (54). Clearly, Corinne has a vivid imagination; equally clearly, she is deeply resentful of George. She fears she may be going crazy, inventing his transgressions. As readers, we are hostage to her vision—we can mistrust it but cannot see through it to the truth. *A Lifetime Burning* suggests that beneath the quiet domestic surface, women may lead lives of raging imaginative obsession.

Neither Douglas nor her characters regret domesticity. But her sensitive characters want to enlarge the community beyond the family and to limit its claims upon them. These characters feel that election, not by grace but by marriage or clan, is absurd, but they have no standards other than the family's for justifying their deeds. Perhaps in *A Lifetime Burning,* Corinne's sexual fantasies are simply a manic version of all Douglas's characters' attempts to live in the family yet not be bound by it. Despite its eccentricities, then, *A Lifetime Burning* continues the themes of all Ellen Douglas's fiction: how to preserve a community without being smothered or obsessed by it, how to break away without being impoverished. Douglas has described that novel as being about "female sexual rage,"[12] but she depicts rage and resentment as masculine too. Douglas deplores the various misuses and abuses of sexuality she sees around her. Though her characters do not manage, as Hawthorne writes at the close of *The Scarlet Letter,* "to establish the whole relation between man and woman on a surer ground of mutual happiness," Ellen Douglas regrets their failures.

Douglas's latest novel, *Can't Quit You, Baby,* pulls together brilliantly the strengths of her previous work. Here again are women both enclosed by and alienated from families, women with cross-racial friendships, women with a strong sense of the South as PLACE, women who are mature sexual beings. The plot and plots of *Baby* emerge naturally out of character and of the circumstances of storytelling. Here Douglas interweaves and juxtaposes two sets of plots focusing upon two different women, one black, one white. Their peculiar closeness was possible in the South of the 1960s and 1970s because one (Cornelia) likes to cook and the other (Julia, called 'Tweet' by everyone except Cornelia) works in Cornelia's kitchen. While Cornelia makes pasta or puff pastry, Tweet does the rest of the cooking and almost all of the talking. The women are very nearly opposites. Tweet has survived several attempted rapes by white men, accomplished robbery, and even attempted murder by her own father. As she tells Cornelia, her grandfather taught her "to make a split oak basket, rob a bee tree, skin a catfish, look in a mule's mouth and know how old he is. Taught me to milk a cow, ride a horse, build a pump to store potatoes and pumpkins in the wintertime." But despite that resourcefulness, Tweet is afraid of ghosts, and she remains disadvantaged.

Cornelia, like Anna with Estella, has little empathy with the black woman's fears. Affluent and white, she has lived a completely sheltered, almost charmed existence. She has skills—especially cooking and ordering the inventory in the bookstore she and her husband own—but these skills flourish only in a protected environment. Her insularity is emblematized by the hearing aid she turns off and in her family's habit of sparing her unwelcome details of their lives. Her "cocoon of dead silence" is the flaw in her perfect life, for "Tweet is the only one who raises her voice and tells Cornelia what is going on."

Douglas organizes the book by moving back and forth between the two women. At first Tweet tells stories from her past, and the narrator tells those from Cornelia's. The narrator acknowledges the disparity in her way of telling these tales. She (clearly the narrator is female) admits having difficulty in imagining Tweet except through her conversations with Cornelia. And she cannot let Cornelia reciprocate by telling her own stories because "her intimate revelations are scarcely formulable," especially to herself. Through describing such "pitfalls" in her method and repeatedly commenting on the options available to the narrator, Douglas raises issues about storytelling itself. She offers fictions within fictions within comments on the nature of fiction making. But, though *Baby* contains elements of what literary critics call "metafiction," it is hardly an academic novel.

Douglas's remarkable achievement is to move from the tales of the two women's pasts into the events that follow when tragedy and guilt shatter Cornelia's charmed existence. Cornelia enters a trance of avoidance expressed in forgetfulness, fatique, and alcoholism. Douglas's stream-of-consciousness presentation of Cornelia's shock over what she sees as her guilt in her husband's death is masterfully hynoptic. Here is a sample:

it occurred to her something had happened in her head. Synapses were not working. She visualized her brain—stacks of grayish worms doubling over and under, netted as if in a shopping bag with throbbing veins and arteries. When John died, she decided, it was as if God had taken a needle and slipped it carefully into her brain . . . and zapped a minute segment of the bland gray custard of thought with a billion volts of lightning. The area he had struck stored recall of new faces.

She could recall the faces of the absent, saw old friends' faces when they called. At night she saw the dead. . . .

A number of factors finally rescue Cornelia from her state of shock, but one is the recollection of Tweet's saying:

Listen to *me,* she says. I'm too polite to say, but I notice you don't hardly ever ax a question, and sometimes *seems* like you're listen-ing—you put on listening—but you ain't. Seems like you think you don't need to ax, don't need to listen, you already got answers, or else you don't want to hear none. But where are all them words, if you don't ax, don't tell, don't answer? They might be out here in the world. Or they might all be shut up in your head, waiting, making your head swell up. You thought about that?

Tweet believes in ghosts' voices. Finally, Cornelia in time of need be-lieves in Tweet's voice. Douglas works out the powerful ending of this book not just by Cornelia's belief in Tweet's voice, but by Tweet's belief in Cornelia's voice. Both women finally have harsh, even profane, but restorative words for each other.

In this fine novel, Douglas conquers whatever problems limited her earlier work. Blacks and whites cease to exist only in stereotypical rela-tions to one another. The dramatic climax is a logical culmination of character and conflict. The interest in storytelling itself becomes subject matter. And female sexuality is explicable. And despite its Southernness and its domesticity, the setting of this novel includes New York City, while its texture ranges through puff pastry making, cropping on shares, and allusions to black songs and Nabokov's art. In her sixty-fifth year, Douglas continues not only to practice her craft but also to improve it.

Writing *A Lifetime Burning,* Douglas deleted many heavily Southern references. She did so because "Southerners are cursed by reviewers who dismiss their books as being southern."[13] Though reviewers do have a stock of clichéd reactions to Southern fiction, no one could dis-miss *A Lifetime Burning* for being merely Southern.[14] One mark of the maturity of *Can't Quit You, Baby* is that in it Douglas does not even attempt to camouflage its Southern setting. In fact, the words of her title could be addressed to the region that has so strongly nurtured her life and art.

All Douglas's fiction is saturated with place, with the places Josephine Haxton knows best, especially Natchez, Greenville, and the country place her great-great-grandfather built near Natchez. Douglas claims she writes about the South only because she is Southern. (Faulkner too claimed that the South was just the region he knew best.) But she also seems to write because she is Southern. Growing up where the "race question" was an issue every day of her life, where three generations lived together, where her intelligence was both discouraged and encouraged, Josephine was compelled to feel and think her way through issues. She saw that regarding blacks as "a structure meant to serve our own self-deception [managed to create] a sort of ghost world, a wholly unreal vision of the lives of the very black people we lived so intimately with."[15] Sometimes the past vied with the present over which would be the ghost world. And being taught to be intelligent but to seem empty-headed raised questions about the real and the ghost Josephine. The South provoked Josephine Ayres Haxton to think and feel beyond hypocrisy toward truth. The Southern setting provokes Ellen Douglas's characters to try to come to terms with responsibilities to others and to themselves.

Her work continues to command interest and respect because, while each book stems from these central issues, each is a fresh exploration, and *The Rock Cried Out, A Lifetime Burning,* and *Can't Quit You, Baby* are bold technical experiments, each different from its predecessor. Douglas's interest in *telling* itself also prompted her to retell those stories that in the 1940s inspired Walter Anderson, an important Mississippi artist, to create huge linoleum block illustrations. In her introduction to this sumptuous book, Douglas explains the "double sense of changing specificity and unchanging type that gives me the courage to retell these tales" (x). She goes on to say: "When I first saw the beautiful Walter Anderson illustrations for these tales . . . , I was sure that he was saying with his pictures the same thing I had been saying to myself about *telling*. For there is a double quality to the illustrations: they are as hieratic, as mythic as images from an Egyptian tomb or a medieval church, and as quirky and individual as a known voice" (xi). The quirky, individual voice Douglas adds to the familiar tales in *The Magic Carpet* is distinctly feminine and self-assertive. Her princesses partially effect their own rescues; her narrative voice comments on storytelling and on character. She ends "Cinderella," for example, with this condemnation: "As for the father, whose weakness in my view was the cause of Cinderella's misery, perhaps his punishment was to have to live the rest of his life with her wicked stepmother" (117). Douglas applies to these retellings many of the same strengths she exhibits in her own fiction.

In 1963, Orville Prescott wrote in the *New York Times,* "Ellen Douglas is not just one of the best of our southern novelists. She is one of the best of our American novelists."[16] After such recognition for her first two books, Ellen Douglas might have continued writing fiction about love and death within extended families like her own, pleasure and guilt in conventional black-white relationships. Instead she moved on, expanding her themes to include new topics and new techniques. But always, as she says, "my works are unified by the need to make my characters move out and affirm, in some way, a humanity larger than they thought themselves capable of."[17]

Susan Isaacs in the *New York Times Book Review* says that Ellen Douglas has "all the qualities a reader could ask of a novelist: depth, emotional range, wit, sensitivity and the gift of language."[18] Ellen Douglas applies those qualities to an ongoing struggle with the forces that shaped her and for the characters she has shaped. Her work itself is a further ramification of the terrible burden of love.

ELLEN DOUGLAS BIBLIOGRAPHY

NOVELS

A Family's Affairs. Boston: Houghton Mifflin; Cambridge, Mass.: Riverside, 1962; Boston: Houghton Mifflin, 1968.
Where the Dreams Cross. Boston: Houghton Mifflin, 1968.
Apostles of Light. Boston: Houghton Mifflin, 1973.
The Rock Cried Out. New York and London: Harcourt Brace Jovanovich, 1979.
A Lifetime Burning. New York: Random House, 1982.
Can't Quit You, Baby. New York: Atheneum, 1988.

SHORT STORIES AND COLLECTIONS

"On the Lake." *New Yorker,* 26 August 1961. Reprinted in *Prize Stories of 1963: The O. Henry Awards,* ed. Richard Poirier, 230–60. Garden City, N.Y.: Doubleday, 1963.
Black Cloud, White Cloud: Two Novellas and Two Stories. Boston: Houghton Mifflin; Cambridge, Mass.: Riverside, 1963.

The Magic Carpet and Other Tales. Retold by Ellen Douglas with the illustrations of Walter Anderson. Jackson: University Press of Mississippi, 1987.

INTERVIEWS

Jones, John Griffin. *Mississippi Writers Talking,* vol. 2, 47–74. Jackson: University Press of Mississippi, 1983.

Speir, Jerry. "Of Novels and the Novelist: An Interview with Ellen Douglas." *Mississippi Studies in English,* n.s. 5 (Fall 1984–87).

Williams, Susan. "A Visit with Ellen Douglas." Unpublished interview, 28 November 1983.

Elizabeth Spencer

*

ELSA NETTELS

E LIZABETH SPENCER was born in Carrollton, Mississippi, in 1921, an auspicious time for the birth of a Southern writer. According to John Bradbury, the literary flowering known as the Southern Renaissance can be dated from that year, marked by the appearance of several publications featuring the work of young Southern writers: *The Double Dealer* in New Orleans, *The Reviewer* in Richmond, the *Lyric* in Norfolk, the first *Yearbook* of the Poetry Society of South Carolina.[1] The group of Nashville poets led by John Crowe Ransom was gathering the poems that would appear the next year in the first issue of their magazine, *The Fugitive.* Four years later, in 1926, Faulkner published his first novel, *Soldiers' Pay.*

As a successor of such writers as Faulkner, Katherine Anne Porter, and Robert Penn Warren, whose achievements called forth the term "Southern Literary Renaissance," Elizabeth Spencer knew the advantages and the drawbacks of belonging to a second generation. The way had been opened; new traditions gained vitality as first novels were followed by masterpieces, yet the work of the first generation could inhibit as well as inspire a later writer fearful of doing less well what had already been done memorably. Spencer has described her predecessors as "tremendously strong influences for a young writer to shake off." Faulkner, whom she first read in graduate school, was not only "a great discovery" but also "a lion in the path, menacing further advance." She read other writers, such as Chekhov, Turgenev, and Hemingway, to neutralize his effect.[2]

Spencer's early fiction, particularly her first two novels, set in her native Mississippi, bears the mark of Faulkner's influence. But although themes, characters, and prose rhythms at times suggest Faulkner, her work is not derivative, because it springs from an original relation of the author to her subject. From her earliest childhood, years before she read Faulkner or knew of a "Southern Literary Renaissance," she was coming into possession of the world she would re-create in her fiction.

Like Faulkner, Elizabeth Spencer was born to parents whose families had lived and farmed in northern Mississippi since the 1830s. Her "visitable past," in Henry James's phrase, stretched back to the Civil War: she knew her grandfather, who could remember the war; her brother's nurse had been a slave. She not only had the born writer's desire to set down stories as soon as she learned to write, but she also grew up in a town, she recalled, "with more than normal share of history and legend," in which life was perpetually being cast in the form of stories.[3] Those she heard about townspeople, alive and dead, imparted their reality to books, making the Bible narratives, the Greek myths, the fairy tales, and the history she read or heard in childhood seem almost as real as local history: "The whole world, then, was either entirely in the nature of stories or partook so deeply of stories as to be at every point inseparable from them."[4]

At Belhaven, a Presbyterian college in Jackson, Mississippi, from which she received her B.A. degree, she continued to write. She edited the college newspaper, was president of the literary society, won awards in short story and poetry competitions, and met Eudora Welty, who lived across the street from the college. A scholarship to Vanderbilt University, which granted her an M.A. degree in 1943, enabled her to study with Donald Davidson, the one member of the Fugitive group still teaching in the English Department at Vanderbilt after Ransom and Warren had left.

With Davidson's encouragement, she resolved to devote herself to the writing of fiction, after the "lean years" as she called them—two years of teaching English in Northern Mississippi Junior College and the Ward-Belmont School in Nashville—and a short stint as a reporter on the Nashville *Tennessean*. Davidson, who read part of the novel she had begun writing at Belhaven, urged her to make revisions and recommended her work to David Clay, an editor at Dodd, Mead. After receiving two installments of the novel, his firm offered a contract and in 1948 published *Fire in the Morning*.[5]

It is a remarkable first novel in a number of ways: in the imaginative power with which Elizabeth Spencer creates the male characters, who are the central figures in the work; in the delineation of different social groups represented by generations of characters whose lives create the history of the north Mississippi town of Tarsus; and above all, in the focus upon mature characters in their relation to the life of a region, rather than upon the psychological development of adolescents, the favorite subject of young novelists. Not surprisingly, the first novel lacks the unity Spencer was to achieve in later works; at times transitions are awkward and time shifts confusing. But the novel shows her power to impart transcendent meaning to scenes realistically conceived and so to sustain the tradition of symbolic realism developed by Faulkner, Robert Penn Warren, and Eudora Welty.

Fire in the Morning introduces the central theme of Elizabeth Spencer's fiction: the passage of characters to freedom from self-destructive obsessions and imprisoning relationships. In each novel, characters relive traumatic events that they must come to terms with if they are to survive; they are shaped by the past and shape themselves by what they make of the past. Actions are not isolated events but, like currents, flow backward and forward, altering perceptions of the past, motivating acts in time present. As Kinloch Armstrong, the protagonist of *Fire in the Morning,* realizes, "the real things . . . depended perhaps on other things before them and so on backwards endlessly." [6]

The past exerts its power in Tarsus in the effects of a feud precipitated by a Snopes-like family, the Gerrards, who arrived in the 1870s, began as dirt farmers and cotton pickers, then took over the hardware store, and by the turn of the century gained possession of a large estate by cheating the rightful heirs. Chief among the victims of Gerrard greed is Daniel Armstrong, the best of the yeoman farmer stock and the exemplar of sanity, tolerance, and courage in the novel.[7] Understanding that revenge on the Gerrards will merely perpetuate injustice and violence in the town, he has renounced his claim to the land and has made peace with his enemy, Simon Gerrard.

Daniel's son Kinloch, however, refuses to adopt his father's view. Instead, he binds or locks himself to his vow to reveal to the town the crimes of the Gerrards and wrest from them the land that belongs to his family. A flashback early in the novel, a memorably symbolic scene, reveals that his purpose shaped itself during his adolescence, on a day when a gang of boys, led by Simon's son Lancelot, tortured and killed Kinloch's dog by repeatedly throwing him into a creek which they had muddied by their swimming. (This is the first of several instances in Elizabeth Spencer's fiction in which the presence of a dog lends an aura of fear, pathos, or mystery to a scene marking a turning point in a character's life.) After Kinloch marries, his desire for retribution is strengthened by his sense of estrangement from his wife, Ruth, a stranger to Tarsus, who, knowing nothing of the past, has innocently formed a friendship with Simon Gerrard's children.

The central action of the novel is Kinloch's search for the truth that lies behind "his whole Gerrard myth" of plunder and violence. His quest, which sends him to old court records and obscure people whose relation to the Gerrards he ferrets out, occupies less than a year. But gradually, as he pieces together facts, rumors, and fragments of stories, the history of three generations of Gerrards emerges. Of the several narrators who tell Kinloch their stories, the most important is his middle-aged bachelor cousin, Randall Gibson, a choric figure who draws universal truths from local history and shifts his burden of the past to Kinloch in a long recital that occupies a fourth of the novel.

As described by Randall Gibson, the victims of the Gerrards constitute a gallery of typical Southern figures: the Negro, "Ole Tuck," whom the Gerrards kill because he inherited from his master land the Gerrards want; his son-in-law, a mulatto, who, "unable to find a pattern towards black or white race because he was neither" (127), allows himself to be killed in a fight with the Gerrards; Dr. Derryberry, a physically stunted, emotionally starved grotesque, who confesses to Kinloch that he was forced by the Gerrards to give false medical testimony in court. Miss Cherry Bell, compared by reviewers to Tennessee Williams's Blanche DuBois, clings to the image of herself as "the sweet young lady" after her name is clouded by scandal, drinks in secret, and tries to crochet "dainty patterns" from tangled threads she cannot see (106).

These figures are familiar literary types, but the central characters have the unconfined quality of living persons. In Daniel and Kinloch Armstrong, Spencer portrays good men of few words and unself-conscious virtue without idealizing them. In Simon and Lancelot Gerrard, she captures the mixture of arrogance and cowardice that impels them to exploit the weak and cower before the truly resolute, such as Daniel Armstrong. Reviewers compared the Gerrards to the Hubbards in Lillian Hellman's *The Little Foxes* as well as to the Snopeses. But the Gerrards do not act with the impunity and amoral ruthlessness of these characters. Their nature is best defined by the word describing Simon Gerrard as he confronts Daniel Armstrong: "inferior" (127). Like Simon, his children, Lancelot and Justin, leave a trail of wreckage in their wake. Their living room after a party is littered with overturned ashtrays and broken glasses, amidst which a friend has passed out. When the Gerrards' car, which Kinloch's wife is driving, accidentally kills a man, they persuade her to conceal the truth. At this point, they remind the reader of the Buchanans in *The Great Gatsby*: "careless people" who "smashed up things and creatures and then retreated back into their money or their vast carelessness, or whatever it was that kept them together, and let other people clean up the mess they had made."[8] But at the end, Lancelot himself is a broken man, deserted by his wife and shamed by knowledge of his father's crimes and his own weakness.

"You're a victim like all the rest" (225), Kinloch tells Dr. Derryberry, the most pathetic of the characters. So long as Kinloch seeks retribution, he too is a victim of the evil he vainly seeks to undo. He is saved by a vision effecting a conversion that transforms the dweller of this modern Tarsus moments after he sees his father vainly try to rescue Simon Gerrard from a pit in which both men die. When Kinloch confronts his hatred in the form of an "enormous, sprawling, vaguely bestial Shape," he realizes at last that "it had the power to destroy him utterly" (267), then watches the vision recede, leaving him free to destroy his evidence against the Gerrards, abandon his claim to the land, unite himself to his wife, and offer his hand in goodwill to Simon's son Lancelot, who declares his intention to sell the ill-gotten land and leave Tarsus.

It is a measure of the power of the novel that the reconciliations at the end do not nullify the suffering of the characters or erase the horror of the mutilations and deaths. The horror seems all the greater in that violent action takes place—not in such Gothic settings as decaying mansions and graveyards at night, but in daylight, in ordinary, everyday surroundings—offices, stores, streets, and fields. The novel thus realizes the idea Spencer derives from the passage in Djuna Barnes's *Nightwood,* which she quotes as her epigraph, that fire in the morning is more terrifying than the conventional fire against a night sky: in Spencer's words, "he who is enemy or vandal is expected to take his prerogative from the night, and the spoiler who will not, troubles a vaster sphere than thought would choose to enter, and something unreconciled is here" (18).[9]

Spencer's first two novels are linked by the character Elinor Gerrard, Lancelot's wife and the daughter of Amos Dudley, the protagonist of the second novel, *This Crooked Way.* The two novels were not planned as a sequence, however, and their themes are different. Like Kinloch Armstrong, Amos Dudley pursues a course destructive to himself and those near him, but he seeks not truth or justice or retribution but worldly power and wealth, symbolized by the gold that the thieves in Chaucer's "Pardoner's Tale" discover when directed by the Old Man to go "up this crokéd wey" if they would find death.[10]

Of all her works, *This Crooked Way* most clearly shows what Elizabeth Spencer owes to Faulkner and how she differs from him. In plot, the novel bears a marked resemblance to *Absalom, Absalom!,* although *This Crooked Way* is set in a later time. The novel begins in 1900, when Amos is sixteen, and ends some forty years later. Like Thomas Sutpen, Amos begins in poverty, the child of hill country farmers. He conceives a far-reaching plan, like Sutpen's "design," which totally possesses him and drives him relentlessly to remove all obstacles to fulfillment. He is impelled—not by social rejection, which starts Sutpen on his fatal way—but by a vision of God's power, which, in a fiery hand, saves Amos from drowning in the Yocona River, where he had baptized himself after a revivalist preacher had chanted to the crowd of the shining ladder God let down to the sinful Jacob. As Sutpen acquires his vast tract, Sutpen's Hundred, marries the daughter of the aristocratic Coldfield family, and fathers children to establish his dynasty, so Amos Dudley buys hundreds of acres in the central delta, labors with a force of Negroes to lift a plantation out of the swamps, marries Ary Morgan, descended from four generations of rich delta planters, fathers three children by her, and sees the town of Dudley grow up around his cotton gin, barns, and commissary. Like Sutpen, Amos Dudley, before his marriage, lives with a woman of mixed blood, whom he later abandons because she does not fit into the design. She bears a son, who, like Charles Bon, returns to his father's house, is attracted to his half-sister, and is eventually shot and killed by a member of his father's family.

In its use of several narrators, the novel is reminiscent of *Absalom, Absalom!, The Sound and the Fury,* and *As I Lay Dying*. The first section of Amos's story, "The Wandering," shows from the view of a third-person narrator a succession of departures, as Amos separates himself from his family, two employers, his mistress, and his best friend, Arney. Amos narrates the final section, "The Return," which reveals both the change within him and the disappearance of his native town, inundated by the TVA dams. The "Indictments" of the long middle section are given by three first-person narrators: Amos's friend Arney; Dolly, the daughter of Ary's dead sister Louise; and Amos's wife, each of whom suffers his cold will to mastery and pronounces judgment. After more than thirty years of marriage, Ary tells her niece Dolly: "To all that I love, hide it as he will, he is sudden and ruthless death" (201).

Not surprisingly, reviewers compared Elizabeth Spencer to Faulkner and called her a "disciple of the master."[11] But similarities in plot highlight essential differences between *This Crooked Way* and *Absalom, Absalom!* Although cold and ruthless, Amos Dudley has little of the demonic force that makes Sutpen a transcendent figure. None of the narrators vicariously enters Amos's inward life, as Shreve and Quentin relive the experiences binding Charles Bon and Henry Sutpen. After the first section, Amos is often a shadowy figure, as the half-caste Joe Ferguson seems to Ary, "a facade shielding a mind coolly at work" (170).

Although Amos's struggle for mastery is the prime motivating force, the novel centers on the opposition of contrasting regions and ways of life represented by the two families: the Dudleys of the hill country, characterized by their primitive religion, their poverty, and their vernacular speech; and the Morgans of Dellwood plantation, a closely bound clan united by their family stories and meals, their "rites of affection" for Ary's dead sister Louise, their hostility to newcomers, and their opposition to the marriages of Louise and Ary to men from the hills. The Morgans show their power in a highly charged scene of a Sunday dinner after Ary's marriage, when they use Louise's daughter Dolly, the child of an outsider, to draw Amos into a quarrel in which they can unite against him. He, in turn, aware of their efforts to isolate and emasculate him, changes the name of his second daughter from Louise to Dinah, perverts her into an ally against them, insists that his wife, when she is forty-two, bear him another child, and forces her to take Joe Ferguson into their house, although Amos is unable or unwilling to admit or deny that Joe is his son.

The chief victim of the struggle is not the outsider, Amos, but his wife, Ary, trapped between two walls of pressure: the power of her family, whose glorification of Louise compelled Ary to prove herself the strongest in dangerous feats of horsemanship; and her husband's determination to break her ties to the Morgans and destroy the symbols of their power. Ary's plight is represented in her failure to move a heavy antique chair from Dellwood to Dudley, an effort which results in her miscarriage and loss of the child Amos insisted she bear.

As in *Absalom, Absalom!*, conflict builds to violent death. Ary's knowledge that Joe Ferguson has violated Dinah and then betrayed her with a half-witted albino Negro drives Ary to shoot him when she comes upon him alone in their house. Far from separating husband and wife, however, the act of violence frees both from the forces that had held them apart. In firing the gun, Ary frees herself from the Morgans, confessing later to Amos, "I don't care what they think" (243). Amos, in seizing the gun to protect his wife, knows that he has bound himself to her and lost his vision of himself as God's chosen one: "So it was over . . . where God had been there was nothing but a big silence" (p. 226).

As in *Fire in the Morning*, violent death, like a sacrificial act, effects resolution and reconciliation. The ending of the novel, a "ritualistic redemption," as Spencer called it,[12] transforms Amos from an egoistic visionary to a penitent who accepts the limits of his common humanity and acknowledges the family bonds he has hitherto denied. He returns to his birthplace, is baptized in the river where he once baptized himself, casts into the river the bag of money that years before precipitated his quarrel and break with his brother Ephraim, rescues Ephraim and his family when their house blows down in a storm, and takes them all to his plantation in Dudley. His journey ends as a caravan of cars and a school bus filled with Dudleys, furniture, mattresses, and dishes comes jolting into the yard, where Ary flinches, then welcomes them. Whether the influx of relatives signifies the redemption of Amos, the union of Amos and Ary, or the triumph of Dudleys over Morgans, the final scene is a comic, not a tragic, resolution of the action.

That such a scene could fittingly conclude the novel shows how far removed from the surreal nightmare world of the Sutpens are the hills and the delta of *This Crooked Way*. In the plantations of the Morgans and the Dudleys, where Negroes talk of portents, omens, charms, and hexes, the white women give luncheons, play bridge, and buy expensive dresses for their daughters, who at night go in cars with their lovers to the bayou. Unlike Faulkner's Quentin Compson, Gail Hightower, and Isaac McCaslin, Spencer's characters, even those like the Morgans, who derive their sense of identity from their family's past, do not deny or seek to escape the modern world of automobiles, radios, movies, and the TVA.

Like *Fire in the Morning, This Crooked Way,* published in 1952, was widely reviewed and praised by most of its reviewers, who recognized Elizabeth Spencer as an artist in the tradition of Faulkner and Warren and Carson McCullers. She wrote the plan for her third novel, *The Voice at the Back Door,* during the next year, while still at the University of Mississippi, where she had been teaching creative writing since 1948. In 1953, she was awarded a Guggenheim Fellowship, for which Stark Young recommended her. She went to Italy to work on the novel, came back to the United States in 1955 to finish it, and the next year returned to Italy, where she married John Rusher, an Englishman and the director of a language school, whom she had met in Rome. They left Italy in 1958 to make their home in Montreal, where they still live.

In a number of ways, the years in Italy marked a turning point for Spencer. She not only finished the third and the greatest of the Mississippi novels, but she also gained a new perspective on the world of these works and began to develop a new subject—the experience of Americans in Italy. In 1957, when the *New Yorker* published an early story, "The Little Brown Girl," after rejecting it in 1944, she began to establish her reputation as a writer of subtle, polished short stories. For the next fifteen years, she was a regular contributor to the *New Yorker,* which published some of her most important stories, including "First Dark," "Ship Island," "The Fishing Lake," "Sharon," and her most popular and best-known work, the novella *The Light in the Piazza*.

None of the later works, however, surpasses in interest and importance her third novel, *The Voice at the Back Door,* widely acclaimed on its publication in 1956. In an interview in 1981, Spencer recalled that after two "beginning novels" she desired to write a "considerable work" dealing with current racial issues in a restricted setting, "a small town . . . in flux," in which "forces working for change" could be studied at close range.[13] The town, Lacey, in the hill country of northern Mississippi, is similar to Tarsus, but for the first time, Spencer centered her narrative upon the relation of blacks and whites, making the novel a case study in racial prejudice, the conflicts in the town a microcosm of national conflicts.

The novel begins dramatically as the county sheriff, Travis Brevard, races in his car through the dusty countryside into the town, to a grocery store, where he dies of a heart attack in the presence of its owner, Duncan Harper, who will succeed him as sheriff until the next election is held. The contradictions of the old order are represented by the dying sheriff, who took protection money from the town bootlegger, Jimmie Tallant; went to Negro funerals but let a Negro under his protection bleed to death in the jail; and is survived by his Negro mistress and by his wife, a desiccated specimen of genteel Southern womanhood and an ardent segregationist. Duncan Harper, the protagonist of the novel, before he becomes sheriff, is known chiefly for his feats as an All-American football star at Ole Miss and for his engagement to Marcia Mae Hunt, the elder daughter of Lacey's richest family, who left Duncan to marry a Yankee army officer. Until the death of Travis Brevard, Duncan has been content to manage his father's grocery store on the old lines and to live an uneventful life with his wife, Tinker, a Lacey girl, and their two children.

The death of the old sheriff inaugurates a new order in Lacey, in that Duncan Harper resolves to enforce the laws: to shut down his friend Jimmie Tallant's illegal whiskey business and to secure the legal rights of the Negroes. Notable for the "fateful simplicity in his character,"[14] like Kinloch Armstrong, he proceeds steadily, undeterred by the prospects of physical injury, social rejection, and defeat in the election. Unlike his friend Kerney Woolbright—a young lawyer from Lacey who argues that liberal views are destined to prevail in "the New South," until his defense of Negro rights threatens his election to the state legislature—Duncan Harper makes no political analyses, he embraces no ideology, he claims no bond with the Negroes; he acts simply to uphold the laws and do justice: "What else is there to say any more but that they should have an equal chance?" (276).

From the beginning of the novel, Duncan Harper's fate seems locked to that of a Negro foreman in a tie plant, Beckwith Dozer, who also represents a force for change in the town. In contrast to the passive, superstitious Negro servants who remain on the periphery in Spencer's first two novels, Beckwith Dozer is assertive and wily in his readiness to use and be used by white men to gain money and protection. He longs also to emulate his father, Robinson Dozer, a man of extraordinary courage and resolution, who in 1919 led twelve Negroes to the courthouse in Lacey to defend the rights of three Negro soldiers accused of killing a white girl but who was shot and killed, along with his followers, by a gang of white men led by Jimmie Tallant's father.

How little the community has progressed since the days of Robinson Dozer is revealed when Beckwith Dozer, like the soldiers his father tried to defend, is accused of a crime, the shooting of Jimmie Tallant. While Dozer stays in hiding, Duncan Harper, in the face of mounting opposition in the town, insists upon Dozer's legal rights to custody and trial. Although Tallant recovers from his wounds, although all the evidence indicates that the gunman was not Dozer but one of a New Orleans syndicate who was in Lacey to do business with Tallant, a mob gathers to hunt the Negro down and kill him. When Beck Dozer comes out of hiding and seeks Duncan Harper's protection, he insists that he be given custody in Lacey, that he may go into town "like my daddy did." On their way to Lacey, a tire on Duncan's car blows out, his car overturns, and he dies in the wreck.

The fate of Duncan Harper shows that racial prejudice is stronger than reverence for football heroes and proves the error of Kerney Woolbright's initial belief that "the old reactionary position of the South has played out to nothing but a lot of sentiment" (30). In defending the rights of Negroes, Duncan becomes an outsider in his own town, thus proving the truth of Randall Gibson's contention in *Fire in the Morning* that the greatest threat to a people is not the newcomer but the "stranger who was born among them. Here you have the battle worth watching, for this kind of stranger has learned early to draw his own sword" (103). Duncan Harper's opponents appear to win the battle, but his death is not without effect. Among the survivors of the wreck is Beck Dozer, who might have been killed had the mob not been diverted by the accident that killed Duncan Harper. Jimmie Tallant, who had once proposed to run against Duncan Harper for sheriff, takes the dead man's cause as his own and refuses to stand for election on segregationist principles. His opposite, Kerney Woolbright, however, after publicly repudiating Duncan Harper and the cause of civil rights, suppresses the evidence in a telegram from New Orleans that confirms

Dozer's innocence, although he has the grace to shed tears as he rationalizes his deceptions and betrayals in the closing paragraphs of the novel.

In a 1981 interview, Elizabeth Spencer said that she wrote *The Voice at the Back Door* "to explore any number of attitudes toward the changing social climate."[15] Most repulsive is the race hatred of the rednecks who try to stop Duncan's car when they see Beck Dozer in the front seat and of the deputy sheriff, Willard Follansbee, most physically loathsome of the characters, who rapes Dozer's wife, having nothing better to do at the moment. Higher on the scale of gentility and hypocrisy is Jason Hunt, the richest and most powerful supporter of the old order, who urges his prospective son-in-law, Kerney Woolbright, to break with Duncan on the grounds that his "Negro stand is a good thing . . . but we gain nothing—we might lose a great deal—by saying so in public" (43). Once they commit themselves to the fight for civil rights, Duncan Harper and Jimmie Tallant are steadfast, although neither is a noble stereotype guiltless of injury to others. While he is fighting for Beck Dozer's rights, Duncan Harper causes his wife weeks of anguish by his affair with Marcia Mae Hunt; Jimmie Tallant, burdened with guilt by the knowledge of his father's murder of Robinson Dozer, abuses his witless wife without compunction, although, unlike Tinker, she seems to have too shallow a nature to suffer deeply.

Because the novel dramatizes issues of national importance, the town of Lacey seems less isolated, less self-contained than Tarsus or Dudley. In *The Voice at the Back Door,* the characters themselves are, unlike the characters in the first two novels, more conscious of the world beyond their region, especially Kerney Woolbright, Jimmie Tallant, and Marcia Mae Hunt, who have lived outside the South. Jimmie Tallant, for instance, watches the endless stream of trucks and cars passing his café and is fascinated by "the sense of the linked immensities of America" (136).

Because they are more aware of the outside world, they are more conscious than the earlier characters of being Southerners, with memories and experiences and traditions that set them apart from other Americans. Likewise, the narrator observes that certain feelings and actions of the characters are typical of Southerners, and from their experiences she generalizes—not universal truths as in *Fire in the Morning*—but truths about the South. When they talk of racial issues, Duncan Harper and his friends are said to know "in common with all Southerners that when the knot got too tangled it was just as well left alone" (28). The narrator notes that Duncan's defense of "right" sounds odd, out of place "in a country where the motives for doing things are given names like honor, pride, love, family, greed, passion, revenge, and hatred" (128). Duncan knows the whole of Robinson Dozer's story without perhaps having heard it all, because "Southerners hear parts of stories with their ears, and the rest they know with their hearts" (233). The "voice at the back door," the Negro calling at night at the house of white people, is "part of the consciousness of a Southern household" (83).

Although the three Mississippi novels are very different from one another, in each the protagonist is a man striving to achieve a clearly defined goal—to expose past crimes, to build a plantation, to enforce the laws. In both *Fire in the Morning* and *This Crooked Way,* the man is freed when he is released from the grip of his purpose, which he himself has conceived. In all three novels, the man remains in the town or region of his birth and casts off the burden of the past without even desiring physical escape. Kinloch Armstrong knows that it is right for him to remain in Tarsus. Duncan Harper knows that he "was a citizen of Lacey. . . . It was his strongest and final quality" (186).

The women in Elizabeth Spencer's first three novels and in a number of the short stories seek a different kind of freedom. They desire not the fulfillment of a particular ambition but escape from the authority of the family, from its traditions, its powers of influence, and its attempts to dictate the choices and actions of its members. Although Ary Morgan cherishes family heirlooms, names her children after members of her family, and defends her family against her husband's attacks, she feels liberated from an oppressive force when she knows that "I was free of them" (217) and no longer cares what they think. Marcia Mae Hunt jilts Duncan Harper because he will not leave Lacey after she pleads, "We couldn't stay in the South and be free. In the South it's nothing but family, family" (176). She married a man without family roots or ties thinking that "at least he's free" (181). When her husband's death in the war frees her from marriage to a bounder and she returns to her family in Lacey, she supports Duncan Harper as a way of asserting herself against the family's corrupting power.

The theme of women's quest for freedom, although clearly stated, is secondary in *The Voice at the Back Door.* However, it becomes the dominant theme of Spencer's fiction after the three Mississippi novels. The protagonists of the two novellas set in Italy, the two novels that followed them, and most of the short stories are women who seek escape from relationships and ways of living that have hitherto controlled their lives. They exemplify what Spencer has identified as the central idea of her later fiction, that "women feel themselves very often imprisoned by what people expect of them."[16]

In several of her most successful stories, the protagonist is a woman of a small Southern town oppressed by demands of family, in which the power of aging parents to bind their daughters grows stronger as the parents grow physically weaker. Death sometimes releases the woman from the bondage of duty, and she marks her freedom by her departure from her native place. Frances Harvey, in "First Dark," is freed from the prison of her family and its past by the self-willed death of her domineering mother, which allows Frances to yield to her lover's determination that they leave her family house forever. Theresa Stubblefield, in "The White Azalea," escapes to Europe after the death of her parents, whom she had nursed for years in the family house in Tuxapoka, Alabama. When letters from relatives reach her home in Rome describing more family crises she is expected to deal with, she buries the letters in a pot of white azaleas, feeling that she consigns the Stubblefields themselves to the earth in *"the most beautiful family funeral of them all."*[17]

Many of Elizabeth Spencer's characters, it is true, draw strength and a sense of identity from their memories of family and place. To Marilee Summerall, the clear-sighted narrator of three stories, it is important that twenty years after she visits the ruins of a plantation, Windsor, she can imagine the mansion still standing "pure in its decay," to satisfy her need of "a sure terrain, of a sort of permanent landscape of the heart" ("A Southern Landscape," 52).[18] The narrator of "The Day Before" gains her heart's wish when her hand instinctively touches the hidden catch of a glass box seen long ago in childhood and she seems to repossess the "great hidden world" (230) of the past she had believed lost forever. A character in "The Cousins," whose words the narrator recalls thirty years later, relives scenes of summer evenings with his four cousins in Martinsville, Alabama, when he felt that "if I live to be a thousand, I'll never feel more love than I do this minute. Love of these, my blood, and this place, here."[19]

Such feelings make liberating oneself a painful process for a number of Spencer's characters. Aline, the protagonist of "Mr. McMillan," illustrates the pull of conflicting desires—to break free yet hold on to one's past life. Like Katherine Anne Porter's Miranda, Aline seeks self-knowledge but discovers that "trying to find it in the bosom of a Mississippi family was like trying to find some object lost in a gigantic attic" (335). Against the wishes of her family, she undertakes at Tulane University an eight-year research program in parasitology (an apt choice of subject) but realizes that she owes her success, "her very capacity to pull through" (335), to the family whose will she defied. At her hotel in New Orleans, she meets her counterpart, Mr. McMillan, who, after sixty years of "doing just what everybody thought he ought to do" (337), finally, after his parents' death, escapes to the city, where he dies, leaving instructions that his ashes be scattered in the water of a Hawaiian bay.[20]

In these stories of memory and escape, Elizabeth Spencer portrays two kinds of women prominent in her later fiction: the passive figure, like Frances Harvey, who is freed by the agency of others; and the active figure, like Aline, who of her own will frees herself and pursues an independent course. The active figure is the protagonist of the first Italian novella, *The Light in the Piazza;* the passive figure is the protagonist of the second, *Knights and Dragons.*

The Light in the Piazza centers on the thoughts and actions of Margaret Johnson, the wife of a businessman in Winston-Salem and the mother of a twenty-six-year-old daughter who has the physical nature of a grown woman but, because of an accident, the mental capacity of a ten-year-old child. In Italy, where Margaret Johnson has taken her daughter to escape the difficulties of their life in Winston-Salem, she resolves on a course of action and achieves, unaided, the desire of her heart—the marriage and the prospect of a happy life for her daughter.

With a few deft strokes, the three main characters are realized as they come together on a June afternoon in the Piazza della Signoria in Florence: the mother, attractive, competent, heartsick over her daughter's infirmity but controlled and determinedly cheerful with her; the daughter, Clara, physically unmarred, pliant and obedient, yet tenacious in her devotion once she falls in love; and her ebullient and irrepressible suitor, Fabrizio Nacarelli, equally tenacious in impressing his attentions upon Clara and her mother. The "light" is Mrs. Johnson's realization that, after all, marriage may be possible for Clara in this foreign culture, that in the well-to-do Nacarelli family, whose members approve her innocence and beauty and seem unaware of her deficiency, nothing beyond her capacity will be required of her.

In effecting the desired end, Margaret Johnson must first subdue her feelings of guilt in concealing the truth about Clara from the Nacarellis. At one point, at a fiesta, when she is about to tell Fabrizio's father of Clara's injury, a cannon going off accidentally, with Hardy-like fatality, wounds a bystander and prevents her from speaking. Once committed to the vision of her daughter married, she proceeds with the determination of a general mapping a campaign. She contrives to keep her husband, who would object to the marriage, from coming to Rome in time to stop it; she matches her skills as a strategist with those of Signor Nacarelli, a coldly intelligent man of the world, who if he perceives what is wrong with Clara never reveals it. When he declares the marriage off on the grounds of Clara's age, she raises Clara's dowry by ten thousand dollars to secure his consent. Because she has bargained for the sake of her daughter's happiness, he for the sake of the money, she can feel that the onus of turning the marriage into a business transaction rests upon him and not her.

Rather like "The Turn of the Screw," the story Henry James wrote as an "*amusette* to catch those not easily caught"[21] and the subject of more critical analyses than any of his other works, *The Light in the Piazza,* written, according to Spencer, in less than six weeks as a "sort of an amusement,"[22] was her greatest financial success and has remained her best-known work. The novel won the ten-thousand-dollar McGraw-Hill Fiction Award, was translated into ten foreign languages, and was made into a successful film starring Olivia de Havilland as Margaret Johnson. A few reviewers had reservations about the book. Elizabeth Janeway objected to the happy ending as unrealistic.[23] George Steiner criticized the book for not portraying Clara's consciousness.[24] Most reviewers, however, praised the novella without qualification for its sensitive perception of emotion, its evocation of the Italian scene, and the subtlety and precision of its style.

That a number of reviewers compared Elizabeth Spencer to Henry James is not surprising, given the emphasis in *The Light in the Piazza* upon the contrast of Italian and American Anglo-Saxon manners and habits of mind and upon the fathomless nature of the Italian character, as Italy itself, as James insisted, in its deepest reaches seems impenetrable, inaccessible to outsiders.[25] Spencer develops the irony suggested by the title: in "the light of the piazza" celebrated by Michelangelo, colors are clear, surfaces are sharply outlined, and "one had the sense of being able to see everything exactly as it was."[26] Yet, as Elizabeth Spencer observed, neither Margaret Johnson nor the reader is ever certain what the Nacarellis know and think. Their motives remain "absolutely opaque."[27]

Elizabeth Spencer's affinities with James are those of craftsmanship as well as subject. In *The Light in the Piazza,* she constructs a narrative on the Jamesian principles of unity and economy, exemplified by his ideal of the "beautiful and blest *nouvelle.*"[28] Her novella portrays the relation of a small group of characters engaged in a single action, which begins near the point of crisis and unfolds in a sequence of tightly connected scenes. The title emphasizes the unifying image of light carried through the book by Clara's name and by repeated references to vision and seeing. Margaret Johnson, like the Jamesian center of consciousness, is both an actor and an observer of the action, presented entirely from her point of view. Like James, for whom "impressions *are* experience,"[29] Spencer makes the impressions and perceptions of the central character the pivotal points of the action. The turning point in *The Light in the Piazza* occurs at the moment when, in the Roman Forum, Mrs. Johnson comes upon her daughter sitting alone weeping, suddenly recognizes in the girl's grief the dignity of a woman's passion, and resolves to take Clara back to Florence. What is not Jamesian is the cannon shot that kills an unknown man—a sudden rent in the bright surface of the festive scene.

In *Knights and Dragons,* her second novella, Elizabeth Spencer portrays Margaret Johnson's opposite, the woman who, instead of imposing her will and shaping events, suffers under the yoke of another's will. The first sentence introduces the central action: "Martha Ingram had come to Rome to escape something."[30] In Rome, where she works at the United States cultural office, she leads a double life—outwardly competent, poised, and self-assured as she performs her official duties; inwardly "demon-haunted," tormented by memories of her husband and former teacher, known to the world as an eminent scholar and writer and admired by countless friends and disciples, but known to herself as a tyrant and egoist who for ten years of marriage had subjected her to his will and who still pursues her in Rome, sending her letters, clippings, messengers, and once, most sinister of all, an empty envelope. Alone in an apartment reached by "devious stairways, corridors," Martha lives in a shadowy phantasmagoric world of the mind, feeling herself cut off from reality, surrounded by masklike faces in a city of deceptive appearances, often ghostlike in the rain—"a house of death" (36).

Her mental torment is transformed into a nightmare by her affair with an American economist, Jim Wilbourne, who is in Rome for the year on a cultural exchange. His ploy to gain her attention—he tells her falsely that her husband has been wounded in a hunting accident—forces her to confront her suppressed desire for her husband's death. In telling her, "You've wanted him out of the way all along. You wanted me to get rid of him" (58), he claims for himself the role of her rescuer, but in an inversion of the legend of Saint George and the dragon, he becomes also a destroyer, as his blunt words "cast her . . . straight into madness" (58). Unlike Saint Martha, the legendary slayer of a dragon, Martha Ingram is freed by agencies outside herself. The actual death of her husband and Jim Wilbourne's departure from Rome finally free her spirit from its old forms: "those intricate structures, having come to their own completion, were no longer habitable. She saw them crumble, sink, and go under forever" (167). As if her self has dissolved, she feels her spirit intermingled with the life of the city flowing about her, and she asks herself, "Was this another name for freedom? Freedom was certainly what it felt like" (168). But release from psychological bondage does not bring to Martha the sense of triumphant escape that Frances Harvey knows. To free oneself from everyone is to belong everywhere and nowhere. "In freeing herself she had met dissolution, and was a friend now to any landscape, a companion to cloud and sky" (169).

Knights and Dragons is not autobiography, but Martha Ingram's feeling of detachment at the end may be reflective of her creator's sense that in leaving the South she had become, as she said, "a sort of roving spirit" and no longer a "fixed planet."[31] Spencer did not break her ties with her native region: after she and her husband settled in Montreal, she made frequent trips to Mississippi to visit her parents in Carrollton, to give readings and lectures, to receive an honorary degree from Southwestern at Memphis, and to participate in conferences in Oxford and Jackson. But she knew that her relation to the South had changed, just as the world of her childhood had changed. Physical separation from the South had a decisive effect upon her definition of herself as a writer and upon her choice of subject. So long as she was writing Southern novels in the South, she observed, she felt no need to question the ultimate purpose of her work; her sense of purpose and identity came from knowing that "she was simply part of the Southern tradition."[32] Departure from the South impelled her to seek her subjects outside the "mystic community" of her Southern past, to write fiction that would "come to terms with, not the Southern world, but the world of modern experience."[33] Her women protagonists rebel not only against domination by Southern families and Southern traditions but against forces in modern life that threaten their integrity.

Elizabeth Spencer continued to set her fiction in the South, but more often on the Gulf Coast and in New Orleans than in the hill towns of northern Mississippi, and now many of her characters, detached from their families and cut off from the past, instinctively seek to complete themselves in relations with others rootless like themselves. Her "new South" is first portrayed in "Ship Island" (1964), which she has described as a "very significant story for me."[34] The scenes take place in restaurants and bars in Biloxi; in a nearby beach town where the protagonist, Nancy Lewis, lives in a shabby rented house with her parents after her father loses his job in Little Rock; and on Ship Island, where she becomes the lover of Rob Acklen, the popular son of a wealthy Southern family. In "Ship Island," as in many of Spencer's stories, sudden inexplicable occurrences give an eerie quality to the sharply defined scenes and characters.

The quality of mystery inheres in the protagonist herself, the first of those figures to whom Spencer has acknowledged herself particularly attracted: "for some reason I began to feel an affinity to kind of waif-like women that were free. They have no particular ties, or no ties that are worth holding them, and so they become subject to all kinds of en-counters, influences, choices out in the world."[35] Nancy breaks out of the conventional upper-middle-class circle to which Rob Acklen has confined her when she leaves him and his friends suddenly one evening at a party at a hotel. In a sequence foreshadowing *The Snare,* she joins a stranger whom she saw that morning on the beach and goes eagerly with him and his companion to New Orleans, where in an undisclosed scene of brutality she is bruised and beaten. As the subtitle, "The Story of a Mermaid," implies, she breaks with Rob not merely because she is conscious of class differences but because she feels that in his world she is not a person but "another order of creature" belonging to another element—free, unconfined, primordial, symbolized by the mysterious shower of blistering hot rain, which only she and the stranger she sees on the beach have felt. On land, Nancy is bitten by mosquitoes in the bayous, is patronized by sorority girls "with tiny voices, like mosqui-toes," and converses awkwardly with expensive-looking people who seem to her like figures in a magazine. In the water, her element, she drifts like seaweed as if asleep there; she is called a nymph; she feels as if she moves underwater, knows that if Rob "gets down as far as I am, he'll drown" (109), and disappears from him at the end as though into the depths of the sea.

Three years later, in 1967, Spencer's fourth novel, *No Place for an An-gel,* her most searching study of modern life, was published. The title suggests the central idea: in postwar America of the 1950s, there is no place for the innocent and uncorrupted. According to Spencer, the "an-gel" refers also to the absolutes that the characters seek and fail to find and to the Catholic conception of angels as intermediaries between God and human beings[36]—an idea without reality in the "grey world,"[37] where the only believer is a crazed member of a sect called the Blood of the Messiah. The characters live in a wasteland of casual sex and corrupt politics, where people talk at parties of the threat of nu-clear attack, live for the day in hedonistic pleasure at beaches and ho-tels, and are momentarily shocked by sudden accidents and acts of violence: a teenage boy on vacation with his family in Florida deliber-ately electrocutes himself; a gun inexplicably goes off, shattering the wall of a room. Characters' lives are like the hotel balcony, "a new post-war structure . . . loosened from the wall" (90), which collapses and nearly kills two people.

Once again, Spencer develops her central theme through the contrast of characters. The novel focuses alternately on the lives of two couples, the Waddells and the Sassers, linked by an impoverished sculptor called Barry Day, who has been taken up by the Waddells, through whom he meets Catherine Sasser in Rome. Charles and Irene Waddell, worldly, energetic egoists, interested in the latest in fashions, entertainment, and people, are well matched. They impose no standards upon each other beyond those of material well-being, and their marriage survives quarrels and separations, Charles's loss of his job, and Irene's affair with an Italian writer. The Sassers, at the opposite ends of the social and moral scales, are mismatched. Jerry Sasser, the son of a religious fanatic, has lifted himself out of poverty and obscurity in a little Texas town and, backed by his father-in-law's oil fortune, has become a prominent lawyer in Washington, where he trades in falseness and corruption. As the political aide to a senator seeking reelection, he engages in whatever chicanery will win votes for his boss and makes out with secretaries and airline stewardesses, while forcing his wife to provide what his own image requires—a young attractive appendage devoted to her husband's career.

As he is the most corrupt of the characters, so his wife, Catherine, whose sister calls her an angel and a saint, is the least corrupted by the modern world, the most vulnerable yet the most resistant to falsehood. After she circulates among guests at a political cocktail party—telling them, " 'I'm here along with the wives of other important people just to present an image which ordinary people enjoy. It makes them feel safe when men on the inside are nicely paired off with attractive women who wear pretty clothes and look nice and smile like this' " (108)—her husband takes her to a psychiatric clinic in Denver, where she is pronounced a victim of "nervous exhaustion." Some months later, she leaves Jerry after he extorts money from her father in a vain attempt to suppress a news story damaging to the senator.

In the Mississippi novels, the outsider, such as Kinloch Armstrong's wife, is absorbed into the life of the town and few of its longtime inhabitants leave. In *No Place for an Angel,* all the characters, including the Southerners—Barry Day and Catherine and Jerry Sasser—have left their native regions and move from place to place, to Florida, New York, Washington, Rome, Sicily. The many shifts in setting reflect the rootless lives of all the characters cut off from their pasts. Barry Day, who undertakes to sculpt the figure of an angel, despite Irene Waddell's pronouncement that "angels don't belong in America" (3), clings to his boyhood memory of the Catholic church near New Orleans, where "there had been a place for angels" (18), but he has cut his ties with the

South, has changed his name and for years lived apart from his wife, whom he had married in Arkansas after the war. For Irene Waddell, "family was a dream you sometimes had, awakening conscience; like an occasional religious phase, they passed quickly out of your mind again as soon as you actually did anything about them" (22).

After Catherine leaves her husband, she becomes "one of those people—numerous in the world we have now—who have lived in so many different points on the globe that they have to think when they wake up, not just what room is this, or what house is this, or what hotel, motel, pension or resort is this, but what city is this in what country and what am I doing in it?" (168). Catherine's one root to the past is the memory of her uncle Dick, whose look of sweetness struck through her like "a glance from an angel" (78) and whose story she often recalls, that of a young boy, an orphan, crushed to death in Sandy Gulch in Texas under the wheels of a wagon in a train going west. When Jerry Sasser confesses himself inwardly driven to meaningless ends, she begins to associate him with the dead boy. Jerry himself, when he is sacrificed to the senator's reputation and cast aside, identifies himself with the boy: "He was buried at Sandy Gulch like the boy beneath the wagon . . . his long trajectory of glory had fizzled out in the sand" (277).

The novel is not entirely dark, however. Jerry Sasser, most guilty of injury to others, is at least allowed to perceive the truth of his life, that "he had been that worst of all human things, a pretender at goodness for where it could get him" (277). When his dream of success collapses, he feels himself severed from his past yet free, "oddly alive, an escapee from a life sentence" (277). Irene Waddell, the most practical and hard-grained of the characters, has her moment of insight—a Joycean vision of vast cycles in which the human power of life alone gives meaning to the never-ending pattern of millions of lives. Catherine preserves her integrity even in madness, while Barry Day, after a failed marriage and unfulfilling liaisons, marries a girl whose love for him transforms his life.

Although the parents have been cut off from their pasts, they gain through their children a sense of connection and continuity. Charles Waddell is spiritually awakened by his discovery of the character and potentialities of his twin sons. Jerry Sasser is saved from obliteration in the "grey world" by choosing to make a life for the girl born to him and his mistress. Catherine has the love and companionship of her son Latham, a biologist, whose crippling from polio seems the sign and the guarantee of his freedom from the ambitions that corrupted his father.

For Martha Ingram and for Catherine Sasser, freedom is escape from the destructive will of another person, a journey through disillusionment and madness to the peace of withdrawal and detachment. For Julia Garrett, the protagonist of Spencer's next novel, *The Snare* (1972), freedom is a more positive state, achieved not in withdrawal but in immersion in life, in willing entrance into "the great life snare."[38] The setting is New Orleans in the 1960s; Julia is representative of her era in her determination to cast off all that she feels confines her to a life of sterile convention and materialism. When the novel begins, she has broken her engagement to a millionaire entrepreneur from northern Louisiana, whose family rejects all forms of unconventional behavior; she has left her home in the house of her aunt and uncle, aristocratic French Creoles whose life of perfect order and propriety in a secluded and exclusive suburb of New Orleans seems to her empty and dead. In this seemingly inviolate household, however, Julia as a child had an abnormally close relationship with her uncle's father, a sensual connoisseur of decadence who quoted Baudelaire and whose voice continues to haunt her after his death. Whether or not he physically violated her, he imbued her with the spirit of his philosophy, that love and corruption are inseparable, that the deepest joy is born out of decay and death.[39]

Elizabeth Spencer has identified Julia as "my threshold" to "that darker world I needed to explore."[40] Julia's threshold figure is a young jazz musician, Jake Springland, who leads her into the labyrinthine underworld of New Orleans. Becoming his lover, she is drawn unwittingly into the tangled net of a sordid murder case, is used as a messenger by drug pushers in league with a jazz combo, is abducted, beaten, and drugged in a night's orgy, but escapes and lives to bear Jake's child. Experiences that would have destroyed the mind and body of another woman only seem to strengthen her desire to shrink from nothing in which she feels the pulse of life. "I'll not refuse any part of it" becomes her creed (402). More like a matrix of experiences than a fallible, vulnerable person, she passes through the depths without being corrupted by what she does and what is done to her. To one of her lovers, journalist Tommy Arnold, who covers the murder case, Julia is "as wicked-innocent as a nymph out of nature" (364).

Spencer reveals the fullest significance of her heroine's life in her repeated association of Julia with the multitudinous life of New Orleans. Springland, to whom she is most deeply bound, "equated her with the city she had come to and grown into, its nerves at last like her own" (287). Tommy Arnold perceives in the dark underworld that ensnares Julia "the hidden bone structure" of the city; she herself incarnates the complex life of New Orleans, which is to him the "nation's true pulse beat" (81, 82). At the end, Julia feels her identity with the city in the sense of joy "special and profound" that "they shared together, she and the city; it was the joy that all came to find there, whether or not they knew it" (406).

In portraying outsiders—rootless figures of the modern world—seeking fulfillment in the historic city, Spencer shows in this novel, as in her earlier fiction, the impact of the modern upon the traditional. In *The Snare,* characters themselves share her purpose of revealing the past through the present, the universal through the particular. Tommy Arnold, through journalism, seeks to " 'get through' to the outside world," to make a New Orleans murder case a revelation of a "whole locale" that is "local to the world" (84). Jake Springland, the jazz musician, comes to New Orleans to realize his ambition of "working with an old tradition to create a new" (114). Julia is not only a vessel of experiences, her life "a great marble basin waiting to be filled to the swelling brim" (287), but she also becomes at the end an artist, making new designs of bits of iron and stone and colored glass, "fragments of a city" (402).

Neither *The Snare* nor *No Place for an Angel* received the attention given the first three novels or the widespread praise bestowed upon *The Voice at the Back Door* and *The Light in the Piazza.* Elizabeth Spencer's career had entered the stage familiar to writers who, in turning to new subjects, encounter neglect or criticism for leaving the world of their popular early works. She was not to publish another novel for eleven years, but her short stories continued to appear in the *Southern Review,* the *Atlantic,* and the *Ontario Review,* among other American and Canadian periodicals. Three stories were reprinted in the annual *Best Canadian Stories:* "Port of Embarkation" (1978), "The Search" (1979), and "Jean Pierre" (1982). In 1981, Doubleday brought out *The Stories of Elizabeth Spencer,* with a foreword by Eudora Welty and all but four of the thirty-six short stories published up to that time, as well as the novella *Knights and Dragons.*[41] A laudatory review by Reynolds Price on the first page of the *New York Times Book Review,* 1 March 1981, and other highly favorable reviews, which ranked Spencer with Katherine Mansfield, Flannery O'Connor, and Eudora Welty, marked the collection as one of the most important works of fiction to appear that year.[42]

The stories are set in Italy, Quebec, and the American South; the central characters include children, parents, students, teachers, husbands, wives, widows, widowers. But the stories, written over a period of more than thirty years, are notable not for their differences but for their unity of effect. Because of their brevity, the stories, more so than the novels, highlight the most distinctive quality of Spencer's fiction: the emanation, in scenes rendered with the utmost clarity, of mysterious forces, indefinable, often sinister, placing characters within the "haunted verge"—in Hawthorne's phrase—between the Actual and the Imaginary. The streets and apartments and hotels of Montreal are created with the same intensity as the towns and plantations of Mississippi, and the power of the visionary and the irrational knows no boundaries of age or place.

It manifests itself in many forms: in the inexplicable evil of a child ("Instrument of Destruction"), in the compulsions of a beautiful woman who craves the subjection of others ("Judith Kane"), in disturbing coincidences and mistaken identities (*Knights and Dragons,* "Go South in the Winter"), in fantasies that seem to tremble on the verge of being true ("The Little Brown Girl"), in the atmosphere of such deserted places as the sandpit in "The Fishing Lake" and the Vermont quarry in "Jean Pierre." Some characters find refuge from the haunting and the sinister in the familiar patterns of marriage ("The Absence") or in the "smooth, safe surfaces" of daily life ("Go South in the Winter"). Others, such as the protagonists of "Ship Island," "The Finder," and "The Girl Who Loved Horses," are, like Julia Garrett, drawn irresistibly to strange figures, often outcasts or criminals who threaten death yet seem to embody a primordial vital force, which, when withdrawn, leaves the protagonist dispossessed even in the presence of a marriage partner or lover.

The routines of seemingly normal upper-middle-class life can themselves become life-threatening forces, as in "I, Maureen," in which the narrator feels herself trapped by her husband's family, the Parthams, who wish her to be "somebody . . . like themselves" (345), just as the Parhams in *The Snare* try to force Julia into their mold. Unlike Julia, Maureen escapes into madness, finding refuge in a shabby apartment in East Montreal, where, despite her sense of attachment to her son and her lover, she learns, as Martha Ingram does, that to free oneself is to suffer a kind of dissolution. The protagonist of a later story, "Jean Pierre" (*New Yorker,* 17 August 1981) lives through a succession of haunted days and strange encounters during her husband's mysterious absence. In the end, however, as in *Fire in the Morning,* husband and wife are reunited, seemingly bound more closely than before the absence by profound experiences that neither can convey to the other.

The aura of mystery that surrounds the everyday world is heightened in a number of stories by allusions to folklore and fairy tales that frame the action and impart symbolic power to the characters. Spencer has linked "First Dark" to the tale of Rapunzel; *Knights and Dragons* to the legend of Saint George (one of Martha's would-be rescuers is named George Hartwell); and *The Light in the Piazza* to the tale of the prince whose love blinded him to the harelip of the princess. In "Ship Island," she makes her most deliberate use of folklore, exemplifying in Nancy Lewis traditional characteristics of mermaids—"their affinity for sailors, their breathing underwater, their unhappiness when on land."[43] Of her novels, *This Crooked Way,* which develops parallels between Amos Dudley and the biblical Jacob, draws most fully on mythic and legendary sources—appropriately, since the Old Testament figures are alive in the consciousness of the hill people who gather at the revivals.

The bizarre and the mundane, the primordial and the contemporary are once again commingled in Spencer's most recent novel, *The Salt Line* (1984), set on the Mississippi Gulf Coast. The world of "Ship Island" is here portrayed after hurricane Camille of 1969 has left in its wake the debris of smashed houses and broken trees. The scene of devastation, now animated by signs of renovation and intrigue among promoters, symbolizes the lives of the main characters, who, having suffered the ruin of hopes and ambitions, are now struggling to build new lives on the wreckage of the past.

The protagonist, Arnie Carrington, four years earlier a highly popular teacher of English literature at a Mississippi university called Southern Pines and a leader of student causes during the Vietnam War, is now, in his sixties, bereft of his position and prestige. Forced by his enemies to resign his professorship, he lives alone in a half-ruined house on the coast, haunted by the ghost of his wife, Evelyn, who died of cancer, impotent as a scholar as well as a lover, unable to complete his masterwork on Byron's last years. He is fisher-king of this wasteland, but rather than passively await a redeemer, he actively strives to restore his ruined world. When the novel opens, he is seeking capital to buy land and rebuild the devastated houses and hotels, to save the coast from operators who would blight it with motels and hamburger stands and miniature golf courses. Calling himself a "guardian," he tells the architect Yates, whom he has interested in his plans, " 'I'm keeping the faith with what I remember. I'm giving it back if I can.' "[44]

Sustained by his sense of mission to salvage and rescue, he draws to himself others who are bereft: Barbra K., a beautiful mulatto woman, childless, married to a ne'er-do-well; Mavis Henley, a young artist suffering the effects of an abortion but still bound to her lover, Frank Matteo, a local promoter with ties to the underworld, who was himself abandoned as a child. Most important is Arnie's relation to a onetime friend and colleague, Lex Graham, with whose wife, Dorothy, Arnie had an affair and who in revenge helped to oust Arnie from the university. The arrival of the Grahams in the opening chapter in quest of a house on the coast to buy with their newly inherited money precipitates the action that changes the lives of all the characters.

For several of them, change brings regeneration. The presence of Dorothy Graham, who still loves Arnie and goes to him in his house, cures him of his impotence. Mavis Henley conceives a second child by Frank Matteo, who, when the child survives a premature birth, exclaims in the closing scene, "Why, that's all there is" (302). A street restored by Arnie becomes a center of creative life, where Yates designs new buildings, Mavis Henley teaches weaving and needlework in her crafts shop, and Barbra K. tends children in her day-care center. Arnie sells to Frank Matteo the island on which he has buried his wife, and no longer engulfed by memories, he works steadily to complete his book on Byron.

But life and death, health and sickness, sanity and madness are inseparable in Elizabeth Spencer's world. She expresses the central theme of her fiction in Arnie's reflection that "distinctions were no longer possible here, that all of life, good and bad together, was simply one thing, a growth, a creature made of many creatures within the area of its original simple structure, yet complicating itself the more it let new creatures in" (193). Survivors are those like Arnie and Mavis, who neither repudiate the past nor remain imprisoned in it, who accept the truth that Arnie voices—"The heart makes houses for itself. They get broken into" (178)—who settle for less than perfection and accept what comes, as Arnie welcomes whatever the storm washes into his house and yard and at the end asks, "How can we gather everything up? Everything we know? Everyone we know? And preferably not as corpses" (277).

Those who go under are the exclusive and the self-absorbed, like the Grahams, whose longing to secure themselves in a perfectly furnished, inviolable dwelling is symbolized by the white house on the coast, which they are destined never to buy. Dorothy escapes a sterile life in nymphomania and incurable madness. On Arnie's island, Lex is bitten by something never identified and in the hospital nearly dies of the mysterious venom, symbolic of his unremitting hatred of Arnie. At the end, he seems almost indistinguishable from the beige Mercedes that perpetually encases him. Neither he nor his wife can live beyond the salt line, the point at which one smells the salt and feels the life-stirring force of the sea as one goes toward the coast.

The title of the novel suggests the importance of boundaries, psychological as well as physical, thresholds that one may encounter anywhere. More powerful than the impression of the characters in Elizabeth Spencer's fiction is the evocation of the spirit of such places—houses, streets, cities, landscapes, where past and present merge, places at once real and visionary, expressive of states of mind and phases of civilization.

In her preface to *The Stories,* Spencer defines the writer as one "walking down a certain path, a personal road," which "itself is always moving on" (xi). The image suggests progression, not conclusion, but the direction of the road is clear. Beginning within a strong, well-defined tradition, she, like her Southern contemporaries, has helped to develop that tradition by moving out from the regional to the national and the universal, from the Mississippi towns of her early novels to the American and European cities of her later fiction, in which she has sought to capture "large patterns of modern experience in American terms."[45] At the same time, she has declared that she is "still a part" of the South, that "you carry the South with you."[46] She credits the three Marilee stories, all set in Mississippi but written in Montreal, to the enduring vitality of memories: "so many scenes sprang to mind, they seemed to wait in line for me to get them down."[47]

The image that most completely suggests her aims as a Southern writer of modern experience appears near the end of *The Snare,* in the scene in which Julia discovers a cache of colored marbles "near the site of an old mansion that was being torn down" (402). By Julia's desire to make a new art of these pieces, which once decorated the furniture of the house, that they be "allowed to find a new voice, though broken, fractured, torn from their original purpose" (402), Elizabeth Spencer symbolized the art of the novelist who would create from the materials of tradition new forms and meanings.

ELIZABETH SPENCER BIBLIOGRAPHY

NOVELS

Fire in the Morning. New York: Dodd, Mead, 1948.
This Crooked Way. New York: Dodd, Mead, 1952.
The Voice at the Back Door. New York: McGraw-Hill, 1956 (Rosenthal Award of the National Institute of Arts and Letters).
The Light in the Piazza. New York: McGraw-Hill, 1960.
Knights and Dragons. New York: McGraw-Hill, 1965.
No Place for an Angel. New York: McGraw-Hill, 1967.
The Snare. New York: McGraw-Hill, 1972.
The Salt Line. Garden City, N.Y.: Doubleday, 1984.

SHORT STORY COLLECTIONS

Ship Island and Other Stories. New York: McGraw-Hill, 1968.
Marilee: Three Stories by Elizabeth Spencer. A Southern Landscape, Sharon, Indian Summer. Jackson: University Press of Mississippi, 1981.
The Stories of Elizabeth Spencer. Garden City, N.Y.: Doubleday, 1981.

INTERVIEWS

Broadwell, Elizabeth Pell, and Ronald Wesley Hoag. "A Conversation with Elizabeth Spencer." *Southern Review* 18 (Winter 1982): 111–30.
Brown, Laurie L. "Interviews with Seven Contemporary Writers." In *Women Writers of the Contemporary South,* ed. Peggy Whitman Prenshaw, 3–22. Jackson: University Press of Mississippi, 1984.
Bunting, Charles T. " 'In That Time and at That Place': The Literary World of Elizabeth Spencer." *Mississippi Quarterly* 28 (Fall 1975): 435–60.
Cole, Hunter McKelva. "Elizabeth Spencer at Sycamore Fair." *Notes on Mississippi Writers* 6 (Winter 1974): 81–86.
Haley, Josephine. "An Interview with Elizabeth Spencer." *Notes on Mississippi Writers* 1 (Fall 1968): 42–55.
Jones, John Griffin, ed. "Elizabeth Spencer." In *Mississippi Writers Talking,* vol. 1, 95–129. Jackson: University Press of Mississippi, 1982.

BIBLIOGRAPHICAL GUIDE

Barge, Laura. "An Elizabeth Spencer Checklist, 1948 to 1976." *Mississippi Quarterly* 29 (Fall 1976): 569–90.
Pilkington, John. "Elizabeth Spencer." In *A Bibliographical Guide to the Study of Southern Literature,* ed. Louis D. Rubin, Jr., 294–95. Baton Rouge: Louisiana State University Press, 1969.

Joan Williams:
The Rebellious Heart

*

JUDITH BRYANT WITTENBERG

A MY HOWARD, one of Joan Williams's characters whose struggle to become a writer mirrors in many ways that of the author herself, wonders, early in the novel in which she appears, "How . . . did people reconcile themselves to things against their nature, or quell rebellious hearts and manage to laugh." Soon after, Amy's mother cries out, "Oh, why can't you be like the other girls?" and Amy herself has "a conflict-ing second thought" about her decision to forsake a social occasion for a visit to a writer whose work she admires (*TW*, 29, 33).[1] Amy's diffi-culties in effecting any sort of workable compromise between her per-sonal need to define herself as a writer and the external demands that she be sociable and feminine are much like those that Anne Goodwyn Jones has described as inevitably confronting any Southern woman who wishes to become an artist. As Jones says, "The woman writer in the South . . . participates in a tradition that defines her ideal self in ways that must inevitably conflict with her very integrity as an artist: voicelessness, passivity, ignorance."[2] Both Joan Williams's personal life and the fiction she has written over the past thirty-five years embody the problems of possessing a rebellious heart in a society that prizes tra-dition and conformity.

Born on 26 September 1928 in Memphis, the only child of Maude Moore and Priestly H. Williams, Joan Williams early discovered both her desire to write and the fact that she was unlikely ever to accept com-pletely the values of the community in which she was raised, although her periodic efforts to strike a balance between her individual needs and the social norms would create, ironically, additional problems. Sent to a fashionable private school, Miss Hutchinson's School for Girls in Memphis, Joan discovered her interest in writing while doing essay assignments for her English class. She showed a natural facility that won her teachers' praise, and although she says she "had no idea what being a writer meant," she decided to become one.[3] When she went on to Southwestern at Memphis, she told her English professor that she wanted to be a writer, but she was unable to achieve the sort of vividness of detail that he admired until after some months in the class.[4] During this same period, however, Joan's ambivalence about her homelife led her, in a moment of romantic impetuousness, to make a runaway marriage, which her parents quickly had annulled.

Feeling that life in Memphis was too constricting, because "it was a place where women weren't supposed to do anything" and because "wanting to be a writer often caused people to laugh at you," Joan spent her second year of college in Washington, D.C., at Chevy Chase Junior College. A friend of hers, Louise Fitzhugh, who was motivated by similar aspirations, had an uncle, the writer Peter Taylor, who advised them to go to Bard College if they wanted to learn to become writers.[5] At Bard, Joan met yet another encouraging English teacher, Joseph Summers, who suggested that she submit a piece of fiction to a short story contest, and she astonishingly produced "Rain Later," which won first prize in *Mademoiselle*'s fiction contest and was given honorable mention in *Best American Short Stories 1949*.

"Rain Later," published before Williams was twenty-one, draws on the impressions she accumulated during childhood visits to her maternal grandmother in the northern Mississippi town of Arkabutla and reveals a certain maturity of sensibility and method. A simple story about a widow awaiting a visit from her daughter and granddaughter, it dramatizes what would become some of Williams's major themes—unspoken tensions between family members that are counterbalanced by a yearning for connection and communication, the complexities of relationships between blacks and whites—and shows her ability at capturing a character's interior life as well as the texture of her daily routine; at the same time, motifs such as a door that will not open smoothly, the grandmother's fatigue, and the imminence of rain serve to mirror aspects of the frustrating human interactions. Williams herself was surprised at the effectiveness and success of "Rain Later," saying years afterward, "I knew nothing technically about writing a short story, I just sat down and it came out; I have no explanation for it."[6] Ironically, this natural facility was related to what would become one of Williams's ongoing problems, her tendency at times to work mainly when "inspired" to do so, which has resulted in long periods of silence and a rather small corpus. As she says now, "No one had ever talked to me about discipline, that to be a writer you sat down and worked every day. So [after "Rain Later"] I just kept waiting for the muse to strike me, and it didn't strike me again for four years."[7]

After Williams completed her first short story and before the honors accorded it were announced, she met William Faulkner, who would become an important figure in her personal life and who would have an impact on her career that was at once helpful and problematic. She read *The Sound and the Fury* in the summer of 1949 and, feeling that it had spoken to her in some extraordinary way, was easily persuaded by a friend to join in making a pilgrimage to visit its famous author, who was shortly to win the Nobel Prize.[8] The personal rapport between the fifty-two-year-old writer and the admiring twenty-one-year-old college student was almost instantaneous, though the relationship was fraught with complications from the outset, including the age difference, the fact that Faulkner was married and a father, and Joan's reluctance to become deeply involved emotionally and sexually.

For Joan, the relationship with Faulkner was also complicated artistically; he was, to be sure, a figure omnipresently *there* for any contemporary Southern writer—Eudora Welty compared him to a mountain always in the background—but he was far more important to Williams than to most comparable writers, playing a role in her life alternately that of father, Pygmalion, and ardent lover. Enthusiastic about the story Joan wrote before she met him, Faulkner eloquently praised it as "moving and true, made me want to cry a little for all the sad frustration of solitude, isolation, aloneness in which every human being lives, who for all the blood kinship and everything else, cant really communicate, touch."[9] Along with asking Joan to collaborate with him on projects, such as the play portion of *Requiem for a Nun* and a television drama, *The Graduation Dress*, Faulkner soon was reading her own subsequent fiction in draft, offering both criticism and encouragement.

Faulkner's involvement in Joan's next short story, "The Morning and the Evening," which she would eventually expand into her first novel, has been well documented. After going over a draft of it, he sent it back, saying, "You could either rewrite, copy it into your language, or use what of it is mine, whatever you like." Fearful she might balk at some of his suggestions, Faulkner added, "I will probably still meet resistance in you which I will hope to vanquish by seeing you face to face. . . . I am only trying to help you become an artist."[10] After "The Morning and the Evening" was rejected by *Harper's*, Faulkner had his agent send it to the *Atlantic Monthly*, where it was accepted and published as an Atlantic First. Reviewers of Williams's short fiction, recently published in book form (*Pariah*, 1983), have repeatedly compared her work to that of Faulkner, and indeed, the protagonist of "The Morning and the Evening" is a moaning idiot who falls in love with a cow, seeming thus to be a combination of Benjy Compson of *The Sound and the Fury* and Ike Snopes of *The Hamlet*. Although Faulkner obviously had an important influence on Williams's work, something she has acknowledged both in her various public statements on the subject and in her dedication of her latest book to him, he was not necessarily the sole influence. Williams remembers reading a 1941 collection of Eudora Welty's short stories, *A Curtain of Green,* about the time she was beginning her own career as a writer of fiction, and one can also see significant traces of Welty stories from that collection in "The Morning and the Evening" and in the novel that evolved from it: the main character in Welty's "Lily Daw and the Three Ladies" is a half-wit whose mother has died and who runs into difficulties buying a ticket for a tent show, much like Williams's Jake Darby; and an incident in Welty's "Clytie," in which a lonely old spinster makes a gesture of affection toward a man, terrifying him in the process, is recapitulated in *The Morning and the Evening*. Still, the Faulknerian impress upon Williams's work is, for both biographical and artistic reasons, the one most likely to interest her reviewers and critics.

Faulkner was very ambitious for Joan. Over the years he knew her, he wrote to Saxe Commins of his fear that she was "not demon-driven enough for art,"[11] and he repeatedly exhorted Joan to "write another," to "keep your sights high."[12] As early as late 1951, almost ten years before her first novel was published, he asserted, "I intend for you to win that prize [the John P. Marquand Award for a distinguished first novel]. Then you wont have to ask anyone for permission to go where you like."[13]

During the early 1950s, however, Williams was having trouble heeding all of her mentor's advice. In the first place, aware that she was unlikely to earn very much money from her writing and anxious to have a life independent of her prosperous but demanding parents, after her graduation from Bard, she worked at a series of paying jobs in different cities. She moved from a clerkship at a Doubleday bookshop in New Orleans to a post in Annandale-on-Hudson, New York, as assistant director of admissions at Bard, and thence to New York City, where she answered letters to the editor at *Look* magazine and lived in an apartment in Greenwich Village. During this period, she was also struggling with her ambivalence about the relationship with Faulkner, who wanted more intensity and intimacy than she did; she began drifting away from him by late 1953 and, on 6 March 1954, married Ezra Bowen, a writer at *Sports Illustrated* who was only two years older than she.

Williams's new husband proved in professional ways to be a useful influence upon her work, teaching her the value of disciplined work habits. His own mother was the famous biographer Catherine Drinker Bowen, so he was used to having a hardworking woman writer in the house and attempted to instill in Joan some of his mother's methods, saying to her, "If you're going to do this, sit down every day and write from 9:00 until 1:00, and that's it, don't make other plans or do anything else."[14] His advice was helpful, but the rapid arrival of two babies, Ezra, born in 1954, and Matthew, born in 1956, prevented Williams from putting it fully to use. Moreover, the example of her mother-in-law, useful though it was in some respects—she was not only a writer, but also an outspoken feminist who encouraged her daughter-in-law to be independent in thought and action—was problematic in others. To Mrs. Bowen, her daughter-in-law believed, "writing was the most important thing in her life; it was [even] more important than her children." Williams, on the other hand, felt her family should come first, being worried about having her boys "grow up with the feeling that my writing was more important than anything else." Hence, "they were trained to respect my solitude, but they could interrupt."[15]

As a result, although Williams continued to work on her fiction, things went rather slowly during the first several years of marriage and motherhood. She did, however, manage to complete "The Sound of Silence," which was purchased by *Mademoiselle* but never published, and to make it and her 1953 story the basis for a novel. Encouraged by Berton Roueche and Nancy Hale, whom she had met at the Breadloaf Writers Conference, and with Faulkner still generously offering criticism and advice, she completed *The Morning and the Evening* and found a publisher for it in mid-1960. She was, of course, worried about its being "too much Faulkner," but he wrote back almost angrily, "Never give one goddam about what anybody says about the work, if you KNOW you have done it as honestly and bravely and truly as you could. Sure some discerning person will holler Faulkner because there will be some Faulkner in it. Every writer is influenced by everything. Whatever touches him, from the telephone directory to God. I was in your life at an age which I think you will find was a very important experience, and of course it will show on you."[16]

The Morning and the Evening is perhaps Williams's favorite among her novels, for, as she says, "It was the easiest; I don't know where it came from, so maybe I like it because it is a kind of mystery."[17] In it, the gentle and mentally defective mute, Jake Darby, based not only on Faulkner's comparable characters but also on a retarded man whom

Williams knew when she was a child visiting the Mississippi town of Arkabutla, attempts to cope with the death of his mother and with a group of well-meaning but limited and uncomprehending towns-people. They, baffled by the prospect of trying to help a man who can neither speak nor think as they do, eventually have him committed to a mental institution. Jake thus serves as a sort of moral touchstone; by their responses to him, members of the community variously reveal their flaws and limitations.

Like Faulkner novels such as *The Sound and the Fury* or *As I Lay Dying* in its use of a central character to whom the others respond in self-revealing ways, it also recalls Sherwood Anderson's *Winesburg, Ohio* in the manner in which it portrays the frustrations and distortions of a number of other members of the community. We become familiar with Mrs. Darby, who before her death confronts the loss of her hus-band and the departure of another son and who believes that the birth of Jake is her "punishment" for her "one infidelity" with the leader of a revival meeting (*TMTE*, 27); with Ruth Edna May, a lonely spinster, who expresses the frustrations of long years spent caring for members of her family by secretly drinking paregoric and by making desultory ef-forts to find a job; and with Frances Morgan, trapped in a bad marriage and seeking to surmount her dissatisfaction with an intense extramari-tal affair. Although a male is the central figure, Williams's sympathy with the special limitations of women's lives in small-town Southern society is evident; the women characters become increasingly important as the novel progresses, and they express angrily rebellious thoughts. Ruth Edna complains that men "have all the advantages in this world. They can hide their flaws, and they can marry if and when they choose," and Frances thinks about "the advantage men had over women—their work. They could always worry about it instead of something they couldn't do anything about" (*TMTE*, 86, 115). Williams's sympathy for blacks—part of the "veiled liberalism" Anne Goodwyn Jones has noted that one frequently finds in Southern women's writing[18]—is also apparent in her portraits of the kindly Jurldeane, the Darbys' "wash girl," the errand boy Little T, whose obsession with obtaining a fishing lure leads to the final tragedy of the novel, and Bald Dave, who hides behind a mask of eccentricity.

Although *The Morning and the Evening* becomes somewhat melodra-matic in a rather contrived way near its close, it is adroit in its handling of dialogue and tone and in its evocation of the physical and social at-mosphere of a small Southern town. It is also effective in its sympa-thetic characterization of a series of individuals struggling with the limitations imposed by poverty, isolation, bad luck, or their own failures of vision. When the novel was published in 1961, it won high praise from reviewers, including Robert Penn Warren and Granville Hicks, and was given the John P. Marquand Award for the best first novel of the year, which conferred both prestige and a cash stipend of ten thousand dollars. Williams was also awarded a National Institute of Arts and Letters Grant for 1962.

Despite the fact that Williams continued to regard her family as of equal importance with her fiction writing, defining herself as "writer (and housewife)" in a profile she prepared for a reference work,[19] her career had begun auspiciously. She accepted a commission to do a project for *Life* magazine and began research for her next novel, which would chronicle both the entire life of a dynamite salesman and the development of levee building along the Mississippi River. She approached this far more consciously than she had her first novel, reading books about dynamite and levee building and spending a summer with the family of an engineer who had helped build the levee system along the Mississippi River (that engineer was the adoptive father of the boy who would become the poet Frank Stanford).[20]

Although Williams's months of careful research had the effect of making brief portions of *Old Powder Man*, which appeared in 1966, a bit too data-ridden, the fact that she based its protagonist, Frank Wynn, on her own father gave the work both autobiographical significance and poignancy. Priestly H. Williams, to whom the book is dedicated, had died some years before of emphysema, so the work has a certain memorial quality; nevertheless, Williams manages to avoid sentimentality in her portrait of her father, showing him as professionally indomitable, even heroic at times, yet personally difficult and seriously flawed in some of his attitudes.

Frank Wynn, the dynamite salesman at the center of the novel, is a self-made man whose literary antecedents go back as far as Howells's Silas Lapham, and whose drive is evident from the outset. He feels "there's got to be a place in the world for a man as willing to work as me" (*OPM*, 46) and after some false starts finds his "life's work" in the dynamite business. A flood emergency gives him his first chance to show the full range of his energy and mettle, and he eventually establishes his own business, which becomes quite successful. Admired by colleagues and increasingly prosperous, Wynn runs the business until ill health finally forces him into retirement.

However successful he might be as a businessman, Wynn is in many respects a failure in his personal life, for "never had he found the self he was when he was not working" (*OPM*, 201). He tends to be sexist and dominating, telling his first wife, "I'll do the thinking around here.

You're not supposed to do any thinking" (*OPM,* 73), and forbidding his second wife access to the checking account, thus forcing her to depend on the allowance he grudgingly doles out. He even harshly criticizes his beloved only daughter when she makes decisions about her education or life-style that are not in full accordance with his wishes. Not surprisingly, his first wife leaves him for another man, his second wife begins to drink heavily, and his daughter moves to another state. Only near the end of his life, when Wynn is forced into idleness by the sale of his business and into torpor by his increasingly bad health, does he face the personal losses he has incurred and make efforts at reconciliation with those who are close to him. Some of the most poignant scenes occur late in the novel as he makes gestures toward his daughter, a young mother (as was Williams herself at the time she began writing the book) and toward his grandchild.

Although Frank Wynn dominates *Old Powder Man,* Williams offers memorable portraits of women and their plights. Wynn's mother, Cally, a character based on family stories about Williams's paternal grandmother, who had died before she was born, is notable for her strong-willed restlessness and the hypochondria that is perhaps a response to unacknowledged frustrations inherent in her situation as a woman; at points, Cally recalls Edith Wharton's Zenobia Frome, but she lacks Zenobia's maliciousness. Wynn's shallow and materialistic first wife, Lillian, is hardly a sympathetic character, but her vengeful departure with another man, leaving behind enormous bills, is far from undeserved, given Wynn's lack of attention to her needs and his absorption in his business. His second wife, Kate, a schoolteacher, sees him as her "only choice" for a husband (*OPM,* 138), but when he refuses to let her work and shows little interest in his family, she despairingly turns to alcohol for solace. His daughter, Laurel, cares for both her parents but attempts to escape the turbulence of life at home, with its quarrels and its alcoholic distortions, as definitively as she can. But once Wynn begins reaching out to Laurel, she has difficulty responding, admitting that " 'for so many years, he paid no attention, never talked to me, that now I don't know anything to say to him' " (*OPM,* 272). After he dies, Laurel is filled with regret and forgiveness but is determined that "she would not make exactly his mistakes" (*OPM,* 312).

Old Powder Man is fictionalized biography more than it is a dramatically conceived novel, a fact that would trouble at least one of its reviewers, who called it "neither dramatic nor imaginative,"[21] but in an article written shortly after the book was published, Williams said that its leisureliness and repetitiousness were a conscious part of her method. "Over and over I touched on how tired [Wynn] was when he came home, and many times I described the hot Southern summers and the dusty, inadequate roads and the difficulties he had getting his car into and out of places where there were no roads at all. By these repetitions I wanted not only to impress on the reader's mind the sense of struggle but also the sense of time."[22] Although the novel marked such a sufficient departure in both scope and method from her previous work that Williams felt "as though I was starting over,"[23] and although five years had elapsed since *The Morning and the Evening* had been published, *Old Powder Man* was widely reviewed, mostly favorably. Joyce Carol Oates called it the "kind of traditional novel that affirms the intrinsic dignity and worth of the novel," and Robert Penn Warren praised it in a *Life* review entitled "Death of a Salesman—Southern Style," in which he compared it to *An American Tragedy.*[24]

The time Williams spent in the South doing her *Life* assignment and the research for *Old Powder Man* also yielded her material for several short stories. "No Love for the Lonely," published in the *Saturday Evening Post* in 1963, returns to some of the characters of *The Morning and the Evening* to tell the affecting tale of Cotter May's effort to find solace after the death of his sister. He turns first to a married couple and then to a longtime friend, the spinster Hattie McGaha; on the verge of marrying Hattie, he lets the moment pass, because "he could not come out of himself after all these years" (*P, 79*). The themes of grief and of the lost chance are recurrent ones in Williams's fiction. Other stories from this period deal with the changes in the civil rights status of blacks during the 1960s and with the varying efforts by whites to cope with them. "Going Ahead" (1964) is about a boy's perception of his grandfather's inability to accept an integrated lunch counter during a Christmas trip to a local city; Tad's loss of faith in Santa Claus is mirrored by his disappointment with his grandfather. He decides "he would have to go on ahead without him" (*P, 93*). "Spring Is Now" (1968) also concerns a young person's growing awareness of her elders' moral inadequacies with regard to racial issues. The local high school is being integrated, and the grown-ups in sixteen-year-old Sandra's world are filled with gossip and fears; Sandra's gradual recognition that a black fellow student is an individual who shares many of her attitudes leads her to reject an heirloom pin given her by her grandmother, for the pin is, like the adults' ideas, antiquated and irrelevant.

Two more stories with an interesting interrelationship, "Jesse" (1969) and "Daylight Come" (unpublished until *Pariah*), use blacks as central characters. Williams met the real-life prototypes when she and a photographer spent time in Tate County, Mississippi, gathering material for *Life*. Jesse is a defeated sharecropper helped by an earnest civil rights worker to find salaried non–farm work and to go to school to gain the literacy that has eluded him all his life. Jesse struggles to overcome, but it is, in one sense, too late for him; he suffers from psychic as well as physical fatigue and, though he decides not to run away from his obligations, he can only "wait and see what will happen in the end" (*P,* 152). Williams basically admired Jesse when she wrote about him but later realized "he was not this struggling man, he was a drunk who had beat his wife and not done anything [worthwhile]."[25] So she portrayed him as Lish, the ne'er-do-well husband who has abandoned his wife, Scoot, the protagonist of "Daylight Come." Now working as a maid in a motel and feeling some pride because it is "the first [job] that was not cleaning house for a white lady" (*P,* 163), Scoot is thwarted in her ambitions when she has to quit her job to devote herself to a troublesome child who has been caught smoking marijuana. "She knew her day had not yet come" (*P,* 179).

While essentially all of Williams's work up to this point has a setting that is identifiably—and distinctively—Southern, a 1967 story, "Pariah," could be set anywhere. It depicts a middle-aged woman, Ruth, who is forced, during the course of a bridge party, to recognize the havoc wreaked on her family and the distaste engendered in her friends by her constant drinking. It is told from the point of view of the main character, so the reader's recognition of the truths of the situation develops in tandem with Ruth's. Though it ends on a mildly hopeful note, as Ruth discusses her drinking with her husband and watches birds in the snow, thinking "how incredible they survive, when there's so much to keep them from it" (*P,* 110), "Pariah" offers a haunting portrayal of the problems of middle-class alcoholism. Another brief story, "Vistas," seems to belong in the same nonspecific but implicitly middle-class suburban milieu. It depicts a middle-aged woman, Amy, concerned about the evidence of her own advancing age, and dreading one of the regular telephone calls from her mother, who is querulous and demanding. Amy tries to be sympathetic but mildly rebuffs the older woman, only to then telephone one of her own children and be rebuffed by him.

Such fiction, though rare in Williams's corpus, suggests that she might find promising material in the contemporary world of exurbia as well as in the small-town South of an earlier era. Indeed, Williams's Southernness has been at once an inspiration and a sort of psychic bondage. She essentially left the South in 1947, when she went to college in Washington, and she has lived in the Northeast almost continuously since, primarily in a suburb of New York City. Yet her work has been almost exclusively about the South, especially the South she knew as a child, and the literary predecessors she found influential include, beside William Faulkner and Eudora Welty, Katherine Anne Porter and Carson McCullers. It is the memories of the sound of Southern conversation, of the character configurations of small-town society, and of the heat, dust, and smells of a Southern summer that provide the largest impetus to her work. Specific people she knew in Memphis and Arkabutla and tales she heard as a child gave rise to many of her works, while later trips South provided background for her most recent novel and several short stories. As effectively as Williams has transformed much of this Southern experience into fiction, she now feels that the fact that "I wanted to write just about the South" has been in some sense a "mistake," limiting both the audience for her fiction and the material available to her imagination. At the same time, paradoxically, she often views her trips south as imaginatively regenerative. She saw, for example, a 1981 trip to Mississippi as designed to help her "come up with some material for a new book."[26] Moreover, she believes that leaving the South more or less permanently in the late 1940s detached her from the source of regular inspiration. As she put it, "[If I had lived there full time], I would have written a lot more because all that Southern flavor would have kept turning me on as I was exposed to it." She finally returned in 1982, spending nearly a year in Memphis, only to discover that "the kinds of things I was writing about are [now] gone," that the contemporary South is "much like anyplace else."[27] Thus her ambivalence about the South, her sense that it was once both hauntingly unique and a place too limiting to live in, is ironically offset by a nostalgic feeling of loss for a now-vanished way of life.

The two milieus of Williams's personal life, urban North and small-city South, are both important to her third novel, *The Wintering* (1971), which is at one level about her decisions to leave the South and to become a writer, the two being necessarily interrelated. The novel could have been a thoroughgoing *Künstlerroman,* had there been more in it about the precise nature of Amy Howard's efforts to find herself as a creative artist, but that aspect of *The Wintering* is relatively sketchy; one could say that the work is about a woman's unacknowledged difficulties in defining herself as a writer, a result of her preoccupation with men and romance. The novel's major focus is on Amy Howard's involvement with a famous writer; she meets him when she is a student and attempts over the next few years to attain some sort of emotional equilibrium in her relationship with the older man, about whose desire for her she is highly ambivalent. In the process, she gets involved with, and even engaged to, other men. The writer, Jeffrey Almoner, is closely modeled on Faulkner, and the novel recapitulates in essential ways Williams's romance with him. Almoner shares with his real-life counterpart a sense of being an alien in the small Mississippi town where he lives and works, a propensity for self-destructive alcoholic binges, and a desire for a relationship with his young protégée that is compounded of emotional intimacy and professional guidance. He goes so far as to give her the manuscript of his favorite novel, just as Faulkner gave Joan Williams the manuscript of *The Sound and the Fury*.

It was not long after Joan met Faulkner that he began encouraging her to write a novel about their affair, which was rather surprising, given his usual instinct for privacy. He even "envisioned it as a rush of letters, a quick exchange the way he conceived our relationship to have been," an idea she eventually discarded as "too boring," although she reproduced or paraphrased many of their letters to each other in the novel. But Williams says she was too young at the time, and "I wasn't able to write the story of our relationship while I was [still] in it."[28] She was unable to begin it until she had completed *Old Powder Man,* at which point their romance had been over for more than a decade and Faulkner had been dead since 1962. Even then she felt inhibited, particularly because Mrs. Faulkner, for whom she felt a good deal of sympathy, was still alive. Mrs. Almoner is different in crucial respects from her real-life model, but other facets of *The Wintering* recapitulate or approximate actual events and people.

The young Amy Howard is self-conscious and shy, uncomfortable with her peers and with conventional social expectations but unable yet to define her own goals and to act assertively in their pursuit. The one thing she is sure of occurs when she begins to read Almoner's books and gets from them "the feeling that everything she had ever asked herself, he had" (*TW,* 29). "What Almoner wrote was a mirror for her soul, Amy felt" (*TW,* 48). After she meets Almoner and he begins his gently ardent pursuit of her, she finds that she has exchanged one sort of difficulty for another. He sees himself as not only lover but tutor, acting as a "catharsis" for her, freeing her from her past so that she can do as she wishes and become a writer (*TW,* 116). In struggling with him as lover, Amy is unable to avail herself of his tutelage as fully as she might, and she spends an enormous amount of time and energy in petty rebellions. In New York, she becomes involved with a parasitic and fraudulent artist, Tony, whom Williams depicts satirically and who is, she says, a "composite" both of people she knew while living in Greenwich Village and of derogatory comments that Faulkner made about such people.[29] She flees from Almoner to Tony and to Billy Walter, a friend from home, and from New York back to Delton (Memphis). When she finally recognizes Almoner's importance to her, it is too late; he dies just before the reunion at which they are to plan their marriage.

Although the novel is not particularly successful, because Amy is frequently too vapid and unformed to carry the intellectual and emotional weight that she must as the central consciousness, and also because Almoner's motives are often too opaque to make him of interest to other than Faulkner scholars looking for correspondences between fact and fiction, it has moments of nice comedy, particularly when Williams turns her satirical eye on her heroine and her satellites. In one of those moments, Amy goes to bed with Tony in a gesture of rebellion against her middle-class roots, only to have the middle-classness reassert itself in the morning and drive her to clean up his appallingly messy apartment; in another, she buys bohemian clothes and longs for "experiences," including "Liquor," "Drugs," and "An affair with a Negro" (*TW*, 204). Williams is also effective, as always, at creating portraits of older women whose rebellions have been thwarted, such as Mrs. Decker, once a "free spirit" who ran away with an itinerant portrait painter, now a liquor-mottled and pretentious middle-class wife, or Amy's mother, who paints numbered canvases to fill up her lonely hours.

When *The Wintering* was published in 1971, it received fewer reviews than Williams's previous novels, none of them in the mass-circulation periodicals and some of them stingingly negative. The lack of attention may have been a result of the fact that reviewers were either unaware of or disturbed by the work's intimate and often disagreeable portrait of Faulkner, who had become by then one of America's most respected novelists; while one reviewer admired its "bittersweet" portrait of a May-December romance and said it was written with "sensitivity and insight," yet another called it "a washed out book" and said that its heroine was "too tentative and indecisive."[30]

Affected by those few hostile reviews and aware that public interest in her work was now negligible, Williams, always a slow writer, began to work at a snail's pace. Events in her personal life also had an impact, for she divorced Ezra Bowen and married John Fargason, a Southerner by birth. Williams's second marriage was more turbulent than her first, and that too ended in divorce. All through the 1970s, as she coped with events in her domestic situation, Williams was struggling to complete her fourth novel, *County Woman*. She was also going through the difficult—and, for some writers, traumatic—procedure of changing editors during this time; Hiram Haydn had seen her previous three books through the publication process, and now Williams made the switch to C. Michael Curtis in the Atlantic Monthly Press division of Little, Brown.

During the period she was working on *County Woman,* Williams was also making efforts to come to terms with what she now realizes is an increasingly feminist-oriented aspect of her fiction. Sympathy for women trying to cope with a patriarchal society that stifled their wishes to be independent and to have sexual freedom had been evident from the first, but it was some years before a woman would occupy center stage in Williams's work; men had been her major protagonists, and even in *The Wintering,* the female character is overshadowed by that of her male mentor. A short critical essay Williams wrote during the early 1980s offers a useful clue to the changes in her thinking; "In Defense of Caroline Compson" attempts to elicit sympathy for a Faulkner character always regarded as monstrously selfish, a failure as a mother and a human being. Williams asserts that Mrs. Compson is a victim of the Southern system of an earlier period, with its strictures to marry early, to bear multiple children, and to adhere to class assumptions; while some of her judgments are precarious, Williams's effort to invoke compassion for this critically maligned fictional character is revealing.[31] Williams's growing feminism may also have led her to say recently that Welty, Porter, and McCullers were greater influences on her work than Faulkner, because "as females there are things and themes they wrote about that were closer to what was going to come out of me than the things he wrote."[32]

While Williams's sympathy for any character confronting the difficulties of a "rebellious heart" in a limiting environment extends to her male characters, whether black or white, the embryonic feminism revealed in her earlier fiction comes effectively to fruition in the 1982 novel *County Woman,* in the character of Allie McCall, whose story is juxtaposed with the racial turmoil of the early 1960s in Mississippi. Constricted both by the girdles she wears and by half a lifetime of having to care for her husband and invalid father, the fifty-year-old protagonist gradually and painfully breaks free.

Allie is filled with terror when we first meet her, "because all her life she had fought against a feeling of nothingness, and in middle age she had the terrible fear that she was losing that battle" (*CW,* 10). In some sense, Allie's plight is a general one; though she is timid enough to be "fearful over a small matter" such as the seasoning of her French toast because "it concerned the wrath of men," she and other "women her age were beginning to discuss how tired they were of catering to men, feeling they had served their sentences" (*CW,* 88, 21). Moreover, it is echoed by the situation of the blacks, who are attempting to change things with their courageous efforts to integrate the University of Mississippi at Oxford. Both women and blacks have been severely inhibited by the rigid traditions of the white male patriarchy. Allie thinks of the brave young black James Meredith as "making a mark on history" and "long[s] more deeply to make some mark of her own" (*CW*, 46). Her first actions are primarily symbolic and potentially self-destructive—a trip to Oxford made despite male admonitions that the racial turmoil there makes it too dangerous for a woman, and also a wanton sexual encounter with a filling station attendant. This encounter, faintly implausible to the reader, is recognized by Allie as having moments of male "domineering" that reveal "men did not very much like women" (*CW*, 129).

Unlike most of Williams's previous female characters, Allie learns to act constructively and politically; she evolves from a frustrated housewife to a public figure. With the Oxford riots in the background serving as an emblematic amplification of Allie's private turbulence, she manages to solve the long-standing mystery of her mother's death and to exonerate a wrongfully accused black in the process; the combination of a detective story and a chronicle of personal growth on the part of the protagonist, all with racial implications, is evocative of Faulkner's *Intruder in the Dust*. Allie, however, does even more than Faulkner's Chick Mallison; she also exposes a hit-and-run killer and agitates for the construction of a new bridge. Already acting like a community spokesperson, she becomes one by running for constable, an office previously held only by men, specifically by "good old boys." Not only is Allies's "liberation" successful, it galvanizes at least a few of the other women of the town in crucial ways.

While the book is overplotted in some respects—an occasional problem in Williams's work, as she seeks to compensate for her tendency to concentrate on thought processes and the slow pace of daily life—its portrait of the political and racial awakening of a woman at an age when so many females are thought to be past the possibility for growth and change is something many readers find cheering. Moreover, its portrait of the texture of small-town life and of a community attempting to cope with radical change is effective, and its protagonist is compassionate rather than harshly militant. Allie accepts the foibles of her cartoon-watching and occasionally deranged old father and thinks of her husband, Tate, not as an oppressor but as one who has also been trapped by conventional expectations on the part of herself and others. By the end of the novel, Tate too has begun "seeming more aggressive" (*CW*, 279), and the possibilities of their achieving a new sort of relationship are apparent. To be sure, the ending of *County Woman* finds honor and truth more triumphant than they usually are in real life, a product of Williams's publicly expressed desire for "moral resolution" in her fiction. As she says, "I have to write in the traditional way, and I think a character has to change or something has to happen in a story."[33]

Nevertheless, Allie McCall's emergent feminism is a new and essentially promising sort of fictional vein that one might expect Williams to continue to mine carefully in her subsequent fiction. Her next novel, which was published by Dutton in 1988 and is entitled *Pay the Piper,* resurrects a secondary woman character from the 1966 novel *Old Powder Man,* Laurel Perry, and brings her forward into middle age. Recently out of a tumultuous marriage to a wealthy Mississippian with a murder and prison term in his past, Laurel finds herself living alone for virtually the first time in her life. Although she is committed to her profession as a writer, Laurel soon realizes that her Southern background has conditioned her to expect romance and subservience to a man to be the central focus of her life; the novel depicts her vicissitudes as a single woman in her fifties struggling to come to terms with her new status. Apparently drawing on some of her own experiences of the past several years, Williams says that the work portrays the discomfiting collision between a woman with traditional values and a modern world in which those values no longer seem completely appropriate.[34] The author's efforts to combine, in this, her fifth novel, autobiographical retrospective with a portrayal of contemporary women's issues suggest that she is still searching for that balance of private and general concerns that often elicits her strongest writing.

There are obvious challenges in properly assessing the corpus of this particular writer, haunted by a powerful male mentor, struggling to keep working through the difficulties of a somewhat turbulent personal life, and attempting to come to terms with her Southernness in the North where she lives and with her femaleness in what has been for her largely a male-dominated world. Nor has she completely fulfilled her early promise; one can see in her work suggestions of the potential for a largely conceived, coherent oeuvre—it is nearly all set in and around Memphis and Arkabutla, and one can find in it recurrent characters and thematic patterns—but Williams has done less than she might have with such intertextual resonances, and her corpus is relatively small. Although most of Williams's fiction has been favorably reviewed, much of it by writers who themselves enjoy distinguished reputations, sales have been relatively small. Moreover, she has received virtually no attention from the academic critics, presumably because her work is relatively traditional, both artistically and socioculturally. Yet her work has been more neglected than it deserves. The best of it documents the constrictions of small-town Southern life and individuals' moving realizations of loneliness, loss, and the limitations of the human condition. It also depicts those moments of imperceptible but significant inner change, when a rebellious heart comes into being. At such times, Williams's fiction speaks eloquently and memorably.

JOAN WILLIAMS BIBLIOGRAPHY

FICTION

The Morning and the Evening. New York: Atheneum, 1961.
Old Powder Man. New York: Harcourt, Brace & World, 1966.
The Wintering. New York: Harcourt, Brace Jovanovich, 1971.
County Woman. Boston: Atlantic/Little, Brown, 1982.
Pariah. Boston: Atlantic/Little, Brown, 1983.
Pay the Piper. New York: Dutton, 1988.

ARTICLES

" 'You-Are-Thereness' in Fiction." *Writer* 80 (April 1967): 20–21, 72–73.
"Twenty Will Not Come Again." *Atlantic Monthly* 245 (May 1980): 58–65.
"Remembering." *Ironwood* 17 (1981): 107–10.
"In Defense of Caroline Compson." In *Critical Essays on William Faulkner: The Compson Family,* ed. Arthur F. Kinney, 402–7. Boston: G. K. Hall, 1982.

Maya Angelou:
Self and a Song of Freedom in
the Southern Tradition

*

CAROL E. NEUBAUER

WITHIN the last fifteen years, Maya Angelou has become one of the best-known black writers in the United States. Her reputation rests firmly on her prolific career as an autobiographer, poet, dancer-singer, actress, producer, director, scriptwriter, political activist, and editor. Throughout her life, she has identified with the South, and she calls Stamps, Arkansas, where she spent ten years of her childhood, her home.

Maya Angelou was born Marguerite Annie Johnson on 4 April 1928 in St. Louis to Vivian Baxter and Bailey Johnson, a civilian dietitian for the U.S. Navy. At age three, when her parents' marriage ended in divorce, she was sent, along with her brother, Bailey, from Long Beach to Stamps to be cared for by their paternal grandmother, Mrs. Annie Henderson. During the next ten years, a time of severe economic depression and intense racial bigotry in the South, she spent nearly all of her time either in school, at the daily meetings of the Colored Methodist Episcopal Church, or at her grandmother's general merchandise store. In 1940, she graduated with top honors from the Lafayette County Training School and soon thereafter returned to her mother, who lived in the San Francisco-Oakland area at that time. There she continued her education at George Washington High School under the direction of her beloved Miss Kirwin. At the same time, she attended evening classes at the California Labor School, where she received a scholarship to study drama and dance. A few weeks after she received her high school diploma, she gave birth to her son, Guy Bailey Johnson.

Her career as a professional entertainer began on the West Coast, where she performed as a dancer-singer at the Purple Onion in the early 1950s. While working in this popular cabaret, she was spotted by members of the *Porgy and Bess* cast and invited to audition for the chorus. Upon her return from the play's 1954–55 tour of Europe and Africa, she continued to perform at nightclubs throughout the United States, acquiring valuable experience that would eventually lead her into new avenues of professional work.

In 1959, Angelou and her son moved to New York, where she soon joined the Harlem Writers Guild at the invitation of John Killens. Together with Godfrey Cambridge, she produced, directed, and starred in *Cabaret for Freedom* to raise funds for the Southern Christian Leadership Conference. Following the close of the highly successful show, she accepted the position of Northern coordinator for the SCLC at the request of Dr. Martin Luther King, Jr.

Her work in theater landed her the role of the White Queen in Genet's *The Blacks,* directed by Gene Frankel at St. Mark's Playhouse. For this production, she joined a cast of stars—Roscoe Lee Brown, Godfrey Cambridge, James Earl Jones, and Cicely Tyson. In 1974, she adapted Sophocles' *Ajax* for its premiere at the Mark Taper Forum in Los Angeles. Original screenplays to her credit include the film version of *Georgia, Georgia* and the television productions of *I Know Why the Caged Bird Sings* and *The Sisters.* She also authored and produced a television series on African traditions inherent in American culture and played the role of Kunte Kinte's grandmother in *Roots.* For PBS programming, she served as a guest interviewer on *Assignment America* and most recently appeared in a special series on creativity hosted by Bill Moyers, which featured a return visit to Stamps.

Among her other honors, Maya Angelou was appointed to the Commission of International Women's Year by former President Carter. In 1975, *Ladies' Home Journal* named her Woman of the Year in communications. A trustee of the American Film Institute, she is also one of the few women members of the Directors Guild. In recent years, she has received more than a dozen honorary degrees, including one from the University of Arkansas located near her childhood home. Fluent in seven languages, she has worked as the editor of the *Arab Observer* in Cairo and the *African Review* in Ghana. In December 1981, Angelou accepted a lifetime appointment as the first Reynolds Professor of American Studies at Wake Forest University in Winston-Salem, where she lectures on literature and popular culture.[1] In 1983, Women in Communications presented her with the Matrix Award in the field of books.

Her personal life has been anything but smooth. As a young mother,

Angelou had to endure painful periods of separation from her son while she worked at more than one job to support them. Often her ventures into show business would take her far from home, and she would put Guy in the care of her mother or baby-sitters. When she was twenty-one years old, she married Tosh Angelos, a sailor of Greek-American ancestry, but their marriage ended after three years. While working in New York, she met and later married Vusumzi Make, a black South African activist who traveled extensively raising money to end apartheid. They divided their time between New York and Cairo, but after a few years their marriage deteriorated. In 1973, Angelou married Paul du Feu, a carpenter and construction worker she had met in London. They lived together on the West Coast during most of their seven-year marriage.

SOUTHERN ROOTS AND LITERARY REPUTATION

Although she is rarely called a regional writer, Maya Angelou is frequently identified with the new generation of Southern writers. She has always called the South her home, and recently, after much deliberation, she settled in North Carolina, ending an absence of more than thirty years. Her autobiographies and poetry are rich with references to her childhood home in Arkansas and to the South in general. For Angelou, as for many black American writers, the South has become a powerfully evocative metaphor for the history of racial bigotry and social inequality, for brutal inhumanity and final failure. Yet the South also represents a life-affirming force energized by a somewhat spiritual bond to the land itself. It is a region where generations of black families have sacrificed their brightest dreams for a better future; yet it is here that ties to forebears whose very blood has nourished the soil are most vibrant and resilient.[2] Stamps, Arkansas, in the 1930s was not a place where a black child could grow up freely or reach her full intellectual and social potential, but the town was nevertheless the home of Angelou's grandmother, who came to stand for all the courage and stability she ever knew as a child.

Her literary reputation is based on the publication of five volumes of autobiography (*I Know Why the Caged Bird Sings, Gather Together in My Name, Singin' and Swingin' and Gettin' Merry Like Christmas, The Heart of a Woman,* and *All God's Children Need Traveling Shoes*) and five volumes of poetry (*Just Give Me a Cool Drink of Water 'fore I Diiie, Oh Pray My Wings Are Gonna Fit Me Well, And Still I Rise, Shaker, Why Don't You Sing?* and *Now Sheba Sings the Song*).[3] In the twenty years of her publishing history, she has developed a rapport with her audiences who await each new work as a continuation of an ongoing dialogue with the author. Beginning with *Caged Bird* in 1970, her works have received wide critical acclaim and have been praised for reaching universal truths while examining the complicated life of one individual. The broad appeal of her autobiographies and poetry is evidenced in the numerous college anthologies that include portions of her work and in the popularity of the television adaptation of *Caged Bird*. In years to come, Angelou's voice, already recognized as one of the most original and versatile, will be measured by the standards of great American writers of our time.

AUTOBIOGRAPHY

In her first volume of autobiography, *I Know Why the Caged Bird Sings* (1970), Maya Angelou calls displacement the most important loss in her childhood, because she is separated from her mother and father at age three and never fully regains a sense of security and belonging. Her displacement from her family is not only an emotional handicap but is compounded by an equally unsettling sense of racial and geographic displacement. Her parents frequently move Angelou and her brother, Bailey, from St. Louis to Arkansas to the West Coast. As young children in Stamps in the 1930s, racial prejudice severely limits their lives. Within the first pages, she sums up this demoralizing period of alienation: "If growing up is painful for the Southern Black girl, being aware of her displacement is the rust on the razor that threatens the throat" (*CB*, 3). The pain of her continual rejection comes not only from the displacement itself, but even more poignantly, from the child's acute understanding of prejudice.[4] A smooth, clean razor would be enough of a threat, but a rusty, jagged one leaves no doubt in the victim's mind.

In *Caged Bird*, Angelou recounts many explosive incidents of the racial discrimination she experienced as a child. In the 1930s, Stamps was a fully segregated town.[5] Marguerite and Bailey, however, are welcomed by a grandmother who is not only devoted to them but, as owner of the Wm. Johnson General Merchandise Store, is highly successful and independent. Momma is their most constant source of love and strength. "I saw only her power and strength. She was taller than any woman in my personal world, and her hands were so large they could span my head from ear to ear" (*CB*, 38).[6] As powerful as her grandmother's presence seems to Marguerite, Momma uses her strength solely to guide and protect her family but not to confront the white community directly. Momma's resilient power usually reassures Marguerite, but one of the child's most difficult lessons teaches her that racial prejudice in Stamps can effectively circumscribe and even defeat her grandmother's protective influence.

In fact, it is only in the autobiographical narrative that Momma's personality begins to loom larger than life and provides Angelou's memories of childhood with a sense of personal dignity and meaning. On one occasion, for example, Momma takes Marguerite to the local dentist to be treated for a severe toothache. The dentist, who is ironically named Lincoln, refuses to treat the child, even though he is indebted to Momma for a loan she extended to him during the depression: " 'Annie, my policy is I'd rather stick my hand in a dog's mouth than in a nigger's.' " As a silent witness to this scene, Marguerite suffers not only from the pain of her two decayed teeth, which have been reduced to tiny enamel bits by the avenging "Angel of the candy counter," but also from the utter humiliation of the dentist's bigotry as well: "It seemed terribly unfair to have a toothache and a headache and have to bear at the same time the heavy burden of Blackness" (*CB*, 159–60).

In an alternate version of the confrontation, which Angelou deliberately fantasizes and then italicizes to emphasize its invention, Momma asks Marguerite to wait for her outside the dentist's office. As the door closes, the frightened child imagines her grandmother becoming "ten feet tall with eight-foot arms." Without mincing words, Momma instructs Lincoln to " 'leave Stamps by sundown' " and " 'never again practice dentistry' ": " 'When you get settled in your next place, you will be a vegetarian caring for dogs with the mange, cats with the cholera and cows with the epizootic. Is that clear?' " (*CB*, 162). The poetic justice in Momma's superhuman power is perfect; the racist dentist who refused to treat her ailing granddaughter will in the future be restricted to treating the dogs he prefers to "niggers." After a trip to the black dentist in Texarkana, Momma and Marguerite return to Stamps, where we learn the "real" version of the story by overhearing a conversation between Momma and Uncle Willie. In spite of her prodigious powers, all that Momma accomplishes in Dr. Lincoln's office is to demand ten dollars as unpaid interest on the loan to pay for their bus trip to Texarkana.

In the child's imagined version, fantasy comes into play as the recounted scene ventures into the unreal or the impossible. Momma becomes a sort of superwoman of enormous proportions ("ten feet tall with eight-foot arms") and comes to the helpless child's rescue. In this alternate vision, Angelou switches to fantasy to suggest the depth of the child's humiliation and the residue of pain even after her two bad teeth have been pulled. Fantasy, finally, is used to demonstrate the undiminished strength of the character of Momma. Summarizing the complete anecdote, Angelou attests, "I preferred, much preferred, my version." Carefully selected elements of fiction and fantasy in the scene involving Dr. Lincoln and her childhood hero, Momma, partially compensate for the racial displacement that she experiences as a child.[7]

When Angelou is thirteen, she and Bailey leave the repressive atmosphere of Stamps to join their mother. During these years, she continues to look for a place in life that will dissolve her sense of displacement. By the time she and Bailey are in their early teens, they have crisscrossed the western half of the country traveling between their parents' separate homes and their grandmother's in Stamps.[8] Her sense of geographic displacement alone would be enough to upset any child's security, since the life-styles of her father in southern California and her mother in St. Louis and later in San Francisco represent worlds completely different and even foreign to the pace of life in the rural South. Each time the children move, a different set of relatives or another of their parents' lovers greets them, and they never feel a part of a stable family group, except when they are in Stamps at the general store with Momma and Uncle Willie.

Once settled in San Francisco in the early 1940s, Angelou enrolls at George Washington High School and the California Labor School, where she studies dance and drama in evening classes. She excels in both schools, and her teachers quickly recognize her intelligence and talent. Later she breaks the color barrier by becoming the first black female conductor on the San Francisco streetcars. Just months before her high school graduation, she engages in a onetime sexual encounter to prove her sexuality to herself and becomes pregnant. *Caged Bird,* however, ends on a note of awakening with the birth of her son and the beginning of a significant measure of strength and confidence in her ability to succeed and find her place in life. As autobiographer, Angelou uses the theme of displacement to unify the first volume of her life story as well as to suggest her long-term determination to create security and permanency in her life.

Between the conclusion of *Caged Bird* and the beginning of Angelou's second volume of autobiography, *Gather Together in My Name* (1974), there is virtually no break in the narrative. As the first ends with the birth of her son, the second starts when Guy is only a few months old. As a whole, *Gather Together* tells the story of his first three years and focuses on a young single mother's struggle to achieve respect, love, and a sense of self-worth. Her battle to win financial independence and the devotion of a faithful man could hardly have been easy in the years immediately following World War II, when racial discrimination, unemployment, and McCarthyism were all on the rise. In spite of her initial optimism, which is, incidentally, shared by many members of the postwar black community who fervently believed that "race prejudice was dead. A mistake made by a young country. Something to be forgiven as an unpleasant act committed by an intoxicated friend" (*GT*, 2), Angelou soon realizes that her dreams for a better America are still too fragile to survive. But worst of all is the burden of guilt that rests on the shoulders of the seventeen-year-old mother who desperately believes that she must assume full adult responsibility. Fortunately, her mother encourages her to set high goals, to maintain her sense of dignity and self-worth, and to work hard to succeed. Her mother's words come back to her throughout her life: "Anything worth doing is worth doing well" (*GT*, 81), and "be the best of anything you get into" (*GT*, 24).[9]

Like many young women who came of age in the postwar era, Angelou easily imagines herself moving into a life modeled on *Good Housekeeping* and *Better Homes and Gardens*. She describes herself as both a "product of Hollywood upbringing" and her own "romanticism" and continually envisions herself smoothly slipping into the role guaranteed by popular culture. Whenever she meets a man who might potentially fulfill her dream, she anticipates the enviable comfort of "settling down." The scenario is always the same: "I would always wear pretty aprons and my son would play in the Little League. My husband would come home (he looked like Curly) and smoke his pipe in the den as I made cookies for the Scouts meeting" (*GT*, 127–28), or "We would live quietly in a pretty little house and I'd have another child, a girl, and the two children (whom he'd love equally) would climb over his knees and I would make three layer caramel cakes in my electric kitchen until they went off to college" (*GT*, 120).[10] These glamorous dreams, of course, never quite materialize, but Angelou maintains a hopeful outlook and a determination to support and protect herself and her infant son. Her primary motivation during these early years of motherhood is to spare her son the insecurity and rejection she faced as a child. During these years, Angelou even works as an absentee madam and a prostitute, in hopes of achieving a regular family life and easing her unabiding sense of guilt over not being able to provide herself and her son with financial and familial security.

Yet Angelou understands that the hurdles she has to cross on her road to success are often higher than those set by her own expectations and standards of performance. Although she spends the first years of her son's life in California, both in the Bay Area and in San Diego, she often faces racial discrimination reminiscent of her childhood experiences in the South. At one point in *Gather Together,* when she suspects that her thriving business as a madam of a two-prostitute house will soon be uncovered by the police, Angelou returns to Stamps with her son, hoping to find the same comfort and protection she had known as a child. Specifically, she seeks her grandmother's "protective embrace" and her "courage" as well as the "shield of anonymity," but she soon realizes that the South is not ready to welcome her and that she has "outgrown" its "childhood protection." The five years she has spent in school and working in California have broadened her horizons and convinced her of her right to be accepted on the basis of her character and intelligence. But the South to which she returns is unchanged: "The town was halved by railroad tracks, the swift Red River and racial prejudice, . . . " and "above all, the atmosphere was pressed down with the smell of old fears, and hates, and guilt" (*GT,* 61–63).

Not long after her arrival in Stamps, Angelou comes face to face with the double standards of racial discrimination during an unpleasant confrontation with a salesclerk in the white-owned general merchandise store.[11] Although she attempts to explain to her grandmother why she refused to accept the clerk's humiliating insults, Momma warns her that her "principles" are all too flimsy a protection against the unrestrained contempt of bigotry: " 'You think 'cause you've been to California these crazy people won't kill you? You think them lunatic cracker boys won't try to catch you in the road and violate you? You think because of your all-fired principle some of the men won't feel like putting their white sheets on and riding over here to stir up trouble? You do, you're wrong' " (*GT,* 78–79). That same day, her grandmother sends her back to California where she and her son are somewhat more distanced from the lingering hatred of the South. Not until the filming of a segment for Bill Moyer's PBS series on creativity thirty years later does Angelou return to her childhood home.

Upon her return to the Bay Area and to her mother's home, she is more determined than ever to achieve independence and win the respect of others. Leaving her son in the care of baby-sitters, she works long hours first as a dancer and entertainer and then as a short-order cook in Stockton. But as is often the case, the reality of her situation falls far below her ideal, and Angelou eventually turns to marijuana as a temporary consolation: "The pot had been important when I was alone and lonely, when my present was dull and the future uncertain" (*GT,*

131). During this period, she also falls in love with an older man who is a professional gambler supported by prostitution. When his luck fails him, Angelou agrees to help him pay his debt by becoming a prostitute herself. She makes this sacrifice fully believing that after her man has regained his financial security, he will marry her and provide her with the fulfillment of her romantic dream. Rationalizing her decision, she compares prostitution to marriage: "There are married women who are more whorish than a street prostitute because they have sold their bodies for marriage licenses, and there are some women who sleep with men for money who have great integrity because they are doing it for a purpose" (*GT*, 135). But once again her dreams are disappointed, and she finds herself on her own at the end.

The second volume of her autobiography ends just before she decides to settle down with a man she pictures as an "ideal husband," who is in fact a heroin addict and gambler. Before it is too late, Angelou learns that she is on the verge of embracing disaster and defeat. At the end, she regains her innocence through the lessons of a compassionate drug addict: "I had walked the precipice and seen it all; and at the critical moment, one man's generosity pushed me safely away from the edge. . . . I had given a promise and found my innocence. I swore I'd never lose it again" (*GT*, 181). With these words, ready to accept the challenge of life anew, Angelou brings the second volume of her life story to a close. In *Gather Together in My Name*, a title inspired by the Gospel of Matthew (18: 20), she asks her family and readers to gather around her and bear witness to her past.

The third volume of Maya Angelou's autobiography, *Singin' and Swingin' and Gettin' Merry Like Christmas* (1976) concentrates on the early years of her career as a professional dancer and singer, her related experience with racial prejudice, and with the guilt suffered through separation from her young son. During her childhood, her love for music grows through her almost daily attendance at the Colored Methodist Episcopal Church in Stamps and through her dance classes in California. Music in fact is her closest companion and source of moral support during her first few months back in the San Francisco area. She calls music her "refuge" during this period of her life and welcomes its protective embrace, into which she could "crawl into the spaces between the notes and curl [her] back to loneliness" (*SS*, 1). Without losing any time, she secures a job in sales and inventory at the Melrose Record Shop on Fillmore, which at the time served as a meeting place for musicians and music lovers of all description. In addition to earning enough money to quit her two previous jobs and bring her son home from the baby-sitter's in the evenings and on Sundays, Angelou also gains valuable exposure to the newest releases in blues and jazz and to an expansive circle of eccentric people.

Her sales position at the record shop is her first step into the world of entertainment. Her hours behind the cashier counter studying catalogs and helping customers make their selections bring her an easy familiarity with the newest stars and songs. Relying on her dance lessons and her trusted memory of popular lyrics, she later auditions for a position as a dancer at the Garden of Allah, where she is eventually hired as the first black show girl. Unlike the three white women who are also featured in the nightly show, Angelou is not required to strip but rather earns her audience's attention on the basis of her dance routines alone. All of the dancers, however, are instructed to supplement their regular salary by selling B-grade drinks and bottles of champagne on commission to interested customers. At first reluctant to put herself at the mercy of fawning, flirtatious spectators, she soon learns to sell more drinks than any of the others, simply by giving away the house secret on the composition of the ginger ale and Seven-Up cocktails and the details of the commission scale. But her success evokes the jealousy of the other women, and soon her first venture into professional entertainment comes to an end.

Through contacts established during her work at the Garden of Allah, Angelou auditions for an opening at the Purple Onion, a North Beach cabaret where she soon replaces Jorie Remus and shares the nightly bill with Phyllis Diller. After lessons with her drama coach, Lloyd Clark, who, incidentally, is responsible for coining her stage name, Maya Angelou, she polishes her style as an interpretative dancer and perfects a series of calypso songs that eventually comprise her regular act at the cabaret. Although the audience at the Purple Onion has never been entertained by a performer like Angelou, she quickly becomes extremely popular and gains much wider exposure than she did as a dancer at the Garden of Allah. Many professional stars and talent scouts, visiting San Francisco from New York and Chicago, drop in at the Purple Onion and some eventually invite her to audition for their shows. In 1954, for example, Leonard Sillman brought his Broadway hit *New Faces of 1953* to the Bay Area. When she learns through friends that Sillman needed a replacement for Eartha Kitt, who would be leaving for an engagement in Las Vegas, she jumps at the chance to work with a cast of talented performers. Even though she is invited to join the show, the management at the Purple Onion refuses to release her from her contract. Her first real show business break, therefore, does not come until after she goes to New York to try out for a new Broadway show called *House of Flowers,* starring Pearl Bailey and directed by Saint Subber. While there she is unexpectedly asked to join the company of *Porgy and Bess* in the role of Ruby, just as the troupe is finishing up its engagement in Montreal and embarking on its first European tour. She accepts, thereby launching her international career as a dancer-singer.

As her professional career in entertainment develops, Angelou worries about her responsibility to care for her young son and provide him with a secure family life. In *Singin' and Swingin',* she continues to trace her pursuit of romantic ideals in the face of loneliness and disappointment. While working in the Melrose Record Shop, she meets Tosh Angelos, a sailor of Greek-American heritage, and later marries him. Her first impression of marriage could not have been more idealistic:

> At last I was a housewife, legally a member of that enviable tribe of consumers whom security made fat as butter and who under no circumstances considered living by bread alone, because their husbands brought home the bacon. I had a son, a father for him, a husband and a pretty home for us to live in. My life began to resemble a Good Housekeeping advertisement. I cooked well-balanced meals and molded fabulous jello desserts. My floors were dangerous with daily applications of wax and our furniture slick with polish. (*SS,* 26)

Unfortunately, after a year, Tosh and she begin to argue and recognize that their different attitudes stand in the way of true compatibility and trust. Her "Eden"-like homelife and "cocoon of safety" begin to smother her sense of integrity and independence. In her autobiography, she describes this difficult period as a time in which she felt a "sense of loss," which "suffused [her] until [she] was suffocating within the vapors" (*SS,* 37). When their marriage ends, Angelou again looks for a way to give her young child a stable home and a permanent sense of family security. Understandably, her son temporarily distrusts her and wonders whether she will stop loving him and leave him behind to be cared for by others.

Before she marries Tosh, she seriously questions the nature of interracial marriage and is advised by others, including her mother, to examine the relationship carefully. Throughout *Singin' and Swingin',* she studies her attitude toward white people and explains her growing familiarity with their life-styles and their acceptance of her as an equal within the world of entertainment. When she first meets her future Greek-American husband, she suspects that her racial heritage precludes the possibility of any kind of permanent relationship. Her Southern childhood is too close, too vibrant in her memory: "I would never forget the slavery tales, or my Southern past, where all whites, including the poor and ignorant, had the right to speak rudely to and even physically abuse any Negro they met. I knew the ugliness of white prejudice" (*SS*, 23). Although she discounts her suspicion in her dealings with Tosh Angelos, her deeply rooted fears stay close to the surface as she comes to associate with a large number of white artists and entertainers during her career as a dancer: "I knew you could never tell about white people. Negroes had survived centuries of inhuman treatment and retained their humanity by hoping for the best from their pale-skinned oppressors but at the same time being prepared for the worst" (*SS*, 104). Later, during her role as Ruby in *Porgy and Bess*, which played throughout Europe, the Middle East, and North Africa, she observes the double standards of white people who readily accept black Americans in Europe, because they are fascinated by their exotic foreignness, but who are equally quick to discriminate against other people of color. In North Africa, she witnesses yet another version of racial bigotry in the way members of the Arab elite mistreat their African servants, "not realizing that auction blocks and whipping posts were too recent in our history for us [black Americans] to be comfortable around slavish servants" (*SS*, 210).

While in Rome, Angelou decides to cut short her engagement with *Porgy and Bess*, not because she has witnessed the complexities of racial prejudice but rather because she realizes that her son has suffered during her extended absence. Throughout her European tour, she carries the burden of guilt, which comes to characterize her early years of motherhood. Although she recognizes the pattern of abandonment emerging in her son's life as it had in her own, she often sees no alternative than to accept a job and, with it, the pain of separation. Finally, upon learning that her son has developed a severe and seemingly untreatable rash in her absence, she decides to return to San Francisco. Once there, she assumes full responsibility for "ruining [her] beautiful son by neglect" and for the "devastation to his mind and body" (*SS*, 233). Shortly after her return, Guy recovers, and together they reach a new level of trust and mutual dependence based on the understanding that their separation is now over for good. *Singin' and Swingin'* comes to a close as mother and son settle into a Hawaiian beach resort where she has just opened a new engagement at a nightclub. She achieves a longed for peace of mind as she comes to treasure her "wonderful, dependently independent son" (*SS*, 242).

In *The Heart of a Woman* (1980), the fourth in the autobiographical series, Maya Angelou continues the account of her son's youth and, in the process, repeatedly returns to the story of her childhood.[12] The references to her childhood serve partly to create a textual link for readers who might be unfamiliar with the earlier volumes and partly to emphasize the suggestive similarities between her childhood and her son's. Her overwhelming sense of displacement and instability is, ironically, her son's burden too. In a brief flashback in the second chapter, she reminds us of the displacement that characterized her youth and links this aspect of her past with her son's present attitude. When Guy is fourteen, Angelou decides to move to New York. She does not bring Guy to the East until she has found a place for them to live, and when he arrives after a one-month separation, he initially resists her attempts to make a new home for them:

> The air between us [Angelou and Guy] was burdened with his aloof scorn. I understood him too well.
>
> When I was three my parents divorced in Long Beach, California, and sent me and my four-year-old brother, unescorted, to our paternal grandmother. We wore wrist tags which informed anyone concerned that we were Marguerite and Bailey Johnson, en route to Mrs. Annie Henderson in Stamps, Arkansas.
>
> Except for disastrous and mercifully brief encounters with each of them when I was seven, we didn't see our parents again until I was thirteen. (*HW,* 34–35)

From this and similar encounters with Guy, Angelou learns that the continual displacement of her own childhood is something she cannot prevent from recurring in her son's life.

In New York, Angelou begins to work as the Northern coordinator of the Southern Christian Leadership Conference and devotes most of her time to raising funds, boosting membership, and organizing volunteer labor, both in the office and in the neighborhoods. Throughout *Heart of a Woman,* she expands her own narrative by including anecdotes about well-known entertainers and political figures. Her account of a visit with Martin Luther King, Jr., at her SCLC office is just one example of this autobiographical technique. When Dr. King pays his first visit to the New York office during her tenure, she does not have advance notice of his presence and rushes into her office one day after lunch to find him sitting at her desk. They begin to talk about her background and eventually focus their comments on her brother, Bailey:

"Come on, take your seat back and tell me about yourself."

. . . When I mentioned my brother Bailey, he asked what he was doing now.

The question stopped me. He was friendly and understanding, but if I told him my brother was in prison, I couldn't be sure how long his understanding would last. I could lose my job. Even more important, I might lose his respect. Birds of a feather and all that, but I took a chance and told him Bailey was in Sing Sing.

He dropped his head and looked at his hands.

. . . "I understand. Disappointment drives our young men to some desperate lengths." Sympathy and sadness kept his voice low. "That's why we must fight and win. We must save the Baileys of the world. And Maya, never stop loving him. Never give up on him. Never deny him. And remember, he is freer than those who hold him behind bars." (*HW*, 92–93)

Angelou appreciates King's sympathy and of course shares his hope that their work will make the world more fair and free. She recognizes the undeniable effects of displacement on Bailey's life and fervently hopes that her own son will be spared any further humiliation and rejection.

From time to time, Angelou sees marriage as the answer to her own sense of dislocation and fully envisions a perfect future with various prospective husbands. While in New York, she meets Vusumzi Make, a black South African freedom fighter, and imagines that he will provide her with the same domestic security she had hoped would develop from other relationships: "I was getting a husband, and a part of that gift was having someone to share responsibility and guilt" (*HW*, 131). Yet her hopes are even more idealistic than usual, inasmuch as she imagines herself participating in the liberation of South Africa as Vus Make's wife: "With my courage added to his own, he would succeed in bringing the ignominious white rule in South Africa to an end. If I didn't already have the qualities he needed, then I would just develop them. Infatuation made me believe in my ability to create myself into my lover's desire" (*HW*, 123). In reality, Angelou is only willing to go so far in re-creating herself to meet her husband's desires and is all too soon frustrated with her role as Make's wife. He does not want her to work but is unable on his own to support his expensive tastes as well as his family. They are evicted from their New York apartment just before they leave for Egypt and soon face similar problems in Cairo. Their marriage dissolves after some months, despite Angelou's efforts to contribute to their financial assets by working as editor of the *Arab Ob-*

server. In *Heart of a Woman,* she underscores the illusory nature of her fantasy about marriage to show how her perspective has shifted over the years and how much understanding she has gained about life in general. Re-creating these fantasies in her autobiography is a subtle form of truth telling and a way to present hard-earned insights about her life to her readers.

A second type of fantasy in *Heart of a Woman* is borne out in reality rather than in illusion, as is the case with her expectations of marriage. One of the most important uses of the second kind of fantasy involves a sequence that demonstrates how much she fears for Guy's safety throughout his youth. A few days after mother and son arrive in Accra, where they move when her marriage with Vus Make deteriorates, some friends invite them to a picnic. Although his mother declines, Guy immediately accepts the invitation in a show of independence. On the way home from the day's outing, her son is seriously injured in an automobile accident. Even though he has had very little experience driving, his intoxicated host asks Guy to drive. When their return is delayed, Angelou is terrified by her recurring fear for Guy's safety. Later, in the Korle Bu emergency ward, her familiar fantasy about harm endangering her son's life moves to the level of reality, as she relates the vulnerability she feels in her role as mother with full responsibility for the well-being of her only child. In a new country, estranged from her husband and with no immediate prospects for employment, she possesses very little control over her life or her son's safety. After the accident in Ghana, Guy is not only fighting for independence from his mother but also for life itself. The conclusion of *Heart of a Woman,* nevertheless, announces a new beginning for Angelou and hope for her future relationship with Guy.

Her most recent autobiography, *All God's Children Need Traveling Shoes* (1986), has swept Angelou to new heights of critical and popular acclaim. Her life story resumes exactly where it ended chronologically and geographically in *The Heart of a Woman,* with Guy's recovery from his automobile accident in Accra. Although only portions of two earlier volumes of her autobiographical narrative occur in Africa, her latest addition to the series takes place almost exclusively in Ghana. In *All God's Children Need Traveling Shoes,* however, Angelou focuses primarily on the story of her and many other black Americans' attempts in the early 1960s to return to the ancestral home in Africa. As in her four previous autobiographies, she explores the theme of displacement and the difficulties involved in creating a home for oneself, one's family, and one's people.

In choosing to live in Ghana following the deterioration of her marriage to Vus Make, Angelou hopes to find a place where she and her son can make a home for themselves, free at last from the racial bigotry she has faced throughout the United States, Europe, and parts of the Middle East. While Guy is recuperating from his injuries, she carefully evaluates her assets and concludes that since his birth, her only home has been wherever she and her son are together: "we had been each other's home and center for seventeen years. He could die if he wanted to and go off to wherever dead folks go, but I, I would be left without a home" (*TS,* 5). Her initial expectations, therefore, for feeling at ease and settling down in West Africa are, understandably, considerable: "We had come home, and if home was not what we had expected, never mind, our need for belonging allowed us to ignore the obvious and to create real places or even illusory places, befitting our imagination" (*TS,* 19). Unfortunately, the Ghanian people do not readily accept Angelou, her son, and most of the black American community in Accra, and they unexpectedly find themselves isolated and often ignored.

Taken as a whole, *All God's Children Need Traveling Shoes* recounts the sequence of events that gradually brings the autobiographer closer to an understanding and eventually to an acceptance of the seemingly unbreachable distance between the Ghanians and the black American expatriates. Within the first few weeks of her stay in Ghana, Angelou suspects that she has mistakenly followed the misdirected footsteps of other black Americans who "had not come home, but had left one familiar place of painful memory for another strange place with none" (*TS,* 40). In time, she understands that their alienation is most likely based on the fact that they, unlike the Ghanians, are the descendants of African slaves, who painfully bear the knowledge that " 'not all slaves were stolen, nor were all slave dealers European' " (*TS,* 47). No one in the expatriate group can feel fully at ease in Africa as long as they carry the haunting suspicion that "African slavery stemmed mostly from tribal exploitation" (*TS,* 48) and not solely from European colonial imperialism.

Angelou, nevertheless, perseveres; she eventually settles into lasting friendships with both Americans and Africans and finds work through her talents as a journalist and a performer. With her professional and personal contacts, she meets many African political activists, as well as diplomats and artists from around the world. These acquaintances, in addition to a brief tour in Berlin and Venice with the original St. Mark's Playhouse company of Genet's *The Blacks,* enlarge Angelou's perspective on racial complexities and help her locate a place in Africa where she can live, albeit temporarily, at peace.

In *All God's Children Need Traveling Shoes,* Angelou continually reminds the reader that the quest for a place to call home is virtually endemic to the human condition. During her time in Ghana, she comes
to understand that the search is seldom successful, regardless of the political or social circumstances involved. Toward the end of her personal
narrative, Angelou sums up her conclusions about the struggle to find
or create a home: "If the heart of Africa still remained allusive, my
search for it had brought me closer to understanding myself and other
human beings. The ache for home lives in all of us, the safe place where
we can go as we are and not be questioned" (*TS,* 196). In a 1984 interview conducted during the period when she was completing an earlier
draft of *All God's Children Need Traveling Shoes,* Angelou voices the
same illuminating insight:

Neubauer: How far will the fifth volume go?

Angelou: Actually, it's a new kind. It's really quite a new voice. I'm
looking at the black American resident, me and the other
black American residents in Ghana, and trying to see all the
magic of the eternal quest of human beings to go home again.
That is maybe what life is anyway. To return to the Creator.
All of that naivete, the innocence of trying to. That awful
rowing towards God, whatever it is. Whether it's to return to
your village or the lover you lost or the youth that some
people want to return to or the beauty that some want to return to.

Neubauer: Writing autobiography frequently involves this quest
to return to the past, to the home. Sometimes, if the home
can't be found, if it can't be located again, then that home or
that love or that family, whatever has been lost, is recreated or
invented.

Angelou: Yes, of course. That's it! That's what I'm seeing in this
trek back to Africa. That in so many cases that idealized home
of course is non-existent. In so many cases some black Americans created it on the spot. On the spot. And I did too. Created something, looked, seemed like what we have idealized
very far from reality.

Whatever vision of home Angelou creates for herself and her son in
Ghana, she discovers a heightened sense of self-awareness and independence. By the end of her stay in West Africa, she has a renewed image of

herself as a woman, lover, mother, writer, performer, and political activist. In her state of fortified strength, she decides to leave Africa and return to the country of her birth, however disturbing the memories of slavery and the reality of racial hatred. In fact, Angelou ends her sojourn in foreign lands to commit herself to Malcolm X's struggle for racial equality and social justice in the United States, by planning to work as an office coordinator for the Organization of Afro-American Unity. She has finally freed herself from the illusion of claiming an ancestral home in Africa. Ironically perhaps, with the writing of *All God's Children Need Traveling Shoes* and the brilliant clarity of the autobiographical present, "this trek back to Africa," Maya Angelou also decides to return to the South, and for the first time since her youth, make her home there. Although she has learned that "the idealized home of course is non-existent," she leaves her readers to suspect that her traveling shoes are never really out of sight; if nothing else, we will soon find ourselves following her paths of autobiographical discovery once again.

POETRY

Most of the thirty-eight poems in Maya Angelou's *Just Give Me a Cool Drink of Water 'fore I Diiie* (1971) appeared several years earlier in a collection called *The Poetry of Maya Angelou,* published by Hirt Music. Among these are some of her best known pieces, such as "Miss Scarlett, Mr. Rhett and Other Latter Day Saints" and "Harlem Hopscotch." The volume is divided into two parts; the first deals with love, its joy and inevitable sorrow, and the second with the trials of the black race. Taken as a whole, the poems cover a wide range of settings from Harlem streets to Southern churches to abandoned African coasts. These poems contain a certain power, which stems from the strong metric control that finds its way into the terse lines characteristic of her poetry. Not a word is wasted, not a beat lost. Angelou's poetic voice speaks with a sure confidence that dares return to even the most painful memories to capture the first signs of loss or hate.

The first twenty poems of *Cool Drink* describe the whole gamut of love, from the first moment of passionate discovery to the first suspicion of painful loss. One poem, in fact, is entitled "The Gamut" and in its sonnet form moves from "velvet soft" dawn when "my true love approaches" to the "deathly quiet" of night when "my true love is leaving" (*CD,* 5). Two poems, "To a Husband" and "After," however, celebrate the joyous fulfillment of love. In the first, Angelou suggests that her husband is a symbol of African strength and beauty and that through his almost majestic presence she can sense the former riches of the exploited continent. To capture his vibrant spirit, she retreats to Africa's original splendor and conjures up images as ancient as "Pharoah's tomb":

> You're Africa to me
> At brightest dawn.
> The congo's green and
> Copper's brackish hue . . .

In this one man, she sees the vital strength of an entire race: "A continent to build / With Black Man's brawn" (*CD,* 15). His sacrifice, reminiscent of generations of unacknowledged labor, inspires her love and her commitment to the African cause. "After" also speaks of the love between woman and man but is far more tender and passionate. The scene is the lovers' bed when "no sound falls / from the moaning sky" and "no scowl wrinkles / the evening pool." Here, as in "To a Husband," love is seen as strong and sustaining, even jubilant in its harmonious union, its peaceful calm. Even "the stars lean down / A stony brilliance" in recognition of their love (*CD,* 18). And yet there is a certain absent emptiness in the quiet that hints of future loss.

In the second section, Angelou turns her attention to the lives of black people in America from the time of slavery to the rebellious 1960s. Her themes deal broadly with the painful anguish suffered by blacks forced into submission, with guilt over accepting too much, and with protest and basic survival.

"No No No No" is a poem about the rejection of American myths that promise justice for all but only guarantee freedom for a few. The powerfully cadenced stanzas in turn decry the immorality of American involvement in Vietnam,

> while crackling babies
> in napalm coats
> stretch mouths to receive
> burning tears . . .

as well as the insincere invitation of the Statue of Liberty, which welcomes immigrants who crossed "over the sinuous cemetery / of my many brothers," and the inadequate apologies offered by white liberals.

The first stanza ends with the refrain that titles the complete collection of poems, "JUST GIVE ME A COOL DRINK OF WATER 'FORE I DIIIE." In the second half of the poem, the speaker identifies with those who suffered humiliation

> on the back porches
> of forever
> in the kitchens and fields
> of rejections

and boldly cautions that the dreams and hopes of a better tomorrow have vanished (*CD,* 40–43). Even pity, the last defense against inhumanity, is spent.

Two poems that embody the poet's confident determination that conditions must improve for the black race are "Times-Square-Shoeshine Composition" and "Harlem Hopscotch." Both ring with a lively, invincible beat that carries defeated figures into at least momentary triumph. "Times-Square" tells the story of a shoeshine man who claims to be an unequaled master at his trade. He cleans and shines shoes to a vibrant rhythm that sustains his spirit in spite of humiliating circumstances. When a would-be customer offers him twenty-five cents instead of the requested thirty-five cents, the shoeshine man refuses the job and flatly renounces the insulting attempt to minimize the value of his trade. Fully appreciating his own expertise, the vendor proudly instructs his potential Times Square patron to give his measly quarter to his daughter, sister, or mamma, for they clearly need it more than he does. Denying the charge that he is a "greedy bigot," the shoeshine man simply admits that he is a striving "capitalist," trying to be successful in a city owned by the superrich.

Moving uptown, "Harlem Hopscotch" celebrates the sheer strength necessary for survival. The rhythm of this powerful poem echoes the beat of feet, first hopping, then suspended in air, and finally landing in the appropriate square. To live in a world measured by such blunt announcements as "food is gone" and "the rent is due," people need to be extremely energetic and resilient. Compounding the pressures of hunger, poverty, and unemployment is the racial bigotry that consistently discriminates against people of color. Life itself has become a brutal game of hopscotch, a series of desperate yet hopeful leaps, landing but never pausing long: "In the air, now both feet down./Since you black, don't stick around." Yet in the final analysis, the words that bring the poem and the complete collection to a close triumphantly announce the poet's victory: "Both feet flat, the game is done. / They think I lost.

I think I won" (*CD*, 50). These poems in their sensitive treatment of both love and black identity are the poet's own defense against the incredible odds in the game of life.

Within four years of the publication of *Just Give Me a Cool Drink 'fore I Diiie,* Maya Angelou completed a second volume of poetry, *Oh Pray My Wings Are Gonna Fit Me Well* (1975). By the time of its release, her reputation as a poet who transforms much of the pain and disappointment of life into lively verse had been established. During the 1970s, her reading public grew accustomed to seeing her poems printed in *Cosmopolitan.* Angelou had become recognized not only as a spokesperson for blacks and women, but also for all people who are committed to raising the moral standards of living in the United States. The poems collected in *My Wings,* indeed, appear at the end of the Vietnam era and in some important ways exceed the scope of her first volume. Many question traditional American values and urge people to make an honest appraisal of the demoralizing rift between the ideal and the real. Along with poems about love and the oppression of black people, the poet adds several that directly challenge Americans to reexamine their lives and to strive to reach the potential richness that has been compromised by self-interest since the beginnings of the country.

One of the most moving poems in *My Wings* is entitled "Alone," in which carefully measured verses describe the general alienation of people in the twentieth century. "Alone" is not directed at any one particular sector of society but rather is focused on the human condition in general. No one, the poet cautions, can live in this world alone. This message punctuates the end of the three major stanzas and also serves as a separate refrain between each and at the close of the poem:

Alone, all alone
Nobody, but nobody
Can make it out here alone.

Angelou begins by looking within herself and discovering that her soul is without a home. Moving from an inward glimpse to an outward sweep, she recognizes that even millionaires suffer from this modern malaise and live lonely lives with "hearts of stone." Finally, she warns her readers to listen carefully and change the direction of their lives:

Storm clouds are gathering
The wind is gonna blow
The race of man is suffering. (*MW,* 70)

For its own survival, the human race must break down barriers and rescue one another from loneliness. The only cure, the poet predicts, is to acknowledge common interests and work toward common goals.

A poem entitled "America" is no less penetrating in its account of the country's problems. Again Angelou pleads with the American people to "discover this country" and realize its full potential. In its two-hundred-year history, "the gold of her promise / has never been mined." The promise of justice for all has not been kept and in spite of "her crops of abundance / the fruit and the grain," many citizens live below the poverty line and never have enough food to feed their families. Similarly, racial bigotry has denied generations of Americans their full dignity and natural rights, while depriving them of the opportunity to contribute freely to the nation's strength. At the close of the poem, Angelou calls for the end of "legends untrue," which are perpetrated through history to "entrap" America's children (*MW*, 78–79). The only hope for the country is to discard these false myths once and for all and to guarantee that all people benefit from democratic principles.[13]

In one poem, "Southeast Arkansia," the poet shifts her attention from the general condition of humanity to the plight of black people in America. The setting of this tightly structured poem is the locale where Angelou spent most of her childhood. At the end of the three stanzas, she poses a question concerning the responsibility and guilt involved in the exploitation of the slaves. Presumably, the white men most immediately involved have never answered for their inhumane treatment of "bartered flesh and broken bones." The poet doubts that they have ever even paused to "ponder" or "wonder" about their proclivity to value profit more than human life (*MW*, 99).

Any discussion of *My Wings* that did not address the poems written about the nature of love would be necessarily incomplete. The entire volume is dedicated to Paul du Feu, Angelou's husband from 1973 to 1980. One very brief poem, "Passing Time," speaks of a love that is finely balanced and delicately counterpoised. This love stretches over time, blanketing both the beginning and end of a day: "Your skin like dawn / Mine like dusk" (*MW*, 62). Together is reached a certain harmony that carries the lovers through the day, perfectly complementing each other's spirit. Equally economical in form is the poem "Greyday," which in nine short lines compares a lonely lover to Christ. While she is separated from her man, "the day hangs heavy / loose and grey." The woman feels as if she is wearing "a crown of thorns" and "a shirt of hair." Alone, she suffers in her solitude and mourns that

No one knows
my lonely heart
when we're apart. (*MW*, 64)

Such is love in the world of *My Wings*; when all is going well, love sustains and inspires, but when love fades, loneliness and pain have free rein.

As the title of Maya Angelou's third volume of poetry, *And Still I Rise* (1978), suggests, this collection contains a hopeful determination to rise above discouraging defeat. These poems are inspired and spoken by a confident voice of strength that recognizes its own power and will no longer be pushed into passivity. The book consists of thirty-two poems, which are divided into three sections, "Touch Me, Life, Not Softly," "Traveling," and "And Still I Rise." Two poems, "Phenomenal Woman" and "Just for a Time" appeared in *Cosmopolitan* in 1978. Taken as a whole, this series of poems covers a broader range of subjects than the earlier two volumes and shifts smoothly from issues such as springtime and aging to sexual awakening, drug addition, and Christian salvation. The familiar themes of love and its inevitable loneliness and the oppressive climate of the South are still central concerns. But even more striking than the poet's careful treatment of these subjects is her attention to the nature of woman and the importance of family.

One of the best poems in this collection is "Phenomenal Woman," which captures the essence of womanhood and at the same time describes the many talents of the poet herself. As is characteristic of Angelou's poetic style, the lines are terse and forcefully, albeit irregularly, rhymed. The words themselves are short, often monosyllabic, and collectively create an even, provocative rhythm that resounds with underlying confidence. In four different stanzas, a woman explains her special graces that make her stand out in a crowd and attract the attention of both men and women, although she is not, by her own admission, "cut or built to suit a fashion model's size." One by one, she enumerates her gifts, from "the span of my hips" to "the curl of my lips," from "the flash of my teeth" to "the joy in my feet." Yet her attraction is not purely physical; men seek her for her "inner mystery," "the grace of [her] style," and "the need for [her] care." Together each alluring part adds up to a phenomenal woman who need not "bow" her head but can walk tall with a quiet pride that beckons those in her presence (*IR*, 121–23).

Similar to "Phenomenal Woman" in its economical form, strong rhyme scheme, and forceful rhythm is "Woman Work." The two poems also bear a thematic resemblance in their praise of woman's vitality. Although "Woman Work" does not concern the physical appeal of woman, as "Phenomenal Woman" does, it delivers a corresponding litany of the endless cycle of chores in a woman's typical day. In the first stanza, the long list unravels itself in forcefully rhymed couplets:

I've got the children to tend
The clothes to mend
The floor to mop
The food to shop
Then the chicken to fry
Then baby to dry.

Following the complete category of tasks, the poet adds four shorter stanzas, which reveal the source of woman's strength. This woman claims the sunshine, rain, and dew as well as storms, wind, and snow as her own. The dew cools her brow, the wind lifts her "across the sky," the snow covers her "with white / Cold icy kisses," all bringing her rest and eventually the strength to continue (*IR*, 144–45). For her, there is no other source of solace and consolation than nature and its powerful elements.

In two poems, "Willie" and "Kin," Angelou turns her attention from woman to her family. "Willie" tells the story of her paternal uncle, with whom she and her brother, Bailey, lived during their childhood in Stamps, Arkansas. This man, although "crippled and limping, always walking lame," knows the secret of survival. For years, he suffers humiliation and loneliness, both as a result of his physical affliction and his color. Yet from him, the child learns about the hidden richness of life and later follows his example to overcome seemingly insurmountable hardships. Willie's undying message echoes throughout the poem: "I may cry and I will die, / But my spirit is the soul of every spring" and "my spirit is the surge of open seas." Although he cannot personally change the inhumane way people treat their brothers and sisters, Willie's spirit will always be around; for, as he says, "I am the time," and his inspiration lives on beyond him (*IR*, 141–42).

As in "Willie," the setting of "Kin" is the South, particularly Arkansas, and the subject is family. This powerful poem is dedicated to Bailey and is based on the painful separation of brother and sister during their adult years. As children, Marguerite and Bailey were constant companions and buffered each other somewhat from the continual awareness of what it meant to grow up black in the South. Then, she writes, "We were entwined in red rings / Of blood and loneliness. . . ." Now, distanced by time and Bailey's involvement with drugs, the poet is left

>   . . . to force strangers
>   Into brother molds, exacting
>   Taxations they never
>   Owed or could pay.

Meanwhile, her brother slips further and further away and fights

>   . . . to die, thinking
>   In destruction lies the seed
>   Of birth. . . .

Although she cannot reach him in his "regions of terror," Angelou sinks through memory to "silent walks in Southern woods" and an "Arkansas twilight" and is willing to concede that her brother "may be right" (*IR*, 149–50).

But ultimately, the poet challenges her readers to fight against the insipid invitation of destruction and death. Throughout *And Still I Rise*, the strong, steady rhythm of her poetic voice beckons whoever will listen to transcend beyond the level of demoralizing defeat and to grasp life on its own terms.[14] The single strongest affirmation of life is the title poem, "And Still I Rise." In the face of "bitter, twisted lies," "hatefulness," and "history's shame," the poet promises not to surrender. Silently, she absorbs the power of the sun and moon and becomes a "black ocean, leaping and wide, / Welling and swelling I bear in the tide." Her inner resources, "oil wells," "gold mines," and "diamonds," nourish her strength and sustain her courage. Her spirit will soar as she transforms "the gifts that my ancestors gave" into poetry, and herself into "the dream and the hope of the slave" (*IR*, 154–55). Through all of her verse, Angelou reaches out to touch the lives of others and to offer them hope and confidence in place of humiliation and despair.

Her fourth volume of verse, *Shaker, Why Don't You Sing?* (1983), is dedicated to her son, Guy Johnson, and her grandson, Colin Ashanti Murphy Johnson. As do her three previous collections of poems, *Shaker* celebrates the power to struggle against lost love, defeated dreams, and threatened freedom, and to survive. Her poetic voice resonates with the control and confidence that have become characteristic of Angelou's work in general and of her determination that "life loves the person who dares to live it." The vibrant tone of these poems moves gracefully from the promise of potential strength to the humor of light satire, at all times bearing witness to a spirit that soars and sings in spite of repeated disappointment. Perhaps even more than in her earlier poems,

Angelou forcefully captures the loneliness of love and the sacrifice of slavery without surrendering to defeat or despair.

More than half of the twenty-eight poems in *Shaker* concern the subject of love between woman and man, and of these, most deal with the pain, loss, and loneliness that typically characterize unrequited love. In many of these poems, a woman awakens at sunrise, with or without her lover by her side, wondering how much longer their dying relationship will limp along before its failure will be openly acknowledged. An underlying issue in these poignant poems about love is deception—not so much the intricate fabrication of lies to cover up infidelity but rather the unvoiced acquiescence to fading and failing love. In "The Lie," for example, a woman protects herself from humiliation when her lover threatens to leave her by holding back her anger and pretending to be unmoved, even eager to see her man go:

> I hold curses, in my mouth,
> which could flood your path, sear
> bottomless chasms in your road.

Deception is her only defense:

> I keep, behind my lips,
> invectives capable of tearing
> the septum from your
> nostrils and the skin from your back. (*SW,* 33)

Similarly, in the very brief poem "Prelude to a Parting," a woman lying in bed beside her lover senses the imminent end when he draws away from her touch. Yet neither will acknowledge "the tacit fact" or face the "awful fear of losing," knowing, as they do without speaking, that nothing will "cause / a fleeing love / to stay" (*SW,* 25).

Not all of the love poems in this collection suggest deception or dishonesty, but most describe the seemingly inevitable loss of love. The title poem, "Shaker, Why Don't You Sing?," belongs to this second group. A woman, "evicted from sleep's mute palace" and lying awake alone in bed, remembers the "perfect harmonies" and the "insistent / rhythm" of a lost love. Her life fills with silence now that love has withdrawn its music, its "chanteys" that "hummed / [her] life alive." Now she rests "somewhere / between the unsung notes of night" and passionately asks love to return its song to her life: "O Shaker, why don't you sing?" (*SW,* 42–43). This mournful apostrophe to love serves as a refrain in an unsung song and, in its second utterance, brings the poem to a close unanswered.

The same determined voice comes through in a number of other poems that relate unabiding anguish over the oppression of the black race. Several of these poems deal specifically with the inhumane treatment of the slaves in the South. "A Georgia Song," for example, in its beautifully lyrical cadences, recalls the unforgotten memories of slavery, which linger like "odors of Southern cities" and the "great green / Smell of fresh sweat. / In Southern fields." Angelou deftly recounts the "ancient / Wrongs" and describes a South broken by injustice and sorrow. Now, "dusty / Flags droop their unbearable / Sadness." Yet the poet calls for a new dream to rise up from the rich soil of Georgia and replace the "liquid notes of / Sorrow songs" with "a new song. A song / Of Southern peace" (*SW*, 8–10). Although the memories of "ancient / Wrongs" can never be forgotten, the poem invites a renewal of Southern dreams and peace.

Perhaps the most powerful poem in this collection is "Caged Bird," which inevitably brings Angelou's audience full circle with her best-known autobiography, *I Know Why the Caged Bird Sings*. This poem tells the story of a free bird and a caged bird. The free bird floats leisurely on "trade winds soft through the sighing trees" and even "dares to claim the sky." He feeds on "fat worms waiting on a dawn-bright lawn" and soars to "name the sky his own." Unlike his unbound brother, the caged bird leads a life of confinement that sorely inhibits his need to fly and sing. Trapped by the unyielding bars of his cage, the bird can only lift his voice in protest against his imprisonment and the "grave of dreams" on which he perches.[15] Appearing both in the middle and end of the poem, this stanza serves as a dual refrain:

> The caged bird sings
> with a fearful trill
> of things unknown
> but longed for still
> and his tune is heard
> on the distant hill
> for the caged bird
> sings of freedom. (*SW*, 16–17)

Although he sings of "things unknown," the bird's song of freedom is heard even as far as the "distant hill." His song is his protest, his only alternative to submission and entrapment. Angelou knows why the caged bird and all oppressed beings must sing. Her poems in *Shaker, Why Don't You Sing?* imply that as long as such melodies are sung and heard, hope and strength will overcome defeated dreams.

At the end of *All God's Children Need Traveling Shoes,* Angelou hints at her association with Tom Feelings, a young black American artist who lived in Ghana during the early 1960s. Angelou cites Malcolm X's introduction of this newcomer to the black American expatriate community: " 'A young painter named Tom Feelings is coming to Ghana. Do everything you can for him. I am counting on you' " (*HW,* 193). By introducing Feelings at the conclusion of her latest autobiography, she subtly sets the scene for her most recent publication, *Now Sheba Sings the Song* (1987), a single poem, illustrated by eighty-two of Feelings's drawings of black women, sketched throughout the world over a period of twenty-five years. Together the poem and the sepia-toned drawings royally celebrate the universal majesty of the black woman. In his introduction to the book, Feelings credits Angelou as the "someone who shared a similar experience [with the women he drew], someone who traveled, opened up, took in, and mentally recorded everything observed. And most important of all, it [his collaborator] had to be someone whose *center* is woman" (*NS,* 6). Angelou's poem, in turn, glorifies the spiritual, physical, emotional, and intellectual powers of black women or what Feelings calls "Africa's beauty, strength, and dignity [which are] wherever the Black woman is" (*NS,* 6). Angelou affirms the black woman's "love of good and God and Life" (*NS,* 48) and beckons "he who is daring and brave" (*NS,* 54) to meet the open challenge of the radiant Queen of Sheba. Maya Angelou's songs, like Sheba's, testify to the creative powers inherent in the works of today's Southern women writers.

MAYA ANGELOU BIBLIOGRAPHY

AUTOBIOGRAPHIES

I Know Why the Caged Bird Sings. New York: Random House, 1970; Bantam, 1971 (paper).

Gather Together in My Name. New York: Random House, 1974; Bantam, 1975 (paper).

Singin' and Swingin' and Gettin' Merry Like Christmas. New York: Random House, 1976; Bantam, 1977 (paper).

The Heart of a Woman. New York: Random House, 1981; Bantam, 1982 (paper).

All God's Children Need Traveling Shoes. New York: Random House, 1986; Bantam, 1987 (paper).

POETRY

Just Give Me a Cool Drink of Water 'fore I Diiie. New York: Random House, 1971; Bantam, 1973 (paper).

Oh Pray My Wings Are Gonna Fit Me Well. New York: Random House, 1975; Bantam, 1977 (paper).

And Still I Rise. New York: Random House, 1978; Bantam, 1980 (paper).

Shaker, Why Don't You Sing? New York: Random House, 1983.

Now Sheba Sings the Song. Illustrated by Tom Feelings. New York: Dutton/Dial, 1987.

INTERVIEWS

"The AFI-Aspen Conference." *American Film* 5 (July/August 1980): 57–64.

Benson, C. "Out of the Cage and Still Singing: Interview with Maya Angelou." *Writers Digest,* January 1975, 18–19.

"The Black Scholar Interviews: Maya Angelou." *Black Scholar* 8, no. 4 (January/February 1977): 44–53.

Elliot, Jeffrey M. "Author Maya Angelou Raps." *Sepia* 26 (October 1977): 22–27.

———. "Maya Angelou: In Search of Self." *Negro History Bulletin* 40 (1979): 694–95.

"Maya Angelou: Interview." *Harper's Bazaar,* November 1972, 124.

Neubauer, Carol E. "An Interview with Maya Angelou." *Massachusetts Review* 28, no. 2 (1987): 286–92.

Oliver, Stephanie Stokes. "Maya Angelou: The Heart of a Woman." *Essence* 14 (May 1983): 112–14.

Paterson, Judith. "Interview: Maya Angelou." *Vogue* 172 (September 1982): 416–17, 420, 422.

Tate, Claudia. "Maya Angelou." In *Black Women Writers at Work,* 1–11. New York: Continuum, 1983.

Weston, Carol, and Caroline Seebohm. "Talks with Two Singular Women." *House and Garden* 153 (November 1981): 128–29, 190, 192.

BIBLIOGRAPHICAL GUIDE

Cameron, Dee Birch. "A Maya Angelou Bibliography." *Bulletin of Bibliography* 36 (1979): 50–52.

Shirley Ann Grau's Wise Fictions

*

LINDA WAGNER-MARTIN

A S EVERY REVIEWER of Shirley Ann Grau's fiction points out, she was born in New Orleans in 1929 and spent her childhood between that city, which her mother preferred, and Montgomery, Alabama, the location her father liked. She was educated in the now defunct Booth School, receiving much training in languages, and then, because Booth School was not accredited, transferred to Ursuline Academy for her senior year. She wanted to attend Tulane University but, being female, was accepted instead into Tulane's women's division, Sophie Newcomb College, which she describes as "a kind of finishing school."[1] While there, however, she enjoyed creative writing classes and announced her intention of becoming a professional writer. Her professor in the writing program, John Husband, remembers her initially as a student more diligent than talented, though she quickly became one of his best students.[2] Evidently, despite the clear signals Grau was receiving about the kind of life a Southern woman should be preparing herself to lead, she had already determined what her direction would be.

Grau began publishing her fiction soon after graduation from college in 1950. Part of this need to publish resulted from her father's conviction that writing was not "doing anything" and that she needed to find real work. She was able to appease him only by being published in prestigious places. That Grau won the Pulitzer Prize for fiction only ten years after her first book appeared (in 1965, for *The Keepers of the House*) was evidence of her dedication and professionalism. By 1965, Grau had given birth to three children, with a fourth to arrive in 1967. Her household, in a suburb of New Orleans and, in summer, on Martha's Vineyard, has never been the scene of monastic calm or attention focused on Grau-as-writer.[3] But with what seems to be typical equanimity, she continues to write and work in the directions she early established.

143

By virtue of her birth, education, life experiences, and residence, then, Shirley Ann Grau could clearly be labeled a "Southern" writer. And in her fiction, she not only uses the South as setting and cultural milieu, but she also focuses attention on some of its most striking characteristics and finds her central themes in its current and pervasive concerns. The issue with Grau's writing is not so much whether she is a "Southern" writer—*that* she obviously is—but whether or not she is working in strains of "Southernness" that in some way either enhance or diminish her art.

Frederick J. Hoffman, in his classic *The Art of Southern Fiction* (1945 and 1967), identifies some of the characteristics of the mode, to that time. Southern fiction often attends to history and is an "act of considering, staring at, brooding over the past-as-legend."[4] Such a constant interest, according to Hoffman, stems in part from a sense of both "self-awareness" and "guilt"[5] and, at its worst, may lead to self-justification—and to ultimate falsity. The interest may also lead to repetitious themes and characters: one wonders how many times the Civil War can be the subject of great fiction (obviously, many).

More often, however, as John Stewart points out, the Southern writer is less concerned with the facts of history than with the use made of that history by the culture: "the gesture of trying to distinguish between legend and actuality is in itself a major preoccupation with Southern fiction."[6] Such motivation places emphasis on the *way* stories are told, on the *process* of telling. Hoffman defines a Southern "rhetoric" as being "the style of the folk tale, the story told and retold, filled out by hazard and guess."[7] And for the Southern writer—who may be shying away, even if unconsciously, from the guilt and grief of the Southern past, with its freight of both slavery and defeat/destruction—the most compatible method of narration is that based on concrete images. Southern fiction includes less authorial intervention; it relies frequently on metaphor (and often on metaphors of the land).

The Southern writer, ultimately, benefits from all of this sense of history and concern with the past because, through it, the writer is forced to acknowledge tradition, and the Southern tradition, as Hoffman points out, usually included "a complement of ceremony, belief, and dynastic observance. Those were forms of behavior that were regionally distinctive."[8]

Grau's fiction meets most of these criteria. The most noticeable departure is that it seldom focuses on history per se (many of her narratives take place in the present time, or close to it) but her characters are often concerned with Southern history and its traditions. They may be fighting to preserve what is best from it (Abigail Howland in *The Keep-*

ers of the House), or they may be intent on amassing property as a means of self-identification (many of her male characters). In some cases, their very practical ignorance presents an escape of sorts from history's weighty burdens (the primitives of her early fiction, for example).

And when her characters are obsessed with the past and its effects on their lives (as occurs in only some of her work), their focus is less on the past as past, for itself, than it is on their immediate lives, on bringing themselves to fruition and self-understanding. A reader will become much more involved in what is happening to Annie, to Joan Mitchell, to Abigail than in what has happened to their families in some relatively remote past. Grau's approach tends much more often to be that of Faulkner as he presents Joe Christmas—a life fully realized, though not explained, through detail and image—than that of Faulkner as he works, and worries, the character of Quentin Compson, whose life and death are inextricably part of the reconstruction of Southern history.

Grau's highly stylized method of narration (having a named character tell his or her own story through parts of a novel) blunts the sense of her method as being "the style of folk tale," but in many ways it is that. One of the most problematic areas of critical response to Grau's work lies in her choice of narrative method: the charge that she has too objective a tone, too great a "distance" from her characters, can be answered through attention to her choices of structure and perspective. The other trait of the Southern writer's method, reliance on concrete image and scene, is integral to Grau's fiction, but then this method has been so much a part of nearly all modern writing that describing it as characteristic of Southern work may be misleading.

One of Grau's most distinctive traits is what Hoffman defines as an interest in ceremony, in ritual, as if these external forms were in themselves images of the larger "meaning" of the lives portrayed. Grau's fiction is rife with rituals of holidays, births, marriages, and, especially in her last novels, death; in fact, the novels move almost from one scene of ritual to another. Ritualized interaction and the departures from the expected interaction constitute many of Grau's "plots." And this narrative focus also provides a means for Grau to go beyond concentration on the forms of the white aristocratic life, which often is the dominant setting of her fiction, to include the rituals and ceremonies of the Cajun and black cultures. It is perhaps this latter area of interest that makes Grau the important novelist she is: her consistent concern with nonwhite culture, its traditions and rituals, and the way that culture impinges on the patriarchal matrix that seems to dominate Southern life. Grau's best fiction deals, relentlessly if subtly, with that impingement.

Because it does—and because this thematic focus is relatively rare among Southern writers, even today—it seems necessary to consider Grau as not only a Southern writer but also as a woman writer. One way of doing that is to compare her with other Southern women writers. In background and family life, she is much like Ellen Glasgow, whose fiction was tolerated by the family that felt real outrage at her choosing to be "independent." The protected Southern woman, kept from "doing" anything, elevated to pedestals and proprieties, is surely as alive in Grau's adolescence as it was during Glasgow's in the 1890s. In these respects (the lack of independence, the presence of an ultimately censoring shelter), both writers must have at least known what Sandra Gilbert and Susan Gubar have called "the anxiety of authorship."[9] For these important critics, most women writers had to push through so many barriers, psychological as well as physical, that the act of coming to write was already perilous. Their feelings of inadequacy, of sheer guilt, led women writers to revise the genres male writers worked in easily. Because the stories they had to tell were so different, were so much their own, women writers could not simply copy male forms. But because they carried such anxiety about their narratives, they usually were forced to disguise what they were actually about. It is rare, then, that a woman writer will tell a woman's story in identifiable terms. Often, a woman's novel seems to be "about" a male protagonist, with a strong secondary protagonist who is female. Or the structure of a novel will be layered, one story juxtaposed against another, "palimpsestic" as a means of what Gilbert and Gubar term "necessary evasion." And in their earliest works, most women writers are careful to imitate the forms and themes of successful fiction written by men.[10]

Anne Jones, in her recent *Tomorrow Is Another Day,* claims that the Southern woman writer may have less anxiety than women writers who work from a shorter tradition (there have been a great many Southern women writers throughout history), but she admits readily that the South did its own kind of disservice to the literary profession. The Southern patriarchy accepted literary pursuits, to a certain extent, but it succeeded in relegating literature to the category of a frill. In Jones's terms, the South equated "women, beauty, literature, and irrelevance."[11] And finally, the essence of the South was "a rigid southern patriarchy that subjected women, blacks, children, and nonslaveholding white men to the control and authority of the slaveholding men. If only in his subculture, he ruled patriarchally."[12] In fact, one might point out that a man who feared his real standing (given the defeated South, the indefensible practice of slavery, the sense of imminent loss the Southern male would be privy to) might be an even more oppressive "master."

A study of Shirley Ann Grau's fiction suggests that far from being an autonomous, successful, modern woman writer, she too has felt the same kinds of anxieties Gilbert and Gubar identify. She has, however, managed to write, consistently, and not fall prey to Tillie Olsen's "silences."[13] She has managed to produce a body of work that shows developing patterns, characters, insights, themes—a true oeuvre that is characteristic of Shirley Ann Grau. In her comparatively short career, such an accomplishment *is* an achievement.

But Grau's work has also received unexpected critical reaction. It has frequently been misread. Grau shares this kind of uneven response with other writers such as Glasgow, Cather, Wharton, O'Connor, and Welty, women whose works have become important to the canon of American fiction in spite of the reception those works have had. (Response may be positive and still be misleading, as when Louise Y. Gossett claims that all Grau's best work is about "primitives," into which category she places blacks as well as bayou people, and that because of the primitive quality of these people, Grau's fiction is filled with violence.[14]) This essay will not attempt to correct these misreadings, but the fact that they exist in such quantity proves once again the separateness of women's writing, its relative inaccessibility so long as it is approached only through established literary categories and perspectives.[15]

Grau's first novel, *The Hard Blue Sky,* was published in 1958, four years after her first collection of stories, *The Black Prince and Other Stories,* had been well received. Reminiscent of the fiction of Paul Bowles and Albert Camus, *The Hard Blue Sky* attempted to create an environment of disinterest, of a nature oblivious to its creatures, and to suggest the powerlessness of any human culture. But in this book, as in her later fiction, Grau quickly let the real force of the narrative rest on a single character, that of the sixteen-year-old maturing but neglected Annie Laundry. In this role, Annie foreshadows Grau's concern with Joan Mitchell, protagonist and central consciousness of *The House on Coliseum Street,* the 1961 novel that was considered a great departure from her earlier fiction. But if the stories in *The Black Prince* and much of her first novel are seen to be explorations of the unknown, the emotional, the unreasonableness of life, as they well might be, then Grau's focus on the lonely young Mitchell as she faces an abortion is less a departure than it is an extension.

One key to the development between Grau's first novel and the second lies in the titles of the respective books. *The Hard Blue Sky* suggests the impersonality of natural forces, and the novel accordingly traces relatively meaningless deaths (in the course of the opposing families' feuds) and relationships. The mood of the novel is one of impoverished emotions, of people taking what they can find and can get quickly, before even that acquisition is taken from them. These are placeless people, Grau's bayou families, belonging to one of the several islands that chain the Gulf of Mexico. Flooded annually, subject to death-dealing storms at intervals, these pieces of earth are, ironically, havens for the fishermen who live on them. And Annie, with the street knowledge of the very poor, knows that her only real way of escaping the island malaise is to leave, which she does with Inky and his boat.

The House on Coliseum Street, in contrast, images a relatively settled society. In the house, Joan's mother—five-times married but still in possession of both property and five daughters, one from each of her marriages—rules, as she does in parts of the city's society. Whereas Grau's structure in *The Hard Blue Sky* emphasized the randomness of life patterns, her tactic in her second novel is to emphasize the ravages of time. The four-part structure suggests the kind of division she tries in her third novel, each section named for the narrating character, a device that allows her to pay less attention to chronology and to focus more steadily on creating a mood that can become identified with respective characters. But in *The House on Coliseum Street,* the sections—"June," "End of Summer," "House on Coliseum Street," and "Winter"—are evocative of not only time (and for the newly pregnant Joan, months and seasons are crucial) but also of changes within the protagonist's psyche. Joan as she is in "June" is a very different woman than she is by "Winter." In effect, Grau's named sections do present a different character in each segment.

But central to the novel, to Joan, and to the pattern of Grau's fiction remains the house of the title. The opening preface, which is spoken by Joan just after she returns from her abortion and marks the midpoint of the book, is entitled "House on Coliseum Street," as is the third, and turning, segment of the novel. In that section, Joan discovers that the effects of her abortion cannot be forgotten, washed away, or celebrated, as in the haunting dinner scene with Michael. Permanently scarred by her experience, Joan is forced to accept her own position in her mother's house: the oldest, and therefore first abandoned, child; the observer of all her mother's lovers and children; the real victim of the chic, inhuman life-style. And in that knowledge lies the seed of self-destruction. Grau draws the distraught Joan carefully and plausibly, and when she turns her self-destructive impulses to anger and is able to blame Michael for her pregnancy (to the dean, costing Michael his position at the college), the reader breathes a sigh of relief. Joan is safe, at least for a while. The quick move to the last scene of the book, with Joan locked out of the house but willing to wait in the cold, huddled in a borrowed sweater, allows Grau to express, even if somewhat didactically, the source of Joan's personal strength—her identity as "keeper of the house," here the house on Coliseum Street: "I'll own it some day, she thought, because I'm the oldest and Aurelie will leave it to the oldest, whether she likes me or not. . . . Maybe I can come back to it. And maybe I won't even want to. Maybe. But I'll have to go away now."[16] Grau's progression through Joan's consciousness takes her to her incredible, angry loneliness, and the loss of the child who might have been company for her ("ghost child"), to the thought of her father's money, here a positive gesture: "I'll have to go away now. Once they know what I've done, I couldn't stay in the house. But I can go. It's only a question of where. My father knew I would have to leave some day. And he fixed it so I can go . . . " (241).

In her first two novels, Grau used almost opposing techniques to create her structure. *The Hard Blue Sky* includes a list of characters as a preface page, identified as though a drama were to be acted. Structure is time oriented, with setting presented first, Inky introduced through the appearance of his boat, and lines of conflict carefully, if busily, set up. The reader can almost see Grau's charts of characters and actions being implemented, as chapters alternate between the "rivalry" plot and the "Annie-Inky" plot. Thematically, however, the novel is filled with children who are parentless, with adolescents making mistakes in life because of so little adult direction or concern, with images of the loveless culture that affects every action on the islands. One might be tempted to blame the tragedies on fate, the force of nature, the existential position. But when seen from the perspective of Grau's later work, most of the tragedies even here result from lack of love, as Annie says when she goes to her former boyfriend to talk about leaving for New Orleans:

> "Thought you want to go to New Orleans, me," he said.
> "Maybe," she said automatically, "maybe not."
> She swung her body forward catching her weight on her hands. "I'm not sure." She sounded miserable; she knew it. And she knew she hadn't intended to. . . .

Perique shrugged. "What's keeping you?"

She didn't believe it. She just didn't believe it. Even when she knew she should stop, she tried again: "You want me to go?"

"Maybe you got a taste for New Orleans now."

"You don't want me to stay?"

Perique was smoothing his left eyebrow with his right finger. "None of my business."

"Why not?"

"Free country."

Annie got down from the rail. She stood at the top of the steps. "I reckon you won't miss me," she said. "I don't reckon nobody will."[17]

A word from Perique would have made the difference, but his doctrine of noninvolvement (under the guise of her "freedom") prevented his statement. Although this is a long and somewhat slow scene in its entirety, Grau catches the temper of the uncommitted character.

Buried in detail and scenic blur, the structure of *The Hard Blue Sky* ends with a sprawl of oddly named characters, so many that keeping track of them is difficult for even the most interested reader. In contrast, *The House on Coliseum Street* errs in being so singly focused. Unless Joan Mitchell becomes the most fascinating woman since Emma Bovary, Grau has little chance of holding our attention through the novel. Part of the difficulty is that Joan, in her present circumstances, has very little idea who she is herself; the novel is a coming-to-understanding, a bildungsroman for Joan as protagonist. But Grau chooses to handle narrative from an objective point of view, rather than from a more impressionistic, personal perspective. Because it is focused only on Joan, and because Joan herself has trouble deciding how she feels about any of these experiences, the novel moves slowly and seems oversimplified in its execution. As one of the earliest fictions about the abortion experience and its effect on the woman undergoing it, this novel could have been an important statement, a central evocation of many of the issues involved in the ongoing abortion controversy. It is an interesting novel, and one that deserves to be "rediscovered," but it pales in comparison with her third novel, *The Keepers of the House,* published in 1964.

In this, her best novel, Grau manages to combine the multiple characters and the panoramic scene of *The Hard Blue Sky* with the masterful mood of *The House on Coliseum Street.* She also draws back into her own sense of the past as she creates characters heavy with the weight of history (whereas the characters from her first novel were defiantly oblivious to history of any kind, of themselves or of their country). As Grau has said, discussing writing fiction, "Aspiring writers must learn that writing is making a structure, and it is putting thoughts into that structure for the total effect."[18] The most important change in *The Keepers of the House* is Grau's use of the part structure to order both the chronology and the various sets of moods and characters integral to the novel's action. *The Keepers of the House* builds in an amazing way to a culminating scene that works perfectly to realize not only the plot of the novel but, more importantly, the theme.

Like *The House on Coliseum Street, The Keepers of the House* begins with a short preface section, this one entitled "Abigail," which occurs later in the ostensible action. The tone of these first four pages is peacefully rigid, dulled by what might have been excessive emotion: "November evenings are so quiet, so final. This one now. It is mistfree; you see for miles in all directions. . . . "[19] Sometimes in Grau's short fiction, the pace and sound of her words create tone poems, but this is the first novel to be grounded so consistently in a single tonal base. As Abigail continues reminiscing, we understand that this soliloquy takes place at the end of all the novel's action, that the reasons for her behavior throughout the story are explained here: "I was a child in this house once too, rushing through those halls and up and down those stairs. It was not as nice as it is now—that was before the war, before my grandfather made his money—but it was the same house. For them, for me. I feel the pressure of generations behind me, pushing me along the recurring cycles of birth and death" (5). Grau saves the preface from oversimplification by taking Abigail immediately from this monologue to the taut, image-centered paragraph that follows, leaving the reader with many questions: "They are dead, all of them. I am caught and tangled around by their doings. It is as if their lives left a weaving of invisible threads in the air of this house, of this town, of this county. And I stumbled and fell into them" (6).

The other three parts of the novel, which are its major divisions, trace the lives of William Howland, Abigail's maternal grandfather, and Margaret Carmichael, his second wife, who is part Negro, part Choctaw (and their children, Robert, Nina, and Crissy, who are sent North to school to assume white lives and never return), as well as Abigail's own life as the wife of an ambitious politician. The segment entitled "William" gives the history of the Howland fortunes and land, the land Abigail comes to claim. It recounts the life of the hardworking man, his first courtship, and his wife's death soon after the birth of their second child. Alone, Howland rears his daughter (the second child dies). Once she is married, he then finds the arresting young Margaret, "earth-colored . . . her hair black as her skin." Impulsively, thinking she is the demonic black Alberta, lover of Stanley (from Grau's story "The Black Prince"), Howland offers her the job of housekeeper, and they are soon lovers. The dignity of the relationship is maintained throughout the narrative, as Grau closes this first section with a coda: "That was the way it began. That was how he found Margaret, washing clothes by a creek that didn't have a name. She lived with him all the rest of his life, the next thirty years. // Living with him, she lived with us all, all the Howlands, and her life got mixed up with ours. Her face was black and ours were white, but we were together anyhow. Her life and his. And ours" (78).

In the second major section, entitled "Margaret," Grau describes the Freejack way of life, the need for the daughter, at eighteen, to find her own existence, and her years with the Howlands (married secretly, they live as housekeeper and master, and their children are *her* children). Her implicit mysticism colors Grau's accounts of her realizing that she will need to leave her family and move away, that Howland's offer is "sent," and that she has no recourse but to become his wife. Margaret's proud serenity is well established in this short section.

With the third segment, "Abigail," the ostensible narrator takes over from her own perspective. Abandoned by her father, she and her mother, another Abigail, return to the Howland place and learn to care for, and be cared for by, Margaret. After her mother's death, Abigail really does depend on Margaret, who acts as buffer between her and her grandfather, as well as stable support, though unobtrusive, throughout her life. Her marriage to John Tolliver takes her away from the Howland place, and as he rises politically, she assumes the wifely duties expected of her—having children, running a good home, never complaining about his many absences. But in the course of her life, her grandfather dies, and Grau takes this occasion to draw on her belief in the inexplicable and to clarify the man's real worth. Howland appears to Abigail as she drives out to Freejack territory to visit Margaret, who has returned home now that her husband is dead. At the close of their drive, Abigail thinks to herself (and the theme of male/female dominance is finally established, as it needs to be for Grau's denouement):

He'd protected and cared for so many females in his life, that he just looked on us as responsibilities and burdens. Loved, but still burdens. There'd been his wife, the vague little bumbling girl, who'd been so lovely and who'd died so young. There'd been my mother, who'd read poetry in a summerhouse and married a handsome Englishman, who'd come scurrying home, heartbroken, with another girl. She'd lingered around the house and around the bed until she died. And there was me, the orphan, and my two daughters.

Sometimes he must have felt that he was being smothered in dependents. There hadn't been a man of his blood in so long. And that must have worried him too.

All those clinging female arms. . . . And then there was Margaret. Who was tall as he was. Who could work like a man in the fields. Who bore him a son. Margaret, who'd asked him for nothing. Margaret, who reminded him of the free-roving Alberta of the old tales. Margaret, who was strong and black. And who had no claim on him. (222–23)

Or so Abigail thinks, at this point in the novel. The revelation of Howland's marriage to Margaret, of course, is the provoking action: it loses John Tolliver his election and turns the white "friends" of the Howlands into raging avengers who burn the barn, kill their stock, and are poised to fire the house when Abigail singlehandedly turns their anger into fear.

The great irony of the novel is that the Howland son, Margaret's Robert, has been reared in the North and has forgotten the ways of Southern righteousness. When Robert reveals his parentage and also, and most importantly, the fact that Howland had married Margaret, he intends to destroy only Tolliver's political career. He in fact destroys the Howland name and property and the life his mother has sacrificed to give him. Not the Howland son, but rather the Howland daughter—Abigail—saves the family home, and she saves it from none other than Robert Howland, the only son.

And in the teeming action, one of the best depictions of class and race prejudice in modern fiction, Abigail turns from the pampered, mindless Southern wife to a vindictive woman of proud courage, who delivers her best weapons at fashionable tea parties and then returns home to live out the life she has chosen for herself, as a Howland, alone.

Grau succeeds in telling Abigail's story so deftly, with so much involvement in the tale of the Howland family and its traditions, that the reader is hardly aware that *The Keepers of the House* is a feminist novel. She is able to achieve this partly because of the book's structure. As it is organized, Abigail inherits the stories of both her grandfather and Margaret; the information in them, the tone of their characters and their relationship, become part of our knowledge about Abigail. Were we to have been told only Abigail's story (as we were told only Joan's

in *The House on Coliseum Street*), we would know far too little to understand—her husband's hypocritical nature, Oliver's loyalty. And Abigail, through most of the novel, would not have been capable of
explaining the layers of complexity the book reveals; she is, in much of
the book, a childlike narrator.

Part of Grau's skill accrues in the fact that the motivating action, the
denouement of the Howland story, comes at the end of Abigail's section, so that she is narrating it even while she is innocent of its far-
reaching consequences. We thus are caught up in the events; we are experiencing them with Abigail. Her rage as she realizes what is going to
happen, her capacity to act in the face of that lonely outrage, is also
ours.

And so too is her peace, her sense of calm resolution, when the attack
is over: "I circled the house, slowly, finding nothing else disturbed.
When I was sure of that, when I was quite sure that I had checked
everything, I stood—with the shotgun held crosswise in my hands and
my scratched and torn legs aching feebly under me. . . . I looked briefly
at the house behind me, lit dimly by those two distant fires; it was
white and smooth and lovely and unruffled. It would belong to my children. It would come to them the way it had come to me. Howlands
were not run out, nor burned out" (289). Abigail does not need the re-
assurance of her grandfather, but he, and a host of other Howlands, appear to her at the close of this scene: " 'You didn't think I could do it,' I
said. . . . You do what you got to do, he answered me" (290).

Grau succeeds in giving us the impression that Abigail is well
launched. She acted when she needed to act, of her own volition. Her
family spirit was of no material help, except in helping her nurture her
own spirit. As a Howland, Abigail will go on doing what she knows is
right, despite the petty prejudices of the community; she will, in fact,
avenge their wrongs as she withdraws the family wealth from the area.
In times as muddled and sinister as the epigraph from Ecclesiastes suggests, humankind deserves punishment rather than help.

Grau's next two novels, *The Condor Passes* (1971) and *Evidence of
Love* (1977), continue the theme of the decaying society that needs
guidance, again using "the old gentleman" as central character. Her
success with the William Howland figure in *The Keepers of the House*
and the dying patriarch in "One Summer," a major story from *The
Black Prince* collection, evidently led her to attempt to use the character
of the rich, powerful, but aging male as the focus for a number of relationships in both these novels. The books differ, but in structure and
assortment of characters, they are surprisingly similar.

The Condor Passes hints that the black bird of Mr. Oliver's imagination has a connection with his black valet, Stanley (whose name echoes that of the "black prince" of Grau's early published story). Working for Oliver for twenty years, both Stanley and his wife, Vera, have been well paid; they are wealthy and look forward to retirement. Divided into named sections, as was Grau's third novel, *The Condor Passes* opens with a Stanley section, in which he explains the family, the financial genius of the Old Man, and his solace in the specially built greenhouse, complete with birdcage and collection of birds. The second section that concerns Stanley is entitled "The Secret Thief." It advances the present-tense plot (much of the novel flashes back to Oliver's rise to wealth) and also incorporates what seems to be a key image, as Stanley ponders: "I been thinking that I was the big black hawk spying on people's lives. But now it looks like there was a skinny sparrow right up under my nose, watching everything, watching me. Who's fooling who? The Old Man. It's always the Old Man."[20]

In the "Old Man" segment, Grau traces the childhood and life of her protagonist and also creates some effective brushes with death for the aging, weary man. His grief at the time of his wife's death is another evocative scene. But Grau's real interest lies in the character of Robert Caillet, a Cajun. Oliver adopts him in spirit (and marries him to his older daughter, Anna, in order to have the son he would himself choose). In the third part of the book, Robert's development into the completely amoral man he will become begins. Part of his anger at the Old Man, his benefactor, stems from his poverty and misuse as a child, Grau suggests, but she draws Robert as such an unpleasant character that feeling any sympathy is difficult.

She creates a detailed description of Anna, Oliver's daughter, in the section titled for her, but she is so completely absorbed by her role as wife that she too becomes unreal. Hardly a parody of the adolescent reared to think only in terms of Cinderella and charming princes, the character of the adult Anna is frightening.

Margaret, Anna's younger sister and supposedly her foil, is both frightening and appealing as Grau presents her. Hungry for sexual experience, Margaret becomes involved with many men, including her brother-in-law, but never gives up her own wily perspective. Seeing the relationship with Robert become more and more tawdry, the reader comes to have more sympathy for Anna, and to see that Oliver has devalued his own child to try to create some fantasy relationship for himself. *The Condor Passes* is a double narrative: the story of Oliver's disillusion with his chosen "son" and of Anna's disillusion with her chosen life. To be a wife and mother, when neither husband nor child appreciates that role, leaves only bitterness and regret: Robert's many affairs and her son's withdrawal, final illness, and suicide leave her numb with her wasted sacrifices.

Grau alternates sections between Robert and Margaret, as their affair changes through the years. The denouement of Robert's obsession with sex occurs when he begins to need adolescent girls, and Margaret finally realizes that his indiscriminate taste is venal. Because we have so little concern for either of these characters, much of the later part of the novel moves slowly, and Grau's return at the end to Stanley, observing the Old Man's death, does little to confirm earlier directions in the novel. Stanley's renunciation of the remaining family—with Robert vomiting out on the lawn and the women oblivious to their father's death—may be positive, but it seems strangely added on. If *The Condor Passes* is Grau's *The Sound and the Fury,* describing the fall of what might have been a great and powerful Southern family, it is disappointing. The immensity of the cultural forces displayed in *The Keepers of the House* in this novel reach only to Robert's perversity, Anna's self-centeredness, and Margaret's insatiable appetites. Racial issues are not important, even though the Old Man adopts for himself both a black man and a Cajun, and all characterizations seem both flat and predictable.

Evidence of Love (1977) is marred by some of the same qualities. Again, named sections portray characters we care little about. The novel opens with a segment about Edward Milton Henley, scion of a very wealthy family, and the second segment portrays his son, Stephen, a minister. For all the difference in occupation and life-style, both men are distant, manipulative, and self-centered.

In *Evidence of Love,* Grau uses her by now commonplace structure for a new ironic effect. In both *The Keepers of the House* and *The Condor Passes,* the patriarchal male wants desperately to produce a son. Supposedly, the son would both continue the family name and husband the inheritance. In each of these novels, the chosen son and heir is an utter disappointment. So too in *Evidence of Love,* Stephen Henley is a vapid, pretentious, and judgmental son, who, in effect, chooses a life-style to spite his father. But his father, Edward, has earlier committed the most loveless act in the book, when he hires a woman to be a surrogate mother rather than having the child with his legal wife. Edward is not only going to create his own dynasty; he is—singly—going to create his own line. In Edward's words:

> I knew that my child must, so to speak, burst from the brow of Jove, or rise like Venus from the sea foam. It must be mine alone,

it must have no blood attachment to any of my wives—by then I could predict, quite accurately, a series of them.

Within two months of my sister's death, I found the perfect incubator for my child. A young Irish girl, of no importance whatever. She met all my requirements: she was quite young, sixteen, intelligent, a virgin. She was very well paid for her trouble, which can't have been all that onerous to a young healthy woman. . . . [21]

(From the tone of this excerpt, one can see why many critics, not realizing that this is precisely Edward's pomposity and has nothing to do with Grau as author, have objected to the tone and voice that prevails in Grau's fiction.)

The famed male line does continue through Stephen's sons, Thomas and Paul. Thomas, an affable "user" like his grandfather, will get along, hurting his wife and defiling his other relationships, but the conscience of the family exists in the younger son, Paul. He has, in fact, managed to find the "lost" mother, the woman who gave birth to Stephen, now an old artist whose self-portrait, as well as her early paintings of a young boy, resemble Stephen. Grau's scene between Stephen and his son Paul, as the latter explains his collection of Mary Morrison Remick's work, characterizes the two men perfectly. It is a long passage and comes to this ending as Paul speaks:

"And do you know why her portrait looks familiar to you? That's yourself you're seeing. That's your mother."

I blinked.

"Look at it."

I sat down, propping the small piece of canvas against the flower-filled silver centerpiece. Red anemones peeped around the frame.

"Well, Paul, I suppose that is possible."

"So you see, she was all right after all. She was a talented painter, she had a fine family, and they all did very well. She wasn't hurt by you."

Hurt by me? I had never thought of it that way. . . . "I hardly think bearing a single child could hurt a healthy young woman, Paul."

"But giving him up. . . ."

I became impatient. "When it is possible to have many more children, one is not so important. There is a story of Catherine Sforza on the ramparts of Bologna, when the city was under siege and the enemy held two of her children as hostages. . . ."

"I know the story, Father."

"Do you? Paul, you are remarkably well read."

"You aren't interested, Father!"

It was a cry of pain. No less. From a thirty-three-year-old man. My stomach lurched. (125)

The scene continues, with Stephen wondering, "Was the presence of blood so important to him? What strange evidence of love was this?" (125). All Stephen's reasons that it does not matter who his mother was force the reader to adopt the silence of the son who *does* recognize love, values, the stuff of immortality—and has given years of his life and his resources to finding the lost woman, his grandmother. Grau's method works through that silence, while the reader closes ears to the rationalizing verbiage of both Stephen and his father, Edward.

In this novel, as in *The Keepers of the House,* the moral center of the story appears late and goes almost unnoticed. After the segments titled for the father and the son, Grau introduces "Lucy." A strong, quiet woman, Lucy marries Stephen several years after her first marriage has ended with her husband's suicide, and her own near-murder. That relationship had been one of frightening passion, and in the creation of Lucy, Grau achieves what she may have been aiming for with Margaret in *The Condor Passes.* (One dimension of the proper Southern lady was surely her disinterest in sex: Anna is a cold illustration of that quality. But both Margaret and Lucy find sexual pleasure a necessary part of their lives as women.)

Like the structure of *The Keepers of the House,* that of *Evidence of Love* builds toward a final, defining act. Here Lucy offers her father-in-law, Edward, a killing dose of Seconal, to free him from the life he hates. It is an act of courage that saves "the house" in much the same way Abigail saves hers under very different circumstances.

There is little question that these two later novels are less successful than *The Keepers of the House,* but then Grau has consciously chosen to work with the archetypal Southern theme—the creation of a dynasty that burdens its creator until it is "handed down," handed down to sons. A patriarchal theme, one that pervades much fiction in a country where material prosperity still remains the only important kind of achievement, Grau manages to treat it with new insight each time. It should be noted that in each case the patriarchal plan fails. Either no heir worthy of the inheritance exists, or the patriarch himself cares only about dying.

So much attention to the act of dying is also unusual. Writers have seldom tried to show the movement from the dying consciousness into

death, but Grau seems fascinated with that image. From the moment
the black prince made his appearance in her short story, his eyes like silver pennies, it was clear that Grau was intrigued by folk legend and fantasy, and that she would use those subjects throughout her fiction. Her
treatment of death—the mystic, the fantastic, and always the elusive
and unknowable—seems to illustrate that interest.

Throughout her fiction, Grau seems to be trying to present human
consciousness as it exists. In *The Hard Blue Sky,* Annie must choose between leaving "home" (accepting the fact that no one cares whether or
not she stays) and going to New Orleans with a man who may or may
not love her. Romance is secondary to survival: a hard lesson for a sixteen-year-old to learn. In *The House on Coliseum Street,* Joan must decide whether to accept her abortion as her responsibility, with its
resultant guilt, or to feel anger, toward both the father of the child and
the society, represented by her mother, that created such death. In *The
Keepers of the House,* choices become both more complex and simpler.
White men do not marry black women, but when they do, society
knows nothing but vengeance. Sympathy, compassion, love—the virtues women are taught to cultivate—have no part in the real, patriarchal world. In this novel, Grau's female protagonist operates, finally,
with a full range of resources. Abigail is a capable woman, drawing on
knowledge she has never realized, strength she has never tested, and a
moral position her society would have preferred to deny.

Grau's most recent book, entitled simply *Nine Women* (1985), continues the themes, and some of the characterization, of *The Keepers of
the House.* Nine separate women protagonists survive everything from
a plane crash that kills all survivors except the one woman, to divorce
(celebrated at the only daughter's fashionable wedding), to crisis in a
lesbian relationship, to self-discovery. Understated, drawing for their
effect on cool, plot-oriented narrative, the fictions convey tones that
often jar with the cataclysmic events occurring in them. But the basic
tenor of the collection—equanimity, poise, peace—accrues from the
narrative pace that draws each story into the fabric of calm. Exemplary,
these stories could almost be examples. Women such as these have en-
dured, another Southern tradition, and have done so with quiet acceptance of what kinds of acts might be necessary.

"The Beginning," Grau's first story, introduces both theme and
method: " 'You are,' my mother would say, 'the queen of the world, the
jewel of the lotus, the pearl without price, my secret treasure.' "[22] The
unmarried black woman nurtures her illegitimate daughter with such
loving praise, steals clothing for her, and creates from her beauty a
prosperous livelihood in designing clothes for her. That the child has

had no childhood and no identity other than as her mother's model seems a small price to pay for the survival that drives the woman throughout her life. Here reverence for a female child motivates all action, contrary to the obsessive male demands for sons.

Self-sufficiency is the mode of each of these women's lives, none more so than the strangely remote protagonist of the closing story, "Flight." The account of a woman's death, this story retells her modest, impoverished life, the few moments of satisfaction, the images that visited her during her last hospital stay. In an ending that is tranquil and composed, Grau depicts the stasis of relinquishment, the shadowy ease that leads to actual death: "She was flying, alone, complete. She saw rushing toward her, rushing past her, everything. Leaves uncurled, people rose from their beds. Cats crouched, claws tearing fur across backs. . . . She saw bitches strain in birth and puppies born like chains of pearls. She saw suns rise and stars dance in their paths across the seasons. She saw ants and oceans and curving endless space. She saw her house, the one she had lived in all her life . . ." (202).

A fitting conclusion to the nine stories of struggle and victory, "Flight" also suggests death as reward, repose. As the protagonist, Willie May, says at one point in her hospital stay, "My world grows smaller, the edges peel back, an orange shedding its skin" (201). In Grau's lexicon, the journey from life to death is natural, just one of the recurring cycles she is wise enough to recognize and to chart, through her steady fiction, in her miraculous sense of detail and her equally miraculous understanding of women's lives.

SHIRLEY ANN GRAU BIBLIOGRAPHY

NOVELS

The Hard Blue Sky. New York: Knopf, 1958.
The House on Coliseum Street. New York: Knopf, 1961.
The Keepers of the House. New York: Knopf, 1964.
The Condor Passes. New York: Knopf, 1971.
Evidence of Love. New York: Knopf, 1977.
Nine Women. New York: Knopf, 1985.

SHORT STORY COLLECTIONS

The Black Prince and Other Stories. New York: Knopf, 1954.
The Wind Shifting West. New York: Knopf, 1973.

Doris Betts at Mid-Career:
Her Voice and Her Art

*

DOROTHY M. SCURA

IN A THIRTY-FIVE YEAR career, Doris Betts has established herself as a woman of letters—short story writer, novelist, contributor to magazines and journals, participant in writers' conferences, winner of awards. Although her books are seriously reviewed and she has been recognized by some critics as a major talent, she has not received the wide public recognition her work deserves. In a *Washington Post* review of her 1981 novel *Heading West,* Jonathan Yardley predicted that because this novel had been selected by Book-of-the-Month Club as a dual main selection, "it should liberate Doris Betts from the relative obscurity in which she has labored for most of her career." Yardley introduced Betts's work to the reader by explaining that she "writes clear, vivid prose, creates distinct and interesting characters, and is a master at conveying the nuances of psychological conflict; she is a serious writer whose books are unfailingly intelligent and readable." He goes on to call Betts "one of the best writers of fiction in the country, and a very important figure among those Southern writers who have come to prominence since the '60s. . . ."[1]

Betts's reputation is perhaps highest among academics, critics of Southern literature, and other writers, but there are signs that her reputation will continue to grow among the general public. The American Film Institute's short film entitled *Violet,* adapted from her short story "The Ugliest Pilgrim," won an Academy Award in 1982, and the same story is now under option for a full-length motion picture. *Heading West* has been bought by an independent movie producer.

She has published seven books—three collections of short stories and four novels. *The Gentle Insurrection,* her first book, the two-thousand-dollar first-prize winner in a contest sponsored by the publisher

G. P. Putnam and the University of North Carolina, marked an auspicious beginning for the twenty-two-year-old writer. Evelyn Eaton, in a review entitled "A Fine Debut" in *Saturday Review,* heralded the appearance of this new, young, and serious writer and noted that the volume is "free from banality of thought and commonplace theme, exploring deep dimensions of experience with a mature authority." Eaton called it "a properly polished piece of work" and its publication "an occasion for excitement."[2]

A close reading of Betts's work reveals that her themes, her preoccupations, have remained fairly consistent throughout her career, from the earliest published work to the most recent. She says her themes are "time and mortality," and she has written tellingly about children, old people, relationships among family members, growing up, the relationship of the races, isolation and loneliness, death, and the possibilities of love. Along with a certain consistency in subject matter, there has also been much development in her art. She has written better and better, her long fiction becoming more complex, more layered, more subtle, and more optimistic. She has been experimental in her work, not breaking the conventions of short story or novel, but stretching herself with each work, never repeating herself, trying new things. Overall there seems to be in her recent work more hope expressed about the possibilities of earthly love and more importance given to the implications of religious experience.

Place is always important in her fiction, and her characters are intimately connected to North Carolina. She depicts ordinary people. In discussing her great theme of mortality with one interviewer, she talks about character and quotes Thornton Wilder, who observed that each human being lives " 'an unbroken sequence of unique occasions.' " Betts explains:

> And that's what fascinates me about character. I think it's true that I write about the lower and lower-middle class, because the mortality is much closer to the edge of the veil there. It's a more primitive way of living, and one is conscious every time you sing old down-home, thumping hymns that death is always present, and that one is talking about it in terms of blood, flesh, and perishing. And I do think every human being is so unique and is not going to be duplicated.[3]

In a recent talk, Betts describes "the tribe I know best":

> Mostly Scotch-Irish, with a featherweight of Cherokee. Farmers, beauticians, policemen, millworkers, squirrel hunters, army pri-

vates. Earthy, joking people without college degrees, often without high school diplomas, living hard in piedmont North Carolina—red clay, red rivers. Use-it-up, wear-it-out, make-it-do people. Thrifty, stubborn, honest, hot-tempered. Their occasional fist fights were over money or sex but rarely ideas.[4]

These are the ordinary people of Betts's fiction. She is most gifted at creating living, breathing, changing characters, each one unique.

Her ear for spoken language is true, and her prose style is rich, allusive, metaphorical, suggestive, economical, and flexible. In an unpublished paper entitled "The Fingerprint of Style," Betts talked about her own style, which was influenced by her early churchgoing and Bible reading. She explains:

"I retain strong membership in my first tribe, where the fingerprint was inked and an early working life drew its own lines in the hand. In parts of my style that old membership always shows, since the ARP's [Associate Reformed Presbyterians] taught, not Greek logic, but Hebraic psychology. Their Bible cared less about how ark or temple looked than how they were built. God could be immanent in prickly bush and baptizing river, but also transcendent, outside the story altogether, sometimes vocal. . . .

Elsewhere Betts explains that "style should be like that pane of glass through which you can see the heart of the story absolutely clearly without distortion."[5]

Because she is a woman and she is from the South, Betts is often categorized as a Southern writer or a woman writer. She disapproves of attempts to categorize her art and feels that the only adjective a writer wants before that designation is "good." Her life itself is grist for a feminist's mill—a veritable Hortense Alger story, from mill town girl to distinguished professor and author—and her works, with their sensitive portrayals of women's lives, are appropriate subject matter for the feminist critic. Betts is tolerant of the feminist interpretation of *Heading West,* for example, that it is a story of a woman coming to terms with herself and her family and asserting her freedom and independence, but Betts herself does not interpret Nancy as feminist heroine. She sees Nancy's journey as one that changes her from pharisee to publican. Betts has said, "I'm much more interested, say, in theodicy—which has to do with divine good versus evil in the world—than I am in ERA, although I support ERA."[6] She is impatient with women's complaints of having been oppressed, and she is absolutely opposed to politics in literature, fiction that embodies a political message.

And Betts dislikes literature courses that include only women writers, preferring not to separate writers according to sex. She admits that she does a better job in fiction with women characters because she knows them better, but she is uncomfortable with a classification that would limit the way a reader approaches her work or any other writer's work. Among her contemporaries, she feels, for example, a closer affinity with Walker Percy than any woman writer.

In the same way that Betts's knowledge of women informs her work, so does her personal Southern geography. She knows the South—its climate, its seasons, its look and feel—and that is apparent in her fiction. She has come to accept that her work does indeed reflect many of the concerns that critics of Southern literature have designated as peculiarly characteristic of literature of the South. But she says that "what a good regionalist is doing is taking what he knows and building upon it and hoping to write the sort of material that does not need translation in another region, even though it draws upon the weather, the language, the culture, the habits where he grew up."[7] She objects to being categorized as a woman writer, a Southern writer, or even a Christian writer, though she herself fits comfortably into those categories. Her fiction, however, is written in a conscious attempt to transcend geography, sex, and religion, categories that she believes are limiting.

Doris Waugh was born on a farm in her grandmother's house on 4 June 1932 in Statesville, North Carolina. Her mother and father had grown up on neighboring farms. William Elmore Waugh was an illegitimate child, adopted by a sharecropper family who took him in when he was four years old. He and Mary Ellen Freeze attended school together. He was a shy young man who stuttered, and Mary Ellen, born with a cleft palate, was the shyest and quietest member of her large family. In the tenth grade, William ran away to the navy, and when he returned, he married his childhood sweetheart. Ten months later, their only child, Doris, was born.[8]

They lived in a concrete block house not far from the cotton mill where Doris's father worked. Sometime later, they moved to an apartment, where they resided until Doris was fourteen, when the family moved to the first house Doris's parents owned. It was a big, old, remodeled house with a long backyard complete with fishponds, a place Betts remembers as a "wonderful house for a child." The neighborhood was safe for exploration, and Betts remembers rambling for miles. Her own family was small, but many relatives lived close by, and the farm where she was born stayed in the family. For many years, young Doris spent summers with her grandparents on that farm.

She adored her grandfather and explains that he appears occasionally in her fiction. His death was a signal event of her childhood. He had a stroke and fell on a fence on Christmas Eve. Eleven-year-old Doris was sent to tell members of the family on neighboring farms, and she ran the distance of perhaps two miles. Because the family was poor, they had drawn names for Christmas presents on Thanksgiving Day. That year Doris had drawn her grandfather's name and had saved her allowance to buy him a white dress shirt from Penney's for $4.95. On New Year's Day, her grandfather was buried in the white shirt. Moving accounts of the deaths of Esther's grandfather in *The Scarlet Thread* and Nancy's in *Heading West* owe much to the death of the author's beloved grandfather.

Betts says that in retrospect she understands that her family was poor, but as she grew up, she was not aware of that fact. Everybody in her mill town lived in similar circumstances, and surrounded by a loving family, she had no sense of material poverty.

Perhaps a small mill town in rural North Carolina seems an unlikely place for the development and nurture of a writer, especially since Betts grew up in a family that was, as she explains, "not bookish." But Doris Betts seems to have been a born writer, making up poems even before she could write the words. Her mother, a loving, supportive parent who wrote down the poems, gave Doris the feeling that her writing was important. Young Doris continued to write poems all through her childhood and teenage years. And she wrote fiction too. While in junior high school, she wrote "novels," filling perhaps four composition books with text and illustrating the stories with pictures cut out of magazines. One of these "novels" featured a woman who was kidnapped and raped, although she was bound hand and foot at the time. Betts now explains that this showed her naive notion of "how sex worked."

Not until she was a freshman at Women's College of the University of North Carolina (now UNC-Greensboro), however, was she introduced to the idea of evaluation of her work. Her freshman English teacher told her that her poetry was "not very good," but, he explained, "your prose is not bad." This was an important event in her development, and this teacher introduced her to Dostoyevsky and Dos Passos and other writers whom she read greedily.

But she seems to have been aware always that she would be a writer, to have taken the idea for granted, and not to have questioned her vocation. She had learned to read early. The public library offered reading

material, and when not in school and not playing, she read omnivo-
rously without any sense of quality or selectivity. She says she read
comic books, great literature, and Bible stories. She liked it all
"equally." It took her many years to develop a critical ability because
the written word captivated her in all its manifestations. Even today
Doris Betts describes herself as "addicted" to reading; she will read la-
bels or scraps from a wastebasket if there is nothing else available.

Betts claims that her wonder at the power of words comes out of her
fundamentalist religious background. The members of her family were
dedicated and regular attendees of the Associate Reformed Presbyterian Church. The rhythm and the concreteness of biblical stories gave
her background as a writer. "And you come out of them [the stories],"
she has said, "with a great sense of the flesh, and the blood, and the
same material which I did see about me, and about which I have written
extensively."[9] In her church, she explains, everybody was always talking
about the word, and that was "quite magical to me in a primitive, sav-
age way." She has told one interviewer that she "grew up very much on
the King James version of the Bible, and on the entire philosophy of
the language which goes with that. Whether you talk about the opening of the Book of John or about the opening of the Book of Genesis,
in which the universe appears to be created not by action or event but
by an imperative sentence, you learn early of what I suspect all the
primitives know: that the Word is magic somehow."[10] In her church,
Betts says, "Words and the Word were almost sub-sacraments themselves, could work wonders, could transubstantiate any old thing by
the side of a redclay road."[11] This sense of the power and mystery of
language is at the very heart of her fiction.

Doris Waugh married Lowry Matthew Betts of Columbia, South
Carolina, in 1952. Lowry attended law school at Chapel Hill beginning
in 1954. Doris attended UNC-Chapel Hill in 1954, but she never completed work for the bachelor's degree she had begun at UNC-Greensboro. There are three children in the Betts family: Doris LewEllyn was
born in 1953, David Lowry in 1954, and Erskine Moore II in 1960.
Doris Betts explains that she has given up things to be a writer, but
none of the important things. She wanted to be a writer, to have a
family, and to have a career, and she "didn't want those things in any
order."[12] She has had them all.

Betts began writing for a local newspaper, the *Statesville Daily Record,*
when she was a teenager and went on to other newspaper jobs, serving
as a UPI stringer for several years and working with the news bureau at
UNC-Greensboro while she was a student there. She wrote a daily col-

umn for the *Sanford Daily Herald* in 1957–58 and in 1960 assumed the editorship of the *Sanford News Leader.*

She began teaching a course in creative writing at the University of North Carolina at Chapel Hill in 1966. From that part-time beginning, she has moved up the academic ladder and now holds the alumni distinguished professorship in the English Department and has served a three-year stint as the first chairwoman of the faculty at the university. Along the way, she has directed the freshman English program (1970–77) and served as dean of the honors programs (1977–80). Highly respected as a teacher, as a colleague, and as an administrator, Doris Betts's academic career is a distinguished one.

In addition to raising a family, writing fiction, teaching, and serving on literary panels and boards, Betts served two terms on the Sanford City School Board (1965–72). She is a Democrat and an elder in the Presbyterian church.

The Betts family lived for many years in Sanford, North Carolina, and Doris drove to Chapel Hill to teach. Now, a son and his wife live in the Sanford house, and Doris and Lowry have a farm outside Pittsboro, in Chatham County. Their farm is named Araby for both the James Joyce short story and the Arabian horses they raise. They now have fifteen Arabians and have had regional champions and have taken horses to the nationals. Their library includes many volumes on the care and raising of horses. Her life at home and work are separate, and she says she feels herself shake off one role and assume another as she drives to Chapel Hill from Pittsboro and then home again.

At home, Betts writes in a room off the kitchen that also serves occasionally as sleeping quarters for a visiting daughter or son. She works in an easy chair, surrounded by books and papers, writing in exquisite longhand, putting pen to paper for all first drafts. An IBM personal computer serves as a mechanical aid, not a writing aid. She has never had a formal study, a room of her own, but has produced her fiction writing at the kitchen table or during her lunch hour at work or in laundromats. She is a sensible, calm, practical person with great reserves of energy, excellent health, and immense talent.

Betts's natural forte is the short story. She began her career in this genre, and she has continued to publish stories. In 1969, she stated that she wrote novels only so that her publisher would take her short stories. Short stories do not make money in the book market, she explained, "So for me, the novel is like the bread on the sandwich, I just slip in the bread so they'll let me do the filling."[13] In 1974, she pointed out some of the restrictions of the short story, such as the inability to get depth of character, the impossibility of showing progress over time, and the lack of social complexity, but she still claimed this genre as her favorite. She suggested that the mind works differently for writers of short and longer fiction, that people "most naturally given to long forms write a different rhythmic sentence and think on a larger scale." She continued, "I honestly suppose this has something to do with metabolism, that their hearts probably beat at a different rate from mine. If you are a brisk, intense, fast sort of person and drive too fast and smoke too much, you are probably going to be more of a short story writer."[14] One of the advantages of the short story for her is that "it seems to *stop* time, to gather it together, to make it dense and glowing."[15]

Betts stops time in short stories that show much variety in content, style, and point of view. She has a great ability to show within a brief time the ordinary experience of ordinary people and at the same time reveal depth, complexity, ambiguity, and, ultimately, its symbolic meaning. Often her characters are emotionally repressed, with a buried life that is revealed in the story—some escape the tortured existence; others do not. There are no easy answers in the Betts universe, no sentimentality, no clichés, infrequent "happy" endings. She sometimes focuses on handicapped characters, damaged physically, crippled in some outward way that seems to reflect the human condition. These special characters—the girl with the brutal scar dividing her face or the boy with the harelip wrinkling his upper lip—receive their author's special affection. Indeed, all of her characters, even the most despicable, are recipients of her love. Her characters are individually identified in all their uniqueness, but the cumulative effect on the reader is often to recognize himself as the stories illuminate with meaning.

She has been called tough; her vision, ironic. Critics comment upon her humor. Often she surprises the reader with a comic turn of phrase, the humor sometimes becoming dark comedy, sometimes farce.

The Gentle Insurrection and Other Stories (1954), Betts's first published book, consists of twelve short stories. Reviewers have chosen a number of them to discuss, suggesting the high quality of the volume. Seven deal with death in its various manifestations. The darkly comical "A Sense of Humor," for example, depicts two children in the midst of a family funeral coming to terms with their Uncle John's death. Uncle John, always joking and always the life of the party, was a jolly person. The children realize that the last joke is on him, locked in a box in the ground, unable to escape, and they are convulsed with laughter. In another story, Betts depicts the terrible conflict a character undergoes when suppressed feelings suddenly surface. "Miss Parker Possessed" tells of a middle-aged spinster librarian who experiences an overwhelming passion for a townsman, Lewis Harvey: "after forty placid years there had erupted within her a wild springtime of thinking. . . . " The townspeople think she has gone mad, and eventually she suppresses this buried part of her self, which has briefly surfaced, and she is "safe" again.

The relationship of the races is treated in "The Sympathetic Visitor." A white woman, a middle-aged shop owner, pays a courtesy visit to a young black woman who works for her. The black woman's brother had gone berserk, brutally murdered his mother, and then killed himself. The separation of the races, the failure of humans to communicate, the buried life of a character—all are depicted in this story. Two people do communicate in "Child So Fair," which tells of the transcending power of love in the relationship between a grandmother, almost blind with cataracts, and her grandson, abandoned by his mother. The grandson is retarded and has a cleft palate, but the grandmother does not see nor care about that. She thinks to herself, "He was as high grown as my heart," and she sees his aureole of golden hair, a "fair" child. The simplicity and surpassing power of love in ordinary circumstances are depicted in this story.

The title story of this collection is about a mother, daughter, and son, all trapped in a hard and mean life on a tenant farm. Each deals with reality in a different way—the mother through illusion and the son through denial, but the daughter seems about to escape with a lover. She does not; her lover is a fantasy, or he abandons her, or she cannot leave.

All of these stories deal with ordinary people who might be neighbors in a small town in the South. Each story depicts a "gentle insurrection" on the part of a character. Betts presents in different guises the failure of people to touch one another, to communicate, to understand. Robert Tallant, writing in the *New York Times Book Review,* observed that "the characters, all alive and very believable, are varied, leading different kinds of lives and having different kinds of troubles. Yet, basically, it is their inability to understand or to be understood that is their tragedy."[16] The reviewer for *Catholic World* called this volume "one of the most distinguished of the year."[17] Certainly, it is a phenomenal work for a young writer's apprentice effort.

The Astronomer and Other Stories (1966), Betts's second collection of short fiction and her fourth book, consists of seven short stories and a novella. This volume further develops themes from the first collection, as characters grow up, suffer isolation, encounter love, live a proper life while suppressing powerful feelings, and face death. Two of the stories,

"All That Glisters Is Not Gold" and "Spies in the Herb House," are told in the first person and are autobiographical. The latter is a lyrical and nostalgic story about an imaginative eight-year-old girl growing up in the 1940s. She already knows that she will be an artist.

"Clarissa in the Depths" tells of a motherless young black woman's coming of age. Clarissa quits school at eleven, goes to work for a white family, and is given her own room. The preparation for sexual initiation provided to her by the men in her family—her father, uncle, and grandfather—leads her to arm herself with a knife when the delivery man from the grocery store enters her bedroom one night. But her own feelings compel her to put the knife aside and touch his chest with her hand.

"The Dead Mule" and "Careful, Sharp Eggs Underfoot" are comic tales. The first is a grotesquely humorous account of a bootlegger who gets caught by the sheriff with fifty-six bottles of white mule buried in a dead mule. The second is the farcical tale of a lawyer at a local egg festival.

"The Proud and the Virtuous" features one of Betts's sexually suppressed women, outwardly quite proper, who impulsively and provocatively invites a chain gang up to her house for ice water and then waits for the men (who never come) to rape her. And "The Mandarin" tells of a bored, lonely, rich old lady who loves nobody. She despises her paid companion, a nurse. Her useless life is symbolized by her pastime of making "thin lace for the edges of nothing." When she confronts death, she realizes she has not had enough of life: "I wish I were young! I wish it were all new."

The most important selection in this book, however, is the novella "The Astronomer," the finest piece Betts had published up to that time. It remains a small masterpiece. Here all of her themes merge in the story of Horton Beam, a reclusive widower, who retires from Corley Knitting Mills with a gold watch engraved "WELL DONE!" A withdrawn, quiet, uncommunicative man, he decides after reading a Whitman poem to devote himself to the study of astronomy. He gets books from the public library, becomes interested in mythology, and determines to buy a telescope.

Into his life abruptly comes Fred Ridge with a "face like a rat terrier, all eyes and bones." Ridge rents a room from the astronomer. Shortly afterward, Eva, who has left her husband and children, joins Fred. Eva is pregnant. Gradually, the astronomer comes to know Eva, to share a relationship with her, and to love her. From his previously withdrawn life, he changes and is now willing to give, share, and do anything to keep Eva—even give her and Fred his house. He comes to realize that he had been hard on his sons and always let his wife down: "they thought I was a cold fish." This is Eva's story too, as she struggles with the question of whether or not to abandon her family, chooses to undergo an abortion, takes a short trip into prostitution, suffers mightily, seeks forgiveness, and ultimately decides to return to her husband. In the end, the astronomer is left alone in his "house of thunderous silence," looking up to the stars, crying out to the universe: " 'Listen! Say something to me!' "

This collection was well received critically. In the *New York Times Book Review,* Benedict Kiely praised the volume and observed, "Up among the stars or at home in small towns in North Carolina, Miss Betts displays equally a rich imagination and disturbing vision."[18] And the reviewer for *Virginia Quarterly Review* ranked Betts "among the finest writers of contemporary fiction" and commented upon her great powers of observation and imagination, her feeling for time, place, and character as well as her "wonderful sense of form and structure."[19]

Beasts of the Southern Wild and Other Stories, published in 1973, consists of nine stories, seven with women characters at the center of the story, one with a young boy, and one an otherworldly piece with a man, apparently dead, at the center. "The Spiders of Madagascar," Betts's most terrifying story about childhood, tells of a young boy whose father dies in an automobile accident. Surrounded by women, he is emotionally abandoned by all of them—his neurotic mother, his grandmother, and his teacher. He develops an interest in science and begins raising spiders, finally cultivating a black widow spider with her egg case. The story ends with a surprising variation on the-lady-or-the-tiger question; he is deciding whether to turn the deadly spider loose in his mother's room or in his own.

Three of the stories are about isolated women, unconnected to other human beings. "The Ugliest Pilgrim" tells of a mountain girl's setting out on a bus in a quest to a television faith healer for a miraculous cure of her disfiguring facial scar. Violet Karl has carefully planned her journey, but grace comes to her in an unanticipated form. She is disappointed by the faith healer, but she finds love with a soldier she meets on the bus. Violet finds redemption, but Rose Marie Duffy in "The Hitchhiker" does not. She suicidally drives her car into a river. And Wanda Quincy, a reclusive widow, breaks out of her isolation by running away with an abortionist, to the horror of the townspeople.

Three stories focus, from various perspectives, on women within the context of a family. "Still Life with Fruit" delineates the ambivalent feelings of a mother in giving birth to her first child. "The Mother-in-Law" is the story of a woman's coming to self-knowledge by working out her relationship with and coming to an understanding of her husband's deceased mother. Another story with a woman protagonist is "Burning the Bed," which is about loss. A woman comes home to take care of her dying father, imagining that after he dies she will burn his bed in a primitive ritual. The accidental discovery in a telephone call that her lesbian lover is being unfaithful devastates her. And the title story focuses on Carol Walsh, a high school English teacher, trapped in a boring life with Rob, her insensitive husband, and two children. In contrast to her dull, outward life, Carol enjoys a rich and satisfying fantasy life with a sustained story line. In her imagination, the world has undergone revolution, and blacks control everything. She is the mistress of the provost of New Africa University (which she had attended under its old name), an elegant, rich, and cultured man, who reads Yeats with her. One night after joyless and mechanical sex with her husband, she imagines that she gives her black lover an order to have Rob hunted down and killed for raping her.

Reviewers praised this collection of stories, which can only be partially characterized by brief plot summaries. Michael Mewshaw in the *New York Times Book Review* called them "deceptively simple and entertaining on the surface," but, he explained: "They resist interpretation the way Wallace Stevens said poems should—almost completely." He went on to remark that the "writing escapes categorization and remains very much an index of one woman's intriguing mind, and the finest fruit of her imagination falls to the reader in a shower of startling images, metaphors, and similes."[20]

With these three collections as well as other stories published in journals, magazines, and anthologies, Doris Betts has established her reputation as a superb short story writer. Critics frequently put her in the exalted company of Flannery O'Connor, Eudora Welty, and Peter Taylor. But if mastering the short story has seemed easy for Betts, writing the novel has come with much effort. Although she is an instinctive writer of short stories, she has described herself as "an artificial and contrived and forced novelist."[21] And so Doris Betts has had to work up to the novel, which has not come to her naturally.

She has found that the short story no longer appeals to her as it once did, and she describes it as an "unsatisfactory" form for her fifties. She compares the short story to the lyric poem and remarks, "You can't go on being Shelley when your hair is gray. . . . It's a bore."[22] She has accepted the challenge of writing novels and has had to make a conscious effort with both plot and the intellectual structure of the longer genre. She says the short story has taught her all that it can, and she will not succumb to the "temptation to use the skills" she has. She feels instantaneously whether a short story is "right or it isn't," but the novel does not offer that quick realization. Betts explains, "It's much scarier to write a novel. The sense of failure abounds on every page and I think when you finish a novel what you have mostly is a sense of failure." Despite these difficulties, Betts has had four novels published between 1957 and 1981.

Many of the general observations made about her short stories apply to the novels—the kinds of characters portrayed, the use of humor, the depiction of the buried life of characters, the use of the grotesque, the portrayal of the relationship between the races. With more time and space in the longer fiction, Betts has developed at length the involved, intricate, and complex relationships among family members that are suggested in the short fiction. Her ability to evoke place with all the concrete details that make it come alive is fully developed in the novel. Stone County, North Carolina, is her Yoknapatawpha.

The themes of the novels are similar to those of her short fiction. She is interested in love and death, in growing up and growing old. Often she shows the relationship between the sexes in a variety of situations—young love, married love, incestuous love. More and more she is interested in evil. Her last two published novels feature evil characters, and the next two will take evil as a central subject matter. The growth of her ability as a writer can be traced in the novels. Her first novel is clearly an apprentice work, the last one an achievement of maturity.

Betts's first novel, *Tall Houses in Winter* (1957), appeared when she was twenty-five. An apprentice work, it has a strangely dark tone for a young writer. The central character, Ryan Godwin, is a forty-eight-year-old English professor who has come home to Stoneville with a sentence of cancer in his throat. He had fled this small North Carolina town a decade earlier and vowed never to return. Home again, he confronts the remnants of his family—his stern, moralistic, and materialistic sister, Asa, and a beloved black servant, Lady Malveena. Also in the household is twelve-year-old Fen, who is probably his own son by his brother's wife. Godwin must deal not only with these three, but also with people from his past who are now dead—his hated father; his fat, platitudinous brother, Avery; and his brother's wife, Jessica, who was the great love of Godwin's life. Much of the story is told retrospectively, as Ryan Godwin comes to terms with his past, accepts responsibility for his son, and decides to seek treatment for his cancer.

This is the bleakest work in Betts's shelf of fiction. A philosophical, introspective novel, it focuses on a middle-aged man's interior life. The most interesting part of the work is the retrospective account of the love affair between Ryan Godwin and his sister-in-law, Jessica. Betts shows in this youthful work her gift in describing and evoking place, depicting family relationships, and portraying love between a man and women, ingredients of not only this novel, but her other three as well.

Reviewers made positive comments about the work, but critical response was mixed. Evelyn Eaton observed that this novel "is a substantial first novel, well constructed, well sustained, evocative of a South recognizable to the majority of Southerners." However, Eaton compared this work unfavorably with the earlier short story collection, observing that Betts "is a greater artist in the short story than she proves herself to be—so far—in the novel."[23] Borden Deal in the *New York Times Book Review* called the book promising but observed that it "is a disappointing novel," which was written "from a deep conscientiousness rather than from a deep conviction."[24] The reviewer for the New York *Herald Tribune* observed that Betts has a "literary instinct as sound as it is gifted."[25] The reviews show that critics considered it a respectable work, but this first novel was not so well received as the first short story collection had been three years earlier.

Betts's second novel, *The Scarlet Thread* (1964), is quite different from her first. It has more characters, covers a longer period of time, and deals with a community as well as with people. A historical work that looks back in time to the turn of the century, it focuses on the Allen family—Mildred and Sam, as well as their three children, Esther, Thomas, and David. It is also the story of a small North Carolina village that undergoes dramatic change as a cotton mill becomes the center of life. The action covers the years from 1897, when Esther Allen turns thirteen and the mill comes to town, until 1920, but flashbacks tell of the past; a brief final chapter brings the characters forward in time from 1920.

The canvas for this work is broad, and Betts focuses on different characters in turn, telling the story from various points of view. Sam Allen, competent and ambitious, makes his way dishonestly from manager of the general store to major stockholder of the mill. Mildred, his wife, is religious, and his sister, Rosa, a fat, barren woman, obsessed with having a child, is deranged. The three children in the family have contrasting characters. A bright, loving, independent young woman, Esther is always testing the limits of conventional behavior, whether she is drinking whiskey secretly at a family gathering, peering in the window at a black couple making love, or engaging as a teenager in a sexual relationship with Max Carson, the Northern manager of the mill. She runs away from home and disappears from the novel, reappearing briefly at the end. Her presence, however, continues to be felt throughout the novel. Thomas is hardworking, cold, mechanical, exploitive, materialistic, and sadistic. He satisfied his father by working in the company store and eventually taking over the mill. The younger brother, David, is sensitive and artistic. He rejects going into the mill and instead apprentices himself to a crippled stonecutter, Bungo Mayfield, spending his short life as an artist, hewing monuments out of stone.

More ambitious in scope than her first novel, *The Scarlet Thread* portrays more complex family relationships, delineates more characters, and attempts the double goal of showing both a family and a community over time. It covers much of life—birth, death, madness, religion, sexual relationships, racial tensions. The accidental death of a black sorceress and a visit of the Ku Klux Klan to a black employee of Sam Allen are sensational events. The novel excels in showing the Allen children growing up—the lively sister whose imagination will not allow her to conform, and the two brothers, each in love with this sister, each driven by different demons. The interrelationships of the Allen family are sensitively and realistically documented.

Reviewers praised the characterization and style, but criticized the structure and sensational elements. In *Best Sellers,* C. P. Collier called Betts "an exacting writer" and went on to praise the novel: "She is a vigorous writer, starkly revealing all the ugliness of rape, sadism, brutality, murder, birth, degeneracy, and insanity. She writes with an awareness of irony and passion, of changes wrought within the personality. . . ."[26] And J. M. Carter in *Library Journal* observed that the novel "has beauty and depth and understanding, and, as a book about children, will stand with the best of them." But William Peden in *Saturday Review* claims the novel degenerates "into almost a burlesque of the 'scrambled-genes' school of regional writing" and accused her of Gothic excess. Writing in 1977 in *Survey of Contemporary Literature,* John C. Coleman criticized her "narrative method" and suggested that "Mrs. Betts is not yet fully at ease in the full scope of the novel." He went on to praise her short stories.

Another short story collection, *The Astronomer and Other Stories* (1966), intervened between *The Scarlet Thread* and Betts's third novel, *The River to Pickle Beach* (1972). In the new novel, Betts moved from the past to contemporary 1968, and she moved the setting from rural Stone County to the beach of North Carolina. Bebe and Jack Sellars, a childless couple in their forties, are at the center of the novel. They agree to take over the management of a small beach community. Jack, a gardener, is reluctant to make this move, but Bebe is enthusiastic about it and pleased to leave her waitress job. Their relationship is warm and loving, forthrightly and comfortably sensual. Into their lives intrudes

Mickey McCann, an old Army friend of Jack, who is powerfully drawn to Bebe. McCann is sexually frustrated, racially prejudiced, and mightily attracted to hunting and guns. In an act of sudden and unreasonable violence, McCann shoots a retarded woman and her child.

Echoing in the background of the novel is the violence in this country during the years of the King and Kennedy assassinations. Betts delineates the evil character who perpetrates violence, a colorless man psychologically twisted by his frustrated desires and his hatreds. Set against this random and violent murder is the steady and passionate love of the middle-aged married couple.

This novel was well received. In the *New York Times Book Review,* Jonathan Yardley complained that Betts "has never quite got her due." He called her a "tough, wise and compassionate writer."[27] He predicted that this novel might widen her audience because "it has the ingredients of good popular fiction, and it is also a serious, provocative novel." And the reviewer for *Choice* called it a "superior novel," observing that "current issues—sex and violence, the generation gap, racial unease, family ties, the place of religion, viability of friendship—are treated freshly and vividly. . . . " William B. Hill in *Best Sellers* termed it "a good, serious, crisp novel."

Betts's fourth novel, *Heading West,* was published in 1981. (Again she had produced a volume of short stories, *Beasts of the Southern Wild* (1973), between novels.) For the first time, a Betts novel focuses on a woman, a thirty-four-year-old librarian, and the author moves the action of the novel out of rural North Carolina across the United States to the Grand Canyon. This novel treats a contemporary subject, the kidnapping of a woman by a psychopathic criminal, but it also deals with the old subjects, time, mortality, love, death, family relationships. Nancy Finch is Betts's most literate heroine; she has read books, and literary allusions abound in the text. And with this wry, smart, earthy character Betts makes the fullest use thus far of her comic talents.

Nancy Finch is burdened by her family—her neurotic, complaining mother and her retarded, epileptic brother. Traveling with her superficial sister, Faye, and despicable brother-in-law, Eddie, she indulges herself in escape fantasies in the backseat of the car. She is liberated from her family when she is kidnapped by a man who calls himself Dwight Anderson. Nancy makes ineffective attempts to get help but eventually forgoes escape to travel with Dwight and a wandering, disbarred judge, Harvey Jolley. These three characters travel across the country heading west. On one level, this novel is a thriller that details a kidnapping. On another, it is a psychological exploration of the three characters in the car (and others as well). Ultimately, it is a philosophical book dealing with the nature of evil and delineating Nancy's agonizing journey into her own soul.

Heading West elicited the most interesting reviews Betts has received for a book of fiction. John Leonard's provocative review in the *New York Times* is a thoughtful piece of literary criticism. Leonard explains that Betts "writes as well about the Grand Canyon as she does about the sulking, God-haunted South. She hits the risky road with as much energy and lyrical precision as she stays home with Nancy's invalid mother and epileptic brother and their Freudian family romance." But Leonard claims that "there are three books quarreling inside this ambitious novel," and he does not think that they "quite add up." One is a "taut psychological thriller with metaphysics on its mind"; another is an explanation of this first book; the third is a "subtext to the other two" and "is very modern." Leonard is not satisfied with Betts's ending; he says the book "she began to write was sad and splendid and very different from the valentine to human possibility with which she concludes."[28]

In a generally positive review, Jonathan Yardley writes in the *Washington Post,* that "*Heading West* is actually two novels." The first one tells about an entrapped woman who suddenly "finds herself sucked into a journey of prolonged fear and gradual self-discovery." This novel "is quite brilliant," but the second, in which Nancy Finch is "nursed back to health, falls in love, and returns home to accomplish her final liberation," is, according to Yardley, "superior women's-magazine fiction."[29] Beth Gutcheon, in a review entitled "Willing Victim" in the *New York Times Book Review,* praised the novel, explaining that Betts is "capable of thinking and writing about more than one thing at once, and so, just as the horizontal progress of the Colorado River cuts vertically through stratum after stratum of rock in the canyon that is the central image of the novel, she tells a story that is taut and linear and compelling while simultaneously she cuts through layer after layer of different kinds of meaning."[30]

In other reviews, the novel received praise for characterization and style, with most of the criticism leveled at the plot and structure. For this rich and complex novel, it is appropriate that reviewers chose various aspects to comment upon and that they did not agree. Most reviewers praised the style, but there were dissenters who, for example, found the allusion and symbolism intrusive. In general, the novel received serious reviews from critics who praised Betts as an important writer and the novel as a significant work of fiction.

Betts now has two novels in progress. One, almost completed, *Souls Raised from the Dead,* got its title from a plate glass window in a section of the city of Atlanta which no longer exists, destroyed to make way for an urban renewal project. The sign read:

Keys Made
Knives Sharpened
Palms Read
Souls Raised from the Dead.

In this novel, Betts deals with a subject that continues to preoccupy her, the presence of evil in the world. The soul in despair is that of Frank Thompson, a North Carolina highway patrolman. His beloved daughter, Mary Grace, suffers from kidney disease and needs a kidney transplant. For the first time in a novel, Betts will use Chapel Hill and environs as the setting.[31]

The second novel, entitled *The Wings of the Morning,* will be a big book. The title comes from the Book of Psalms, and the central character is a Presbyterian minister. This work will depict the decline of religion in the United States.

At fifty-eight, Doris Betts is vigorous physically, mentally, and creatively. She is a stunning woman—witty, articulate, warm, earthy, expressive. She and her husband have added a greenhouse on their farm and raise plants from seeds and cuttings. Her first grandchild, Matthew Palmer Betts, was born in 1988. Money from a movie producer's purchase of *Heading West* will be used in the spring to build a new home on the farm. Her personal life is a rich one. Family, farm, classroom—all enrich her fiction. With a grandmother who lived to be ninety-four, Betts may be at mid-career. In looking to the future, she says she would like to "write one good novel," and at the risk of sounding "corny," she would "like to ripen in soul." Her voice promises to be heard in contemporary fiction for many years.

DORIS BETTS BIBLIOGRAPHY

NOVELS

Tall Houses in Winter. New York: Putnam, 1957; London: Gollancz, 1958.
The Scarlet Thread. New York: Harper & Row, 1964.
The River to Pickle Beach. New York: Harper & Row, 1972.
Heading West. New York: Knopf, 1981.

Doris Betts

SHORT STORY COLLECTIONS

The Gentle Insurrection and Other Stories. New York: Putnam, 1954; London: Gollancz, 1955.
The Astronomer and Other Stories. New York: Harper & Row, 1966.
Beasts of the Southern Wild and Other Stories. New York: Harper & Row, 1973.

The Southern Imagination
of Sonia Sanchez

*

JOANNE VEAL GABBIN

Death is a five o'clock door forever changing time. And wars
end. Sometimes too late. I am here. Still in Mississippi. Near the
graves of my past. We are at peace . . . I have my sweet/astringent
memories because we dared to pick up the day and shake its tail until it became evening. A time for us. Blackness, Black people. Anybody can grab the day and make it stop. Can you my friends? Or
maybe it's better if I ask:
Will you?[1]

THE WOMAN who utters this challenge at the end of Sonia Sanchez's
play *Sister Son/ji* has the gift of second sight: she is a visionary, a
prophet, a revealer of truths. She has touched love, births, deaths, danger, tumult, upheaval, and change and has distilled from these experiences "sweet/astringent memories." Willing to pick up the day and
"shake its tail until it became evening," she helped to bring into being
an order that transformed time and defied death itself.

In many ways, *Sister Son/ji* becomes a metaphor for the poet herself
and the visionary quality and sense of the past that pervade much of her
poetry. Like *Sister Son/ji,* Sonia Sanchez has been a singer during turbulent times, a translator of the needs and dreams of black people. Sanchez has written to challenge black people—all people—to change the
world, "to make people understand . . . that we are here to perpetuate
humanity, to figure out what it means to be a human being,"[2] "to show
what is wrong with the way that we are living and what is wrong with
this country . . . to correct misinterpretation and bring love, understanding, and information to those who need it."[3] If this all sounds
idealistic, it is. For Sanchez matured as a writer in an era in which ideas
took on an elasticity heretofore unheard of. It was a time when a visionary president challenged the nation to land a man on the moon be-

fore the end of the decade; when a black power movement, led by such political thinkers as Malcolm X, Stokely Carmichael, H. Rap Brown, Angela Davis, Huey P. Newton, and Elijah Muhammad, ushered in a change in race relations in America; when 250,000 people, culminating several difficult years of boycotts, sit-ins, voter registration drives, marches, and riots, marched on Washington to make America accountable to black and poor people. It was a time when Americans protested an undeclared war in Vietnam, and the country mourned and immortalized its fallen heroes: John F. Kennedy, Robert Kennedy, and Martin Luther King, Jr. This era shaped the mettle of the poet, and like the Mississippi woman, Sanchez has become an armed prophet whose voice is at once a prod and a sword.

In her eight volumes of poetry, which appeared between 1969 and 1987, Sanchez's voice is sometimes abrasive but never as profane as the conditions she knows must be eradicated; her tone ranges from gentle to derisive, yet the message is one of redeeming realism. Also undergirding her poetic expression is a deep concern for heritage; for the sovereignty of time with all its ramifications of birth, change, rebirth, and death; for the impress of the past and memories; and for nurture, nature, and God. Moreover, these themes reveal Sanchez's strong Southern imagination, one that was born in the impressionable times of her youth in Alabama, where the tensions of struggle were fed with mama's milk.

Homecoming (1969), Sanchez's first book of poems, is her pledge of allegiance to blackness, to black love, to black heroes, and to her own realization as a woman, an artist, and a revolutionary. The language and the typography are experimental; they are aberrations of standard middle-class Americanese and traditional Western literary forms. As such, they reflect her view of American society, which perceives blacks as aberrations and exploits them through commercialism, drugs, brutality, and institutionalized racism. In this book and the poetry that follows, the vernacular and the forms are clear indications of her fierce determination to redefine her art and rail against Western aesthetics. *Homecoming* also introduces us to a poet who is saturated with the sound and sense of black speech and black music, learned at the knees of Birmingham women discovering themselves full voiced and full spirited. The rhythm and color of black speech—the rapping, reeling, explosive syllables—are her domain, for she is steeped in the tradition of linguistic virtuosity that Stephen Henderson talks about in *Understanding the New Black Poetry*. Black music, especially the jazz sounds of John Coltrane, Ornette Coleman, and Pharoah Sanders, pulse, riff, and slide through her poetry.

In her second volume, *We a BadddDDD People* (1970), Sanchez is wielding a survival sword that rips away the enemy's disguise and shears through the facade of black ignorance and reactionism. Arranged in three groups, "Survival Poems," "Love/Songs/Chants," and "TCB/EN Poems," the poems extend the attack begun in *Homecoming* and tell black people how to survive in a country of death traps (drugs, suicide, sexual exploitation, psychological slaughter via the mass media) and televised assassination. Her message, however, is not one of unrelieved gloom, for it is rooted in optimism and faith: "know and love yourself." Like Sterling A. Brown's "Strong Men" and Margaret Walker's "For My People," "We A BadddDDD People," the title poem of the volume, is a praise song that celebrates black love, talent, courage, and continuity. The poems appear rooted in a courage learned early from aunts who spit in the face of Southern racism and sisters who refused to be abused by white men or black men. In this volume, Sanchez reveals her unmistakable signature, the singing/chanting voice. Inflections, idiom, intonations—skillfully represented by slashes, capitalization (or the lack of it), and radical and rhythmic spelling—emphasize her link with the community and her role as ritual singer.

In *It's a New Day* (1971), a collection of poems "for young brothas and sistuhs," Sanchez nurtures young minds, minds that must know their beauty and worth if the nation is to be truly free. Her belief in the seed-force of the young led her to write the children's story *The Adventures of Small Head, Square Head and Fat Head* (1973).

In 1973, her fourth volume, *Love Poems,* appeared. Haki Madhubuti calls this "a book of laughter and hurt, smiles and missed moments."[4] The poems are collages of the images, sounds, aromas, and textures of woman-love. With the clarity and precision of Japanese ink sketches, Sanchez skillfully uses the haiku to evoke emotion:

did ya ever cry
Black man, did ya ever cry
til you knocked all over?[5]

Using the haiku, the ballad, and other traditional forms that advance her preference for tightness, brevity, and gemlike intensity, she fingers the raw edges of a woman's hurt and betrayal:

When he came home
from her
he poured me on
the bed and slid
into me like glass.

And there was
the sound of splinters.[6]

The poet also celebrates the magic that love has to transform and transcend:

i gather up
each sound
you left behind
and stretch them
on our bed.
   each nite
i breathe you
and become high . . . [7]

A Blues Book for Blue Black Magical Women (1974) is a dramatic departure from the poetry of earlier volumes. The scope here is large and sweeping. The language is no longer the raw vernacular of *Homecoming,* though, as in *We A BadddDDD People,* it is possessed by the rhythms of the chants and rituals. At its most prosaic, it is laden with the doctrine of the Nation of Islam and ideologically correct images. At its best, it is intimate, luminous, and apocalyptic. Tucked inside *A Blues Book* is a striking spiritual odyssey that reveals the poet's growing awareness of the psychological and spiritual features of her face.

In 1978, Sanchez culled some of her best poetry from earlier volumes in *I've Been a Woman: New and Selected Poems.* To these she adds a collection of haiku and tankas that is dominated by the theme of love: the sensual love of a man, the love of old people and young, the love for a father and spiritual mothers. She brings to this theme a style that is replete with irony, wit, and understatement. And in most of her poetry, her feelings are intensified and her symbols, those of nurturing, birth, growth, freedom, civilization, are deeply feminine. Here, as Margaret Walker Alexander states, is poetry of "consistently high artistry that reflects her womanliness—her passion, power, perfume, and prescience."[8]

In *homegirls & handgrenades* (1984), Sanchez shows the further deepening of the poet's consciousness, for it is a sterling example of her going inside herself, inside the past, to pull out of her residual memory deeply personal experience. From the past, she draws images that explode the autobiographical into universal truths. The predominant genre in this volume is the sketch, much like those that stud Jean Toomer's *Cane.* Bubba, "the black panther of Harlem," lost in a sea of drugs and unfulfilled dreams; Norma, black genius that lay unmined;

or the old "bamboo-creased" woman in "Just Don't Never Give Up on Love" all live again and vividly show Sanchez distilling "sweet/astringent memories" from her own experience.

Distinguishing much of her poetry is a prophetic voice that brings the weight of her experience to articulating the significant truths about liberation and love, self-actualization and being, spiritual growth and continuity, heroes, and the cycles of life. Her vision is original because it is both new (a fresh rearrangement of knowledge) and faithful to the "origins" of its inspiration. Therefore, it is not surprising that in her most recent volume of poetry, *Under a Soprano Sky* (1987), the mature voice of the poet is giving expression to the sources of her spiritual strength, establishing and reestablishing connections that recognize the family-hood of man/womankind, and singing, as another Lady did, of society's strange fruit sacrificed on the altars of political megalomania, economic greed, and social misunderstanding.

Throughout her poetry, which will be the focus of this study, Sanchez demonstrates the complexity of her Southern imagination. Though she spent a relatively short period of her life in the South, her way of looking at the world is generously soaked in the values she learned during her childhood in Birmingham, Alabama. The importance of the family and love relationships, her fascination with the past and her ancestry, her search for identity amid the chaos and deracination of the North, her communion with nature, her exploration of the folk culture, her response to an evangelical religious experience, and her embracing of a militancy nurtured in fear and rage are Southern attitudes that inform her poetry. Especially in *A Blues Book, I've Been a Woman,* and *Under a Soprano Sky,* Sanchez's fascination with the concept of time, her faith in the lessons of the past, and her deep notion of continuity firmly root her in the tradition of Southern imagination.

In *The Immoderate Past: The Southern Writer and History,* Hugh Holman explores the relationship between the concept of time and the Southern writer:

The imagination of the Southerner for over one hundred and seventy-five years has been historical. The imagination of the Puritans was essentially typological, catching fire as it saw men and events as types of Christian principles. The imagination of the New England romantics was fundamentally symbolic, translating material objects into ideal forms and ideas. The Southerner has always had his imaginative faculties excited by events in time and has found the most profound truths of the present and the future in the interpretation of the past.[9]

In part two of *A Blues Book,* the poet invites her readers to:

Come into Black geography
you, seated like Manzu's cardinal,
come up through tongues
multiplying memories
and to avoid descent
among wounds
cruising like ships,
climb into these sockets
golden with brine.[10]

Describing history as the spiritual landscape of events and images, she invites the reader to travel back in time, through what George Kent calls her "spiritual autobiography," her "own psychological and spiritual evolution in the past."[11] Sanchez has the past define the features of her identity and uncover her origins. Calling on the earth mother as the inspiration and guide on the journey, she implores her to reveal the truths locked in time:

Come ride my birth, earth mother
tell me how i have become, became
this woman with razor blades between
her teeth.

      sing me my history O earth mother
about tongues multiplying memories
about breaths contained in straw.[12]

The poet realizes that the essential clues to who she is are there in the dusty corners of history, in the myths and tales preserved by "tongues multiplying memories," in the seemingly inconsequential bits that can be gleaned from those who live in the spirit and in the flesh. Because she is in tune with her oral tradition, she shares with other Southern black writers, such as Ralph Ellison, Richard Wright, Margaret Walker, Ernest Gaines, Maya Angelou, and Alice Walker, what Ellison calls some of the advantages of the South:

I believe that a black Southern writer who does know his traditions has some of the advantages which William Faulkner or other white Southern writers have had: the advantage of contact with a long accumulation of history in a given place; an experience which has been projected in other forms of artistic expression, which has traditional values and variants, and which has been refined by being defined by generations of people who have told what it seemed to be: "This is the life of black men here. . . . "

This is one of the advantages of the South. In the stories you get the texture of an experience and the projection of values, and the distillation of a kind of wisdom.[13]

For Sanchez, who she is and who she is to become have much to do with the texture of experience, the values, and the wisdom alive in the folk community of Birmingham, Alabama.

Sonia Sanchez was born in Birmingham on September 9, 1934. Her parents, Wilson L. Driver and Lena Jones Driver, faced with naming a second girl (the first daughter was named Patricia), gladly turned over the task to relatives, who returned quickly enough with the name Wilsonia Benita. The communal name turned out to be a portent of the role relatives would play in her upbringing, for when she was one year old, her mother died in childbirth, and she thus began a series of moves from one relative's home to another during the next nine years.

After her mother's death, Wilsonia and her sister were cared for by her father's mother. Elizabeth "Mama" Driver, whom Sanchez describes as a "heavy-set, dark complected woman," was the head deaconess in the African Methodist Episcopal Church. In an interview, Sanchez remembers her grandmother: "My grandmother spoiled my sister and me outrageously. She loved us to death . . . she loved us so much that she used to walk us to Tuggle Elementary School. This old, old woman used to walk very slowly up that hill. . . . "[14] Mama Driver brought the girls into the circle of the rituals of the A. M. E. Church. They experienced the sonorous roar of the minister, who strode across the pulpit of the wood frame church; the buzz of the congregation when a sister got "happy" and threw her pocketbook "clean across the aisle"; and the wonderment of the spirituals when all those choir members, dressed in white, sounded like the angels at the gates of the city.

Sanchez remembers the many occasions her grandmother had allowed them to sit quietly at her knees while she talked with the women who visited their modest house in a Birmingham housing development. In "Dear Mama" in her most recent book, *Under a Soprano Sky,* she recalls vividly the Saturday afternoons when she "crawled behind the couch" and listened to the old deaconesses as they told of their lives "spent on so many things":

> And history began once again. I received it and let it circulate in my blood. I learned on those Saturday afternoons about women rooted in themselves, raising themselves in dark America, dis-

charging their pain without ever stopping. I learned about women fighting men back when they hit them: "Don't never let no mens hit you mo than once girl." I learned about "womens waking up they mens" in the nite with pans of hot grease and the compromises reached after the smell of hot grease had penetrated their sleepy brains. I learned about loose women walking their abandoned walk down front in church, crossing their legs instead of their hands to God. And I crept into my eyes. Alone with my daydreams of being woman. Adult. Powerful. Loving. Like them. Allowing nobody to rule me if I didn't want to be.

And when they left. When those old bodies had gathered up their sovereign smells. After they had kissed and packed up beans snapped and cakes cooked and laughter bagged. After they had called out their last goodbyes, I crawled out of my place. Surveyed the room. Then walked over to the couch where some had sat for hours and bent my head and smelled their evening smells. I screamed out loud, "oooweeee! Ain't that stinky!" and I laughed laughter from a thousand corridors. And you turned Mama, closed the door, chased me round the room until I crawled into a corner where your large body could not reach me. But your laughter pierced the little alcove where I sat laughing at the night. And your humming sprinkled my small space. Your humming about you Jesus and how one day he was gonna take you home. . . . [15]

Mama Driver also gave the children a sense of continuity as she acquainted them with the long line of aunts, uncles, and cousins who made up their extended family. She acquainted them with a community that held dear the notion of family ties and took for granted the willingness of family members to take another member in: "My life flows from you Mama. My style comes from a long line of Louises who picked me up in the nite to keep me from wetting the bed. A long line of Sarahs who fed me and my sister and fourteen other children from watery soups and beans and a lot of imagination. A long line of Lizzies who made me understand love. Sharing. Holding a child up to the stars. Holding your tribe in a grip of love. A long line of Black people holding each other up against silence."[16]

When Mama Driver died, the small frail child of five experienced the manufactured adult mystery of death and the insensitivity of relatives who shut children out of this fact of nature. As a way of managing the loss and the pain, she withdrew behind a veil of stuttering that remained with her for the next twelve years. When she and her sister lived with her father and his second wife, the stuttering protected her from the brunt of her stepmother's cruelty. In part two of *A Blues Book,* she raises the specter of this woman:

> And YOU U U U U U U —step/mother.
> woman of my father's youth
> who stands at a mirror
> elaborate with smells
> all shiny like my new copper penny.
> telling me through a parade of smiles
> you are to be my new mother. and your painted lips
> outlined against time become time
> and i look on time and hear you
> who threw me in angry afternoon closets
> till i slipped beneath the cracks
> like light. and time stopped.
> and i turned into myself
> a young girl breathing in crusts
> and listened to those calling me.

to/	*no matter what they do*
be/	*they won't find me*
chanted/	*no matter what they say*
	i won't come out.[17]

The collective images of the woman—her stepmother's resentment, her rages, her neglect, and her authoritarianism that weighed heavily on the two girls—had the effect of distorting time itself ("and your painted lips / outlined against time"). The mature sensibility records the prominence of the cruel punishment that loomed prodigiously in the child's mind ("and time stopped / and i turned into myself") and indelibly marks her personality. She, the youngest, had hidden behind her "black braids and stutters"; she, the strange one, the quiet one, would not come out. When her father learned of his second wife's treatment of the children, he sent them to live with relatives, and they remained with relatives or friends until their father married again and took them to New York, reenacting the solemn ceremony that many thousands of black people performed as they migrated to Northern cities.

Reflecting on her childhood, Sanchez said that, despite the unhappy experiences, she had "a good Southern girlhood."[18] Her grandmother had initiated her into the rituals of black life; aunts and uncles and cousins had given connections, continuity to her sense of self, and Birmingham, Alabama, had rooted her in a history of black struggle, with its lessons of fear, segregation, rebellion, and an awareness of her place. Years later, in her first published poem, she urges from her subconscious the memory of a cousin who, when made to move from her seat on the bus, spits in the white driver's face.

From 1944 until she graduated from Hunter College, Wilsonia Driver lived in Harlem at 152d and St. Nicholas Place, where there was "no space." In the small apartment she shared with her sister, her father, and his third wife, she felt hemmed in. Her tiny bedroom, whose window faced a redbrick wall, further mocked her sense of loss, now far from the greener, open space of the South. She also felt hemmed in by the kind, yet restrictive, care of her new stepmother and by the unwritten expectation placed on a young girl growing up in an environment that did not offer its girl-women protection but demanded that they protect themselves or run the risk of scorn and censure:

coming out from alabama
to the island city of perpetual adolescence
where i drink my young breasts
and stay thirsty
always hungry for more than the
georgewashingtonhighschoolhuntercollegedays
of america.
    remember parties
    where we'd grinddddDDDD
    and grinddddDDDD
    but not too close
    cuz if you gave it up
    everybody would know. and tell.[19]

In those early Harlem days, the young girl was hungry for more than the restrictions of the island city, so she daydreamed and began to write. In an *Essence* magazine article, Sanchez recalls that she started writing because it was a way to express herself without the annoying stuttering. She remembers writing a poem about George Washington's crossing of the Delaware. The poem, which was left out while she rushed to rewash dishes, was found by her sister, who began reading the poem to their parents in a singsong rhyme. "I reached for the poem, but she pulled it away and finished reading it to everybody in the kitchen. They all laughed. I don't really remember it as cruel laughter, but I was a very sensitive little girl. So I was very much upset and after that I began hiding my poems. I doubt if anyone knew I was still writing."[20]

This incident recalls a similar experience related by Richard Wright in his book *Black Boy*. After he read one of his stories to a woman in his neighborhood, he realizes that she cannot possibly understand his desire to write: "God only knows what she thought. My environment contained nothing more alien that writing or the desire to express one's self in writing."[21] According to Ladell Payne in *Black Novelists and the Southern Literary Tradition,* Richard Wright's life of imagination sustained him in his estrangement but also served to isolate him further from his family and community.[22] Similarly for Sanchez, from the very beginning, writing was a solitary endeavor that simultaneously isolated her from others and gave her the distance that she needed to see herself, her family, and community reconstituted in a new light.

As the young woman matured, her estrangement extended into most areas of her life. At Hunter College, she wanted more than the benign indifference that left her sense of self unnourished. She was not only alienated from those at school, but she was also separated from those on her block. They left the serious-eyed, quiet, college girl alone.[23] However, in "Bubba" in *homegirls & handgrenades,* the poet remembers one who saw more in her than she was prepared to acknowledge: "One summer day, I remember Bubba and I banging the ball against the filling station. Handball champs we were. The king and queen of handball we were. And we talked as we played. He asked me if I ever talked to trees or rivers or things like that. And I who walked with voices for years denied the different tongues populating my mouth. I stood still denying the commonplace things of my private childhood. And his eyes pinned me against the filling station wall and my eyes became small and lost their color."[24]

And the alienation reached her in her home. She had not really known her father. Though she lived with him from the time she was ten until she left college, on many levels, they remained strangers. "A Poem for My Father" in *We A BadddDDD People* and "Poem at Thirty" in *Homecoming* tell poignantly of this relationship.

But more significantly, the young poet felt alienated from herself and her roots. In *A Blues Book,* she recalls those times when she "moved in liquid dreams":

and i dressed myself
in foreign words
  became a proper painted
  european Black faced american
  going to theatre parties and bars

and cocktail parties and bars
and downtown village apartments
and bars and ate good cheese
and caviar with wine that
made my stomach stretch for artificial warmth.

danced with white friends who
included me because that was
the nice thing to do in the late
fifties and early sixties

and i lost myself
down roads
i had never walked.

and my name was
without honor
and i became a
stranger at my birthright.[25]

Perhaps it was this sense that she had lost her birthright that turned her thoughts to her past. And the South became the place where the mysteries of her past could be discovered. There too was the knowledge of her mother.

It was not until she graduated from college that she learned anything about her mother. When her father showed her a photograph of Lena Jones Driver, a beautiful Latin-looking woman with fair skin and dark eyes, she became aware of the void that existed in her life. On a pilgrimage to the South in 1980, she found a wizened old man who held the knowledge that had long since been lost in county records. He told her that her mother was the daughter of a black plantation worker and her white boss by the name of Jones. The revelation convinced the poet of her intimacy with historical events and finds its way into her upcoming novel, *After Saturday Night Comes Sunday,* in which a woman who is going crazy because of a man must spiritually find her mother's mother. Only then, when she had traversed the void, can she become the kind of woman she is capable of becoming. In *After Saturday Night Comes Sunday,* as in part two of *A Blues Book,* the reader experiences an almost cinematographic sensation, as Sanchez reverses the projector, making the frames from the past flick in rapid retrogression. In much the manner of Alejo Carpentier as he envisions a "journey back to the source" (*Guerra Del Tiempo*), the poet manipulates time and harnesses the power and magic of the rivers to give birth to herself:

tell me. tellLLLLLL me. earth mother
for i want to rediscover me. the secret of me
the river of me. the morning ease of me.
i want my body to carry my words like aqueducts.
i want to make the world my diary
and speak rivers.[26]

The ritual invocation of the earth mother has its analogue in the rituals of the Orisha, the Yoruba gods. As if drawing on the Jungian collective unconscious, the poet reveals a close relationship between the riverain goddesses who reside at the bottom of the river, and Earth, whom they recognize as the pure force, the *ashe,* the power to make things happen.[27] In *Flash of the Spirit,* Robert Farris Thompson gives a description of one of the riverain goddesses, who has an uncanny resemblance to the spirituality revealed in *A Blues Book:*

> Divination literature tells us that Oshun was once married to Ifa but fell into a more passionate involvement with the fiery thunder god, who carried her into his vast brass palace, where she ruled with him; she bore him twins and accumulated, as mothers of twins in Yorubaland are want to do, money and splendid things galore. . . . When she died, she took these things to the bottom of the river. There she reigns in glory, within the sacred depths, fully aware that so much treasure means that she must counter inevitable waves of jealousy with witchcraft, by constant giving, constant acts of intricate generosity. Even so, she is sometimes seen crowned, in images of warlock capacity and power, brandishing a lethal sword, ready to burn and destroy immoral persons who incur her wrath, qualities vividly contrasting with her sweetness, love, and calm.[28]

Oshun, in fact, can well be a metaphor for Sanchez's power. For in her poems, one senses a power that is feminine, and consciously so. It comes from her understanding of her connections with the universe, her connections with her ancestors, and her strong matrilineal ties with a universe that has given to its kind not only the responsibility but, indeed, the power to bear the children and nurture seed. Her power comes from a faith in continuity; seeds grow into flowers and produce their own seeds. Sanchez clearly presents the life cycle and cherishes it.

Sanchez calls the phenomenon that makes sense out of these mystical connections and recurrent archetypal images "residual memory." It is her capacity to draw on this memory that deepens the implications of her poetry. And on another level, it provides a source of implications that even the poet cannot fathom. Some would call this simply—inspiration.

In speaking about how she writes, Sanchez explains a process in which one sees the art of the poet and the role of the prophet merging. In an interview that appeared in *Essence* magazine (July 1979), she says that sometimes lines of poetry come and she jots them down and that sometimes a feeling comes and she will write down lines that respond to that feeling. Often for Sanchez, the inspiration comes after rereading a favorite book or the work of a poet she admires. During her best time for reflection—early in the morning, from twelve midnight until four, she reads and reworks lines, "fussing at those things that obviously don't work."[29] However, sometimes the poet gives way to the prophet, whose voice "derives its authority, not from some inner reservoir, but from an outside . . . source."[30] Sanchez says: "Sometimes I actually see something that moves me or makes me angry or whatever, and then line by line just pours out from God knows where. Whenever people compliment me after a reading or tell me they enjoyed one of my books, I'll say, 'Thank you so much.' But inside I'll say to myself, 'It's not just me.' Everything that you or I could write has been written before; there's that energy there in the universe for us to pull from. Many of us just become attuned to that energy."[31]

It was this energy that helped Sanchez begin her career as a writer. While attending New York University, she began to write seriously. At NYU, she took a course from poet Louise Bogan, a prolific writer and teacher who disliked intensely "bad writing and bad writers."[32] Sanchez found Bogan fascinating and sincerely interested in her growth as a writer, and she did not sense in her the patronization and indifference that she had encountered at Hunter.

Encouraged by this experience, she organized a writers' workshop that met every Wednesday night in the village; there she met Amiri Baraka (LeRoi Jones) and Larry Neal, the poet-critics who became the architects of the black arts movement, and began to read with them in jazz night spots. She also joined the New York CORE and the Reform Democrats Club. At this time, she was married to Albert Sanchez, a first-generation Puerto Rican American. He did not understand her intense commitment to causes or her need to write. After four years of marriage and the birth of her first child, Sanchez found herself moving away from the narrowly defined bounds of that relationship:

and visions came from the wall.
bodies without heads, laughter without mouths.
then faces crawling on the walls

like giant spiders,
came toward me
and my legs buckled and
   i cried out.[33]

And when the break was complete, she

woke up alone
to the middle sixties
full of the rising wind of history . . . [34]

In 1967, Sanchez started teaching at San Francisco State College. Her two-year tenure there was marked by student unrest, demonstrations, and the fledgling stretching of the black power movement. She found herself in the midst of the struggle to make black studies a part of the college's offerings. She, along with psychologist Nathan Hare, played a significant role in the establishment of the first black studies program in the country. She also began to document the ironies and nuances of the overall struggle for black awareness in poems that would appear in her first volume, *Homecoming*.

Also during this time, Sanchez met poet Etheridge Knight through Gwendolyn Brooks and Dudley Randall. While he was in prison, they began to correspond, and in 1969, they married. Twin sons, Mungu and Morani, were born to them. After little more than a year, the marriage ended in an uneasy alliance. "Poem for Etheridge," "last poem i'm gonna write bout us," and other poems in *We A BadddDDD People* and *Love Poems* reveal the often poignant, sometimes tragic nature of their relationship. However, what is significant in these poems is the ability of the poet to transcend the bounds of her own experience and speak with an authority that comes from going many times to her own personal wailing wall. For example, in "Poem No. 8," Sanchez brilliantly captures the sense of interminable waiting that only a woman knows intimately:

i've been a woman
  with my legs stretched by the wind
    rushing the day
      thinking i heard your voice
        while it was only the night
          moving over
            making room for the dawn.[35]

From 1967 to 1975, Sanchez was intensely involved in continuing her career as a poet and a teacher. During that time, she completed nine books and published her poems and plays in several periodicals, including *Black Scholar, Black Theatre, Black World, Journal of Black Poetry, Liberator, Massachusetts Review, Minnesota Review, New York Quarterly,* and the *Tulane Drama Review.* She also taught at the University of Pittsburgh, Rutgers University, Manhattan Community College, and Amherst College. While at Amherst, from 1972 to 1975, she taught one of the first courses on black women writers offered in an American college. For a brief period from 1972 to 1975, she was a member of the Nation of Islam, directing its cultural and educational program and writing for *Muhammad Speaks.* She resigned from the Nation of Islam in 1975 and one year later came to Philadelphia to teach at the University of Pennsylvania. After a year, Sanchez began teaching at Temple University, where she has taught Afro-American studies, English, Pan-African studies, and creative writing since then.

In 1978, Sanchez published *I've Been a Woman: New and Selected Poems.* In this volume, she concludes with a group of new poems that fall under the rubric "Generations." These poems attest to the significance she places on the vestiges of the past that have been gathered to bring meaning, value, direction, and inspiration to an individual's present.

In "A Poem of Praise," which is dedicated to Gerald Penny, a student who died on September 23, 1973, and to the Brothers of Amherst College, Sanchez reconciles the loss of a young warrior by giving promise to the cycles of his life. The truth of the poem is that the man has been on earth and has experienced a life that is no less beautiful, dramatic, or meaningful because it has been short. One sees the poet developing a view of the universe that holds man as a traveler, who comes from another space, walks from the morning through day, to evening, tasting "in himself the world":[36]

In your days made up of dreams
in your eyes made of dawn
you walked toward old age,
child of the rainbow
child of beauty
through the broad fields
and your eyes gained power
and your limbs grew long like yellow corn
an abundance of life
an abundance of joy
with beauty before you, you walked
toward old age.[37]

This traveler brings to mind another one who came "trailing clouds of glory." William Wordsworth's youth must travel from the East, farther from the splendid vision of celestial light that was his when he was born. However, consistent with the teaching of Islam (during the writing of this poem, the poet was a follower of the teachings of Elijah Muhammad), Sanchez envisions a universe in which the young man walks toward the light, wisdom, and rebirth:

> For i am man
> and i must
> run with the evening tide
> must hold up my hands
> for my life is opening
> before me.
>
> I am going to walk far to the East
> i hope to find a good morning
> somewhere.[38]

This youth need not content himself with the memory of radiance that once was, for life moves in cycles and progresses toward endings that have, at their center, beginnings.

Sanchez's poetic kinship with Native American tribal poets is striking here. There is the same understanding of "the cyclic continuities" that make up the circle of life.[39] There is the same respect for the generative power of language, a language that is medicinal, rooted in nature, dignified, and spare. Kenneth Lincoln, in his book *Native American Renaissance,* writes:

> Oral tribal poetry remains for the most part organic, for tribal poets see themselves as essentially keepers of the sacred word bundle. . . . They regard rhythm, vision, craft, nature, and words as gifts that precede and continue beyond any human life. The people are born into and die out of a language that gives them being. Song-poets in this respect discover, or better rediscover, nature's poems. They never pretend to have invented a "poetic" world apart from nature, but instead believe they are permitted to husband songs as one tends growing things; they give thanks that the songs have chosen them as singers.[40]

In a real way, Sanchez's attitude about her purpose as a poet is rooted in a way of thinking about the world that is similar to that of the poet-singers of more than five hundred Native American cultures who send out the voice. Her early Southern experience watered her sensibility—the greening of her mind—and nourished her purpose as a poet: to create positive values for her community. She writes in "The Poet as a Creator of Social Values" that the poet is a manipulator of symbols and language—images that have been planted by experience in the collective subconscious of a people. She believes that "the poet has the power to create new or intensified meaning and experience" and, depending on the visibility of the poet and the efficacy of the poetry itself, "create, preserve or destroy social values."[41]

However, even more than these conditions, the poet's power depends on the clarity of her vision, her ability to interpret human nature, and her willingness to speak in tongues that will confirm her vision. For Sanchez, poetry is "subconscious conversation." She says, "When I say something on stage, I make them remember similar experiences that they have not even brought up, but I bring them up and say look remember and people say, 'Yes, I remember.' " And given this process, "poetry is as much the work of those who understand it as those who make it."[42] Thus, when Sanchez eulogizes the Amherst student whose life ended prematurely, she is sending a voice among the people who hear and speak:

> There is nothing which does not
> come to an end
> And to live seventeen years is good
> in the sight of God.[43]

The cycle-of-life theme that provides the frame for "A Song of Praise" gets a deeper, subtler exploration in "Kwa mama zetu waliotuzaa." Significantly, the poem begins with the line, "death is a five o'clock door forever changing time," which first appeared in *Sister Son/ji,* a play written in 1970. By repeating the line, the poet emphasizes the consistency, the predictability, and the weight she attributes to this theme. According to critic Joyce Ann Joyce:

> This line along with the title of the poem echoes the "In the beginning/there was no end" of *Blues Book.* Just as Sister Son/ji reaches out to the audience and asks if they will "grab the day and make it stop," "Kwa mama zetu waliotuzaa" illustrates how the physical, temporal, historical reality becomes an embodiment of the spiritual. For if we grab the day and make it stop, we will see that death is a concrete reality (a five o'clock door) that rules the process of life. For the death of the natural world brings forth the birth of the spiritual (forever changing time) as Sister Son/ji learns.[44]

The lines that follow dramatically show the cyclic nature of life and ironically reveal the human attempt to still a process that is as unrelenting as waves against a shore:

> and it was morning without sun or shadow;
> a morning already afternoon. sky. cloudy with incense.
> and it was morning male in speech;
> feminine in memory.
> but i am speaking of everyday occurrences:
> of days unrolling bandages for civilized wounds;
> of guady women chanting rituals under a waterfall of stars;
> of men freezing their sperms in diamond-studded wombs;
> of children abandoned to a curfew of marble.[45]

The poem, whose title translates "for our mother who gave us birth," is at once a praise poem for the mothers (biological and spiritual) of black women and a eulogy for Shirley Graham DuBois, biographer, teacher and lecturer, whose career spanned over forty years and took her to Africa, Asia, and Europe. In the opening passages, the poet remembers her father's third wife, Geraldine Driver, a kind, caring Southern woman who was saddled with notions of her place and feared breaking loose to ride out her potential. Here, however, in memorializing her (she died of cancer in Detroit), Sanchez uses the symbolism of nature to represent continuity, growth, fruitfulness, and joy, and in effect, she undercuts the pain and unfulfillment that were hers in life:

> mother. i call out to you
> traveling up the congo. i am preparing a place for you:
> nite made of female rain
> i am ready to sing her song
> prepare a place for her
> she comes to you out of turquoise pain.
>
> restring her eyes for me
> restring her body for me
> restring her peace for me
>
> no longer full of pain, may she walk
> bright with orange smiles, may she walk
> as it was long ago, may she walk
>
> abundant with lightning steps, may she walk
> abundant with green trails, may she walk

abundant with rainbows, may she walk
as it was long ago, may she walk . . . [46]

For Shirley Graham DuBois, who was "a bearer of roots," who
taught the poet the truth of the African past, who "painted the day
with palaces," Sanchez, in broad sweeps of pantheism, calls up the
bells, Olokun (the goddess of the sea), the spirits of day and night. For
through their persistence, their repetitiveness, their predictability, they
reassure the poet of her mentor's continuity and her triumphal passage
to the land of the ancestors.

At several turns in the poem, the privileged perception cuts through
the eulogy:

as morning is the same as nite death and life are one.
. . . .

at the center of death is birth
. . . .

death is coming. the whole world hears
the buffalo walk of death passing thru the
archway of new life.[47]

From the very first metaphor, the poem is unified by the epigrams concerning death. Death is one with life and continuity; at its center is a
beginning.

The dimensions of Sanchez's Southern imagination become imposing in *Homegirls & Handgrenades*. Her fascination with time and the
past, her communion with nature, her reverence for the folk, her search
for identity and self-actualization through meaningful relationships,
and her intense spirituality born of a faith in roots and continuity predict the themes and metaphors that unify the book. With a language
pregnant with the images of war, armaments, and nuclear proliferation,
the poet suggests that love and the greening of the mind are the only
reasonable weapons in a world dangerously toying with annihilation.
In the most effective vignette in the volume, "Just Don't Never Give
Up on Love," the poet recounts her meeting with an eighty-four-year-old
woman who inveigled her to hear her message on the power of love:

". . . C'mon over here next to me. I wants to see yo' eyes up close.
You looks so uneven sittin' over there."

Did she say uneven? Did this old buddah splintering death say
uneven? Couldn't she see that I had one eye shorter than the other;
that my breath was painted on porcelain; that one breast crocheted
keloids under this white blouse?

I moved toward her though. I scooped up the years that had stripped me to the waist and moved toward her. And she called to me to come out, come out wherever you are young woman, playing hide and go seek with scarecrow men. I gathered myself up at the gateway of her confessionals.[48]

As Mrs. Rosalie Johnson talks with her about her husbands and love, the young woman cries for herself and "for all the women who have ever stretched their bodies out anticipating civilization and finding ruins." Mrs. Johnson's message is cathartic; by allowing the old woman's healing words to slough off the bitterness and fear built up from past relationships, she is again open to love.

Moving the urgency of her message to global relationships, she concludes the volume with "A Letter to Dr. Martin Luther King" and "MIA's." Though very different in form, they are companion pieces that share Sanchez's urge to articulate the democratic evils (racism/apartheid/imperialism) that stunt the spiritual growth of black youth, corrupt hope by gradualism, and stall freedom. On the occasion of Martin Luther King's fifty-fourth year (the poet addresses the slain leader as a living spirit), she declares anew a faith in the regenerative power of blackness, which eschews fear and moves toward "freedom and justice for the universe." The letter ends with an explosion of feeling as the poet, remembering the chanting of black South African women at the death of Stephen Biko, adopts the chant "Ke wa rona" (he is ours) and calls the roll of black deliverers:

... On this your 54th year, listen and you will hear the earth delivering up curfews to the missionaries and assassins. Listen. And you will hear the tribal songs.

Ayeeee	Ayooooo	Ayeee
Ayeeee	Ayooooo	Ayeee
Malcolm...		Ke wa rona
Robeson...		Ke wa rona
Lumumba...		Ke wa rona
Fannie Lou...		Ke wa rona
Garvey...		Ke wa rona
Johnbrown...		Ke wa rona
Tubman...		Ke wa rona
Mandela...		Ke wa rona
(free Mandela free Mandela)		
Assata...		Ke wa rona

As we go with you to the sun,
as we walk in the dawn, turn our eyes
Eastward and let the prophecy come true
and let the prophecy come true
    Great God, Martin, what a morning it will be![49]

In "MIA's (missing in action and other atlantas)," the datelines—
Atlanta, Johannesburg, El Salvador—serve to show the world of
oppression in microcosm, and the machinations that promote death
(murder / assassination / "redwhiteandblue death squads"). The centerpiece of the poem is a disturbingly accurate account of the death of
Biko. Here one is aware of the substantial capacity of the poet to work
with the ironic voice, which gains power by the incremental repetition
of "we did all we could for the man":

    sept. 13:
hear ye. hear ye. hear ye.
i regret to annouce that stephen
biko is dead. he has refused
food since sept. 5th. we did
all we could for the man.
he has hanged himself while sleeping
we did all we could for him.
he fell while answering our questions
we did all we could for the man.
he washed his face and hung him
self out to dry
we did all we could for him.
he drowned while drinking his supper
we did all we could for the man.
he fell
        hanged himself   starved
drowned himself
we did all we could for him.
it's hard to keep someone alive
who won't even cooperate.
hear ye.[50]

Whether conjuring up Stephen Biko, or the "youngblood / touching
and touched at random" in the killing fields of Atlanta, or the young
men with "their white togas covering their / stained glass legs" in Central America, she exhorts the men and women to harvest their share of
freedom.

201

In Sanchez's most recent volume, *Under a Soprano Sky,* she captures in the poem "for Black history month/February 1986" the essence of her Southern sensibility as she reflects on her visit to the Great Wall of China. As she "started to climb that long winding trail of history and survival,"[51] her thoughts turned to voices and visions that propelled history, demanded survival, and forged the cultural links of which continuity is made. Moving deeply within her culture, Sanchez "had to peel away misconceptions about Blacks." As she sang the blues, hummed the spirituals, explored the myths, and walked "a piece" down the road with Nat Turner, Douglass, Harriet Tubman, Garrison, John Brown, Martin Delany, Malcolm X, Rosa Parks, David Walker . . . her racial memory nourished in Southern soil bears fruit. Her sense of reality, her sense of history rejected Old Black Joe, one of the plantation tradition's favorite sons, "Sambo-hood," and Jim Crow. Her sense of history embraced Lady Day's voice as she sang of strange fruit and blood on the magnolia, embraced Robeson's voice as he sang of deep rivers and the quest of the soul for peace on the other side of Jordan or the Mississippi or the Ohio. Her sense of the past, her roots, her ostensibly Southern imagination has allowed her to keep sight of her vision, a vision of peace and community that was first conceived in the green days of an Alabama childhood.

SONIA SANCHEZ BIBLIOGRAPHY

BOOKS

Homecoming. Detroit: Broadside, 1969.
Liberation Poem. Detroit: Broadside, 1970.
We A BadddDDD People. Detroit: Broadside, 1970.
Ima Talken bout the Nation of Islam. Astoria, N.Y.: TruthDel. Corp., 1971.
It's a New Day (poems for young brothas and sistuhs). Detroit: Broadside, 1971.
Three Hundred and Sixty Degrees of Blackness Comin' at You. Ed. Sonia Sanchez. New York: 5X Publishing, 1972.
Love Poems. New York: Third Press, 1973.
The Adventures of Small Head, Square Head and Fat Head. New York: Third Press, 1973.
We Be Word Sorcerers: 25 Stories by Black Americans. Ed. Sonia Sanchez. New York: Bantam, 1973.
A Blues Book for Blue Black Magical Women. Detroit: Broadside, 1974.
I've Been a Woman: New and Selected Poems. Sausalito, Calif.: Black Scholar Press, 1978.

A Sound Investment: Short Stories for Young Readers. Chicago: Third World Press, 1980.

Crisis in Culture: Two Speeches by Sonia Sanchez. New York: Black Liberation Press, 1983.

homegirls & handgrenades. New York: Thunder's Mouth Press, 1984.

Under a Soprano Sky. Trenton, N.J.: Africa World Press, 1987.

PLAYS

The Bronx Is Next. In *Drama Review* 12 (Summer 1968).

Sister Son/ji. In *New Plays from the Black Theatre.* Ed. ED Bullins. New York: Bantam, 1969.

Uh, Uh; But How Do It Free Us. In *The New Lafayette Theatre Presents.* Ed. Ed Bullins. New York: Anchor, 1974.

Malcolm/Man Don't Live Here No Mo. Philadelphia, ASCUM Community Center, 1979.

I'm Black When I'm Singing, I'm Blue When I Ain't. Atlanta, OIC Theatre, 23 April 1982.

Gail Godwin and Her Novels

*

ANNE CHENEY

THE MANLESS LITTLE FAMILY: A BIOGRAPHICAL SKETCH

B Y THE AGE of five, Gail Godwin was settled in her "preschool occupation . . . [which] . . . consisted of being the adored Child on
whose behalf this family had been created." This small family included
her "elegant, feminine grandmother," Edna Rogers Krahenbuhl, the
widow of a Southern Railways employee; Kathleen Krahenbuhl Godwin, divorced from the charming but unreliable Mose Godwin; and
Gail. In 1942, women with careers were rare in Asheville, North Carolina. But Kathleen supported herself and her mother—and bought
Gail's clothes, storybook dolls, subscriptions to children's magazines—
with income from her reporter's job at the *Asheville Citizen-Times* and
from stories published in such magazines as *Love Short Stories*. Thus,
Godwin describes her "manless little family": "On weekend mornings
my mother sat at the typewriter in a sunny breakfast nook and wrote
stories about women, young women like herself, who after some difficulty necessary to the plot, got their men. In the adjoining kitchen, my
grandmother washed the breakfast dishes and kept asking, 'What do
you two think you could eat for lunch?' "[1]

As an only child, Kathleen Krahenbuhl had led a comfortable life,
riding the train on her father's passes and shopping almost daily for
clothes with her mother[2] (in *The Odd Woman*, Edith often shops with
her granddaughter at Blum's). Later, Kathleen earned her B.A. at Fur-
man College and then her M.A. in English at Chapel Hill, where "her
main problem had been choosing between men." Sometimes she had
five dates a day. But this dilemma was resolved one weekend in Selma,
North Carolina, as she sat on the porch. A handsome young bachelor,
who had hurt his ankle playing tennis, hobbled by. The limp so vexed
Kathleen's "nasty little dog" that he rushed out and bit Mose Winston

Godwin on his *good* leg. Kathleen and Mose were soon married.[3]

During the summer of 1937, the Godwins lived in Birmingham, Alabama. Kathleen was delighted that her husband had a job—even at her cousin's lake resort near the city. Here Mose spent his time "teaching tennis, being around in a pretty white suit, and making sure the guests were happy." On June 18, their daughter Gail was born. The Godwins moved to Durham, North Carolina, in the fall and then to Weaverville, North Carolina (next to Asheville), three years later.[4] A few years later, Mose Godwin moved out and resumed his old playboy ways.[5] Finally, Kathleen—a devout Episcopalian—felt compelled to file for divorce.[6]

By 1943, Gail Godwin was studying at home with her mother (she did not go to first grade), and Kathleen Godwin began to have some interesting assignments for the newspaper. She interviewed wounded soldiers returning from World War II, and she spent a day with Eleanor Roosevelt, who chagrined Asheville citizens by bringing along a black friend. Later, Kathleen used her college French to interview Béla Bartók.[7] Young Gail Godwin began to absorb two lessons from her mother: to meet deadlines and to have a "shapeliness" to her stories. She also observed her mother's being summoned to 48 Spruce Street every time Mrs. Wolfe "remembered something else about Tom"[8] (in 1981, Gail Godwin delivered an unpublished paper to the Modern Language Association entitled "Getting Away from Tom").

In 1944, Gail Godwin enrolled in the second grade at St. Genevieve's-of-the-Pines. Established in 1908 by French nuns, whose order is called Religious of Christian Education, St. Genevieve's provided Asheville's brighter and/or more affluent young ladies with a superb education. (The school was named for St. Genevieve, the patron saint of Paris, and the pine trees on the mountain ridge that encircles the city of Asheville.)[9] Early on, Gail Godwin began to distinguish herself as one of the top three students in her class of twenty to twenty-two. She excelled at languages (especially French), mathematics, and literature. The second of these students was "Prissy" Hursh, now of Cambridge, Massachusetts.[10]

The third top student was Margaret (Pat) Merchant,[11] the daughter of Lawrence Merchant, president of an established contracting firm, and Norma Merchant, a cultivated Southern lady—a lover of Edna St. Vincent Millay's poetry in college, a nurse before her marriage, the mistress of an immaculate, tasteful home, and a loving, demanding mother.[12] Immediately, Pat Merchant and Gail Godwin formed a friendship—which has now spanned four decades (Godwin dedicated *A Mother and Two Daughters* to Pat). Young Gail was fascinated by the comforts of the Merchant home on 94 Marlboro Road, particularly given her own family's financial limitations; Pat was intrigued by the "style" and culture of Gail's family, especially the "glamour" and independence of Kathleen Godwin. The girls began to spend time together after school and on weekends—studying; taking the bus downtown to Haywood Street, where all the expensive shops were then located; attending Girl Scout meetings, with Mrs. Merchant as troop leader. Later, Gail and Pat shared a desire to "escape" from the small town of Asheville.[13]

By 1949, St. Genevieve's had grown to six hundred students from forty states and several foreign countries. For a time, the school included a four-year college, where Kathleen taught. Alumnae became university professors and diplomats; an early graduate became a doctor; Miss America of 1962 had attended St. Genevieve's.[14]

In 1950, Sister Kathleen Winters became principal of St. Genevieve's, when Gail Godwin and Pat Merchant were eighth graders. Diminutive and perceptive, Sister Winters held a B.A. in English from the University of North Carolina and an M.A. in history from Boston College; she also earned summer session grants to study physics at Arizona State, communism at Vanderbilt, and Oriental studies at Hawaii.[15] Her wit and stubborn spirit recall her Irish ancestry. She became, as Gail Godwin said, "a formative influence on my life."[16] She describes Godwin's work as "energetic, highly organized" and proudly relates an incident that typifies a quickness and maturity unusual in a twelve year old. Every day, Sister Winters read to her students; one of the readings happened to be from Browning; a week or so later, Gail Godwin ended her essay with "a man's reach should exceed his grasp."

But Gail Godwin had her mischievous side. One Friday night, after seeing *Arsenic and Old Lace* with the other students, she dashed up a flight of stairs to the sleeping quarters, shouting, "Charge!" On the darkened top landing stood an older nun[17]—nearly frightened out of her habit. And there was the "reserved" side, pushing deep within herself, abetted by the petty snobberies of those girls with more money and less intellect. Later, Godwin wrote: "I was the poorest girl in the class, the one who could not fork up the twenty-five dollars for the eighth grade trip to Washington."[18] Sister Winters said that the amount was "more like seventy dollars." Grandmother Krahenbuhl sacrificed to help with tuition,[19] but there was no money for luxuries.

Thus, Gail Godwin's extended "manless little family" became complete with Sister Winters, whom she had not fictionalized overtly until *A Southern Family*. In *The Odd Woman*, Edna Rogers Krahenbuhl becomes Edith Dewar Barnstorff, and both Kitty Clifford Sparks, who teaches medieval history at the local college and attends Mass daily in *The Odd Woman,* and Lily Quick in *A Southern Family* are clearly based on Godwin's mother, Kathleen. In *A Mother and Two Daughters,* Nell Strickland is based on Norma Merchant. Pat Merchant Verhulst, who becomes Cate Strickland Galitsky, embodies the idealism of the 1960s: she marched on Washington and attended peace rallies; she has written 150 poems and an unpublished novel with a title borrowed from Bob Dylan, *You Know My Baby Will.* But Godwin has a little fun with her friend: Pat *never* dated an exterminator (or Termite King), nor was she ever jailed.[20] In *A Southern Family,* she reemerges as Julia Richardson Lowndes, the Southern historian who writes poems in her doggerel book. Women and the South remain at the center of Godwin's work, but some male characters began to enter her life and works.

By the sixth grade, her home on Charlotte Street[21] in Asheville had a new resident. An attractive, ambitious ex-GI had enrolled in Kathleen Godwin's romantic literature class. Edna Rogers Krahenbuhl did not approve of the suitor,[22] ten years her daughter's junior. Nevertheless, on June 19, 1948, Frank Cole married Kathleen at St. Mary's Episcopal Church, where Gail Godwin was confirmed on November 28, 1948.[23] In *The Odd Woman,* Frank Cole becomes Ray Sparks (the sparks ignite the coal?). Both men are contractors. Sparks lovingly calls Kitty his "Belle Dame Sans Merci." Eventually, they have three children: Emily, a law student (Franchelle Cole Millender is now an attorney); Jack (Tommy Cole); and, Ronnie (Rebel Cole). Godwin's novel, however, exaggerates the real-life tension between daughter and stepfather.[24] In *A Southern Family,* the Coles become the Quick family.

At the end of the spring term in 1952, Gail Godwin bid St. Genevieve's and Sister Winters farewell. Frank Cole was moving his family to Anderson, South Carolina.[25] There he would pursue the first of several jobs before he returned to Asheville in 1957 to found his own construction firm.[26] In 1953, the Cole family, which now included baby Franchelle, moved to Norfolk, Virginia. The next year, they settled across the river in Portsmouth. As graduation drew near in 1955, Gail Godwin and her mother talked about whether they should invite the man who abandoned them years ago to the ceremonies. They did, and the day was "dramatic": "My father floored everyone by showing up for my high school graduation. He had to introduce himself, as I had no idea who he was. I flung myself, weeping, into his arms and he invited me to come live with him.[27]"

From 1955 to 1957, Gail Godwin attended Peace Junior College in Raleigh, North Carolina, while she lived with her father and his second wife. Then, in the fall of 1957, she began her junior year on scholarship at the University of North Carolina at Chapel Hill. On January 8, 1958, the tragedy occurred. Mose Godwin had pointed a pistol at his head, but the gun misfired. The second shot killed him. He had put his head off the rug to avoid the need for dry cleaning. He did not leave a note.

Gail Godwin was unprepared for this loss: "Someone from the Dean of Women's office came and got me out of class and told me. I went back to class afterwards and took notes on the rest of the lecture, as I didn't know what else to do. It didn't sink in until a couple of weeks later, when I really went to pieces and had to go briefly for a stay in the University's psychiatric wing. I did my course work there and took my mid-terms on a bed next to a lady who was having shock treatments." She graduated in 1959, but twenty years elapsed before she grappled with the suicide in her fourth novel, *Violet Clay*.[28] Uncle Ambrose Clay, who commits suicide at forty-nine, remains her best, most sympathetic male character.

In 1959, Gail Godwin became a reporter for the *Miami Herald*, but the bureau chief fired her in August 1960 for "embellishing stories." Immediately, she married a *Herald* photographer, Douglas Kennedy, but they were divorced three months later.[29] (Several years after the divorce, Kennedy was shot in the back by American Marines—a case of "friendly fire"—while he was photographing fighting in the Panama Canal Zone. He was consequently crippled and later married his nurse.[30]) Godwin then moved to London, where she was a travel advisor for the American Embassy from 1962 to 1965. Much of the material in *Mr. Bedford and the Muses* (1983) is drawn from her European days. Nineteen sixty-five marked her marriage to Dr. Ian Marshall, a psychotherapist and father of a beautiful but disturbed three-year-old son. This marriage, which served as the basis for *The Perfectionist,* ended after a year.[31]

Back in the States, Godwin became a student at the University of Iowa, arguably the best school for aspiring writers in America. Here she earned her M.A. in English in 1968 and her Ph.D. in 1971, and she returned as a teacher in the writers' workshop in 1972. In Iowa City, she met two writers who have influenced her work. Kurt Vonnegut, her teacher, wrote: "[She] started out with considerable stature. What remained was simply to put on a little weight, a little muscle and gain some wisdom." One of her favorite classmates was John Irving. Later, as she was writing *Violet Clay* and he, *The World According to Garp,* they exchanged chapters as they wrote them. As Godwin recalls: "It was funny. In my first draft I started off with Violet's birth, and in his he began with Garp as a grown man. . . . He advised me to change mine, to start when Violet is mature enough for the reader to be interested in her, and he was right. Then later he decided to start his novel with Garp's birth, and that decision made the book."[32]

In 1972, Gail Godwin began to share her life and her home with Robert Starer, to whom she dedicated *The Odd Woman* and *Violet Clay*. A large man with a deep laugh, Starer is a pianist, classical composer,[33] and former Julliard professor. In their home near Woodstock, New York, she spends her days writing in her journal, working on her current novel, cooking gourmet dinners, and reading such authors as James, Lawrence, and Austen. In the afternoon, Godwin and Starer used to drive into town to swim at an indoor pool. The woods that surrounded their first house provided ample stalking territory for Gingie, their large tomcat,[34] to whom Godwin dedicated *Mr. Bedford* and who died in 1985. In early 1984, Godwin completed her sixth novel, *The Finishing School*, published in February 1985. The advance for her seventh novel, *A Southern Family*, published in September of 1987, enabled the couple to build a new home in Woodstock, complete with its own swimming pool.

Gail Godwin has become a significant voice in Southern and contemporary American literature. Her travels in England, Denmark, Spain, and the United States; her teaching posts at Vassar, Columbia, and Iowa; her knowledge of music, art, and literature—all have added polish and depth to her work. But as she returns to her "manless little family" in her novels, her most memorable characters (with the exception of Uncle Ambrose Clay) are women. Many can trace their lineage to the extended family of women in Asheville, North Carolina, the most remarkable being Kathleen Krahenbuhl Godwin Cole. Of the many gifts she bestowed on her daughter, the most important was an unconditional belief in her "adored Child." As Godwin writes, "She always took it for granted I would be a novelist."[35]

Gail Godwin has also become a significant voice in Southern literature. She has inherited from Faulkner, Welty, and Wolfe a love of the land, a "sense of place." *A Mother and Two Daughters, A Southern Family,* and nearly half of *The Odd Woman* are set in her native North Carolina, while the heroines of her other four novels grew up in Charleston, Fredericksburg, the mountains of North Carolina, and an unspecified Southern locale. A character in Wolfe's fiction would observe the beauty, the power of the mountains; a Welty heroine would see and smell the pine needles on the Natchez Trace. But Godwin's heroines have become a bit too numbed by their urban adulthoods to react spontaneously to the land per se. Nevertheless, to them, the South and its lush landscape represent beauty, permanance, and unequivocal love.

In Godwin's fictional world, the family is as close, as respectful of ancestors (especially grandmothers), at times as suffocating as any clan in Faulkner, Wolfe, and many of Welty's short stories. Problems arise between stepparents and children, whose uneasy unions lack the strength of Southern "blood ties": the young wife is tormented by her brattish three-year-old stepson in *The Perfectionists;* the young professor is belittled and bedeviled by her materialistic stepfather in *The Odd Woman*. Godwin's marriages are generally troubled, but they rarely have cold, resigned fury playing beneath the surface—as does that of Eliza and W. O. Gant in *Look Homeward, Angel*. When the going gets tough, the contemporary Godwin heroine gets a divorce.

Although Gail Godwin values her Southern and European (especially Swiss) ancestry, she is very much a Southern writer of the new generation. Legally and socially, the white Southern family has been dominated by men; in antebellum times, of course, wives, slaves, and livestock bore the same relationship to the male master—as property. But Godwin's families consist of strong women and few men—more a result of her early life than of any feminist vision.

Traditional Christianity does not affect the Godwin heroine as profoundly or overtly as it did earlier Southern protagonists. Godwin and her characters would not concur with W. J. Cash's belief in *The Mind of the South* (1941) that Southern religion is self-denying "puritanism." Her characters are rarely of Scotch-Irish descent, which Cash and Cratis Williams stress as norms in the Southern and Appalachian past, nor are they usually Presbyterians as are Wolfe's Gants or several characters in Faulkner's *Light in August*.

Unlike earlier male Southern writers, Godwin does not usually see the sexuality of women as a matter of religious or moral anguish. In *The Sound and the Fury* (1929), Caddy Compson's promiscuity leads to diverse persecutions by her brother Jason, who takes away her child; the forward action of the novel takes place during Easter weekend. In *Lie Down in Darkness* (1951), Peyton Loftis's promiscuity culminates in her brilliant, tortured monologue, then her suicidal plunge in Harlem. Illicit sex was the only religious or moral transgression Caddy or Peyton committed. Godwin's women do not deal with the Episcopal belief that divorce involves breaking a covenant with God. When one of Godwin's heroines has an abortion, her reservations are intellectual, not religious.

Within the Godwin canon, however, religion is a persistent but usually subdued theme. The heroine's mother in *The Odd Woman* goes to church each morning, lighting candles for her children. Four novels later, in *A Southern Family,* she has evolved, as her friend Sister Patrick says, into "not an angel of mercy, but an angel of dignity" to the elderly whom she visits in nursing homes and, as her daughter, Clare, says, into a believer in God, not art. In Godwin's last five novels, each heroine has been raised and probably confirmed in the Episcopal church, though none attend services regularly as an adult. Four of her heriones went to private schools, usually Catholic, whose descriptions—complete with pine trees—match St. Genevieve's. Godwin's educated women seem to find more *intellectual* than emotional power in religion, in the Episcopal and Catholic churches—with their long histories; rich liturgies; quiet, aesthetic services, heightened by the aroma of incense and the music of Bach.

The 1960s civil rights movement improved race relations in the South and thus enabled Godwin and other younger writers to depict blacks as a part of a more egalitarian society. In 1941, Cash had described the white Southern male as obsessed by the "hypnotic Negro-fixation," an "ancient fixation on Negro," and "the taboo on the white woman"—attitudes even the least-prejudiced Southern writers could not wish away, if they were to write honestly. Carson McCullers's brilliant Dr. Copeland is paralyzed by white social rejection and self-doubt because he cannot protect his children. His son, Willie, is jailed for a minor infraction, denied due process, and loses both feet to gangrene because of poor prison conditions. Faulkner's Ringo, who Colonel Sartoris says is brighter than his own son, can receive no formal education, while Bayard Sartoris studies law.

Certainly a post-1960s woman, Dr. Renee Peverall-Watson is Godwin's most memorable black character. She has a Harvard Ph.D., owns a renovated historic home and a large, unruly dog, loves Chopin, and is the best friend of the heroine's sister in *A Mother and Two Daughters*. Her companion, Calvin Edwards, is a television producer, a fellow "upwardly mobile pilgrim," a man usually at peace with his white neighbors. But Godwin is too principled a writer to force a false utopia. For many years, Azalea Clark, another black character in *A Mother and Two Daughters,* has been the housekeeper and subservient friend of a Mountain City grande dame, who will give her "anything but the minimum wage." The heroine of *The Odd Woman* gives her student, Portia, inflated grades because she is black. With no loss of verisimilitude, though, Godwin could have included a Renee or Calvin, a black professional, in *A Southern Family* with its 1983–84 setting; in 1985, North Carolina's neighboring state of Virginia elected L. Douglas Wilder as the first black lieutenant governor since Reconstruction.

Thus, Gail Godwin shares a "sense of place" and some ideas about the Southern family with earlier writers. She becomes, however, a member of the new generation in her views of woman's place in the family, Southern religion, and race. She has studied the novels of Faulkner, McCullers, O'Connor, Walker Percy, Wolfe, and other Southern masters. She absorbed the best of European culture from the nuns in Asheville. She cherished the independence and love of her "manless little family." But she is her own person. She is innovative, intelligent. Like Justin Stokes in *The Finishing School,* Godwin remains "fluid," continues to grow, and is in no danger of "congealing."

FROM MAJORCA TO MOUNTAIN CITY: THE NOVELS

At the age of thirty-three, Gail Godwin published her first novel, *The Perfectionists* (1970). Joyce Carol Oates dubbed it "an engrossing and mysterious first novel [and] a perfectly structured story." Oates found Godwin's work "intelligent" and praised her as "a young writer of exciting talent."[36] Robert Scholes in the *Saturday Review* went further: "*The Perfectionists* is . . . too good . . . to be patronized as a 'first novel.' " He compared Godwin's work to Jane Austen and D. H. Lawrence; he admired the "complex relationship" of this "excellent piece of work, shrewdly observed and carefully crafted."[37] At the onset of her career, then, the critics noted the "shapeliness" of plot that marks all seven of her novels—part of her legacy from her mother. Godwin's work is also enriched by her sense of humor and her catholic knowledge of the arts and such diverse fields as psychology and business.

Scholes, however, did fault Godwin for her "resolute femininity," whereby she creates interesting, sympathetic women characters but men who are "all fatuous and self-centered."[38] Indeed, Godwin does not have a compelling man serve as a major character until her fourth novel. One might wish for more than silhouetted male characters in the psychotherapist, lawyer, and art historian of the first three novels, but women—not men—in search of meaning are the subject of Godwin's earlier novels.

The heroine of Godwin's novels is prototypically bright, attractive, educated, and witty. She is twenty-five to forty-two years old and is searching for happiness, academic or artistic achievement, love, respect, or, more generally, meaning in life. She is a professional—an artist, a writer, a professor, an actress—or is married to doctor or lawyer. Reared in the South, she is ambivalent about Southern values. To test these values, she leaves. The itinerary of Godwin's seven novels forms a sweeping, then narrowing arc from a Carolina setting—Europe, California, the Midwest, New York, then the South, then up to New York, then back to the South. The heroine gains a necessary tension, a painful fragmentation in parental or marital relations, often artistic or academic self-doubts, which are resolved if and when the heroine goes home—to the South.

Godwin has often been called a feminist writer, a label she dislikes. Marilynn J. Smith considers her more recent novels "more feminist."[39] In truth, the changes in Godwin's portrayals of women have been an accurate barometer of feminist concerns in this country from the late 1960s to the present. Her first two novels depict women to whom *work* is not especially important; they are trapped in unfortunate marriages to men who are insensitive and "chauvinistic." These women are victims. By 1974, in her third novel, Godwin presents the "odd" or single woman, who teaches, attends MLA conventions, and seeks love and enlightenment from Gabriel Weeks. In Godwin's last four novels, in 1978, 1982, 1985, and 1987, women now are not necessarily victims of men or society; the power to change lies within women themselves. Violet Clay is an artist, committed to painting something of more value than Gothic paperback covers. Cate S. Galitsky seeks a more permanent position as an English professor and finds qualified happiness with a rough but intriguing businessman. Justin Stokes is an established actress, who pauses to sort out the meaning of a troubling adolescent summer. Clare Campion is a novelist, intent on deepening her fiction, on understanding the enigmatic life and violent death of the brother she left behind during her ascent to national prominence.

Unlike some other modern American novelists, Godwin produces books on a dependable schedule. She learned well another lesson from Kathleen Krahenbuhl Godwin Cole: to meet deadlines. Since 1970, Godwin has had a novel or short story collection published every two years. The only exception was 1980 during the writing of *A Mother and Two Daughters,* a manuscript double the length of her earlier novels. But her reliability—surely an agent's or publisher's dream—does nothing to diminish her artistry. In a 1983 interview, she said: "I've proved to myself that I've got perseverance. What I'm after is the glow; I'm after the art."[40] Some years earlier, she had written: "My task is simple. 'Try to be one of the people on whom nothing is lost,' urged Henry

James. I try. I listen more than I used to. I force myself to be more adventurous. . . . Anecdotes, experiences, gossip, dreams . . . I try to be open to them all."[41]

Set in Majorca, Spain, *The Perfectionists* chronicles the one-week vacation of a recently married American woman, Dane Tarrant Empson, and her psychotherapist husband, Dr. John Empson. They have brought with them John's precocious, illegitimate three-year-old son, Robin, and one of John's patients, Penelope. As usual, Godwin describes the setting with an artist's sensibility: the eastern coast of Majorca, Cala d'Or, had "colors . . . raw and primeval: scalding azure sky, burnt sienna earth, leaves of dusty green." John has set goals for all in his party: Penelope is to realize that she is "normal"—easily accomplished by her amour with a married Dutch painter. But then her most pathological behavior has been a "crack up" in the jam, jelly, and marmalade section of Fortnum's.

John Empson's own goals in Majorca are to write and to work toward a more perfect union (hence the title of the book). His research for his psychological writing leads him to conclude that "the basic pattern of human thought [is] in the shape of a snowflake" and to venture from the hotel at night to have a spiritual and sexual relationship with a tree. Oates's puzzle about whether John Empson is "perhaps a genius, perhaps a fool"[42] becomes easier to solve as he explores marriage. He and Dane read Yeats and Count Keyserling's *Book of Marriage*. He keeps a diary about the progress of the marriage. He seeks "total truth" and cautions Dane not to attack the "tender shoots of me." One is cheered when Dane mentally compares sex to "nuns, when their hair is being cut off." As one reviewer notes: "John . . . will discuss anything at any time, and only wants to share, and Dane is buckling under the strain."[43]

The heart of this novel, however, is Dane Empson's search for meaning—in her abstraction of a marriage, in her imposed relationship with her stepson, and, though critics have missed it, her distant link to her father. She is twenty-seven years old (though age is not stated in the novel, Godwin married Ian Marshall at twenty-seven). Prior to her marriage, Dane is a writer for a magazine; she meets John while covering his lecture to a Mensa chapter. She is genuinely attracted to his mind and his "rare talent of explaining people to themselves." Only gradually does she realize that intellect is not enough. They do not share private jokes; he does not understand her need for privacy; they never argue, they "discuss." Near the end of the novel, she inspires pathos as she thinks: "How could she leave John? Who else could footnote her dreams?"

Robin Empson is demonic and beautiful in the tradition of the troubled children of Henry James. John's tacit insistence that Dane nurture the child speeds the erosion of their marriage. (John's standing on the "crumbling ruins of the old fort" at the end of the novel indicates the Empsons' ultimate course). A mute violence envelopes the child: he enjoys a game in which he hits John, who pretends to be a cringing dog. Robin shrieks and turns red when disappointed; he wets his bed; he fixes his "icy blue-eyed stare" on all around him; he sleeps with his eyes open; unaccountably, he kicks his kindly riding instructor in the groin; he refuses to speak to his stepmother. On a practical level, the parent-child relationship here is a travesty, because John will not grant Dane, the stepmother, authority to discipline the child. John reasons with him as though he were an adult.

When Dane finally beats Robin till her hands sting, she is only superficially meting out tardy punishments. More symbolically, she is trying to force life and feeling into the wordless replica of the glib father. Earlier, she sees Robin as "a small divinity, utterly untouchable." John had studied for the Jesuit priesthood (a testament to his intellect), but he could not make the commitment, perhaps emotional, to enter the order, a situation that causes a coldness between him and his mother. Godwin foreshadows the Gabriel Weeks dilemma in *The Odd Woman* as she has Dane muse: "What would it be like to make love with an angel? Cool, pure, remote." Dane Tarrant Empson, then, fails to find meaning in John or his son because they lack the human qualities of passion, warmth, and love.

Ironically, Dane derives meaning from the most practical, realistic character in the novel: her Southern father. Mentioned only nine times in the novel, Captain Tarrant is the antithesis of his son-in-law: he is "stodgy, but comforting"; he prizes neatness, discipline, duty; his heroes are the stoic philosopher Marcus Aurelius and General Robert E. Lee. His book, *The Unsung Brothers Tift,* tells of Civil War shipbuilders who dynamite their new ship to prevent Union capture. In Dane's first flashback to the captain, he hires an exterminator: hence, he straightforwardly has the "bugs" removed from their house (and their lives). We learn that when Dane was three, her mother left her father, who simply put his energies into caring for his daughter:

It was a sunny Saturday morning in spring. While Dane watched through the window and saw her mother put her suitcases into a big car, helped by a big, jolly-looking man, her father went from room to room collecting pairs of shoes—his and Dane's. . . . "Do you know what day this is?" he called. . . . Her favorite event of the week was this very time. . . . "Shoe polishing day!" she cried, running to her father.

Had Dane Empson recalled her father's values, she might not have married an intellectual bully and boor. As a single woman, she enjoys the culture and history of London—and her independence. She has a flat on Cheyne Walk with window seats, bay windows, and velvet curtains; she visits Trafalgar Square and reads the London *Times;* she has friends in the American Embassy. She has a good job as a writer for a magazine, which she quits immediately upon marriage. On Majorca, Dane dreams that her father has died in "dryest Italy," where nothing grows. Perhaps then Dane realized that the wasteland was not Italy, or England; rather, the wasteland was the soul of a man who presumed to believe that human perfection—especially in the absence of human love and warmth—was possible.

Glass People (1972) is Godwin's allegory of striking beauty that denies a woman her freedom. Joyce Carol Oates deems it "a formally executed, precise, and altogether professional short novel."[44] Anatole Broyard considers it a breakthrough, a "good novel . . . for contemporary woman's 'new consciousness' " and more than "a well-written surface story of a beautiful woman who makes an abortive bid for freedom."[45] Another reviewer says the "short novel . . . seems a minor literary feat" and praises the "stunning last few chapters, when the husband literally transforms Francesca into a Byzantine madonna. . . ."[46] But *Glass People* has its detractors, including the *New Yorker:* "Miss Godwin is clearly capable of writing good fiction, but . . . her characters [seem] childish or somewhat demented."[47] Indeed, *Glass People* is the only unsatisfying of Godwin's seven novels, a work atypical of such a talented writer.

In 1972, *Ms.* magazine was in its first year of publication; Gloria Steinem, Kate Millett, and Germaine Greer were media names, and "I am Woman" became an anthem as surely as had "We Shall Overcome" a decade earlier. But Godwin insists that her second novel was not a feminist work: "I wrote *Glass People* in 1970–1971, before the media had taken up The Women's Movement. I was at the time studying at Iowa for my Ph.D. comprehensives in English, and one of my specialties was allegories. This meant reading lots of allegorical poetry, prose, and fairy tales. *Glass People* was supposed to be a modern allegory about beauty and freedom, perhaps with Beauty and the Beast as an inspiration. (One scholar, so far, has caught this: Karen C. Gaston.) The initial draft had a sci-fi element, which my editor at Knopf asked me to take out. I did reluctantly (he wouldn't publish the book unless I did), and I have felt sorry ever since."[48]

Francesca Fox Bolt, age twenty-five, is the beautiful, bored, none too bright protagonist of the novel. Growing up in the North Carolina mountains,[49] she is adored by her beautiful mother, Kate, who teaches her to *shop*—the only skill Francesca ever attains—and her wealthy father, who unceremoniously dies when Francesca is eighteen. The two women speedily squander his estate on travel, jewels, clothes. But their aimless, opulent lives are saved when the affluent Jonathan appears, sends Francesca on a trip to Amsterdam because she "likes" Van Gogh, and marries Kate. Then Jonathan's friend, Cameron Bolt, a district attorney from California, visits; within two years, he marries Francesca for her astonishing beauty. She marries him because she has little to do after graduation from a local college, where she took "appreciation" courses in music, theater of the absurd, and astronomy.

In California, Francesca feels "frozen, paralyzed" by marriage. She imposes meaning on her life by tweezing the hairs from her legs every other day. Cameron does all the cooking and cleaning, since he does not want Francesca to mar her beauty, which he, as a candidate for attorney general, needs. He suggests that she visit her mother (now twice widowed) to dispel her ennui. She then flies to North Carolina, via New York, where she discovers her formerly chic, doting mother now pregnant, poor, taciturn, and married to a natural foods enthusiast. In the mountains, Francesca sunbathes and is frightened by a snake.

On her return flight, Francesca meets an attractive man named Mike, who spirits her off to a La Guardia motel. Francesca believes she will leave Cameron and get a job, so Mike moves her to a run-down hotel in the mid-Fifties. In New York, Francesca shows some sparks of autonomy. A *Village Voice* ad leads to a job for M Evans, a lesbian writer with a shaved head; she cleans M's foul apartment and pays her bills. But Francesca becomes seriously ill, and Cameron comes to care for her. Later, he takes her to Bergdorf's, where he buys her a designer original, encrusted with semiprecious stones. As she looks in the triple mirror, she *becomes* the Byzantine Madonna of the dress—an experience which somehow propels her to return to California. As the novel ends, she is pregnant with Mike's child, whom Cameron will be honored to raise.

In *Glass People,* marriage is stifling for women but useful to men. Francesca is "paralyzed," while Cameron will become attorney general. He also delivers a gratuitous monologue on marriage as a "sacrament."

Women are viewed as "sex objects"—or in Francesca's case, a fragile "glass person," a goddess, a Madonna. Men are insensitive, true of Cameron, except in his job: he champions the Crystal Gardens, an outdoor "crash pad" for drug users; he cares about his constituents; he works on his speeches. He is a lover of Bach and Dürer.

The allegory of Beauty vanquishing Freedom, however, is not the problem in this novel. Sara Blackburn writes, "The author . . . doesn't give us much to care about. . . . Are we really to root for blank-minded Francesca to break free, when her author has promised us throughout that she's totally incapable of doing so?"[50] Francesca is afraid of telephone operators; she asks Mike, "How does a person go about getting a job?"; she drifts into relationships—with Cameron, Mike, M Evans. This book suffers especially when compared with Joan Didion's *Play It as It Lays* (1970), in which the heroine seems equally catatonic. But there is a difference. Maria Wyeth has real concerns at stake: a retarded child whom she futilely loves, a waning career as a film actress, an unwanted abortion, dead parents who gave her solid values. As she drives the freeways with no clear destination—the counterpart of Francesca's hair tweezing—Maria has *reason* to be depressed.

Thus, Francesca Fox Bolt fails to find meaning in California or New York. The South is usually a repository of solid values, love, and permanence for Godwin. Francesca is loved until she is twenty in her North Carolina mountain home but is imbued with oddly materialistic values. Unlike the heroines of two later novels, she does not gain nurturance from her mother on her adult trip home. Late in the novel, she says that Francesca Fox was a name in which she took pride. Perhaps she should have emulated the smart, swift mountain fox and realized that she should bolt—for self-knowledge, from marriage. Perhaps Godwin should have written about real, not glass, people.

In *The Odd Woman* (1974), Godwin returns to her typical heroine—as bright and incisive as Dane Empson—and permits Dr. Jane Clifford, thirty-two, a long visit (seven of the eighteen chapters) to North Carolina.[51] Doris Betts praises the book for "its intelligence and verbal richness.[52] Lore Dickstein of the *New York Times* compares the novel to "the best of Doris Lessing and Margaret Drabble" and adds that "Godwin's prose is elegant, full of nuance and feeling, and sparkling with ironic humor.[53] The *New York Review of Books* states that "Gail Godwin's quiet, canny writing presents the awareness of an intelligent woman without sentimentalizing it."[54] Others admired the "brilliant opening stream of thoughts,"[55] the maturity and intelligence,[56] and her "awareness of human loneliness."[57] A few reviewers seem to forget that the heroine is a university professor: the *New Yorker* faults Godwin for "dialogue . . . couched in flat, dull universityese";[58] the *Times Library Supplement* considers the novel "exceedingly literary and allusive."[59] Only novelist Larry McMurtry is nasty: "I have reviewed more than a dozen Iowa City novels in the last 15 years and the task has left me with an abiding urge to go and explode several canisters of laughing gas in the English building's solemn and serious halls."[60]

In some respects, Godwin's third novel prefigures her most popular work, *A Mother and Two Daughters*. In both novels, the protagonist is an untenured English professor at a Midwestern university; she is single and attractive; a death in the family prompts her return to her Southern home; there she enjoys the near-perfect love of her mother, a reunion with her younger sister, and memories of her elegant grandmother. But the novels differ. *The Odd Woman* is partly based on Godwin's own family,[61] whereas the seed of *A Mother and Two Daughters* was a 1977–78 Merchant "family squabble" that Pat Merchant Verhulst described to Godwin.[62]

The Odd Woman begins and ends in Jane Clifford's apartment in a university town "much like Urbana, Illinois."[63] During her bouts with insomnia, she thinks of her black student, Portia, to whom she has ironically given a grade higher than she deserves, and of her colleagues and friends. Jane's night thoughts wander to what has become the central concern of the novel: "Perhaps she would write the Dickens article. Play the academic game and pose as a 'professor' while secretly pursuing her real profession: researching her salvation."

She researches her salvation in the story of George Eliot's unwedded, contented life with George Henry Lewes. She rereads the book she will teach her women's studies class, George Gissing's *The Odd Woman* (1893), whose characters "think" and "come to horrible ends . . . but . . . keep track of themselves so beautifully along the way." But Jane Clifford does not find her salvation in the frozen flatlands of the Midwest—or of her profession. Instead, she must seek the grail in the South and New York.

The one-week odyssey is set in motion by news of the death of Edith Dewar Barnstorff, Jane's beautiful, patrician grandmother. Jane flies home for the funeral and later helps her mother, Kitty, sort through Edith's belongings, including fifteen pairs of white gloves. With Jane's romantic sensibility—her stepfather is a "villain," and her married lover is named Gabriel—she cannot see that her salvation could be found in the unconditional love of Edith and Kitty. As a child, Jane detested the Pinner School for Young Ladies, so Edith shortly transferred her to a local convent school, run by caring French nuns. When Kitty married Ray Sparks, Edith allowed the girl to spend weeknights at her apartment. Often Edith would put aside her sewing or reading as Jane studied and would "brood at her granddaughter from the shadows in her own study of possessive love." Jane understands her mother's immersion in medieval history but not her religious mysticism or her attendant love for her daughter. Instead, Jane the romantic continues to "research" Great Aunt Cleva Dewar, who in 1905 ran away to New York with the villain of a melodrama, *The Fatal Wedding,* returned in 1906 in a coffin, and left an infant girl as her legacy. This subplot exemplifies Jane Clifford's Southern sense of the history, the continuum of the family.

Two days after the funeral, Jane flies to New York to meet Gabriel Weeks, her married lover and author of *Lessons on Love by Three Pre-Raphaelite Painters.* She first saw him at an MLA convention; they are now trysting for the fourteenth time in two years; she loves him for "his refusal to deal in finite concerns" and for his lovemaking, which reminds her of angels. If possible, Gabriel Weeks is more exhausting than John Empson of *The Perfectionists:* he is always punctual; he dislikes room service; he has accumulated eleven shoe boxes of index cards, notes for his second book; he is given to such statements as "The self is like a great warehouse, where we can go and take whatever we need— or like a library. . . . " When he begins to visit museums and take meals with a colleague from his own university, Jane pursues other activities.

Her trip to Saks is funny and "harrowingly real."[64] Jane finally buys a dress to appease the saleslady and escapes to the library, where she researches *The Fatal Wedding.* By chance, she discovers the actor's name in the phone book, calls, and goes to his apartment. Hugo Von Vorst, the villain, becomes Godwin's best adult male character so far. He is ninety and sprightly; he lives with his cat, Ethel Barrymore; he gives Jane a plant, Drambuie, and a kiss. With relish, he describes one of his favorite roles: "I dragged poor Nancy round the stage by the hair . . . I dragged her round again. . . . Then I . . . dashed her brains out. . . . " More seriously, he adds, "Melodrama is the naturalism of the dream life."

Abruptly, Jane leaves New York. Somehow she has learned that her salvation does not lie with angels—who categorize love in books. Later Jane discovers that Great Aunt Cleva eloped with a good man, not with the villain Van Vorst, so her quest is still unfulfilled. Jane Clifford is not "increasingly tiresome,"[65] nor are she and her story "disorganized."[66] She is too eager to organize, to footnote; she reads widely but misses nuances, especially in her family and friends. She does not envision Gabriel as weak and intellectually lazy. She only observes Ray Sparks's manipulation of his wife and home and his "twangy" accent; she does not pause to consider how a childhood of Appalachian poverty can make a man (or woman) hoard woolen shirts, candy, and bread; keep the house too hot; and niggle over phone bills. Jane Clifford is a finely sketched study in loneliness and of the "odd," or single, life. But she must learn to look beyond her Victorian and romantic books—and her own ordered life—to find the loneliness in others.

Edith Dewar Barnstorff, a widow for many years, had a recurring dream in which she missed a train (death) that her husband Hans rode. Edith's passion, which transcends death, would surely have enabled her to understand those hungers in her granddaughter. And therein Jane would have found her Southern "roots," her grail—polished by Edith's white gloves and lighted by Kitty's candles.

Violet Clay (1978), a contemporary portrait of the artist as a young woman, ranks with *The Finishing School* as one of Godwin's finest novels. Susan Shreve of the *Washington Post* writes, "*Violet Clay* is about the integrity of work, the responsibility of the artist to his talent," adding that Godwin is "among the best fiction writers in this generation."[67] Comparing Godwin to Margaret Drabble, Frances Taliaferro of *Harper's* deems the novel an "unpretentious exploration of the creative process" and calls Godwin "a very good novelist indeed."[68] In the *Saturday Review,* John Fludas finds Godwin "one of our major novelists" and praises "the novel within Godwin's novel," *Capriccio* by Violet's Uncle Ambrose, a "flash of greatness."[69] Others admire her wit,[70] her "unsentimental and observant style . . . and crisp prose,"[71] and, as usual, her portrayals of women.[72] A few have quibbles. The *Times Literary Supplement* thinks "Miss Godwin is more critic than novelist,"[73] and John Leonard of the *New York Times* is troubled that nearly "everybody in *Violet Clay* sings, plays the piano or the oboe or the phonograph. . . ."[74]

Set in New York in 1975, the novel opens as Violet Clay, thirty-two and a native of South Carolina, learns within a single day that she is fired and that her beloved uncle has committed suicide. Since she was orphaned as an infant, Violet has shared a "symbiotic bond"[75] with Uncle Ambrose Clay. Not only is he, as her friend Milo says, "the nearest thing you had to a father," but Violet feels that Ambrose's career as a writer somehow portends hers as an artist. At twenty-three, Violet had arrived in New York to become a painter. Instead, she succumbs to a "nine-year-long Era of Compromise" at Harrow House, where she paints book covers of Gothic heroines fleeing from villains. In the two-month forward action of the book, Violet Clay leaves for her uncle's funeral upstate in Plommet Falls, moves into his cabin there, and finally becomes a serious artist with her oil sketch *Suspended Woman,* which a Manhattan gallery leases for a national tour.

Through numerous effective flashbacks, Godwin depicts Violet's New York years. In her first week in the city, Uncle Ambrose takes his niece to the Top of the Sixes in the "sweet lemon-colored air of spring." As they drink and talk at dusk, Violet thinks: "There below was the city I had come to conquer. . . . Slowly the island of Manhattan turned pink, then gray, then blue. . . . The lights began to go on. One here, a whole string there, as an entire floor of a skyscraper suddenly came ablaze, or a suspension bridge outlines itself. . . . I would stare hard at a certain building, willing a light to come on . . . and it would!" Within weeks, Violet becomes a part of her New York world: Washington Square, the Sheridan Square bookstore, Madison Avenue, coffeehouses, the corner bar, brownstones. In Greenwich Village, she meets Elvira, a pornographic painter, who owns a thousand-dollar Shih Tzu. Violet's lover, Jake, plays the oboe and pours sherry on her head. Her hairdresser, Michel, has a poodle named Beatrice. In the *New York Times* (which occasionally gives Godwin mixed reviews), she reads a review of a brass recital by nude women.

Sometimes Violet pauses in the happy chaos of New York, with its exotic dogs and musicians, to remember her Southern childhood. Only in the love of fine clothes does her grandmother resemble Edna Rogers Krahenbuhl. Otherwise, Mrs. Clay is an alcoholic widow, living in a heavily mortgaged "antebellum mansion on the Battery, one of the most prestigious sections of Charleston," and still ruing her exchange of a beginning career as a concert pianist for marriage to an "antique poor lawyer."[76] But Grandmother Clay is not the most important influence from her Southern past.

Eight times in the novel, Violet recalls Pine Hollow School for Girls (St. Genevieve's-of-the-Pines) in the "mountains of North Carolina," where she received a fine education. Here she also absorbed a sense of self and habits of discipline—traits that might have saved Uncle Ambrose from his suicide. Part of her "search for meaning" entails trying to understand Uncle Ambrose Clay, who represents the South to Violet. But the core of Violet's "search" is the quest for maturity as an artist.

A study in creativity, *Violet Clay* explores the reasons for her paralysis. As several gallery owners tell her in 1966, she is a representational painter in an age of abstraction. Violet experiments with different techniques, various media (oil, tempera, watercolors), diverse subjects, light angles, textures, colors. But Violet's problem is not one of technique. As early as the fifth grade, she had become the "class artist." By twenty-three, she had a deep, intimate knowledge of art history, from Dürer to Bosch to Picasso and Braque. Wisely, Godwin juxtaposes Violet's problem—a lack of faith in her imagination and in herself—with the creative dilemmas of two writers.

Milo Hamilton, tall, slim, and thirty-five, is Violet's constant and platonic friend. When she learns of Uncle Ambrose's suicide, Milo invites her to spend the night at his Brooklyn Heights brownstone, decorated with bowls of flowers from his garden and good reproductions of Demuth's watercolors for *The Turn of the Screw*. They had met six years earlier when she illustrated the cover for his Gothic novel, *The Secret of Seven Towers*. He wants to write a book " 'a bit more challenging to the old imagination.' " During his recent trip to Greece, he had delivered a baby for his obese cleaning lady. Since then, he has had a recurring dream. He is trying to pull a baby's head out of a body—of water. On the shore stands the mother who will kill Milo and the baby. He accepts Violet's advice to communicate with the dream lady, who replies: " 'I had my dreams, just like you. And you'd better make it your business to find out what they were.' " He is now writing her story, *Kaatje's Curse*.

Ambrose Valentine Clay, age forty-nine at his death, is a combination of Rhett Butler and Ernest Hemingway—and is based on Mose Godwin. Born in Charleston, Ambrose is charming, bright, and talented. At seventeen, he goes to war, parachutes into Normandy with the 101st Airborne,[77] and returns a decorated hero four years later. *Looking for the Lora Lee*, his novel based on the suicide of Violet's mother, becomes a best-seller. For the next twenty-eight years, he tries to write a second novel, *Capriccio*. He also seduces women, especially by reading them the novel's one completed chapter, wherein a lonely, Southern boy finds his mother in bed with another man. For a time, he lives in an apartment in Greenwich Village, his "Left Bank," and signs his magazine articles with A. Valentine. He moves to Mexico, where his calling cards read: Ambrose V. Clay, *escritor norteamericano*. He alludes to Hemingway's "one true sentence" and "hills like white elephants," but he cannot emulate his favorite writer's discipline. He killed himself. Unlike Mose Godwin, he leaves a suicide note: "Violet honey, I'm sorry, there's nothing left."

Part of Ambrose's difficulty lies with his Southern heritage. Charm, women, and success come too easily to Ambrose, the Charleston blue blood. He tells Violet: " 'I polish it [his Southern accent] up once a month or so, like the family silver. Yankees love family silver—look how much they stole from us.' " But he has retained a vestige of the Southern sense of family—in his unreserved love of Violet. At her fifth birthday party, he jumps from the top of her swing to show the little girls how paratroopers land safely.[78] When she is eight, he comes from New York to her North Carolina school, where he lectures in a "perfect tone for children." He sends Violet a gift from Tiffany's. When she is twenty-three, he lets her live in his Waverly Place apartment while he is away. In return, Violet vows after his death to "make good a few Clay promises"—which Godwin's best male character could not keep.

Thus, Godwin frees Violet Clay from her artistic paralysis by involving her in the creative maladies of others. Milo is cured when he contacts Kaatje, whose story will transcend Gothic novels. Likewise, Violet abandons Gothic heroines. As she paints *Suspended Woman,* she trusts her instincts—as well as dreams,[79] imagination, and myth—and produces a mature painting of a "silver blonde Valkyrie."[80] Unlike Milo, Ambrose is not cured; in fact, his inability to write leads to suicide. Violet tells a friend: " 'I think I've known for years that he wasn't going to write that novel. I . . . didn't want to face it because it might mean . . . that I might never get serious about my painting.' " But Ambrose's failure is only a warning to her, not her destiny. For at Pine Hollow, she learned discipline, a lesson that Uncle Ambrose could not master.

Violet Clay is shot through with colors, music, characters—and brilliance. The heroine has not wasted her years in New York—with its coffeehouses, eccentrics, brownstones, and sparkling lights—for New York polishes and tests the finest artists. This contemporary portrait of the young woman as artist stands with *The Finishing School* as Godwin's finest work.

A Mother and Two Daughters (1982), now translated into eleven languages,[81] is Godwin's most popular novel. Here she broadens her "canvas," abandons the Jamesian idea of "one center of consciousness,"[82] and creates three protagonists and some twenty minor characters. Anne Tyler praises her storytelling, realistic portraits of men, and meticulously documented "little world of Mountain City."[83] In the *Washington Post,* Jonathan Yardley calls Godwin a "stunningly gifted novelist of manners" and predicts that "*A Mother and Two Daughters* . . . will find a permanent . . . place in our national literature."[84] The *New York Times* finds the book "remarkable,"[85] while the *Wall Street Journal* typifies reaction to Godwin's women in "the wisest, most sensitively balanced novel about women in the enormous social transitions of our time."[86] But some critics have reservations. The *Saturday Review* finds the novel "straightforward but a little dull,"[87] while the *Times Literary Supplement* notes it is "far from innovative."[88] The *New Yorker* faults Godwin for lack of a "plausible plot" and sees the three heroines as "sociological specimens."[89] Many consider the thirty-nine-page epilogue unnecessary.[90]

As the novel opens, attorney Leonard Strickland dies in a combined heart attack and car accident on 16 December 1978 in Mountain City (Asheville), North Carolina. His survivors include his widow, Nell, age sixty-two; and his two daughters, Cate Strickland Galitsky, twice divorced at thirty-nine, and Lydia Strickland Mansfield, thirty-six and separated. After the funeral, six months pass until the three women reunite on Ocracoke Island, where Lydia and Cate argue beyond reconciliation and the family cottage burns to the ground. The novel ends at a 1984 picnic (Godwin's ill-conceived epilogue).

During the first six months of 1979, Cate S. Galitsky returns to Melancthon College in Iowa. Despite her Ph.D. in English and her teaching position, she somehow feels a failure. Cate has a "greater need than others to fling themselves against the world, to let it pierce them and knock them about." In 1970, she had been fired from a private school in New York for protesting the invasion of Cambodia. In the Davenport, Iowa, winter, she meets Roger Jernigan, the wealthy president of an extermination company. He lacks education but not intelligence. Once Cate asks him when he stopped believing in God, and he replies: "When I was in the Army . . . in Italy. . . . One of the men in our detail went berserk. There was this chicken. . . . He picked it up and just started tearing it to pieces. I don't mean just wringing its neck. . . . Up until then I never questioned that . . . God was on our side. . . . I was nineteen." When she becomes pregnant, Jernigan asks her to marry him. But she flies to Chicago for an abortion. Later she reads in Emerson's *Essays:* "We think how much time is gone, that might have been saved." Nell thinks of Cate's life as "wasteful . . . movement for movement's sake." But Pat M. Verhulst writes: "When Cate, the rebel daughter, reads a book, she is looking for wisdom. . . . "[91]

Meanwhile, Lydia S. Mansfield almost becomes a "sociological specimen" as she reenters college and discovers feminism. The mother of two teenaged sons, she trades her stockbroker husband for a podiatrist lover. An "exceptionally organized woman," she swims to retain her trim shape and has her Christmas cards ready by early November. She becomes friends with her professor—of sociology—Dr. Renee Peverall-Watson. Lydia's quality of being "strong as steel without forfeiting one ounce of her femininity" is translated into "media chic by starring in a television cookery show."[92]

Nell Strickland spends her six months in Mountain City. She is the only woman in the novel capable of total love. At one point, she despairs: "It would have been simpler . . . if I'd died in that accident, too." But Nell is fundamentally a strong, resilient Southern lady. She tells a flippant nurse to quit calling her "honey." In April, she hosts the meeting of the Mountain City Book Club (founded in 1886). Here Godwin conveys the "solid reality of these people and their North Carolina world"[93] with humor and affection. By custom, the hostess must "circulate," continuously pour coffee and pass hot rolls but never "sit down at her own table." The aristocratic president, Miss Theodora Blount,[94] wears a diamond brooch low on her ample bosom. But Nell prefers the solitude of her well-ordered home. She observes a family of crows, "interesting, intelligent birds." In a fine, understated scene, she digs with bare fingers in her garden. "Nell's vision misted over and she bowed her head. . . . It was purple . . . the first crocus of the year"—which Leonard had planted twenty years ago. Later, her loneliness subsides when she meets the Anglican priest, Father Marcus Chaplin.

A Mother and Two Daughters is, in many ways, a "work of complete maturity and artistic control."[95] Certainly, Godwin deserved "a real . . . [commercial] . . . breakthrough"[96] and another American Book Award nomination much earlier (both *The Odd Woman* and *Violet Clay* were nominated for the National Book Award). She has, indeed, written a "populous . . . expansive novel in the Victorian tradition."[97] But her broad canvas needs more fine brushstrokes, such as Nell's crows and crocus. Cate and Nell are compelling, and at least two minor characters are highly innovative: Wickie Lee Blount, the Appalachian doll maker, and Dr. Renee Peverall-Watson, who researches her *white* ancestors and black elitism. Brigette Weeks sums up the great appeal of *A Mother and Two Daughters:* "Anyone from an average family will [say]: 'Yes, that's how *I* felt, that's how it always is.' "[98]

The Finishing School (1985) is as delicate, balanced, even whimsical as a Miro painting—especially in the renderings of the adolescent Justin Stokes, enchanted by an older woman, Ursula DeVane. *Time* considers it Godwin's "most artful and accomplished novel,"[99] a judgment *The New Republic* shares.[100] The *New York Times* praises her characterization, small details, plot, and "power to isolate and elevate subtle feelings."[101] *Harper's* editor Frances Taliaferro calls it a "wise contribution to the literature of growing up."[102] A few reviewers miss key points. The *Wall Street Journal* is troubled by Godwin's "wimpy men"[103]—forgetting, no doubt, that male concert pianists rarely possess the raw animal appeal of quarterbacks or truckers. In her *Ms.* review, Brigette Weeks, who adored *A Mother and Two Daughters,* laments that the forty-year-old Justin is less "fresh" than the teenage Justin.[104] Perhaps

Weeks has been fortunate enough to escape middle-age exhaustions. She is also distressed by Godwin's "flashbacks intercut with adult musing,"[105] although many reviewers applaud the technical virtuosity of Godwin's intricate time shifts.[106] There is a minor flaw: again, Godwin tidies up the lives of too many characters in the ending. But *The Finishing School* is an important book, a "finely nuanced, compassionate psychological novel."[107]

Much of the power and the beauty of *The Finishing School* rests in Godwin's deft handling of her Faulknerian time shifts and sequences. The novel opens in 1982 in New York, as Justin Stokes, forty, looks back on a summer of her adolescence. She is a successful stage actress, excelling at O'Neill, Pinter, and Ibsen roles, and the unscarred survivor of two brief marriages. She is between plays, a time in which she ironically notes that actors are "notorious trouble-seekers" and "like ghosts looking for bodies to inhabit."

Justin's journey back into memory starts with a dream—of Ursula and herself, sitting in front of the "Finishing School." Later, as she drives to upstate New York, Justin begins to explore the summer when she was fourteen. Within the village of Clove in 1956, she had really lived in two worlds and times. The first was light, airy, and understandable—Lucas Meadows, a subdivision of IBM families, including Aunt Mona and Cousin Becky. Two years earlier, Justin's aristocratic Virginia family had begun dying: first, "Honey," her grandmother who took her to the Episcopal church in Fredericksburg each Sunday, then her beloved physician grandfather, who imbued Justin with an appreciation of J. "Sanity" Bach and who took her on trips to cabins of slaves, those "wonderfully resilient," spiritual people. When Justin's young father died in a car accident in February of 1956, Louise Stokes decided to move north, to transplant her little family of Justin and Jem to her late husband's sister's home.

Aunt Mona Mott is a Dickensian character, a "kind but stereotyped soul who cannot resist mentioning, regardless of context, the advantages that life has failed to bestow on her."[108] She is recently divorced from engineer Eric Mott, and her home is a shrine to the mundane. The living room of her split-level house has a plate glass window and lamps with their shades still covered by cellophane. Overlaying the seafoam green wall-to-wall carpet are plastic runners tacked down on traffic areas. Justin feels oppressed by her room, whose walls Aunt Mona has lovingly repainted an ugly pink, "Raspberry Ice." Worse still, Aunt Mona has made curtains, a dust ruffle and dresser flounce in a fabric decorated with "figures of milkmaids, row after row of them, with their wide skirts and pert, beauty-contest smiles." The house in Lucas Mead-

ows is filled with people who care: Louise Stokes, thirty-two, a temporary martyr in her new widowhood; Mott, who visits, lives to do other
people's chores and to be nice to children; Aunt Mona, who wishes she
was from "one of those creepy old families dating back to God"; Jem,
six; and surly Becky, ten. To escape the house's lack of history and the
milkmaids' warning of conventionality, Justin bicycles through the
countryside. On a May ride, she meets Ursula DeVane.

The DeVane house on Old Clove Road is dark, burnished, full of music and mystery. Originally built by the Huguenots in the early 1700s,
the two-story stone house has only two inhabitants: Ursula DeVane,
forty-four, a former actress, and her brother Julian, forty, a concert pianist who has not fulfilled the promise of his Carnegie Hall recital eighteen years earlier. Even though the DeVanes are gradually selling off
their land to their estranged neighbors, the Cristianas, they still own
the pond and weathered hut, which Justin and Ursula come to call the
Finishing School. This estate and the perplexing woman who rules it,
then, become the other 1956 world of Justin Stokes.

Ursula DeVane is the nerve center of the novel. She enchants, mes-
merizes, bewitches young Justin. Ursula treats her to cucumber and
watercress sandwiches and Chianti. Her living room is a "tabernacle" to
the life Justin wants, one of "art, travel, sensibility, drama, conversation." At the room's center is a grand piano, on which Julian plays
Chopin scherzos, Bach, Debussy, Beethoven, and, once, in a fury,
Liszt's "Mephisto Waltz." Ursula makes Justin her confidante: she
laughs over childhood pranks with Abel Cristiana; she romanticizes her
engagement to her French cousin, Marius DeVane. Most critically, she
gives her a credo of art, which begins to shape Justin's future career as
an actress: "If you are an artist, you learn to trap the yearning and put
it where you want it, put it where it goes." She urges Justin to remain
fluid, to keep moving, changing, not to *congeal* or to let her life solidify
into a "repetition of what you have done before." By early August, she
calls Justin her "dream daughter."

Godwin's tour de force in this novel, rivaling Julian's delicate, nuanced performances of Chopin and Bach, lies in her skillful ordering of
time sequences. At precisely the right points, Godwin embeds the ten
compelling episodes in which Ursula and Justin meet, ranging from
two to forty pages, into the narratives of Justin's 1982 present and the
1956 ennui of Lucas Meadows. These episodes make us heed, almost
against our will, Godwin's admonition: "Fourteen. Be fourteen again."
A lesser writer would have gone for the intensity, content to thrill and
exhaust us with the chronologically ordered story. But Godwin is careful to let Ursula (through the teenage Justin) present the story, as one

might to a lover, with psychological care: first, known facts and phi-
losophies; then, shared biases and jokes; soon after, a few secrets to
establish trust; later, affirmation of one's unique worth; then finally, the
darker details.

Justin is sent spinning from the tenuous present of her other 1956
world, being bounced like a metal ball in a pinball machine, through
the complex field of Ursula's past. The Huguenot ancestry, dating back
to the early 1500s. Julian's 1938 graduation from Julliard. Ursula's
voyage on the *Normandie*. Her French engagement. Sappho on Lesbos
in 600 B.C. Julian's concert tour in Argentina during World War II. Ursula's imagined meeting with George Bernard Shaw. The bizarre tale of
the lesbian student, Kitty, and her father. Finally, Justin lands, off-balance, in 1922, horrified to learn of the ten-year-old Ursula's betrayal of
her own mother.

Most friendships cannot withstand the darker details. Godwin has already forewarned us of doom with mentions of the July 25 sinking of
the *Andrea Doria*. But neither we nor Justin want to accept that betrayal is, like tragedy, inevitable.

The Finishing School resembles a Miro painting, with its strong lines,
its bold and muted colors, its power to stay in our memory. Gail Godwin has called it a "private" book.[109] But it is also a more universal
work: we can all remember the first person who encouraged us to become more than we thought possible. A teacher, like Sister Winters; a
parent, like Kathleen Godwin Cole; a family friend, like Norma Merchant. Godwin's portrait of Ursula DeVane is stunning; William Pritchard compares her to Lawrence's Winifred Unger in *The Rainbow*.[110]
Justin Stokes is funny, awkward, bright; her story is as "happy-sad in
its textures as life itself."[111] She survives, as most young people do.
Much of her strength derives from her first thirteen years in the South,
when she was unconditionally loved by her grandparents, lived in the
historic home on Washington Street in Fredericksburg, and looked out
from her room, under the eaves, at the flowers and "thick foliage of the
backyard" and listened to the birds in spring.

In *A Southern Family* (1987), her seventh novel, Godwin tries to come
to terms with the life and death of her younger brother, who challenges
her to write a book about the insoluble, " 'something that can *never* be
wrapped up.' " The *New York Times* finds it a "rich, complex book" in
which the author is "in full bloom and at her mindful best."[112] Jonathan Yardley of the *Washington Post* admires the "dense, populous
world" of this "psychologically acute" novel, an "ambitious book that
entirely fulfills its ambitions."[113] *Time*'s Paul Gray is delighted that she

abandoned her New York novel, *Gotham,* and returned to the South, where she "inherited a subject for life," making her "birthright seem constantly fresh and enthralling."[114] But others see hairline fissures beneath the smooth obsidian surface. On "All Things Considered," a National Public Radio program, Alan Cheuse laments the story's lack of "real depth, sense of history and psychology" and absence of a "fluid and beautiful prose" for such a long book.[115] Linda Taylor in the *Times Literary Supplement* is more blunt: "The weakness of the novel lies in the sheer quantity of material used to say very little. The Quicks . . . might just as well be living in Tooting [a sleepy, downscale London suburb] for all the narrative excitement they generate."[116]

Spanning a year and a day, the novel opens in October of 1983 in Mountain City, North Carolina, as the Quick clan gathers to celebrate the birthday of Lily Buchel Campion Quick, lovely, petite, and intelligent. Her steadfast refusal to give her age, sixty-five, is in the tradition of her own mother and other Southern ladies of bygone times. Lily's daughter from her first marriage flies down from New York for the occasion. Clare Campion, forty-two, is a successful novelist who lives with Felix Rohr, fifty-six, an executive theatrical producer. Also invited is Clare's best friend of thirty-five years, Julia Richardson Lowndes, forty-two, a college professor. Warmed by champagne and Lily's pleasure in her gifts of perfume, love, and respect, the guests almost forget how acrimonious her thirty-three-year marriage has become during the last ten years. Ralph Quick, fifty-seven, a contractor, upsets Lily by his reluctance to pay bills, clean the carport, or haul away the rotting lumber, rusting old cars and wheelbarrow, and corroding tin sheets beside the road leading to their house. But Ralph is the solicitous host until son Theo, twenty-eight, typically off-center, says, "Women rape men, too." The party is over.

The next day Clare and Julia go on a mountaintop picnic at Pinnacle Old Bald, once an Indian burial ground. They have always been able to "strip down to the current essentials of their inner lives in a matter of minutes." What begins as a leisurely novel of manners explodes, at the end of two chapters and one day. Brother Theo is dead. He has shot his estranged girlfriend and then himself as her small son watched from the car's backseat. The remaining ten chapters become a painful examination of life and death, of Theo and self, narrated by various Quick family members and friends.

Should a future scholar compile a *Who's Who in Godwin,* a concordance, he or she would first mine *A Southern Family,* her most autobiographical novel. The 540 pages contain all members of her "manless little family"; her mother's second family, the Coles; the Merchants;

and other friends. Her first overt depiction of Sister Winters sparkles with the brilliance of a small, perfectly cut emerald as Sister Patrick recalls her Irish father and heritage, the beloved colt of her childhood, Shadow. Godwin juxtaposes the free spirit of Shadow, who must be sent to school to "learn to be a horse," with the independence of Sister Patrick, who wears only Amalfi pumps despite her vow of poverty. The nun's facets of faith and reason fuse as she teaches mathematics to the young: "They tell students now that to divide a number by zero is impossible. We used to teach that if you divided a number by zero, you got infinity." Godwin's mother has evolved from Lily Campion, reporter and believer in art, into Lily Quick, visitor to nursing homes and believer in God. Grandmother Krahenbuhl now lies beneath her tombstone, sans birthdate, simply etched with "Ellen Harshaw Buchel, January 20, 1972." Gail Godwin herself becomes Clare Campion who lives with Felix Rohr, modeled on composer Robert Starer.

The Cole family has changed. Younger sister Franchelle, the attorney, does not exist—at her request.[117] Rebel Cole is now Rafe Quick, twenty-six, a boozing, woman-chasing Ph.D. candidate in business at the University of North Carolina. Tommy Cole becomes Theo Quick, father of little Jason and ex-husband of Snow Mullins, the Appalachian enchantress. The contractor stepfather is a more sympathetic character than he was in *The Odd Woman*. Ralph Quick is at his most poetic when ruminating about Dr. Hannah Ullstein, his lost love, whom he had "at some point stopped thinking of as being 'Jewish.' " This affair ten years earlier has reduced his and Lily's marriage to a purgatory of domestic boredom. He has the fascinating mind of a builder, believing that "a house, if it's designed right, should fit into its landscape like it grew there." He is a good friend to Alicia Gallant, sprightly at eighty-seven, with whom he happily buys the contents of a small drugstore. Godwin probes beneath his facade, forever scarred by deprivations of his Appalachian and part-Cherokee heritage, to discover why he beat his teenage stepdaughter.

Godwin's friend, Pat Merchant Verhulst, has evolved from Dr. Cate S. Galitsky, English professor in *A Mother and Two Daughters,* into a history professor. Dr. Julia R. Lowndes is a bit grating as she assigns such theme topics as "What Is Civilization?" and endlessly discusses W. J. Cash and his seminal work, *The Mind of the South* (1941). She now has a father, Neville Richardson, seventy-nine, proud of Clare's "big book" about his family, *The Headmaster's Daughter*. Norma Merchant, so lovingly transformed into Nell Strickland in *A Mother and Two Daughters,* is now Marie Richardson, her memory debased by postmortem tales of her alcoholic antics. The black characters are a disappointing lot—maids, cooks, a masseuse, a stonemason, Theo's child-hood friend now in prison, a doctor's *wife*. For realism's sake alone, in 1983–84, the novel needs a fully human black professional.

The core of this autobiographical novel is the absorbing portrait of the writer and her work. As she molds Asheville family and friends into Mountain City characters, her creativity in turn is shaped by her North Carolina milieu. In stating her artistic credo, she alludes to her educa-tion by European nuns during her eight most formative years. "The kind of fiction I was trying to write [was] deep-breathing, reflective, and with that patience for detail I admired in those medieval stone carvers who would lavish their skills on the lowliest gargoyle simply be-cause" they worked for "the glory of God." Clare's well-plotted novels owe much to Lily's love of "forms." Trained to be a careful observer, Clare knows when and why to alter a detail. She makes a South Caro-lina debutante "Cinderella of the St. Cecilia Ball" because Northerners had never heard of the actual Spoleto Ball. She questions her subjects, ability, motivations until Julia finally says, "You are too hard on your-self." She concedes that knowing so many life stories, "being on every-body's side is good for a writer." Then Clare has a vintage Godwin dream, one of self-acceptance. Aboard a spaceship (writing, her vehicle to the future), she climbs up circular stairs (journey to self-knowledge), opens a heavy metal door, and falls in love with the captain, Clare her-self.

Godwin, of course, aspired to create two other centers in *A Southern Family*. She told the *New York Times* she "wanted to explore, but not ex-plain" both the "class system" of the South and the actual death of her half-brother Tommy Cole, who died in the same manner as Theo Quick in 1983.[118] She falls short in both cases.

The class system in the South is as multilayered and ever-shifting as the sands and underlying land formations of the South Carolina coast, where she sets one-fifth of her novel. She has apparently read Cash's often-mentioned *Mind of the South* and assigned the Fauquiers of South Carolina to the "aristocrat" class, most townspeople to the "yeo-man farmer" class, and, erroneously, Ralph Quick and Snow Mullins to the "poor white" class. They are not "hillbillies," but Appalachians, members of a separate culture within the South. True to his subcul-ture's Scotch-Irish tradition, Ralph *is* a Presbyterian. But his father's and Snow's offensive racism is atypical of Appalachians, who neither owned nor desired to own slaves. Within each of Cash's three classes are many subclasses, the subtleties of which can be gleaned by carefully reading Faulkner or novelist Lee Smith.

Godwin waited twenty years to fictionalize another suicide, her father Mose Godwin, the wonderful Uncle Ambrose of *Violet Clay*. Had she waited longer than a year to begin committing Tommy/Theo to paper, perhaps his true character would have emerged. Clare never answers her unspoken question to Theo, "What have you done to make you a main character in *anybody's* book?" Felix tells us, twice, "This brother is a mensch. He feels things." A coworker writes that he was a "team player." Snow tells us that his "religious places" are his deepest self. Sister Patrick tells us how young Theo washed his hands before shaking them with the reverend mother general; the nun's dream makes Lily believe he is now shaking hands with God. Theo is not a racist. He loves his son, Jason, and shows him the stars. He hates being an accountant, helping "rich people get richer," and at twenty-eight wishes he were a patrolman. He once tried to take his snake to an Episcopal service, the Blessing of the Animals. He is off the mark, off-balance, off. Yet everyone is devastated by his death. Why? Readers strain to care, but they do not know Theo.

The structure of *A Southern Family*, however, is as sound as one of Ralph Quick's houses. Early in the novel, Clare and Julia enjoy a "walk of celebration" during their mountaintop picnic, while Lily Quick and Sister Patrick close the book with their mountaintop walk of "experience."[119] The ending is Godwin's best so far, as she refuses to "rescue the Quicks" and "allows them their separate uncertainties."[120] The temperas still hanging on the line to dry—of Theo, of blacks, of Southern social classes—are unbefitting such a major novelist. But in *A Southern Family*, Godwin gives us an absorbing portrait of herself as a writer and a lush tableau of Sister Patrick, Ralph Quick, and other fascinating residents of Mountain City.

Thus, Gail Godwin makes the long journey in seven novels from Majorca to Mountain City. The arc of her itinerary sweeps from Spain and England to California, narrows as she visits Iowa, Illinois, and New York, rests in the Carolinas, swerves back to New York, then ends in North Carolina. The South, especially North Carolina, becomes a repository of solid values, love, perhaps stagnation. At times, the Southern family is an "unsafe haven," as her friend John Irving would put it. The family is sustained by the history, liturgy, aesthetic appeal of the Episcopal church—occasionally, the Catholic church—but few Godwin characters attend services regularly. Blacks, especially Renee Peverall-Watson and Calvin Edwards, are a part of the New South's more egalitarian society. But Godwin rarely forgets Asheville, with the permanence of its mountains.

Godwin's novels are filled with women drawn from her extended "manless little family": her mother and grandmother, her sister, the Merchant family. Sister Winters becomes Sister Patrick in *A Southern Family;* she resembles Ursula DeVane in intellectual prowess and joie de vivre but, of course, not in amorality. All of Godwin's women are bright, except for Francesca Bolt. All are searching—for love, respect, meaning in life. Some also seek artistic or academic distinction. All have difficulty loving, even selecting men. Godwin herself comes to terms with her father, Mose Godwin, by creating Uncle Ambrose Clay, her most memorable male character.

Gail Godwin is a significant figure in Southern and American literature. *Violet Clay* and *The Finishing School* are her best novels; *A Mother and Two Daughters* and *A Southern Family* are her most popular. Entering Gail Godwin's fictional world is an experience, as Violet says of Milo's book, that has "the power to make you want to change your life."

GAIL GODWIN BIBLIOGRAPHY

NOVELS

The Perfectionists. New York: Harper & Row, 1970; London: Cape, 1971; New York: Warner, 1979.
Glass People. New York: Knopf, 1972; Warner, 1979.
The Odd Woman. New York: Knopf, 1974; London: Cape, 1975; New York: Warner, 1980.
Violet Clay. New York: Knopf, 1978; London: Gollancz, 1978; New York: Warner, 1979.
A Mother and Two Daughters. New York: Viking, 1982; New York: Avon, 1983.
The Finishing School. New York: Viking, 1985; Avon, 1986.
A Southern Family. New York: Morrow, 1987.

SHORT STORY COLLECTIONS

Dream Children. New York: Knopf, 1976; New York: Avon, 1976.
Mr. Bedford and the Muses. New York: Viking, 1983; New York: Avon, 1984.

UNCOLLECTED SHORT STORIES

"Liza's Leaf Tower." *North American Review* 6 (Fall 1969): 41–44.
"An Intermediate Stop." *North American Review* 7 (Summer 1970): 21–25.
"To Noble Companions." *Harper's,* August 1973, 5.

"His House." *Triquarterly* 35 (Winter 1976): 32–34.
"Fate of Fleeing Maidens." *Mademoiselle,* May 1978, 130.
"Inner and Outer Landscapes." *Anataeus* 28 (1978): 31–40.
"A Tale of the Literary Life." *Cosmopolitan,* August 1979, 278–81, 288, 292–97, 323.
"Afternoon Interlude." *Cosmopolitan,* August 1982, 246–47, 290, 295.
"My Face." *Anataeus* 45 (1982): 95–103.

ARTICLES

"Becoming a Writer." In *The Writer on Her Work,* ed. Janet Sternburg, 231–55. New York: Norton, 1980.
"Discovering the Form for Your Fiction." *Writer,* December 1976, 11–14.
"Finding the Right Shape for Your Story." *Writer,* September 1975, 9–11.
"If She Hadn't Called Herself George Eliot, Would We Have Heard of Marian Evans?" *Ms.,* September 1974, 72–75, 88.
"Keeping Track." In *Ariadne's Thread: A Collection of Contemporary Women's Journals,* ed. Lyn Lifshin, 75–85. New York: Harper & Row, 1982.
"The Southern Belle." *Ms.,* July 1975, 49–52.
"Southern Men, Southern Lies." *Esquire,* February 1977, 126–29.
"Toward a Fully Human Heroine: Some Worknotes." *Harvard Advocate,* Winter 1973, 26–28.
"A Writing Woman." *Atlantic Monthly,* October 1979, 84–88, 92.

Sylvia Wilkinson: Passages
through a Tarheel Childhood

*

ANN M. WOODLIEF

THE FICTION, indeed all of the writing, of Sylvia Wilkinson is intricately but imaginatively tied up with her life. The characters she has created all live in the same North Carolina world she grew up in. The journal she began as a child is the base of many of the incidents and insights her characters experience. The result is fiction with voice and immediacy, not so much autobiographical or confessional as honest and curious. As Fred Chappell notes of her first three novels: "Everything is alive. Every page bristles, quivers, stammers with the forces of organic change."[1] Although Southern in their presentation of place, person, and tale, the novels are also universal portraits of the maturing child who reaches for knowledge and wisdom embedded in nature and in people, especially the aged. They are far more than "coming of age" novels, with their unsentimental insights into the ways of human nature.

Sylvia Wilkinson, like her central characters, was born in April 1940 near Durham, North Carolina. Unlike them, however, she did not have to struggle with the disadvantages of poverty or wealth. Her father and mother had a construction business and were ideal parents for a writer because they understood she and their other two children needed freedom to develop in their own ways. Eventually, her mother became an artist, joining the creative ranks of both daughters (Sylvia's sister Margot became a well-known potter). Sylvia spent much time at the farm of her maternal grandparents, Mama and Papa George, who are reflected in the grandparents of her books, especially *A Killing Frost*. Her books attest that she had a childhood rich in experiences and sustaining relationships. Unlike many writers, though, she was not a reader, preferring to stay outdoors and in the movie house.

When Wilkinson once wrote about what growing up in the South meant to her, she focused on two aspects: nature and prejudice. "School I would endure," she writes, but it was outdoors where she learned, especially after her parents gave her a horse. She "was allowed a closeness with the things of the earth like no other child anywhere," free to "reconcile violence and bloodshed that was not criminal but normal." She believes those fertile years of childhood were lengthened because she did grow up in the South. She resisted the inevitability of changing and growing up, but she also recognized resistance to change as the "ugly face of the south." Though rarely conscious of "attitudes that weren't so important but should have been," she says she later found them "lodged in my memory between the land and the people to be shaped into understanding when I spread them out in front of me in fiction."[2]

Moss on the North Side is a bildungsroman in more than one sense, for it is the novel that Wilkinson grew up writing. At the age of twelve, she hesitantly offered her seventh-grade teacher her first story, about her grandmother patiently and affectionately picking ticks off her dog while he licked the sores on her legs. The teacher was disgusted, brushing off her creative work with, "You write what I tell you to write." Her apparently cruel response made Wilkinson all the more determined, defiantly private as she probed her own experiences and fantasies, filling Blue Horse notebooks at night in her attic room with the incidents, descriptions, and characters that would eventually become a novel.[3]

For eight years, she kept her secret close. Her time outside school was filled with hours of roaming the Durham countryside on her horse, playing fierce competitive tennis, and painting. When she went to Women's College (now University of North Carolina at Greensboro), she chose to major in physical education, planning to be a physical therapist to support her writing. In her junior year, she slipped a manuscript under the office door of poet Randall Jarrell, tentatively inviting his reaction. She had picked the right mentor this time, for Jarrell, an inspired teacher, immediately recognized her talent. The moment was right also, for she needed verification that others would appreciate what she felt she must write. Wilkinson added a creative writing major, graduated, and won a creative writing scholarship to Hollins College, where she earned an M.A. under the tutelage of Louis Rubin, Jr.

As she says, she grew up as both writer and woman on the pages of this book, which expanded at one time to eight hundred pages and went through eleven full revisions before it was published in 1966. Much of the vivid immediacy and emotional integrity of the novel undoubtedly stem from this long and personal foreground. Cary, however, is a main character in her own right, not Sylvia in pale disguise, struggling through adolescence. They obviously share much, including a passion for the outdoors, acute awareness of sounds and colors, an instinctive compassion, a driving curiosity, and a fierce individuality. But Cary, the illegitimate daughter of a Cherokee farmer and a white town prostitute, has many experiences that Wilkinson has only imagined, not lived.

The novel spans Cary's fourteenth year, beginning with her father's sudden death from rabbit fever. Ironically, he is denied treatment because the doctor is in town delivering her mother of a stillborn child. Numerous flashbacks reveal the bond of affection and understanding between Cary and her father, even though he sent her to live in an orphanage for two years. After the doctor confirms the death, Cary sets fire to the contaminated house and body, almost without thinking, and then hides in the night shadows, watching the futile attempts to extinguish the blaze and rescue her. But the story does not lie in events, for there are no more on such a dramatic scale. It emerges from Cary's consciousness and reactions to many small encounters, often involving death, cruelty, and sexuality, both in the natural world she feels akin to and with people.

Underlying each experience is the subtle process of Cary coming to understand and accept herself, though she is a racial and social misfit in her provincial Southern town. But it is the reader who must infer the changes, for Cary simply lives them, without analysis or much evident thought. There is no sense of an older and wiser Cary looking back; the point of view is consistently of this innocent yet perceptive child who feels with her body and sees and hears everything (far more than she wants to understand). Yet at the end, when she discovers her grandmother's notes about Cherokees who "would not be hunted like wild beasts," waves to an old black woman and laughs with her at a chicken dancing comically in the dust, and briefly cuddles a chick though its claws scratch her, the reader realizes how far she has come to resolve her dark confusion.

Her metamorphosis from an asexual child—roaming through the woods, wearing coins flattened by trains, and swimming in a pond clutching a stolen watermelon—to puberty is particularly traumatic. Her social class and poverty do spare her the burden of the stereotypical ideal of Southern femininity but leave her vulnerable to males who assume her sexual availability, like her mother's. From the beginning, she has spurned her mother, feeling abandoned. Just the suggestion from an envious orphan that she once nursed at her mother's fleshy breasts makes her vomit. She never allows any bond with her mother, even when she must live and sleep with her, and soon finds a way to leave after she catches her in bed with a dark-skinned man.

But going to live with and work for Mrs. Strawbridge, a widow with two teenage sons who owns the farm her father worked, does not solve the conflict. Though she has found a more respectable and nurturing mother figure, the boys are both attracted by her half-wild ways. Eventually, she does find herself able to respond to Johnny, the younger son, who is also emerging from a childhood close to nature. It proves difficult for her to continue trusting her body and feelings as she matures, especially when she realizes what a "half breed female" connotes to men, but she gradually makes the transition without losing any of her independence of spirit.

It is not difficult to understand why the young Wilkinson was able to select such outstanding mentors, for her style in this first book would delight any writing instructor. The marks are here from the first sentence: as Cary lies in bed, half listening to her father's labored breathing, "each time her thoughts faded, her body jerked awake again." There are no clichés and few abstract nouns, but there are concrete and fresh verbs that detail explicitly. The descriptions often combine the metaphoric density of poetry with the colors and forms of painting, but the words are always simple and palpable: "as the gray square of light slowly turned a thin green, the whole room became light," for example. Sometimes the deeply embedded metaphors are repeated, carrying a symbolic force, as in the association of indoor rooms with boxes or cages: "The whole room was built only of vertical and horizontal shafts that ran straight across the room stabbing into the wall or driving themselves into the floor without wobbling." Even though written in the third person, Cary's voice throughout the book is clear and authentic, centering the novel. The only drawback is that her well-phrased and detailed observations sometimes take on a tangential life of their own.

Most reviewers liked this first novel, praised its "fresh vision" and lack of sentimentality,[4] "expert command of scene and character,"[5] and "images new as dew,"[6] although one found its details and imagery were too rich and intense, "its virtues occasionally carried to excess."[7] As one reviewer phrased an objection, the "book remains transcription," assuming "that personal observation is nearly synonymous with personal vision."[8] The consensus was that Wilkinson was an unusually talented writer with an exciting and "sensitive" first novel. It enjoyed some success, going into four printings and two paperback sales.

Moss on the North Side confirms a design that Wilkinson has generally

239

followed in her subsequent novels. At the center is an energetic, perceptive, and intelligent young adolescent, usually female, who patiently
observes details of nature and the people around her. She—for the
voice belongs to a girl in four of the novels—is almost a complete misfit
in the world she is born into. Though she may go to a town school, she
is usually surrounded by Southern farm grotesques (in Sherwood Anderson's sense of the word), including her parents or grandparents.
They are poor, frustrated, rigid, prejudiced, and sometimes compassionate, and she both loves and fights them. She is subjected to the
stresses of puberty, crystallizing her identity through many crucial
choices about herself and what she will take from her world, especially
the natural world, which she now finds herself outside. She learns many
lessons, instinctively rather than consciously, about what it takes to be
tough but vulnerable and female on her own terms. In the process, she
may create her own alternate universe, developing a kind of internal gy-
roscope to keep her balanced on the edge of chaos as she emerges into
a very individualistic maturity. As long as she is honest, aware, and
imaginative, she has a chance at survival in spite of the odds of social
class and poverty.

Wilkinson's next novel, *A Killing Frost,* written when she studied
creative writing at Stanford University with Wallace Stegner, elabo-
rates this pattern, though it focuses on two characters, the girl Ramie
and her grandmother, Miss Liz. The voice has shifted into a comfortable first person, as Ramie speaks and thinks in the North Carolina
country dialect appropriate to a thirteen-year-old. Nature itself is not so
much at center stage as it was in the previous novel, but it acts more as
a catalyst for revealing character. The other persons in the novel are as
fully created as Ramie—the cranky, rigid, but compassionate Miss Liz;
the grandfather, Papa, now dead but a gentle and loving man who
shaped the child Ramie's affectionate observation of nature; and
Dummy, an old mute fixed in perpetual childhood. Miss Liz is based on
Wilkinson's own grandmother, a natural storyteller whom she credits
with motivating her to be a writer. Ramie, unlike Cary but like the
young Sylvia, is a budding artist, painting and sculpting people and
animals, trying to catch the fleeting colors and shapes of life and personality.

Through—and sometimes against—Miss Liz, Ramie slowly pieces
together qualities to value, absorbing the best from her, Papa, and even
Dummy (defying Miss Liz's stubborn prejudice), from her school life
in town and a sympathetic biology teacher, and from nature. Her care
of a baby bird and her phobia about spiders (made realistic when Miss
Liz tells her how her baby brother was killed by a black widow) some-

how blend to teach her how to handle cruelty and death. Unlike Cary, she has no sexual stereotype to live down, though she does have to come to terms with the memory of her dead parents, a kind of simple-minded country Romeo and Juliet. By the end of the book, Miss Liz seems to be dying of old age strokes, shut up in the tightly closed house with enough wood to last several winters, and Dummy has died of exposure in a barn, denied entrance to the warm inside of anyone's house. Ramie's last action in the book is to write Dummy's name in the family Bible, formally acknowledging his life against her grandmother's unreasonable hatred of him.

As an artist, Ramie is able to express her conflicts more concretely than Cary could. Even her dreams are creative and meaningful, as when she dreams of people in the church congregation, even Miss Liz, turning into square "sodie crackers." Then she realizes that she too is a little square, unable to sing. Eventually, she is able to imagine her own dreams, as she does by visualizing a romantic scene at the beach when a boy she knows gently hands her a delicate butterfly shell, which she will keep at home.

The art objects she makes also reflect her concerns and psychological growth. She paints seven pictures of Miss Liz for a teacher who thinks them all of different people. She also carves Miss Liz in a piece of wood embedded in a cornstalk, which must eventually be pared away as it dies. But she is never satisfied with her representations. When these works take on life and speak to her, she becomes fearful of touching them, often leaving them unfinished. She is fascinated with faces, not landscapes, but she cannot paint the aunt she lives with, seeing only a blank, or her parents, though she does eventually visualize them going hand-in-hand across a field with their backs to her. Later she takes a cake of her grandmother's soap into her closet to carve the baby bird she has tended and puts it in Dummy's hand, but she works too fast and so must turn the soap to the practical function that Miss Liz insists is the appropriate one. Finally, she makes colored prints of a fish, creating a design to capture its flashes of light, "a pale green light darting through the dark water," though she recognizes that the live fish is prettier. Not only do the images and objects merge into symbols, but art seems the key to Ramie's survival in a world divided into artificial town and dying country; since she has no place in either, she will have to make her own.

A Killing Frost fared almost as well as *Moss on the North Side* with reviewers, who generally recognized that its descriptions are woven more tightly with better realized characters. As a second novel, however, it was allowed less margin for not being an obvious masterpiece. The lack of plot and the dominance of poetically written descriptions of the rural South evidently alienated some reviewers, as well as what they perceived as "forced celebration and message."[9] Wilkinson was becoming classified as little more than another Southern woman who specializes in coming-of-age stories. Even positive reviews damned by praising her "delicate and lyrical writing,"[10] scarcely mentioning the authentic *voice* that centers the novel. In retrospect, these judgments seem unduly harsh and impatient, unwilling to weigh the novel for its own merits. But sales were as good as they had been for her first novel.

At this time, Wilkinson decided that she could not both teach and write out of the same creative energy, so she ended the full-time college teaching career of seven years at Asheville-Biltmore, William and Mary, and the University of North Carolina. She was encouraged by winning the Sir Walter Raleigh Award for fiction and being declared as "one of the four most exciting young women in America in 1966" by *Mademoiselle*. But making a living from her fiction alone would not be possible.

Cale, published in 1970, is Wilkinson's longest and most ambitious novel to date, for it spans many years, tracing all the major influences on the development of Cale from the day of his birth until he is ready to leave his small North Carolina town and father's farm at eighteen. This book is more a social drama than a psychological exploration; it defines Cale's personality and potential within the context of the shaping attitudes and resentments he inherits from grandparents, parents, uncle, and townspeople. He is presented as very much a product of and reactor to his environment and progenitors, with little of the sense of free will, perceptiveness, or gumption that characterized Ramie and Cary. He has a dark foil in Floyd, a black neighbor the same age, beat down by the deeply bred racism of the community. Both boys will leave Summit, but only one has any promise for a decent and fulfilling life, and even that promise may be an illusion.

Ironically, the Southern ideal of femininity contributes much, though indirectly, to Cale's struggle to find himself as a man. His grandmother, Sarah Ann, is a perpetually delicate, resolutely pretty, proud and untouchable belle unwilling to sully herself with reality. Her daughter Falissa's free childish spirit is repressed as soon as she reaches puberty, and the girl is forced into her mother's image of ignorant and submissive womanhood. But she carries an additional burden; it takes hard work to support this frail flower, and she is the one to do it. Her father, Papa Lonza, a gentle former telegraph operator, pays court to his demanding wife, as she expects, but fails to see how Falissa's emotional life has been damaged. Denied happiness of her own, especially after she marries a sullen farmer (thus easing her mother's horror that she will be an old maid), she determines to live for her man-child, Cale. Toiling endlessly for the son she smothers with love and protection, even after a daughter is born, she inevitably sees Cale pushing her away as he grows up and defines himself separately.

Being male has as many hazards as being female, especially with such a heritage. Cale's father, Jerome, is so attached to his land, resentful of Cale's place in his mother's affections, and warped by his own emotional deprivation as a child, that he can offer Cale only rough talk and beatings. Papa Lonza lavishes on the baby Cale all the feelings he withheld from Falissa, proud of the male who will perpetuate his line. He teaches Cale much about nature and urges him to become a builder or, more precisely, a destroyer of the two useless smokestacks that mar the sky of Summit. After he dies and Cale enters puberty, his irascible uncle Roe comes "home" after years of drinking and loving all over the globe, bringing energy and a larger world, as well as plenty of trouble. To Falissa's dismay, Cale adores his uncle and learns to imitate him, up to the moment when he watches Roe being run down on the road by an irate moonshiner.

None of the males, then, can be a satisfactory model, and the values Cale absorbs from each keep clashing. He seems to learn little, being passively shaped by others and reacting almost blindly rather than acting or developing. Although as a male he is presumably free to create his own destiny, he is much less independent than Ramie or Cary. He can only run away, not toward anything positive. Cary has her Cherokee heritage and Ramie her art, but Cale has only vague strivings toward "building," with little evidence of the determination or talent that it will take to realize them. In spite of what Falissa thinks, it is clear that being male is no more the route to success than being female dooms one to an empty life. Each role has its own built-in dilemmas, drawbacks, and limitations, if for some reason the cultural sexual expectations cannot be surmounted.

Wilkinson claims that she wanted to see if she could write as well from a male perspective, and she carefully checked with her brother to confirm the details of Cale's experiences, thoughts, and feelings. Still, Cale remains somewhat distant throughout the book, talking and reacting predictably in light of his origins, but he rarely reflects. Perhaps this bland portrait derives as much from Cale's humorless and somewhat passive personality as from the fact that he has no artistic means to express himself. If Wilkinson means to show him as shaped by forces external to himself, it is only logical that she would also reveal little of the inner workings that are so crucial in her earlier books. However, the fact that Cale is male must also be a factor: the few pages devoted to Falissa's thoughts as she labors and delivers her son are full of tension and understanding.

Dialogue—again in authentic Southern country tones—dominates in this book, as is appropriate for its dramatic approach, although there is also much monologue. There is little variation in the speech of different characters, reinforcing the impression of a pervasive and deadly sameness in the community. Some reviewers have found this detailed sameness and extensive dialogue "lethargic," claiming it is of interest only to students of small Southern towns.[11] Perhaps it is the genre they fail to appreciate; another reviewer asserts that "Miss Wilkinson would appear to have few present peers" within her genre.[12]

The novel marks an important change in approach for Wilkinson, as an experiment in moving beyond a character's inner world and private experience into the dynamics of family relationships and their influence on personality. Louis D. Rubin, Jr., sees this book as marking her maturation as a writer, going beyond the lyrical presentation of a single character's sensibility into "separate resolution within various characters and as significant dramatic developments in their own right."[13] But the book did not prove popular, perhaps because of its length. A revised and shorter version, deleting some of the more tedious monologues, was published in 1985.

While she was writing *Cale*, Wilkinson began establishing herself in another career as a professional timer for sports car racing and then, logically, as a free-lance writer of articles for racing magazines. Also, during the 1971–72 racing seasons, she joined the team of a carefully chosen race car driver, John Morton, following him around the racing circuit to record the turning point of his career. As it happened, he was talented but missed the opportunity to become one of the racing greats, partly because the financial and technical circumstances did not mesh at the right moment. The result for Wilkinson was *The Stainless Steel Carrot: An Auto Racing Odyssey,* published in 1973. Wilkinson's eye for detail and ear for dialogue serve her well in this account, and one need not be a racing fan to appreciate the portrait of the conflicts and allure of this dangerous occupation and the men who pursue it.

Although these works were aimed at an adult audience, Wilkinson has never lost her ability to see through the eyes of a child, converting that also into a paying occupation. Between 1974 and 1978, she wrote for a syndicate under a pseudonym, turning out four children's books that mix mystery and racing. Later she wrote ten small books for the World of Racing Series and *The True Book of Automobiles.* For adults, she published in 1983 *Dirt Tracks to Glory: The Early Days of Stock Car Racing as Told by the Participants.*

During the seven years after the publication of *Cale* and before her next novel was published, Wilkinson also turned to teaching on a "visiting writer" basis. She taught in colleges—Hollins, Lenoir Ryne, Sweet Briar, Washington, the University of Kentucky—and public schools in Asheboro, North Carolina, and Richmond, Virginia. She continues teaching, most recently as visiting professor in M.F.A. programs at Washington University and the University of Wisconsin at Milwaukee. According to all reports, she is an unusually effective teacher of writing, perhaps one of the best in the country, able to teach any level of student or teacher. Certainly she has written clearly about the writing process in articles. Wilkinson has unusual reserves of energy and discipline to keep these diverse parts of her life in balance. However, there are limits, and she needed the grants that she received, a National Endowment for the Arts Fellowship for 1973–74 and a Guggenheim Fellowship for 1977–78, in order to complete her next two novels.

Shadow of the Mountain, published in 1977, offers another variant of her design, but with a depressing outcome. The central speaker, Jean, is older at twenty-two than Wilkinson's earlier protagonists, but no wiser, as she has passed through puberty and evidently learned little about life or herself. Born to a "privileged," wealthy family and treated to expensive schools, she perceives that her advantages may be disadvantages, insulating her from a world of strong emotions, the realities of death and poverty, and even self-knowledge. She wishes to reach out to less privileged folk, as much out of curiosity as compassion, and lead them into fuller lives. She keeps venturing out from her secure niche—hiking alone in the mountains, crossing a dangerous train trestle, traveling by herself through Europe for a summer, and working in the Appalachian Corps, trying to bring art, culture, and economic reform to the mountain community of Rocky Gap. Although she does learn much about human nature, which she faithfully records in her journal, she does not learn nearly enough in the time she has, and her reckless naïveté results in her waiting, paralyzed by fear and pride, for her house to be firebombed at the end of the book. She is still too removed from her instincts to survive, and her education and art cannot save her.

However, this is not a tale of righteous "come-uppance" for a rich girl drunk on curiosity and naïve idealism, but a tragedy of a talented young woman, trapped more subtly but just as surely by the limitations built into her environment, especially those directed at females, as others without "privileges" are by theirs. It is Jean's remarkable journal that gives a reader entry to her submerged conflicts and potential so that the necessary bond of sympathy can be forged. Here, marked by italics, are the inner workings, not just of Jean, but of every person she comprehends well enough to project dramatically. Tensions build naturally, for the authenticity of her portrayals of how these people talk and think has little correlation with her ability to deal with them in person. What she can see and imagine in striking detail is not necessarily what she actually knows and needs to know. Even toward the end of the book, she can unravel the twisted logic of the drunk's mind as he rambles through the woods to her house one cold night, understanding his childish desire to show off his penis decorated with a rubber dragon, but she still locks him out, half aware that his drunken condition will mean that he will freeze to death.

The image of freezing to death hovers over the novel, as if to remind the reader that Jean herself may be freezing, emotionally if not literally. The book starts with her discovery of the frozen body of young Jane Booey, a mountain mother left by her husband, sitting facing the sunset on top of Mount Le Conte, and Jean's subsequent fruitless efforts to understand the sense of futility that drove Jane to suicide. Somehow she finds herself identifying with Jane but has no idea why.

Jean recalls a trip to Lost Cove, a town suddenly emptied in the 1930s when the passenger train stopped because its only entrance was over a train trestle a quarter of a mile long spanning a chasm. She crosses the narrow trestle, just in front of a long freight train, explores the houses emptied of anything that could be carried, and runs back fearfully over the trestle after dark. This outing reflects her plunge into the empty lives of the mountain folks, looking for some hidden vitality surely produced by their intimacy with nature. Her quest sends her in other directions also—to Europe, to a Klan meeting in eastern North Carolina, to a snake-handling revival, to visit college girlfriends, and into a talking friendship with tough old Molly, a wise but limited mountain woman. The scenes are memorable in their detail, for they capture not only the cadence of rural Southern speech but the dark undercurrents of prejudice and paranoia. Jean paints them accurately and objectively, without judgment or, significantly, without insight into her own predicament. She seems to understand the quality of everyone's dilemmas but her own.

The shifts in perspective, as different characters speak and think aloud through the medium of Jean's journal, and in time through her flashbacks to earlier moments that now take on meaning, keep a reader alert trying to make connections. The story is carried along less by Jean's building insight—because neither her skill to describe others or to analyze herself seems to change much—than by growing suspense. There are harbingers of the coming tragedy—the possible death of an acquaintance in a train wreck in Germany, a palm reader's prediction that Jean will meet an untimely and violent death, letters of warning from friends and family, and the rumors gradually confirmed of the recent firebombing death of a union organizer in Rocky Gap. Though the reader is more aware of the ominous possibilities than Jean seems to be, the ending still comes as a shock. It simply does not seem fair that such an intelligent and compassionate person should be betrayed by her own ideals and trust, the makings of a tragic fall. But it is more depressing than cathartic, for those men who will kill Jean seem stereotypically wicked, with none of the redeeming qualities shown by those mountain people she has been able to re-create in her journal.

In *Bone of My Bones,* published in 1982, Wilkinson returns to the basic pattern of her first two books, focusing exclusively on the point of view of a young girl growing up in Summit, North Carolina. But there is a crucial difference: this girl, Ella Ruth Higgins, is not only a survivor but a budding writer, learning to see and to say. She does not re-create the people around her as she writes, as Jean did, but she draws from them to create entirely new characters. The book is not so much a bildungsroman—for Ella Ruth is the same witty, tough but sensitive person at eighteen as she was at ten—as it is a portrait of how the artist learns to transform experience into fiction as well as turn art into a tool for psychic survival.

Like Cary and Ramie, Ella Ruth does not really fit into her family, but at least she does have one—a mother, simple and almost illiterate, who is loving but has a weak grasp on her identity (so she cooks and eats constantly), and a father, a critical and prejudiced house painter who turns to alcohol for comfort. He does have a sharp sense of humor, though on the vulgar side, which Ella Ruth inherits and fashions into an affectionate weapon of her own against her parents' limitations. She learns how to defend her growing sense of identity without wounding, absorbing only the few lessons that fit her. When her mother dies, ironically eaten up by cancer, she decides to stay with her father for a while, but strictly on her own terms, hiding the money her mother saved for her. His petty tyranny does not have a chance against her spunk and wit and his need to be taken care of.

But Ella Ruth is more vulnerable than her parents know. She begins writing at ten in her Blue Horse notebooks after a teacher rejects her first story about her grandmother's "tick-picking" relationship with her dog (a writer's revenge can be sweet). She hides her stories about her alter ego, Starrie Dawn, a strong, half-breed Indian cripple, in a carefully crafted box, along with other childish treasures, which she repeatedly buries and digs up. This is her time capsule, written to strangers in the future, not anyone in her world. The stories begin to include her dreams, an attempted rape, and dramatic deaths, as Ella Ruth copes with the realities of sex and death herself. She also includes witty descriptions of how teenagers act in her time.

Then Ella Ruth is raped in the barn by a group of boys she grew up with, going to movies and trading bad jokes. She is more bruised emotionally than physically, but she tells no one. Her journal perspective shifts, now written in first person by Miss Ella Ruth Darwin, the great female scientist and granddaughter of Charles Darwin. Only the real Ella Ruth cannot bring herself to accept the kind of dissection that Miss Darwin must do. She takes refuge in the objectivity of the scientist, though, staying clear of her dangerous dreams for a while. Eventually, she comes to terms with one boy, Al (who did not participate in the gang rape), slowly understanding why they jumped her. But she resolves that she will never have "lots of babies," that she can be herself without depending on a man.

After Ella Ruth finds a job at the hospital and comes to know two older women, mostly by overhearing their long conversations about life and men, her journal takes another sharp turn. Ella Ruth Darwin, her foot caught in a bear trap in the forest, slowly dies, writing gallantly to the end. Ella Ruth's next literary creation is a play about the two women, reconstructing their lives as they converse. More importantly, she imagines the play as a world premiere, presented not to the future but to her friends and family at a reunion, which includes her dead mother and grandmother. The dialogue, drawn from a variety of her own experiences with an imagined story line, is transmuted into dramatic form. It may not be great art yet, but the writer is on her way.

The triumph of the play is that Ella Ruth learns she can let it go and look for other experiences she can quilt into something permanent. Not only can she accept change outside herself, unlike her parents, but she can enjoy the changes within, the "different levels" of herself, of fiction, and of memory. The book ends with an imaginary conversation with her mother. She finds a luna moth and shows it to Al, who runs to find alcohol to preserve it. But Ella Ruth, no longer Darwin, wants the moth free, not dead; she is unwilling to hurt anything that does not have a shell, as she does. She hears her mother whisper, "Ella Ruth, all you have to do is cut off the light," and the moth is freed. At that moment, Ella Ruth seems to be released from the light that represents all the anger and hatred she feels, so she can make her own heritage.

One reviewer claims that in *Bone of My Bones,* Wilkinson "tops her own triumphs with her poignant, bawdy, humorous story."[14] A harsh review in the *New York Times,* however, did much to dampen the book's reception with its claim that the book "lacks shape."[15] In a sense, the first comment encloses and nullifies the second. There is shape, but it is to be found not just here but in all five of Wilkinson's novels. *Bone of My Bones* is a kind of culmination, bringing together the strongest aspects of style and theme of each book, highlighting the tenuous dynamics of life as related to art. Ella's triumph at the end is not forced but natural, the emergence of a golden thread that has woven restlessly through all the novels. Wilkinson, like her central characters, has sorted through her experiences and perceptions, looking for the shapes embedded there, and she keeps finding them. As Jane Vance shows, this novel is Wilkinson's best, bringing together "astuteness of psychological insight, clarity of narration, and complexity of characterization."[16]

Wilkinson's reputation as a writer after five novels has not yet quite matched her level of achievement. Ironically, her latest, more complex novels are not presently in print and have received little attention. But her talent has been fully acknowledged, by other writers and by awards and fellowships. The wunderkind image may have hurt more than helped, especially since her novels focus on the dense world of childhood. It has been too easy for critics to dismiss her work as adolescent novels or depictions of Southern themes, interesting only to other Southerners. They have both raised and deplored, sometimes in the same breath, her use of vivid details, imagery, and voice. However, Wilkinson learned to resist criticism in the seventh grade, and she has continued to write from her own personal and artistic strengths, even if they may be misunderstood. As she says, in the words of Miss Liz, "I knowed it was a snake when I picked it up." In time, though, her fiction may find the literary reputation it deserves and already has among writers, when the unfair stereotype of a "Southern woman writing about adolescence" will be ignored.

It is hard to imagine what Wilkinson's next work (now in progress) will be, since so much of her childhood vision and conflicts seems to have found artistic resolutions. As one critic notes of her last novel, "she has by now explored the rites-of-passage novel for all it is worth and then some."[17] There will be more novels for this determined writer—tucked between teaching and timing races—and they will continue to explore, in well-crafted sentences and striking images, what it means to be human as well as female with Southern roots, aware of both the bright and the dark undercurrents of nature and the contemporary world.

Sylvia Wilkinson Bibliography

NOVELS

Moss on the North Side. Boston and Toronto: Houghton Mifflin, 1966; London: Rupert Hart-Davis, 1967; Wiesbaden: Limes Verlag, 1967; New York: Avon, 1972; New York: Pocket Books, 1978.

A Killing Frost. Boston and Toronto: Houghton Mifflin, 1967; Wiesbaden: Limes Verlag, 1967; New York: Avon, 1973; New York: Pocket Books, 1978.

Cale. Boston and Toronto: Houghton Mifflin, 1970; New York: Avon, 1972. 2d ed. Chapel Hill, N.C.: Algonquin, 1985.

Shadow of the Mountain. Boston and Toronto: Houghton Mifflin, 1977; New York: Pocket Books, 1978.

Bone of My Bones. New York: Putnam, 1982.

NONFICTION

The Stainless Steel Carrot: An Auto Racing Odyssey. Boston and Toronto: Houghton Mifflin, 1973.

Change: A Handbook for the Teaching of English and Social Studies in the Secondary Schools. Ed. Sylvia Wilkinson and E. Campbell. Durham, N.C.: LINC Press, 1971.

Dirt Tracks to Glory: The Early Days of Stock Car Racing as Told by the Participants. Chapel Hill, N.C.: Algonquin, 1983.

ARTICLES

"Writing a First Novel." *Writer* 80 (January 1967): 18.

"A Time to Live, A Time to Write." *Writer* 81 (July 1968): 9–11, 44.

"Growing Up in America: The South." *Mademoiselle* 68 (April 1969): 208, 298–302.

"I Like That Eustacia Vye." *Writer* 91 (August 1978): 9–12, 28.

"Chicken Simon." In *New Stories from the South: The Year's Best, 1986,* ed. Sharon Ravenel, 235–38. Chapel Hill, N.C.: Algonquin, 1986.

"Three Teachers." In *An Apple for My Teacher: Twelve Authors Tell about Teachers Who Made the Difference,* ed. Louis D. Rubin, Jr., 132–38. Chapel Hill, N.C.: Algonquin, 1987.

Anne Tyler

*

SUSAN GILBERT

ANNE TYLER, with ten novels, the last the winner of the National Book Critics' Circle Award, has a secure critical reputation and a large and faithful audience. Her fictional world is well defined. It is a personal world. The concerns of her characters are the persistent and primary psychological anxieties of life. Children hunger for their mothers' approval. They feel grief and guilt at the death or disappearance of a parent. Siblings' rivalries and dependencies, loves and angers, last for lifetimes. Sons and daughters spend decades running away from, or back to, their homes.

On these private lives, the great world impinges little. Except to her artist characters, envied in their absorptions, neither work nor politics, social status nor religious devotion matters much. Familial relationships consume the reader's attention as well, for her families are for the most part unhistorical and unchanging, groups wherein types persist unaffected by changes in social patterns in the towns where they live.

Time passes; things change; the characters live on streets in changing neighborhoods without noticing the changes. Pearl Tull of *Dinner at the Homesick Restaurant* wonders where the years have gone and what has become of the aunts to whom she used to write, but the reader has little sense of the changing South in her long life. In *Earthly Possessions,* Charlotte Emory, married seventeen years and living still in her parents' house, looks out "at the crumbling buildings across the street: the Thrift Shop, newsstand, liquor store, Pei Wing the tailor . . . not a single home in the lot, come to think of it. Everyone else had moved on, and left us stranded here between the Amoco and the Texaco" (185).

It is a telling passage. The want of a historical dimension is what makes many of Tyler's characters seem anachronisms: Pearl Tull, wearing her hats to work as a checkout clerk; Emily of *Morgan's Passing,* in her long skirts and leotards, out of place on the city streets of Balti-

251

more. The families are close, insular, isolated. The Pecks of *Searching for Caleb* are "very close knit, a *fine* family" who have always "stuck together" (13) in a snobbish clannishness from which a few in every generation flee. Pearl Tull, with her three children, lives all alone barely making ends meet after her husband deserts them. They do not relate well to others. Once, waiting for Beck, Pearl "walked around with a broken arm for a day and a half. . . . She was a stranger in town and had no one to turn to" (5). These families lack not only neighborliness; they lack any sense of belonging to a larger social order.

In twenty years, Tyler's focus has not broadened. Her books run deeper but not wider. Her concerns are at opposite poles from the historical novelists in this collection. One does not look here for Mary Lee Settle's tracing of political ideas across countries and generations, for Harper Lee's examination of racial conflict, for Lee Smith's evocation of a place where a whole culture vanishes in a generation. Nor, looking outside the South, does one see likeness to Joan Didion's habit of working very close to the headlines of the news or to Joyce Carol Oates's attempts to bring her characters' lives into focus against the panorama of historical crises. In the all-Southern settings of Tyler's novels, children trundle off to schools never touched by *Brown v. the Board of Education*; her young men never receive or burn their draft cards; their parents never keep vigil on courthouse steps in protest against a war; no women parade with placards for, or against, the ERA.

Agoraphobics such as Jeremy Pauling of *Celestial Navigation,* who cannot venture off his block; Pearl Tull of *Dinner at the Homesick Restaurant,* who for decades does not go beyond the grocery where she is checkout clerk by day and the house where she hammers and putters in the evenings; Charlotte Emory's mother in *Earthly Possessions,* confined first to one big lawn chair and then to bed; and Morgan's mother in her wing chair by the hearth are just the most extreme cases of the class to which they all belong, characters living in oblivion of sexual or political revolutions, characters whose problems are described in psychology texts, not news clippings.

Thus Tyler's work and characters occupy a timeless world of fiction, and the plots move back as often as they go forward. The pattern of the novels is, repeatedly, circular. Characters who feel themselves imprisoned within the routines and encumbering possessions of their own and others' lives seek to break away. They flee or dream of flight. Then most of them return, or they find that the bonds and the stuff that they sought to leave behind have followed them, to make another place, envisioned as spare and stripped, become moldy, cluttered, heavy with earthly freight, buried under layers of the past.

Tyler's first novel, *If Morning Ever Comes* (1964), begins with the hero's coming home and ends with his leaving. His sister leaves her husband and then goes home again. Tyler's stories are as likely to be about fleeing as returning, and whichever the case, the meaning seems to be the same.

The point of view is that of Ben Joe Hawkes, only son in a family of several sisters, a mother, and their "Gram." Theirs is a large Southern family in a big comfortable house with an ill-tended lawn. The father, now dead, was a doctor and an alcoholic and kept a mistress on the other side of town. Ben Joe visits her and her child. Most of the rest of the time, he wanders about home, vaguely in the way.

Most of the themes of Tyler's mature work are to be found in this remarkably crafted first novel, published when she was twenty-three. There is the central character's ongoing sense of deep attachment to his family. He leaves law school to go home because he thinks they need him. But at home he feels neither needed nor close, but vaguely estranged. He elopes at the last without telling them and rides off on the train, wondering if he will always feel this separation, even from his wife and the child they may someday have: "One part of them was faraway and closed to him, as unreachable as his own sisters, and blank-faced as the white house he was born in. Even his wife and son were that way. Even Ben Joe Hawkes" (266). In this sense of remoteness from his present life, he sets a type for many Tyler characters to come, a tribe "unable to realize a thing's happening or a moment's passing" (263).

As in all later Tyler novels, there is the repeated emphasis on movement without change, on change without movement. The sister who left her husband did so for fear that "history was repeating itself" (239). Her parents' marriage had been unhappy and hers was becoming so. But she tells Ben Joe, "It's not the same place I'm coming back to, really. Not even if I wanted it to be" (74). At that stage, he does not see her point, but later, foreseeing her decision to return to her husband, he says, "I don't know that I would call it going backwards instead of forwards. Sometimes it's not the same place when a person goes back to it, or not . . . the same person" (248). This realization of the hero's is all there is to forward movement of the plot, and he is left with the unresolved doubt of his ability to grasp the present.

The novel is fine in its depiction of families, their internal strifes and their physical features, and in its descriptions of house and furnishings and photographs and the ways these preserve the past. To all these themes, she will return.

The Tin Can Tree (1965) is a small masterpiece. Two characters run away and then return. A little girl, Janie Rose Pike has died. Her brother Simon runs away from home because those around him are grieving for her so much that he feels himself unnoticed. In the days before he goes, he says, time after time, when asked if he's had lunch or combed his hair, that his mother "won't care" (19). When he is found and she comes to bring him home, he beams with a joy he cannot contain because she has come "specially" to get him: "You mean you're here on *account* of my going off?" (250) he exclaims.

Interwoven with the family's loss and Simon's sense of loss of his own significance is the romance of his cousin Joan, who has been living with them, and James, one of two brothers living in the adjoining triple house. Joan runs away for much the same reason as Simon, not displaced in a mother's eye by a dead sister, but in her lover's eye by his living brother, Ansel, an alcoholic hypochondriac who has claimed and will claim much of James's attention all his life. A third set of family breaks is the brothers' with their family. This break remains unhealed, though their father tells James they still have his old bed.

Two significant technical achievements and one major thematic advance stand out in *The Tin Can Tree*. Tyler uses the house to anchor a larger set of unrelated characters and to make of them Simon's and Joan's real family. She makes much of photography to point the significance of life's fleeting moments. Thematically, she introduces, in polished form, the needs of the two characters, Joan and Simon, to be seen and loved for themselves alone. Simon is satisfied. His mother has been jolted from her daze of grief to be grateful to have him home. For him, the plot has moved forward.

For Joan, the advance is only in her perception. In the excitement of Simon's running away, her own leaving goes unnoticed. Her return is to the same relationship. In looking for Simon, James neglects his brother's supper. He will cook him a steak tomorrow; Joan will never hold all his attention. And she knows this as, in the last scene, she is photographing Simon's homecoming party. Though all the characters are moving, looking into the camera, she foresees the image in which they will be still, forever: "they could leave and return, they could marry or live out their separate lives alone, and nothing in this finder would change. They were going to stay this way, she and all the rest of them, not because of anyone else but because it was what they had chosen, what they would keep a strong tight hold of. James bent over Ansel; Mrs. Pike touched the top of Simon's head . . . " (273). Though Joan will not have her love all to herself, this is one of the happiest endings in Tyler's fiction, for she sees life as choice, not fatality, and she too has chosen to be where she is, and she knows it.

A Slipping-Down Life (1970) presents the most bizarre of her characters' ploys to gain attention. A homely, fat high school girl, Evie Decker, carves, with fingernail scissors, a rock singer's name in her forehead. They do marry and very briefly find a quiet haven. He puts up household gadgets. Her old friend envies her that she is an outsider no longer but one of those married people "so cozy with someone they belong to" (150).

Their barely broken loneliness soon returns. He loses his job. She quits going to school. In their worry, she neglects to tell him she is pregnant. Suddenly, in the midst of a wild escapade to gain him publicity, Evie's father dies; she finds her husband in bed with his "kidnapper." Within a year from the start, Evie is home again in her father's empty house, to await the birth of her baby.

Evie's is the smallest of the families Tyler draws. Without a mother, she has had only a distant relationship to her father. At the end, she is in the house with photographs, one in her father's room: "An ancestor, maybe; no one could tell her anymore" (198), and another in the living room, a picture of her mother, "remembered now by no living person" (200).

In its characters and in its humor, *A Slipping-Down Life* differs markedly from the earlier two works, filled with the most ordinary people. Tyler insisted that such as the alcoholic father of the first and brother in the second were part of normal families. But Evie, with her grotesque scar, her friend Violet, enormously fat and dressed always in purple or chartreuse, and Drumstrings Casey, the would-be rock star, dark and mesmerizing as he sings, apparently to no one present—these are oddities indeed, more strange as a complete cast than those of any books to follow, but introducing Tyler's large company of weird characters. They are types, especially the serious, brooding singer, much like Flannery O' Connor's creations.

The humor of Tyler's first two novels derives from close observation of the incongruities in daily family life, a homey humor, much of it in the careful rendering of the folk speech of small-town Southerners. *A Slipping-Down Life* has scenes with as violent mixture of humor and horror as John Irving's *The World According to Garp:* the commotion when Evie brands herself; Evie's carving the letters backward, in a mirror image; the disruption of a revivalist's preaching coupled with the deep wound of Casey's insult to Evie; the juxtaposition of a hospital, an empty house, and Evie's finding Casey on top of "Fay-Jean Lindsay, in her orange lace slip" (207). That Tyler describes the macabre externals at these moments of unexpressed hurt and grief gives the humor a dark, dark tone.

The first three works employ love stories for plots—Ben Joe's court-ship and elopement, Joan and James's romance, Evie's marriage—without ever describing sex. In a short story about a rape, Tyler tells only that the feel of the rapist's hand on the girl's mouth differs little from the feel of her boyfriend's; at the scratchy sound of a zipper unzip-ping, she interrupts the scene. She does not go beyond this in the de-scription of sexual feeling or experience.

In the next two novels, *The Clock Winder* and *Celestial Navigation,* Tyler draws a pair of heroines competent to all the exigencies of daily life, managing households of inept, dreamy men, old people, or chil-dren. Both Elizabeth Abbott and Mary Tell have run away from their first families only to have families accrue to their solitary strengths. They are capable and inexpressive, loved and loving, but shying from examination of deep emotion.

The Clock Winder (1972) is the story of the Emersons, a widow and her seven grown children, and Elizabeth Abbott, who comes to live with Mrs. Emerson as her house handy-woman. Elizabeth is courted by two of the sons, Matthew and Timothy, leaves when Timothy commits suicide, returns to nurse Mrs. Emerson after a stroke, is shot by Timo-thy's twin, Andrew, stays, marries Matthew, and lives, as happily ever after as folk do in Tyler's world, with Matthew, their children, Andrew, and Mrs. Emerson, and with the other brother and the sisters return-ing from time to time.

Not one of Tyler's best books, *The Clock Winder* is yet important, presaging in technique and theme what she will add in the next ten years to what she carries over from her first ten years as a novelist.

She handles more time than she has before, 1960 to 1972, and em-ploys multiple points of view, including letters at one point. She con-tinues to draw insular families. The turbulence of America in the sixties touches none of the young Emersons. Though the youngest son is in Vietnam, no one else in the work notices that a war is going on; his mother writes to ask if he is visiting any tourist sights, and only he seems to feel reproach that she lives in a "sealed weightless bubble float-ing through time" (300).

Fathers in Tyler's work play insignificant roles as heads of house-holds; Dr. Hawkes of the first leaves permanent scars and gaps in his family by his absence, not his presence; Mr. Pike of *The Tin Can Tree* is colorless; Evie's father is colorless, kind, and uncommunicative; Mr. Emerson, who has died just before the novel opens, is dimly remem-bered.

A distinct mark of Southern life, if not of Southern literature, promi-nent in Tyler's works is the degree to which families are female affairs.

Men go off to work; some of them make money; and some have a bit of public reputation. These things matter not at all "at home," the locus of all the life that concerns Anne Tyler. It is surprising, faintly amusing to one of Mr. Emerson's sons to remember that as a real estate tycoon the father had a name some thought worth dropping. Elizabeth Abbott is surprised that some of her preacher father's congregation lean on him. Indeed, here and in *Earthly Possessions* (1977), Tyler makes humorous swipes at the stereotype of the Southern patriarch, the Protestant preacher. They are humored by their wives and families. Elizabeth Abbott's mother makes her funeral casseroles by the dozen; her husband wishes she did not act as though she were playing tea party when she does it. Neither wife is a believer; no one at home accords these men the pontifical importance they think they should have.

Nor does money count in Tyler's world, a strikingly immaterial mid-twentieth-century America in which concern for finances or status is a permanent foible only of humorous characters, rarely directing the lives of the central ones. Mrs. Emerson, a rich woman, is stingy in small affairs and disappointed that her children are not successes. Elizabeth, like most of Tyler's heroes and heroines, is oblivious to worldly success. Rarely and briefly does money seriously affect her characters' lives: their poverty affected the teenagers' marriage in *A Slipping-Down Life*; in *Celestial Navigation,* the heroine hates to interrupt her artist husband with the bother of finances; several well-off youngsters turn their backs on respectable careers. But it is personal, not economic, forces that shape all their lives. Real need or desire for money is more rare in Tyler's world than it would be in a monastery or commune; few of her characters bother enough with it to renounce it.

In family motifs and themes, *The Clock Winder* outlines Tyler's ongoing concerns: family dinners interrupted by quarrels, brothers courting one girl, and the influence of one generation on the next. There are two disparate views on the awful responsibility of parents, that of the anxious Mrs. Emerson, whose children flee her, and that of Elizabeth at the end, humorous, all accepting, calmly nursing one baby while her son plays with bugs on the kitchen floor. Of Mrs. Emerson's sons, one is a mental patient, one a suicide; her daughters' loves and marriages do not suit her. She laments: " 'They say it's the parents to blame, but what did we do? I'm asking you, I really want to know. What did *we* do? . . . Just loved you and raised you, the best we knew how. . . . Made mistakes, but none of them on purpose. What else did you want? I go over and over it all, in my mind. Was it something I did? Something I didn't do?' " (132–33). Elizabeth tells her of watching a parade and thinking of an unending line, stretching back beyond history, of hu-

man beings caring for their children, all the years of feeding, protecting, and teaching that a human child must have from at least one adult
simply to survive: "People you wouldn't trust your purse with five minutes, maybe, but still they put in years and years of time tending their
children along and they don't even make a fuss about it. Even if it's a
criminal they turn out, or some other kind of failure—still, he managed to get grown, didn't he? Isn't that something?" (274). In a richer
characterization in Pearl Tull of *Dinner at the Homesick Restaurant,* Tyler will bring the two points of view together.

Unlike the meddlesome Mrs. Emerson, Elizabeth is passive, and her
passivity reveals a constant feature of Tyler's work more clearly than
any of her other characters do. She can fix anything with a screwdriver,
caulking gun, or drill, but she exerts energy and initiative only on
things that can be literally manipulated, never on people. At the outset,
she says she accepts all invitations. She seeks nothing and makes no
choices. But the awful blame for what people do and do not do in others' lives seems to catch her. She is haunted for years with guilt that she
should have done, or not done, something to prevent Timothy's suicide. In this state, she moves to refusing all invitations, all connections.
She can only go along or flee. Serious as Tyler is, she seizes the chance
for humor this affords for a bride at the altar to say "I don't" (222).

It is a sine qua non of the characters for whom Tyler shows affection
that they rarely, and only ineptly, pursue or seek to hold those they
love. They drift. They watch. Weeping alone, they express little emotion; for loud complainers, Tyler has a caustic wit.

Elizabeth refuses Matthew's suit until she is shot by Andrew. Only
then does she realize, and is she sure all the Emersons realize, that
nothing she did or did not do either time could prevent the shooting.
Thus absolved of guilt for the way human lives turn out, she can stay
and join the parade of people raising children. *The Clock Winder* ends in
forgiveness and in healing, with Elizabeth at the center of a home the
large family will return to as inevitably as the locusts that are featured
in the coda.

Celestial Navigation (1974) covers ten years in a run-down boarding-
house in Baltimore, during which separate, lonely people come together, become part of a family of noisy children, and sink back at last
to loneliness. Mary Tell, a young runaway wife with a small baby, takes
up with Jeremy Pauling, an eccentric artist, lives with him, bears five
children, and runs away again at the end. Of this Tyler makes a dense
jewel of a work, informed by the image of Pauling's creations, collages
of miniatures, scraps rendered in perfectly focused detail to suggest a
life of infinite variety and wonder.

The house and its inhabitants are cut off in space and time, all of them anachronisms. Pauling, an agoraphobic, does not leave the block for decades. Before him, his mother was "a *stagnant* kind of person" who "didn't even notice what the neighborhood had turned into" and who "hardly ever left the house" (6). This is a world seen, as Thoreau saw the universe in Walden Pond, by looking in, not out.

The novel is packed with description, of things and people's feelings, in a style different from the spareness of Tyler's earlier works. At rendering detail, she is here in full mastery. They all complain of clutter, of the house and its "clutter of leaded panes and straggly ivy and grayish lace curtains dragging their bottoms behind black screens" (5), and junk inside, "circus paintings and laughing dolls and plastic horses and coffee cans overflowing with broken crayons" (252), "tattered construction paper Valentines glued to the upstairs panes and the dead Christmas tree on its side in front, dripping tinsel" (195). Packing for her escape, Mary Tell wishes to get away, but the stuff of life sticks to her, "children, grocery bags, stuffed animals . . . Dramamine tablets" (194). When Jeremy the artist drives his children away for interrupting him in his study, he is left lonely and guilty: "How could he have scolded them like that. He knew them so little. . . . He looked around the hall and saw the traces they had left behind—one roller skate, a homemade doll, a chalky hand-print on the newel post" (159).

All the characters wish at times to escape from clutter to spareness, to purity. Mary and Jeremy, like the heroes and heroines of Tyler's earlier works, feel unable to realize the import of life in the present. Mary laments: all of life "can be reduced to a heap of trivia in the end. When I die I expect I will be noticing a water ring someone left on the coffee table, or a spiral of steam rising from a whistling teapot. I will be sure to miss the moment of my passing" (223). Here, if anywhere in Tyler's work, one sees that life is clutter. Its only spareness is in the "great towering beautiful sculptures" (276) that Jeremy makes at the end of his life, alone in a quiet, darkening house.

The narrative technique of *Celestial Navigation,* ten chapters titled by season, year (1960–73), and name of the character whose perspective rules in each one, serves well and is one Tyler will repeat. In their monologues, the central characters articulate their understanding more fully than do the people in any of her other works. The shifting perspective shows starkly the gaps between their feelings and what they can tell others. Whatever Mary or Jeremy understands of their need and love for each other avails nothing toward holding their lives together. For Mary, indeed, it is the urgency to have spoken things that neither of them is capable of saying that makes her pull their life apart.

All the pain and perception will go into his art, but it cannot mend their lives.

The humor in these voices, especially in the brilliant opening monologue of Amanda, is Tyler at the peak of her form. It is as captivating as Lee Smith's *Oral History*. The disjunctions of life are portrayed deftly, in small things, not in the violent, macabre pairings of *A Slipping-Down Life*.

Three of Tyler's works stand out from the rest—this one for its intensity and immediacy. From the opening voice of Amanda to the closing one of Miss Vinton, the characters are at much closer range than they have been before, palpably near. In its density, the novel is not like any of Tyler's other works. The style is a piling on, crowded listing in places and in much fuller characterization with not a single strain, but many threads to each life. The siblings' rivalry is just one example. Amanda is resentful that Jeremy absorbed all their mother's attention; he remembers only being never quite able to please her. A small thread in the dense fabric of this novel, this will be the main theme in *Dinner at the Homesick Restaurant*. For its shimmering surface over more detail than one's senses can absorb, *Celestial Navigation* is a great advance and a different direction from earlier works.

The family in *Searching for Caleb* (1975) covers several generations of the descendants of a Baltimore merchant, Justin Peck. In this novel of broken relationships and unbreakable love, Daniel Peck goes looking, with the help of his granddaughter, Justine, for the half-brother he hasn't seen in more than half a century. Caleb is found and leaves again. Justine is married to her first cousin Duncan Peck, in their generation the chief runaway. At the last, they are seen making one more remove, to live in a trailer and travel with a circus.

Like all Tyler's families, the Pecks live to themselves: "you couldn't say that the Pecks had *friends,* exactly. They kept to themselves. They were suspicious of outsiders" (53). For years, the first Peck is shut up inside, immobilized by a stroke. When his wife arranges mirrors so he can see the street scene below, because she thinks "he might like to keep in touch with things" (56), he sees only his son, descending the steps, and orders the mirrors taken away. Succeeding generations, those who stay in their houses where furniture sits in the same spot for decades and those who live like vagabonds, are out of the currents of history, a family whom history washes over without touching them, unaware of wars or social changes, stranded in time, anachronisms like their predecessors.

The time that does matter in the book is internal family time. The characters divide between those who hold onto stuff and those who do not. Things, Justine notices when she comes home for her parents' funeral, are never simply things: "There was no such thing as a simple, meaningless teacup, even. It was always given by someone dear, commemorating some happy occasion, chipped during some moment of shock, the roses worn transparent by Sulie's scrubbing, a blond stain inside from tea that Sam Mayhew had once drunk, a crack where Caroline, trembling with headache, had set it down too hard upon the saucer" (120). Such are the outward and visible signs of the connections by which individual lives remain part of a longer family life. To throw away such is to cast off memory, as does Duncan, the youngest runaway, who is said to live, "forever in the present!" (120). Preparing for their last departure, Justine looks forward to the escape from clutter, to living in a trailer where everything will be built-in, but she is defeated by things pushed on her as she prepares to drive away, a pot of ivy, a rubber plant, things that serve memory, ties to her former self and to people from her past.

Despite the disruptions of place and the silence between brothers for decades, this novel shows not the impossibility of human expression of love, but its possibilities and endurance, in gestures as ritualized as the Pecks' bread-and-butter letters on monogrammed paper or as spontaneous as a toy. Though they unquestionably belong to Tyler's tribe, who find it impossible to articulate love, the Pecks manage to convey their deepest feelings. Duncan cannot plead with Justine to come with him and leave the old aunts. He makes a little stick figure of twisted wire, looking like her, "looking so straight-backed and light-hearted that even a tribesman in darkest Africa could tell that someone cared for her" (123). Without more said, she leaves with him. Though the main characters in *Searching for Caleb* take off at the last, and Jeremy Pauling of *Celestial Navigation* stays home, this novel points at the thread of continuity even in departures; the earlier one showed the terrible gaps left by severed human ties.

In this novel of four generations, the longest span she has yet treated, Tyler develops for the first time the idea of heredity as fate, a slight motif in several earlier works. In the first novel, characters bear the indelible marks of physical inheritance, the Dower nose, the Hawkes nose. A daughter feels that in her generation history is repeating itself. In *Searching for Caleb,* personality types as well as physical features are handed down, the Pecks' stolid conformity and a forgotten foreign grandfather's wildness. Tyler describes the wandering Caleb: "blond like his half-brother, but his tilted brown eyes must have snuck in from the Baum side of the family, and he had his Grandpa Baum's delight in noise and crowds" (52). However often Justine and Duncan Peck run

away, as they age, they become more visibly Pecks. Heredity, upbringing, the early childhood years—characters may wish to escape these, to
become themselves alone, unique individuals; they never do. Later, in
Dinner at the Homesick Restaurant, Tyler will paint in darker tones the
effects of generations' repeating their parents' failures.

The Pecks are more well-to-do than most Tyler families but are no
more social or stylish. Their house is "bristling with chimneys and lined
with dark, oily wood . . . filled with golden oak furniture and Oriental
screens, chandeliers dripping crystal, wine velvet love-seats with buttons and more buttons up and down their backs . . . curlicued urns,
doilies, statuary . . . great globular lamps centered on tasseled scarves,
and Persian rugs laid catty-corner and overlapping" (50–51). Tyler will
draw a house of wealth but not one of fashion. Here and always she
paints folkways with more affection, Justine Peck in country clothes
peddling goat cheeses, a city-bred girl from this Peck domicile coming
to like the smells of kerosene and fatback. This country domesticity may
have added to Tyler's appeal for some readers in the last two decades,
with their flourishing fads of healthful, simple country-ness.

Artistic sophistication is the only sophistication presented in Tyler's
world, and this artistry is only in nonverbal plastic arts, such as collages
or statues, or in highly stylized simple forms, such as puppetry. Tyler
herself desired a career in painting before writing; she says she sketches
her characters before she describes them in words. But the artworks in
the novels, except for Pauling's barely mentioned late towering sculp-
ture, are homey stuff. Tyler's own work is highbrow, the critical organs
for it are the *New Yorker* and the *New York Times*. Educated and cosmopolitan, a writer married to a psychiatrist, she writes almost entirely
of uneducated folk. When she draws an artist, he is never in an artistic
or—god forbid—an artsy milieu. She describes no fashionable inte-
riors, stylish dress, or bons mots of up-to-date wits. And never does she
draw characters broadly able to think and speak in abstract terms of the
human condition. The only trenchant and comprehensive intelligence
she permits within the pages of her books is her own.

Earthly Possessions (1977) is titled for Tyler's message that the cluttered minutiae of life, though they seem to obscure one's vision of some
life of grander import, are what life is. The title may imply that if there
are "earthly" possessions, then there may be also unearthly ones, accru-
ing in some heavenly mansion, waiting for the individual in some
fairer, faraway place; it isn't so. Her fortunate characters learn this in
time to return and, in learning this, realize what the hero of Tyler's first
novel said, that going forward can look a lot like going backward:

"Sometimes it's not the same place when a person goes back to it, or not . . . the same person."

Charlotte Emory, the heroine of *Earthly Possessions,* is one of the lucky ones. At the novel's opening, she is taking money from the bank to run away from her husband, family, and home. She feels encumbered, buried, unnoticed, and unappreciated. Her parents' home, which she has never left, is crowded with people, with several children, with her husband's brothers, and with the stuff his mother left. At the bank, she is kidnapped by a robber and taken as his hostage on a long drive to Florida, farther from home than she has ever been before. At the last, she is home again, content to stay.

Like Justine Peck and Mary Tell, Charlotte is trying to escape clutter for the "bare essentials." "My life," she says, "has been a history of casting off encumbrances, paring down to the bare essentials, stripping for the journey" (37). In book after book, Tyler's metaphors of weight and freight convey Wordsworthian echoes of mortality: "Full soon thy Soul shall have her earthly freight, / And custom lie upon thee with a weight, / Heavy as frost, and deep almost as life!" In her first novel, the young hero on his first evening home "was beginning to feel the weight of home settling back on him, making him feel heavy and old and tired" (*Morning,* 70). Here Charlotte says, "I have been trying to get rid of all belongings that would weigh me down on a long foot-march" (36). For Tyler, the weight is no intimation of immortality but the inevitable yoke of the only life there is.

Things conveying memory of a human past fill Tyler's characters' houses in "layers" and in "webs." Both figures recur, the first suggesting the connection of the present to the past, and the other that of the individual to his family or surrogate family. In Tyler's first novel, the hero's room seemed to him to be "made up of layers, the more recent layers never completely obliterating the earlier ones" (*Morning,* 219). For him and for Charlotte the layers of the past are clear and bright, the present hard to discern. About to run away, Charlotte fingers bits of past and present, "rolled socks, crumpled homework papers" and the "worn, smudged woodwork, listening to absent voices, inhaling the smell of school paste and hymnals" (189). But deluded, she flees because, as she says of herself, she had not "the knack of knowing I was happy right while the happiness was going on" (189).

These two failures of vision have impelled all of Tyler's characters on their flights, the inability to see the beauty of the present, its outlines obscured in layers of the past, and the inability to see themselves at all, the fear that they are invisible as individuals in the webs of others' lives. Photographs, moments frozen in time, individuals centered in the lens's focus, are a prominent motif in all of Tyler's works. Here Charlotte has taken over, without, it seems, a conscious decision to do so, her father's profession of photographer. She makes portraits in which ordinary folk of their small town seem to stand out as people from another age.

Although the exclusively first-person narration of *Earthly Possessions* should afford Charlotte chance to explain fully the reasons for her return, these remain scantily articulated. She is less revealing of self-understanding than are Mary Tell and Jeremy Pauling in *Celestial Navigation*. In the flashbacks to her past, interspersed with the forward movement of her days with her captor, she does not spell out the lessons she learns in the journey of her soul. In a brief coda, she is back home with her husband, taking pictures of plain people in exotic costumes, and sure to stay. She is no more communicative with her husband or the reader than she has ever been. He lies awake, vaguely disturbed by slight misunderstandings of daily life, questioning whether they are "happy," whether they ought to take a trip. Charlotte is past questioning or seeking afield: "I tell him no. I don't see the need, I say. We have been traveling for years, traveled all our lives, we are traveling still. We couldn't stay in one place if we tried. Go to sleep, I say. And he does" (200).

Without adding much particularly new in characterization or technique, *Earthly Possessions* consolidates several of Tyler's most important themes: the contrast between a muddled web of daily life and a dream life, spare and solitary; the characters' inabilities to feel themselves alive in the present; their desire to be seen for special, individual significance; and the barely articulated return to place.

Earthly Possessions closes with Charlotte Emory's wordless contentment with ordinary life. *Morgan's Passing* (1980) ends with its hero, Morgan Gower, smiling and humming: "Everything he looked at seemed luminous and beautiful, and rich with possibilities" (311). "Passing" is the Southern country euphemism for dying; people "pass" to a greater life. Morgan's passing is from a divided life, in which his earthly situation of dismaying ordinariness is disjoint from his fantasy life, to another in which, though its outline shows little difference, he sees wonder in the commonplace. At the beginning of the novel he is a hardware store manager, filling an unnecessary role in one of the stores his wife has inherited, insignificant at work and at home, where all affairs social and practical are managed by his competent wife. Morgan misses the days when infants ran to greet him. Now they barely notice him. Somehow they have neglected to tell him one of his daughters is to be married. Seeking another identity, he roams Baltimore in costume and so becomes entangled with Emily and Leon Meredith, the other principals of the novel, a pair of young puppeteers whose exotic life fascinates him. They, like Justine and Duncan Peck, are runaways from respectability.

At the end, Morgan has replaced Leon as Emily's husband. He has fled one household, where he felt lost in a clutter of tennis shoes, Triscuit boxes, and pets' feeding bowls, to a life with Emily, which he envisaged as spare, the bare essentials. But he finds, as other of Tyler's characters have, that clutter is life's inescapable condition. Their baby will require a crib and changing table and potty seat, like all others. Though he is not far from where he began, Morgan is content, for the time being at least, looking out at the wonder of his life, freed from the foolish, frantic pursuit of his own identity.

Morgan Gower, dashing about Baltimore in his strange garbs, butting into other people's lives, is the most extroverted character in Tyler's long collection of introverts, but since his interventions are a series of charades, he has no more real links to a historical community than the rest. And for all that he pops in and out of strangers' lives, he is as self-absorbed as his predecessors. Certainly, he and Leon and Emily make a cast that is more exotic than any since *A Slipping-Down Life*. Tyler has remarked that she is pained when people ask about the oddity of her characterizations and insists that all people, looked at closely enough, become odd in their peculiarities, in their uniqueness.

Feeling that they are missing the present, feeling themselves lost and unseen in the layers of past, present, and future, and obscured in the webs of their myriad daily doings with others, Tyler's characters go to extraordinary lengths to break out and be seen. To be seen as an individual, alive in the present, to have focused upon oneself the full, attentive gaze of another, is time after time what lures her characters to their escapes and to drastic measures, momentary or stretching over lifetimes. In the first novel, Ben Joe's sister wears red dresses and jangling bracelets to secure the boys' attention; later she does not know how to live with her husband, or with anyone, after the attention of the first date wears off. More desperate for attention, Evie carves the singer's name in her face. Simon and Joan of *A Tin Can Tree* run from the mother and lover who fail to notice them. Mary Tell of *Celestial Navigation*, taken for granted and unnoticed by Jeremy, succumbs to the gaze of their good friend Brian. Charlotte Emory, feeling herself invisible, falls into a brief affair with her husband's brother because he alone sees her, notices her, as she bakes the cakes, washes the clothes, feeds the dog. Morgan looks for a new life because he is unregarded at home, and Emily, in a marriage where her husband is star and her contribution and creativity are unseen, is irresistibly drawn to Morgan because he watches her. In *Dinner at the Homesick Restaurant,* a girl is again stolen, from one brother by another, because she cannot resist the attention, the notice lavished on her. These characters—imagining themselves unseen in their families, in meshes of domestic chores; angry, with a parent or spouse or lover, feeling, usually with reason, that they are so taken for granted as to be not merely unregarded but invisible in their roles—respond to the inherently sexual appeal of someone else who, looking at them, sees them. The desire to be seen "for oneself alone" is to Tyler romantic delusion.

Usually for Tyler's characters, the sight lasts just a moment, like an expression caught in a snapshot. The photographs that figure prominently in all her books are a foil to the characters' uneasiness that the present is escaping them, their being "unable to realize a thing's happening or a moment's passing." Pictures freeze the moment.

In Tyler's first novel, the hero finds among the "layers" of his room an old snapshot of himself and his sister on tricycles, their mother standing between them. Of this frozen moment and the relationships pictured in it, he is sure; of the present and their relationship, he is uncertain. In the second novel, the face of Janie Rose appears unexpectedly in a picture taken just a few days before her death, her image hard to pick out among little patches of Queen Anne's lace that dot a field. The work closes with a camera's reducing change to permanence; in the lens, Simon's mother bends over him eternally, James leans to his brother. In the third novel, Evie, the expectant mother is alone with pictures of an unknown ancestor and of her own mother, no one in the world left to remember either of them. Charlotte Emory in *Earthly Possessions* resists taking up her father's profession of photographer because she dislikes the way "photos froze a person, pinned him to cardboard like a butterfly" (62). A photograph of a little girl, smiling and dimpled, focuses Charlotte's tortured relationship with her mother. Neither had pleased the other; Charlotte never felt she was her mother's daughter. Finding this photo hidden in her dying mother's drawer, she demands to know who it is, this one she feels is her mother's longed-for daughter, only to be told it is the mother herself.

In *Morgan's Passing* too, pictures trigger several revelations. It takes a picture in the newspaper to make Emily see that her husband is not a young boy any more. Morgan's sister is at last married to the suitor who jilted her decades ago, but she runs out on him because he spends his days mooning over her old graduation photo, jealous, she says, "of my own self . . . of my photograph" (161). However muddled peoples' daily relationships are, in photographs they look out "steadily," with "trust" and with "concentration" (187). It is in looking at Emily's photograph that Morgan sees her most clearly and imagines her seeing him: "Emily herself, marble-pale in folds of black, met his scrutiny with eyes so clear that he imagined he could see through them and behind them; he could see what she must see, how his world must look to her" (187). This vision of himself as seen by another makes him "a man in love" (187).

In photographs, insignificance, ordinariness, transience are lost. Pictures of people taken long ago, or days or hours before, seem, even to those who take the pictures and see their living models, "lost and long ago" (*Tin Can Tree*, 58). For pictures show individuals, and individuals seem always odd.

Tyler's books are full of oddities, alcoholics, hypochondriacs, neurotics, obesities, suicides. These are most understandable seen in the context of their families. In small towns where a person's family place is known, they stand out less than when they are cut off, alone in cities. Emily of *Morgan's Passing,* an orphan married to a runaway, appears like a gypsy in leotards and long skirts on the streets of Baltimore. She, or Justine Peck, a circus fortune-teller, would have been, had either stayed home, one of the Merediths, one of the Pecks, far less strange and far less visible. Human eccentricities thus stand out in sharper focus as characters move toward individuality. Some readers have remarked that individuals in Tyler's large families blur, that the characterization is halting. It is an intended effect; what she draws are families seen as they are seen by older residents of closed communities, in relation to their parents, aunts, or siblings.

They go to great lengths to break out of this ego-deflating invisibility, and they are quickly stirred to love by being seen all alone. Romance is not the only way characters seek to be seen. Sickness is a more effective way to hold the attention of others. The absorption of sexual passion is fleeting in Tyler's world. But malaise, malingering, and mental instability last longer than lifetimes; they affect generations. Alcoholics, invalids, the mentally frail maintain the central position in the vision of the ones who consume their lives caring for them. Some try this game, fail, and therefore flee. Morgan's wife refuses to let his eccentricities become the exclusive concern of the household. Beck, the errant husband of *Restaurant,* has wandered off from his wife and family, and from dozens of women later, it turns out.

It is a war first and last of "normal" families against "odd" individuals. In her first work, the son complains of the "*amazing*" (*Morning,* 190) things that go on in their family; his mother insists, "This family's just like any other family" (190). Morgan says he has a "very ordinary family . . . *determined* to be ordinary" (118). In Tyler's fiction, all families are normal, all are recognizable in their tensions and routines. The works teach not merely that all families have eccentric members but that seen individually all people are odd. Only in the ego-threatening place where one is one of the Dower boys or one of the Gower girls are people ordinary.

Seen alone and still, as in photographs that catch one's expression for a second, her people are stranger than they are familiar, but such a sight lasts just a moment. It flickers; then family life resumes. In a tone more affirmative than resigned, Tyler returns her characters to old relationships or dissolves them in new ones barely distinguishable from those they had known before. The dazzling sight of an individual is, like the flush of first love, merely an illusion. It is a momentary glimpse of a young person's features before they become a "Dower nose," the "Peck eyes," the persistent marks of family, an organism more lasting than any of its members.

Thus the Tulls of *Dinner at the Homesick Restaurant* (1982) are a family in spite of themselves, one generation indelibly marked by the hurts and mistakes of the last. They are a small family living to themselves in a Baltimore row house, cut off from their ancestors and their neighbors. Pearl, an old-maidish woman, married Beck Tull, a bounder. She moved with him half a dozen times, lost track of her past, bore three children, Ezra, Cody, and Jenny, and, after Beck walked out on them, reared them, in rage, frustration, and poverty. Dying, Pearl muses with regret that "something was wrong with all of her children" (22), and she wishes to be excused of blame for the hurt and anger she has passed on to them. She thinks of Cody: "Honestly . . . wasn't there some statute of limitations here? When was he going to absolve her? He was middle-aged. He had no business holding her responsible any more" (22–23). There is in Tyler's world no statute of limitations; the sins and hurts of the fathers and mothers are visited upon the sons and daughters for countless generations.

Like *Earthly Possessions* and *Searching for Caleb,* this family's story is told in flashbacks, from a present in which the mother is old and dying, the children grown. Like *The Clock Winder* and *Celestial Navigation,* it is told from different points of view, which show the gaps in the Tulls' understanding of their single, shared past.

They have weathered it with few external scars. Pearl as a grandmother has a peace and gentleness she never had as a mother. Ezra, if somewhat dreamy and distant, manages a restaurant where he seeks to dispense to the world the warm nourishment his childhood missed.

Jenny, competent and cool, is a pediatrician and mother to a brood of children, her own and those she has acquired in her third marriage. She seems fully recovered from a nervous breakdown when she, as a young medical student, was abusing her daughter as her mother had her. And Cody is a financial success, something of a wizard as a time efficiency consultant. But in Jenny's distant cheerfulness is the defensive armor by which the hurt child learned to cope. And in all his inner life, Cody is the angry sibling, jealous of his mother's preference for his brother, guilty over his father's desertion, unable ever to trust, however desperately he clings to them, the wife he stole from his brother and the son he fantasizes is not his own.

Year after year, decade after decade, they come "home" to family dinners interrupted by quarrels that wait, never settled, to trip them up each time. Pearl has carefully instructed Ezra to "invite" everyone in her address book to her funeral. At the last dinner after the funeral, the absent father is with them, just as, in a sense, he has always been part of all they have suffered and become. He looks around and remarks, " 'Haven't you all turned out fine—leading good lives, the three of you?' " (302). He has been coaxed back to the table after one quarrel but will not stay long, warning them he will leave before the dessert wine is poured.

Dinner at the Homesick Restaurant has been much praised for the qualities Tyler has long been noted for—her wit, her rendering of detail, her compassion—and it has been praised beyond these for its intensity and darkness. John Updike, who has long championed her work, says it shows a "new level of power."[1] Benjamin DeMott says that its truths are "deeper than many living novelists of serious reputation have penetrated, deeper than Miss Tyler herself has gone before. It is a border crossing."[2]

The border is of anger and pain. The depth and power of the book derive from Pearl's barely contained rage that now consumes her son and is clearly marking her grandson Luke. And the work articulates less of tragic insight than Tyler has allowed before. No characters see through mistakes and pain to another vision of the wonder of common life. Less, not more, is articulated of what the Tulls have learned from pounding down life's ruts.

Brief moments of vision do come. The old blind Pearl is humored by Ezra's reading pages of her old diaries and scrapbooks to her. Among these, at the last, they discover an entry from her girlhood, of herself kneeling in a garden, dirty and perspiring, hearing someone play the piano, seeing a fly buzz: "I saw that I was kneeling on such a beautiful green little planet. I don't care what else might come about, I have had this moment. It belongs to me" (277). The book closes with Cody's recollection of a frozen moment from a long-ago family outing that ended disastrously with his shooting his mother with an arrow: "He remembered his mother's upright form along the grasses, her hair lit gold, her small hands smoothing her bouquet while the arrow journeyed on. And high above, he seemed to recall, there had been a little brown airplane, almost motionless, droning through the sunshine like a bumblebee" (303).

Like Virginia Woolf's "Moments of Being," these are occasions when life seems to break through the shell of the characters' consciousness. They are as fine and shining as any Tyler has drawn. It is only the placement of them in the characters' lives that makes this work darker than its predecessors. They are remembrances, for Pearl even a "forgotten" memory, triggered by the diary, for Cody a day long ago in his childhood. The life that is un-being has gathered round and darkened Pearl; there is no hope that this vision will effect any change in Cody's way of seeing himself, his brother, or his wife and son.

In the shifting points of view of *Dinner at the Homesick Restaurant,* none of the characters reveal self-understanding. What in earlier works were much-understated pronouncements, outspoken only in the case of Morgan Gower, of what they had learned of the wonder of everyday life lived piecemeal is here only for the reader to see. Over and over in Tyler's world—she says she has been populating a town[3]—rings the question of *Our Town,* "Do any human beings ever realize life while they live it, every, every minute?" The answer of *Restaurant* is no, not every minute, not any minutes at all.

Reviewing the book, DeMott says that Tyler has taken the reader beyond the "truism" that adversity teaches: "the important lessons taught by adversity never quite make themselves known to the consciousness of the learners—remain hidden, inexpressible."[4] He finds in the book an Emersonian kind of compensation, a psychic ability to endure, which is like a physical attribute, the strength derived from stress. Bruised psyches, like broken bones and scarred skin, heal tougher. What is best in these characters, DeMott says, Ezra's wordless nurturing and Jenny's determined cheerfulness, results from their deprivation.

With her tenth novel, *The Accidental Tourist* (1985), Tyler received the National Book Critics' Circle Award, critical America's recognition of the importance of her rendering of family life and characters in a perpetual pull between returning home and running away. Some, in Tyler's books and in her audience, where most Americans move at least once in five years and half of all marriages end in divorce, dream of a glamour that recedes forever in the distance. Not so is Macon Leary, the "accidental tourist," author of books for people who prefer to go nowhere, guides to tell the business traveler where he can find, in Madrid "king-sized Beautyrest Mattresses," in Tokyo "Sweet'n Low," in Stockholm "Kentucky Fried Chicken" (12).

It is a story that begins in grief and ends in joy. The catalyst to the action has occurred. Leary's only son, Ethan, has been murdered in one of the bizarre phenomena that fill the news, in a shoot-out at a fast-food restaurant. The routine of their lives disrupted, its meaning unclear to her, his wife, Sarah, leaves him. Leary's journey is from solitude in their empty house, back to his childhood home, inhabited by his siblings, to an affair with Muriel, a not-at-all-routine young dog trainer, back to his wife, and finally to Paris, whither both women pursue him, the old and the new claiming his life. The seesaw on which the passive Macon teeters between them is so carefully balanced that the novel feels as if written to go either way. Like reviewers of mystery tales, one hates to tell the end and spoil the reader's fun.

Tyler's novels alternate between those interrupted at the high or the low of her circles of return and departure, between those that suggest the inevitability of the past's wounds and those that proclaim the persistent possibility of happy accident in life. Some, like *The Clock Winder*, end in scenes of homey—"cozy" is a favorite word of hers—family life; there the gathered clan, several generations, a new baby, a new bride, and the seventeen-year locusts symbolize the cyclical rise and fall of the welfare and troubles of the tribe. *Dinner at the Homesick Restaurant* ends with the dinner that is but a momentary interlude in the Tulls' lives of separation. *A Slipping-Down Life* and *Celestial Navigation* close in loneliness. *Earthly Possessions* and *The Tin Can Tree* end in returns, in new visions of people in old settings; *If Morning Ever Comes, Searching for Caleb, Morgan's Passing,* and *The Accidental Tourist* end with departures. Her first novel and her latest end in new marriages.

A corollary to the theme of staying in place and moving on, that of belonging and estrangement, has also a happy twist in this work. The characters, while no less caught up in personal turmoil and no more political than their predecessors, live in less bleak isolation. Though the hero wanders in limbo for most of the book, his sister looks out for her elderly neighbors on the block where she has always lived. Muriel, his girlfriend, has weathered the hurt of a husband's desertion to live on easy terms with neighbors who make themselves at home in her kitchen. When pipes freeze at Leary's home and it floods, neighbors notice, though, like a typical Tyler hero, he has gone off without telling anyone where he is going.

Though the protagonist returns to his family home and to spending evenings playing an old game intelligible only to his siblings, the book holds more of adult struggles and of sexual lure and less of the griefs of children than earlier novels. *Dinner at the Homesick Restaurant* provoked at least one strong attack that Tyler's insistence on the primacy of childhood hurts and rivalries was a case of "arrested development."[5] Here Tyler is closer to such writers as Updike, Oates, Beattie, Didion, who treat frequently the insubstantiality of connections, the breakups of loves and marriages. Still her voice is distinct. To most of her characters, as to Leary's grandfather in this novel, relatives acquired by marriage, even spouses, hardly count.

The third tension in Tyler's work, finally the most important, is between the view of life as a still, bright, timeless present and the dull routine of years, which films sight and blurs the outlines of self, of others, and of earth itself to a smudge of dust and clutter. Leary and the two women form a triangle in what and how they see. He is not surprised by life but has all along, before tragedy struck, seen its capacity for violence. Long before Ethan's murder, he watched helplessly as the child ran into a street before a truck and in "one split second" saw through life's terror and its caprice, "adjusted to a future that held no Ethan—an immeasurably bleaker place but also, by way of compensation, plainer and simpler . . . "(143).

The wife, Sarah, startled by the tragedy, is awakened to bitterness and is resentful of her husband's impassive surface, a trait he shares with most Tyler heroes of being distant and uncommunicative. Hers is a vision of the evil in a world of human atrocity. As one of Tyler's uninitiated, she seeks expression of their grief and complains of his "muffled quality" (142). Like a Tyler hero, reticent and as wary of words as of commitment, he can answer her cries that life has lost its point only with, "Honey, to tell the truth, it never seemed to me there was all that much point to begin with" (5).

Muriel is tough where Sarah was sheltered but has through her suffering acquired a different vision. At the birth of her child, premature and sickly, her husband bolted; she worked for months as a hospital maid. Vision came to her as she stared out a window at ambulances arriving and attendants scurrying. A Martian visitor surprising Earth at such a moment would, she muses, observe "what a helpful planet, what kind and helpful creatures" and would not guess this was not "natural" human behavior (179).

Flashes of vision can be of terror or of loveliness. Another window in the novel is the lens through which Leary sees life as separation. As a dutiful author of guides he visits a round glass restaurant of the sort, the tops of something or other, that dot American cities. Looking out, he observes "the planet curving away at the edges, the sky a purple hollow extending to infinity" (159). He is terrified at the "vast lonely distance from everyone who mattered. . . . He was too far gone to return. He would never, ever get back. He had somehow traveled to a point completely isolated from everyone else in the universe, and nothing was real but his own angular hand clenched around the sherry glass" (160).

In Tyler's writing, the direct point of a plot is to bring people to a still moment of vision. But moments of epiphany seem to come unpredictably, by "accident," and to have little to do with process or progress, to be timeless, disconnected from the daily order.

Most of her characters, caught in the routines of life, travel the same streets for years without seeing them. Caught in the webs of old relationships, they go for decades without acute sense of closeness or distance. Lives fall into patterns that people do not devise, that they perpetuate but do not desire. Over and over, they play the same games, fight the same no-win wars with their kin, living and dead. Patterns triumph over all will to break out, as in the clan of Pecks: "Everything was leveled, there were no extremes of joy or sorrow any more but only habit, routine, ancient family names and rites and customs, slow careful old people moving cautiously around furniture that had sat in the same positions for fifty years" (*Searching for Caleb,* 201).

Routine is comforting to some, terrifying to others for the same reason, that it blinds them to the significance of life or to the sense of self. These come only in momentary flashes, epiphanies stark or tender, always unsettling. At these rare moments, by an altered angle of vision, characters see life's possibilities, not merely its worn outlines. Mary Tell of *Celestial Navigation,* one of the most articulate of Tyler's heroines, reflecting over her life with Jeremy, says, "We have such an ability to adjust to change! We are like amoebas, encompassing and ingesting and adapting and moving on, until enormous events become barely perceptible jogs in our life histories" (216). *Morgan's Passing* closed with its hero's vision of a world aglow: "Everything . . . luminous and beautiful, and rich with possibilities" (311). And Leary, the accidental tourist, rides off to a new life, the dirty windows of a taxi the prism through which he views a bright future: "A sudden flash of sunlight hit the windshield, the spangles flew across the glass. The spangles were old water spots, or maybe the markings of leaves, but for a moment Macon thought they were something else. They were so bright and festive, for a moment he thought they were confetti" (354–55).

Tyler cannot take her heroes very far into a new life, for soon wonder subsides to dullness. Tourists may see things afresh, but the human eye seems able to see, really see, things only once. Then routine films the vision; habit and clutter fill the days; nothing will have changed very much.

But the moments of detachment from time matter as much in her world as the patterns of years that she records so well. They are the moments when time meets eternity. The tension in her work is finally not only between going and staying but also between living and seeing. In attachment, they live; in detachment, they see.

What do her works then teach, with their passive, unchanging heroes, their circular plots? Certainly not the efficacy of human moral resolve, nothing of the energy of a Protestant work ethic, and nothing either of caution against heedless rapidity, headlong careening toward tragedy. Mostly it is a lesson of mundane quietism. It is through contemplation, not action, not even the articulation of the lessons of insight, that some of Tyler's characters move from feeling that life has them trapped in patterns too old and strong for them to break, to the vision of Morgan Gower, one of her least popular but happiest heroes, that there is "virtue in the trivial, the commonplace" (111).

Tyler is still a young writer, celebrating her forty-seventh birthday in October 1988. Tyler is her maiden name; she was born to Phyllis and Lloyd Tyler in Minneapolis, Minnesota, in 1941. The features of her childhood that may have mattered most to her writing are that the family lived for some years in communes and that she felt herself something of an outsider when they moved to Raleigh, North Carolina, very much a small Southern town in her day. As a student, she was bright and precocious, graduating Phi Beta Kappa from Duke University at age nineteen. She has been married since 1963 to Taghi Modarressi, a psychiatrist. They have two daughters, Tezh and Mitra. After working briefly in the Duke University library and McGill University library, she has been "just writing," in her words, since 1965 and living with the family in Baltimore, Maryland, since 1967.

She has said that she spent her adolescence "as a semi-outsider—a Northerner, commune-reared, looking wistfully at large Southern families around me."[6] The notes about the author printed in her books, however, say she "considers herself a Southerner." The primacy of family as her subject, the attention to time, the influence of the past on the present and future, the settings, the use of one setting over and over, the attention to manners and to folk speech, the range of characters from the quaintly anachronistic to the eccentric to the grotesque, the writer's sense of being outside are all qualities for which she and other writers are tagged as Southern.

While these features are wholly true of her work, they do not mark her as exclusively a regional writer; some qualifications may be in order. John Updike has written that her belief "that families are absolutely, intrinsically interesting" is "extinct save in the South."[7] If so, it wasn't always so; Tyler has Jane Austen and Henry James for predecessors here. Novelists of all great traditions draw the locale and the speech patterns they know, but it is true that Tyler has concentrated on her Southern experience. She has exploited only briefly in short pieces the subject of international difference that her marriage to an Iranian might have permitted. Tyler speaks often of the influence of Eudora Welty on her becoming a writer. In her education and reading, her teachers having been Phyllis Peacock in high school and Reynolds Price at Duke, she was also under Southern influence.

On the question of eccentrics, Tyler is as defensive as Flannery O'Connor but for a different reason, individuality itself being the source of peculiarity for Tyler. Her self-absorbed grotesques certainly have their counterparts in Southern fiction, but as some critics of her work have noted, all modern literature is full of pathologically self-absorbed characters. And the posture of the artist as self-conscious outsider knows no regional boundaries.

But putting the locus of value in the private life alone sets Tyler apart from the broad historical concerns of the main current of Southern writing. Like her insular families and anachronistic individuals, Tyler lacks the perspective of those writers—Simms, Page, Cable, Glasgow, Faulkner, Wolfe, Porter, Agee, Warren, Tate, Williams, Settle, Capote, Lee, Betts, Walker, Smith—who have examined Southern American life for the shaping force of cultural habits and beliefs on individual lives. If Tyler has her eyes always to the timeless, as does Flannery O'Connor, she has not O'Connor's attention to the historical versions of her creed. Tyler's characters, whether they find their way or lose it, do so with little effect from any religious or social dogma that they share with any identifiable class or segment in their communities.

Without concern for placing her characters in large social or historical context, Tyler treats them in families, not as lone individuals seeking self-expression or self-identity. She is thus doubly distant from much twentieth-century feminist writing, which frequently does one or the other.

Like Anne Bradstreet, Anne Tyler writes of "thyme and parsley" wreaths, not "bays," nor "wars," "captains," "kings," "cities founded, commonwealths begun." Whether this makes her a pacesetting female writer, taking the subjects of women's lives, marriage, child rearing, housekeeping, and tending the aged as life's most important business, or whether it puts her to the right of Phyllis Schlafly, relegating women and her own art to the backwaters, depends on the critic's bias. Some have sneered that her work falls between high art and stuff for women's magazines. Tyler continues to write for women's magazines, as well as for the *New Yorker*. Her insistence on the primacy of roles of mother, spouse, and tender of the hearth is certainly old-fashioned, if not anti-feminist.

Tyler's work shares the subject matter of the feminist revolution but not its attitudes. In her novels and stories, fathers are often absent, dead or run away. Her heroines live interruptible lives. Her happiest visions of human life as well as her stiffest are of extended families. Rarely she exploits the pathos of children. In one short story, a small boy carries from house to house photographs of foster families he has stayed with. In another, a young single mother of a teenage marriage that failed leaves her retarded son at an asylum.

Tyler regularly makes women the strong centers of the home, but strength is not always benevolent, and she never presents women "achievers," the strong hero models some ardent feminists have called for. Though Tyler's women manage domestic details with ease, when they attempt to exert influence on people, they often become meddlesome, half-humorous harridans, half-terrifying vixens, driving their husbands and children from them. These clean-house busybodies, like Mrs. Emerson and Pearl Tull, are cold and sexless, equaling Eliza Gant in their destructive force. The strong women portrayed with affection are easygoing, passive. They are unaffected by a baby on their hip, milk dribbled or spilt down their clothes; best of all they can nurse the baby, get locusts out of the parlor, branches out of the gutters, and receive unexpected in-laws for dinner with a nary a flap.

Many have used the word "private" about Anne Tyler's life, as she so often describes herself. Her life is centered on her family and her work; anything else, she says, just "fritters" her away.[8] And as she describes it, it is an old-fashioned life of a woman, in which she tends children first and does what she pleases—writing—last. For years, Tyler says, she worked when her children were in school and put aside her writing during vacations or when someone was ill, or when company came, or when the dog had to go to the vet. Still, she has argued against the idea that this interruptible life has been less beneficial to her work, not to mention to her emotional life, than that of her husband, also a writer, who has had to go off to the hospital every day. To such constraint, Tyler has asked for no "liberation." Certainly her production of ten novels and at least one volume's worth of uncollected short stories shows that she has not been "silenced," in Tillie Olsen's word, by her woman's lot.

And she has found in her family the richest emotional lode for her work.

The chief features of Tyler's life are echoed in the critical reception of her work. She has given her own family the central position; she was a precocious young person; she has led an apparently stable adult life. Critics have dwelt on related issues, some praising her examination of the inner life, some complaining that her range is too narrow. Her early work was declared astonishingly good for one so young. The most frequently expressed reservation against her work has been that she has not developed the potential she first promised. Like her adult life, Tyler's development as a writer has been without sudden shifts of direction.

Disagreement about Tyler's work comes not in descriptions of it, where the agreement is fairly widespread, but in estimates of the value of what she does. Her admirers praise her wit, her humor, which by contemporary measure is a kindly, not a sardonic, humor, her sense of detail, her characterization, her emotional power, her compassion, her wisdom, and the understanding she has for inner pain and joy in outwardly unremarkable lives.

Sometimes even her admirers complain that her writing is too literary, that she strains for effect. They may balk at her odd juxtapositions, her wry observations, her method of piling on detail. At worst she has been called "arch," "coy," and "glib."[9]

The place Tyler occupies in American letters seems to have much to do with the fact that she is not in step with the waves of fiction in the last two decades. The absence of a moral dimension, the fact that her characters are often mistaken but are not "evil" or "good," makes them seem without excitement or importance to some. To others, attuned to the newer vogues of a hard-boiled age, she is tender, almost soft. In years when many artists employ violent projection and subdued response, Tyler depicts deeply resonant perception and memory. Although she is of this century, she has been ever more distant from a literary current moving away from her. Her adoption of Eudora Welty as a model was old-fashioned thirty years ago. It is now antique, fine and good to those who appreciate it, not likely to be imitated by a younger generation. Tyler's ardent admirers include those not delighted with the newest modes of American writing, for whom she is a model of timeless worth.

Her last works show greater control over her characterization, a surer sense of balance in descriptive detail, and the writer comfortable at a fairly great distance from her characters, relying less on their explaining themselves and more on dramatic scene. Anne Tyler has never been voguish; she is unlikely to become so even if the movie of *The Accidental Tourist* becomes all the rage with the young set. Her distance may continue to limit her reputation somewhat. With the audience she has, she is probably content.

ANNE TYLER BIBLIOGRAPHY

NOVELS

If Morning Ever Comes. New York: Knopf, 1964.
The Tin Can Tree. New York: Knopf, 1965.
A Slipping-Down Life. New York: Knopf, 1970.
The Clock Winder. New York: Knopf, 1972.
Celestial Navigation. New York: Knopf, 1974.
Searching for Caleb. New York: Knopf, 1976.
Earthly Possessions. New York: Knopf, 1977.
Morgan's Passing. New York: Knopf, 1980.
Dinner at the Homesick Restaurant. New York: Knopf, 1982.
The Accidental Tourist. New York: Knopf, 1985.

BIBLIOGRAPHICAL GUIDE

Gardiner, Elaine, and Catherine Rainwater. "A Bibliography of Writings by Anne Tyler." In *Contemporary American Women Writers: Narrative Strategies,* ed. Catherine Rainwater and William J. Scheick, 142–52. Lexington: University Press of Kentucky, 1985.

Nikki Giovanni: Place and Sense
of Place in Her Poetry

*

MARTHA COOK

NIKKI GIOVANNI's poetry has been most often viewed by literary
critics in the tradition of militant black poetry; the first serious
critical article on her work, in fact, is R. Roderick Palmer's "The Poetry of Three Revolutionists: Don L. Lee, Sonia Sanchez, and Nikki
Giovanni" (*College Language Association Journal*, September 1971).
More recent critics, especially Suzanne Juhasz in her *Naked and Fiery
Forms: Modern American Poetry by Women, A New Tradition* (1976),
have emphasized the developing feminism in Giovanni's poems. No
critic has yet focused on what I see as the key to reading Giovanni, her
position in the rich tradition of Southern poetry, proceeding unbroken
from Richard Lewis in the eighteenth century through Poe, Henry
Timrod, and Sidney Lanier, on through the Fugitives and Jean
Toomer, down to James Dickey and Ishmael Reed today. By focusing
specifically on the sense of place, a vital element in Southern literature,
I have identified a group of poems that represent Giovanni at her best,
technically and thematically.

Before looking at specific themes, subjects, images, and symbols, I
should survey the significant aspects of Nikki Giovanni's life and career.
She was born on 7 June 1943 in Knoxville, Tennessee, to a middle-class
black couple, Jones Giovanni, a probation officer, and his wife, Yolande, a social worker. It is clearly a mark of Giovanni's respect for her
mother that she sometimes gives her formal name as Yolande Cornelia
Giovanni, Jr. When she was young, the family lived "in Wyoming,
Ohio, which is a suburb of Cincinnati, which some say is a suburb of
Lexington, Kentucky."[1] Later they moved to the black community of
Lincoln Heights. Nikki often visited her much-beloved Watson grandparents in Knoxville and attended Austin High School there. She

closely identified her grandparents with their home on Mulvaney Street; when her grandmother Louvenia was forced by urban renewal to move to Linden Avenue, Giovanni explained her own feelings of displacement: "There was no familiar smell in that house." Giovanni's Southern roots were further strengthened during her years at Fisk University in Nashville. She began college immediately after high school; though difficulties in maturing during the turbulence of the 1960s resulted in a gap in her college work, she eventually graduated with honors in history in 1967. She is remembered for her radical activities on campus, especially her role in reestablishing the Fisk chapter of the Student Nonviolent Coordinating Committee. She also studied with John Killens and edited the Fisk literary magazine.

Giovanni continued her involvement in the civil rights movement of the 1960s, primarily through her writing. Right out of college, she began publishing articles, poems, and book reviews in journals such as *Negro Digest* and *Black World*. Consistently attacking elitism in the black arts movement, she praised writers whom she viewed as presenting a realistic yet positive picture of black life, both new voices, such as Louise Meriwether, author of the 1970 novel *Daddy Was a Number Runner,* and established ones, such as Dudley Randall. During the late 1960s, she worked to organize the first Cincinnati Black Arts Festival and the New Theatre in that city, as well as a black history group in Wilmington, Delaware. She also took courses at the University of Pennsylvania School of Social Work and the Columbia University School of Fine Arts and taught at Queens College of the City University of New York and Livingston College of Rutgers University.

Randall's Broadside Press, invaluable for its support and encouragement of black poetry, brought out two small collections of Giovanni's poems, *Black Feeling, Black Talk* (1968), which she had first printed privately, and *Black Judgement* (1969), including many poems that contributed to Giovanni's early reputation as a militant poet who advocated the violent overthrow of the white power structure in America. Many readers found these poems exciting and inspiring, and the poet Don L. Lee pointed to "lines that suggest the writer has a real, serious commitment to her people and to the institutions that are working toward the liberation of Black people." However, he goes on, "when the Black poet chooses to serve as political seer, he must display a keen sophistication. Sometimes Nikki oversimplifies and therefore sounds rather naive politically."[2] Giovanni offered further support for fellow black writers by founding a publishing cooperative, NikTom, Ltd. One of its significant projects is her edition of a collection of poems by black women, *Night Comes Softly: Anthology of Black Female*

Voices (1970), with contributors ranging in age from seventeen to eighty-four, from unknowns to Sonia Sanchez to Gwendolyn Brooks.

In addition to her literary creations, Giovanni marked her twenty-fifth year by having a child, though she did not marry his father. She was living in New York, where she was writing poetry and serving on the editorial board of the journal *Black Dialogue*. One suspects that the humor used to describe her pregnancy and the birth of her son in the essay "Don't Have a Baby Till You Read This" masks to some degree the fears and uneasiness with which she faced life as a single parent. However, she amusingly recounts planning for a daughter's birth in New York, but giving birth prematurely to a son while visiting her parents in Ohio. Through this experience, she learns that one is always a child to one's parents; finally, she asserts herself and goes "home" to New York with her own child. Of her decision to have a child alone, she said later, " 'I had a baby at 25 because I *wanted* to have a baby and I could *afford* to have a baby. I did not get married because I didn't *want* to get married and I could *afford* not to get married.' "[3] Giovanni has remained unmarried and has consistently viewed her single motherhood as a positive choice.

By 1969, Sheila Weller had called Giovanni "one of the most powerful figures on the new black poetry scene—both in language and appeal." Weller goes on to indicate that the woman she is interviewing is not the woman she expected from reading her poetry: "The tense anger that wires many of Nikki's poems is in direct contrast to the warm calm she generates." Giovanni said of herself at the time of the interview, " 'I've changed a lot over the last few months.' "[4] When her next volume of poetry, *Re:Creation* (1970), was published by Broadside, a reviewer for *Black World* was concerned that the poems were not so radical and militant as those in Giovanni's earlier volumes, describing the poet as transformed "into an almost declawed, tamed Panther with bad teeth," yet conceding, "a Panther with bad teeth is still quite deadly."[5] Seeing her changes as positive rather than negative, as strengthening her work rather than weakening it, *Time* noted in a 1970 article on black writers that "already some, like Nikki Giovanni, are moving away from extreme political activism toward more compassionate and universal themes."[6]

In 1970, the firm William Morrow issued Giovanni's first two Broadside books under the title *Black Feeling, Black Talk/Black Judgement*. This publication, followed in 1971 by the prose volume *Gemini: An Extended Autobiographical Statement on My First Twenty-Five Years of Being a Black Poet* (Bobbs-Merrill), brought her such attention as a lengthy review by Martha Duffy in *Time*. Duffy particularly praises the autobiographical sections of *Gemini,* emphasizing: "On the subject of her childhood, Miss Giovanni is magical. She meanders along with every appearance of artlessness, but one might as well say that Mark Twain wrote shaggy-dog stories." Of Giovanni's propagandistic writing, Duffy observes: "Hers is a committed social rage. She is capable of scalding rhetoric, but the artist in her keeps interrupting."[7]

The year 1971 also marked the publication of Giovanni's first volume of poetry for children, *Spin a Soft Black Song.* The poems, enhanced by excellent illustrations by Charles Bible, offer realistic images of black urban life and positive images of black identity. The same year, she recorded the first of several poetry readings combined with gospel music or jazz. "Truth Is on Its Way" includes a number of poems from Giovanni's Broadside volumes, with music by the New York Community Choir under the direction of Benny Diggs. According to *Harper's Bazaar,* Giovanni introduced the album at a free concert in a church in Harlem. Following her performance, "the audience shouted its appreciation."[8]

Peter Bailey summed up Giovanni's public role as follows: "Nikki, the poet, has become a personality, a *star.*" At that time, in 1972, Giovanni seemed to see herself in the tradition of confessional poetry, like so many twentieth-century American women poets, but with the particular perspective of the black American: " 'When I write poetry, . . . I write out of my own experiences—which also happen to be the experiences of my people. But if I had to choose between my people's experiences and mine, I'd choose mine, because that's what I know best.' "[9] Her next volume of poems is entitled *My House* (1972). In the introduction, Ida Lewis, editor and publisher of *Encore,* for which Giovanni was serving as an editorial consultant, calls her "the Princess of Black Poetry," saying lightheartedly: "I've seen Nikki mobbed in Bloomingdale's department store by Black and white customers; I've walked with her down Fifth Avenue and watched a man who was saying 'hi' to her walk into an oncoming taxi." Yet Lewis concludes in a serious vein, emphasizing that Giovanni "writes about the central themes of our times, in which thirty million Blacks search for self-identification and self-love."[10] The star, the princess, at the age of twenty-nine was taken seriously enough to be awarded an honorary doctorate by Wilberforce University, the oldest black institution of higher education in America. Even after the publication of her next two volumes of poetry, Alex Batman considered *My House* her "finest work."[11]

Giovanni's next album, "Like a Ripple on a Pond," again with the New York Community Choir, features selections from *My House.* The volume and the album were criticized by *Black World* reviewer Kalamu ya Salaam for failing to live up to the promise of Giovanni's earlier work. Salaam is particularly hard on the poems, citing their sentimentality and romanticism.[12] He is accurate in some cases, yet he is harshly critical of the sequence of African poems that other critics have seen as one of the strongest elements of the volume. Giovanni's next volume of poetry for children, *Ego-Tripping and Other Poems for Young People* (1973), includes a selection of previously published poems illustrated by George Ford. The title poem is an especially good example of her theme of racial pride and her interest in the places associated with her African heritage.

In 1971, Giovanni had taped a program for the WNET series "Soul!"; this appearance was transcribed, edited, and published in 1973 as *A Dialogue: James Baldwin/Nikki Giovanni*. The volume offers insight into both the works and the personal lives of these two important black writers, as does a similar volume apparently inspired by that experience, *A Poetic Equation: Conversations between Nikki Giovanni and Margaret Walker*, published by Howard University Press in 1974. The latter is perhaps the more interesting, as it gives these black women writers of succeeding generations the opportunity to react to contemporary political and literary issues.

The early 1970s were clearly a period of change and growth for Giovanni, as she was coming to terms with the legacy of civil rights activism and her own personal concerns as a woman and a mother. In 1973, a number of public figures were asked by *Mademoiselle* to describe their views of the previous decade in a so-called epitaph. Giovanni's contribution, a mock radio-drama called "Racism: The Continuing Saga of the American Dream," was obviously a difficult chore; she commented, " 'I had to use a light touch. To approach the '60s any other way right now would be too painful.' "[13] A warmer side of Giovanni is seen in her contribution to a *Mademoiselle* feature entitled "A Christmas Memory," where she concludes, "Christmas to me is a special link to the past and a ritual for our future."[14]

During this period of increasing strength in the feminist movement in America, Giovanni seems to have become more aware of the personal and political significance of sex roles and of sex discrimination. " 'Roles between men and women are changing. . . . We no longer need categories,' " she said in an interview. " 'There is no reason why my son can't cook and rock with his teddy bear as well as swim and play ball.' "[15] Giovanni's next volume of poetry, *The Women and the Men* (1975), reflects her growing awareness of such issues but also hints at difficulties in the creative process. Three years after *My House,* she offers a volume including a number of poems from the 1970 *Re:Creation* (which did deserve wider circulation than it had received); the new poems do not generally demonstrate meaningful development in theme or technique. Yet *The Women and the Men* brought Giovanni further attention in the media, including prepublication of three poems in *Mademoiselle* (September 1975). Jay S. Paul has called it "her richest collection of poems."[16] The mid-seventies also produced another album, "The Way I Feel," with accompanying music by Arif Mardin and liner notes by Roberta Flack.

In addition to Giovanni's growing concern with feminist themes, in the 1970s, she further explored her heritage as a black American. In *Gemini,* she writes of her father's journey from Ohio to Knoxville College as a journey to his "spiritual roots"—his grandfather had been a slave in eastern Tennessee—and also tells the story of how her maternal grandparents were forced to leave Georgia because her grandmother refused to submit to white domination. Another essay in the volume describes her own trip to Haiti in search of "sunshine and Black people"; feeling like a foreigner, she went on to Barbados, where she gained a deeper understanding of the sense of displacement of West Indian immigrants in American society, clearly analogous to the position of blacks who were brought to this country as slaves. In 1975, she traveled to Africa, where she spoke in several countries, including Ghana, Zambia, Tanzania, and Nigeria.

Giovanni continued to receive recognition in the mid-1970s, with, for example, honorary doctorates from the University of Maryland, Princess Anne Campus, Ripon University, and Smith College. Another honor was more controversial. According to Jeanne Noble, "Nikki's winning the Ladies' Home Journal Woman of the Year Award in 1974 meant to some young revolutionaries that she was joining forces with the very people she often considered foes. But, she does not shun confrontation or even violence if whites provoke it."[17] In fact, Giovanni had for some time been more concerned with broader themes of identity and self-knowledge than with her earlier militancy, though she remained politically active. "While her poetry is full of Black pride," *African Woman* explains, "she transcends colour to deal with the challenge of being human."[18]

Giovanni's next volume of poetry, *Cotton Candy on a Rainy Day* (1978), represents a definite, if not wholly positive, change. Paula Giddings's introduction emphasizes the development she sees in Giovanni and her work: "If Nikki, in her idealism, was a child of the sixties then now, in her realism, she is a woman of the seventies." She also notes, "*Cotton Candy* is the most introspective book to date, and the most plaintive."[19] Alex Batman describes the distinctive features of this volume in a similar way: "One feels throughout that here is a child of the 1960s mourning the passing of a decade of conflict, of violence, but most of all, of hope. Such an attitude, of course, may lend itself too readily to sentimentality and chauvinism, but Giovanni is capable of countering the problems with a kind of hard matter-of-factness about the world that has passed away from her and the world she now faces."[20]

Giddings further says of the *Cotton Candy* volume that it represents "the private moments: of coming to terms with oneself—of living with oneself. Taken in the context of Nikki's work it completes the circle: of dealing with society, others and finally oneself."[21] Giddings's description of Giovanni's work may reveal why her development of new themes and techniques was slow. Perhaps she had to come to terms with herself, doing so to a certain degree through her poetry, before she could truly deal with others and with society. Indeed, her poetry is in many ways a mirror of the social consciousness of the 1960s, followed by the self-centeredness of the 1970s. Yet Giddings's comments do not predict what might follow such an inwardly focused collection, what one might expect from Giovanni's poetry in the 1980s. Anna T. Robinson, in a short monograph entitled *Nikki Giovanni: From Revolution to Revelation,* believes that *Cotton Candy* is "a pivotal work in Nikki Giovanni's career. It will mandate that she be evaluated as a poet rather than a voice for a cause."[22]

The title of the volume *Cotton Candy on a Rainy Day* is ironic; the poems are not lighthearted or optimistic, as the positive connotations of cotton candy suggest. Giovanni's next volume has an ambiguous and perhaps also ironic title, *Those Who Ride the Night Winds* (1983). Having read *Cotton Candy on a Rainy Day,* one might anticipate a journey into the further gloom night can symbolize. However, the dedication indicates that night may offer possibilities not readily apparent: "This book is dedicated to the courage and fortitude of those who ride the night winds—who are the day trippers and midnight cowboys—who in sonic solitude or the hazy hell of habit know—that for all the devils and gods—for all the illnesses and drugs to cure them—Life is a marvelous, transitory adventure—and are determined to push us into the next century, galaxy—possibility." The form of the poems shows an interesting development in technique. Most are written in long verse paragraphs with abundant ellipsis marks, a stream-of-consciousness form that is not traditionally "poetic" but produces a sense of openness and forward movement with thematic significance.

The reasons behind the changes in Giovanni's poetry between the

1978 and 1983 volumes may well lie in her decision to move back to Lincoln Heights with her son and share her parents' home after her father suffered a stroke. Although she maintained an apartment in New York City, she devoted time, energy, and money to making a place for herself in Ohio again. She has more than once spoken of the difficulties she has encountered in this situation, not to complain, but simply to explain. For example, she said in 1981, " 'No matter what the situation is or what the financial arrangements are, you are always their child. . . . If you're in your parents' house or they're in yours, it's still a parent-child relationship.' "[23] When her son was born, Giovanni apparently needed to assert her independence, but she had matured enough not to feel her sense of identity threatened by her family. Though she spoke of the need "to feel at home in order to write,"[24] she seems to have made the adjustment rapidly, for during that period, she published her third volume for children, new poems with the title *Vacation Time* (1980).

The poems in *Those Who Ride the Night Winds* transcend such categories as black/white, male/female, reality/fantasy. "In this book," Mozella G. Mitchell points out, "Giovanni has adopted a new and innovative form; and the poetry reflects her heightened self knowledge and imagination."[25] A look down the table of contents reveals new kinds of subjects, with poems to Billie Jean King, John Lennon, and Robert F. Kennedy, as well as to Lorraine Hansberry, Martin Luther King, Jr., and Rosa Parks. Having once stated that she wrote primarily from personal or at least from racial experiences, Giovanni recently contradicted herself in the best Emersonian sense: "I resent people who say writers write from experience. Writers don't write from experience, though many are hesitant to admit that they don't. I want to be very clear about this. If you wrote from experience, you'd get maybe one book, maybe three poems. Writers write from empathy. . . . Writers write because they empathize with the general human condition."[26] *Those Who Ride the Night Winds* is an impressive illustration of the effectiveness of that kind of empathy and the value of change. " 'Only a fool doesn't change,' " Giovanni once commented.[27] In the preface to this volume of poems, she alludes to both Lewis Carroll and the Beatles as she announces: "I changed . . . I chart the night winds . . . glide with me . . . I am the walrus . . . the time has come . . . to speak of many things. . . . " Having changed, Giovanni has reached maturity as a poet, with a volume that satisfies the reader, yet promises more complex and challenging poems in the future.

Giovanni has continued to receive recognition for her work in the 1980s in the academic world, with honorary doctorates from the College of Mount St. Joseph on-the-Ohio and Mount St. Mary College, and with teaching positions at Ohio State University, Mount St. Joseph, and Virginia Polytechnic Institute and State University. She also continues to reach the larger world outside the academy, as indicated by her being named to the Ohio Women's Hall of Fame and as the Outstanding Woman of Tennessee, both in 1985. She was chosen cochairperson of the Literary Arts Festival for Homecoming '86 in Tennessee, the Duncanson Artist-in-Residence of the Taft Museum in Cincinnati in 1986, and a member of the Ohio Humanities Council in 1987.

Some of these honors and positions indicate that Nikki Giovanni has maintained close ties with the South of her birthplace, despite having lived more years away from the South than in it. What the South as a place means to her is of considerable significance in looking at the body of her poetry. Like many writers of the Southern Literary Renaissance before her, Giovanni left the South after her graduation from college. Louis D. Rubin, Jr., speaking of earlier writers such as Allen Tate and Robert Penn Warren, has pointed out: "Almost all the young Southern writers at one time or another packed their suitcases and headed for the cities of the Northeast, toward the center of modernity, toward the new. Some turned around and came back to stay; others remained."[28] These remarks apply to succeeding generations of Southern writers, such as William Styron and Ralph Ellison, and on to Alice Walker and Nikki Giovanni, who continue to be influenced by the South and their often ambivalent feelings toward it, even though they may have felt compelled to leave.

The ambivalence of black Southerners toward the region has been in the past compared to the way Jews might feel about Germany: "They love the South . . . for its beauty, its climate, its fecundity and its better ways of life; but they hate, with a bitter corroding hatred, the color prejudice, the discrimination, the violence, the crudities, the insults and humiliations, and the racial segregation of the South, and they hate all those who keep these evils alive."[29] Though the South has changed, there has been much in Giovanni's lifetime to cause pain for the black Southerner. Still she has acknowledged the South as a symbolic home, commenting earthily: "I can deal with the South because I love it. And it's the love of someone who lived there, who was born there, who lost her cherry there and loved the land. . . ." In the opening essay of *Gemini,* Giovanni describes "going home" to speak in Knoxville, Tennessee, and looking for familiar places—Vine Street, the Gem Theatre, Mulvaney Street. "All of that is gone now," she realizes. Even so, after a tour of the city, "I was exhausted but feeling quite high from being once again in a place where no matter what I belong. And Knoxville belongs to me. I was born there in Old Knoxville General and I am buried there with Louvenia. . . . And I thought Tommy, my son, must know about this. He must know we come from somewhere. That we belong."

This theme of belonging has occurred in Giovanni's poetry since the beginning, in poems set in the South and in other places as well. The best of her poetry throughout her career has been concrete, with references to specific places, rooms, furniture, people, colors, qualities of light and dark. When she is abstract, her poetry is sometimes still successful in a political but not a critical sense. This kind of concreteness has been identified as one of the essential elements in Southern literature by Robert B. Heilman, in a seminal study entitled "The Southern Temper," where he distinguishes between what he terms "a sense of the concrete" and merely employing concrete images.[30] The overriding importance of place in Southern literature has often been noted, for example, by Frederick J. Hoffman, whose essay "The Sense of Place" is a landmark in the criticism of modern Southern poetry and fiction.[31] Looking closely at the body of Giovanni's poetry, one finds places large and small, houses and continents, places she has lived in or traveled to, places important in the history of black people, places from the past and in the present, metaphorical places, places of fantasy, symbolic places. To emphasize this sense of place in her work is to see it, along with the best literature of the South, not as provincial but as universal.

While Giovanni has received more attention first for her militant poems on racial themes and later for her feminist writing, the poems that will finally determine her position in the canon of American poetry are, almost without exception, ones in which place functions not only as a vehicle, but also as a theme. In her most recent work, her themes are becoming increasingly complex, reflecting her maturity as a woman and as a writer. Traditionally in Southern writing, place has been associated with themes of the past and the family; these themes are seen in Giovanni's poems of the late 1960s and the early 1970s, with the added dimension of a desire to understand the faraway places from which black slaves were brought to the American South. Her later poetry reflects a changing consciousness of her role in society as a single woman, the need to adjust her concept of home and family and of the importance of smaller places, such as houses and rooms, to fit her own life, a life that many American women and men, black and white, can identify with. In her best poems, places grow into themes that convey the universal situation of modern humanity, a sense of placelessness and a need for security.

In her first collection of poems, Giovanni expresses themes anticipated by the title *Black Feeling, Black Talk*. But already she demonstrates occasionally her gift for the original, individual image, for example, as she evokes the days and places of childhood in "Poem (For BMC No. 2)":

> There were fields where once we walked
> Among the clover and crab grass and those
> Funny little things that look like cotton candy
>
> There were liquids expanding and contracting
> In which we swam with amoebas and other Afro-Americans

This poem is a striking contrast to the best-known poem from this volume, "The True Import of Present Dialogue, Black vs. Negro (For Peppe, Who Will Ultimately Judge Our Efforts)," with its repetition of the lines "Nigger / Can you kill." Like "Nikki-Rosa" and "Knoxville, Tennessee" from her next volume, "Poem (For BMC No. 2)" recalls a time and place that endure in memory, even in the face of violence and hatred.

One of Giovanni's finest poems is set in this homeland of the past. "Knoxville, Tennessee," written at the height of the unrest of the civil rights movement of the 1960s, develops a theme of security, of belonging, through simple yet highly effective images of nature, of family, of religion. Although it is almost imagistic, it builds to an explicit thematic statement:

> I always like summer
> best
> you can eat fresh corn
> from daddy's garden
> and okra
> and greens
> and cabbage
> and lots of
> barbecue
> . . . .
> and be warm
> all the time
> not only when you go to bed
> and sleep

The simple diction, the soothing alliteration, the short lines to emphasize each word, all create a feeling of love for this place and these people that transcends topical issues.

Giovanni later wrote a prose description of Christmas in Knoxville using images of winter rather than summer, yet conveying the same feeling of warmth: "Christmas in Knoxville was the smell of turnip greens and fatback, perfume blending with good Kentucky bourbon, cigars and cigarettes, bread rising on the new electric stove, the inexplicable smell of meat hanging in the smokehouse (though we owned no smokehouse), and, somehow, the sweet taste of tasteless snow."[32] As Roger Whitlow notes, though, this kind of warmth is "rare" in Giovanni's early work.[33] Still, Giovanni's use of this Southern place from her past speaks to the same aspects of Southern life as poems by James Dickey or prose by Eudora Welty.

Most of the poems in *Black Judgement* are militant in subject and theme; one of the most effective is "Adulthood (For Claudia)," in which Giovanni catalogs the violence of the decade, the deaths of leaders from Patrice Lumumba to John F. Kennedy to Martin Luther King, Jr., and of lesser-known civil rights workers such as Viola Liuzzo. In another poem from this volume, "For Saundra," Giovanni seems to explain why poems of political rhetoric dominate her first two volumes. The persona speaks of the difficulty of composing poems in revolutionary times; for example,

> so i thought
> i'll write a beautiful green tree poem
> peeked from my window
> to check the image
> noticed the schoolyard was covered
> with asphalt
> no green—no trees grow
> in manhattan

She concludes that "perhaps these are not poetic / times / at all." Although the thrust of the poem is toward the civil rights strife of the late 1960s, the reader also senses something of the alienation and displacement of a Southerner in the urban North.

Giovanni uses the South and its people to develop the specific theme of the past in "Alabama Poem" from her next collection, *Re:Creation*. A student at Tuskegee Institute meets an old black man and then an old black woman whose remarks indicate that knowledge must be gained through experience, must be inherited from the past. The persona speculates in conclusion: "if trees would talk / wonder what they'd tell me." Her words do not seem ironic; rather she seems to have learned a valuable lesson in her walk along this Southern country road. Though the images in this poem are sparse, the rural place and its people are seen to be of vital significance to one who seeks knowledge. The theme of the necessity of learning from the past what one needs to live in the present links this poem by Nikki Giovanni to a rich tradition in Southern writing, especially from the Fugitive poets of the 1920s to the present.

A more challenging use of the concreteness of place and the thematic significance of the past can be seen in the complex, ironic poem "Walking Down Park," also from *Re:Creation.* Speculating about the history of New York City, the speaker wonders what a street such as Park Avenue looked like "before it was an avenue," "what grass was like before / they rolled it / into a ball and called / it central park." She even thinks:

> ever look south
> on a clear day and not see
> time's squares but see
> tall birch trees with sycamores
> touching hands

Questioning why men destroy their environment, she returns to days of the past, musing, "probably so we would forget / the Iroquois, Algonquin / and Mohicans who could caress / the earth." Possibly this relationship with nature, which characterized the Indians of an earlier time, can be recaptured:

> ever think what Harlem would be
> like if our herbs and roots and elephant ears
> grew sending
> a cacophony of sound to us

Here through a complex set of images Giovanni connects the situation of blacks in contemporary America with the past of the American Indian, another oppressed minority group, as well as with their African heritage. "Walking Down Park" thus becomes a statement of a longing for happiness, related in the mind of the speaker not only to life in the past, which allowed for a closeness to nature lost in contemporary urban life, but also to a specific place from the past—Africa.

One of the most important examples of the ways Giovanni employs places in her poetry is her use of houses, both literal and metaphorical, from the past and in the present. In "Housecleaning," another poem from *Re:Creation,* the persona speaks first of her pleasure in ordinary chores essential to maintaining a house, then turns tidying up into a metaphor to describe aptly the chores necessary in human relationships as well. The growing sense of independence and identity in this poem anticipates the major themes of Giovanni's next volume, *My House.*

At this point, in the early 1970s, Giovanni is still using the lowercase "i," which R. Roderick Palmer identifies as a common device in revolutionary poetry, more then the uppercase.[34] Perhaps she intends to symbolize the concept she has often invoked, that one retains qualities of childhood, even when striving for maturity. She uses this device in a poem from *My House* set, as is "Knoxville, Tennessee," in a place that now exists only in memory. In "Mothers," Giovanni depicts a woman remembering her mother sitting in a kitchen at night:

> she was sitting on a chair
> the room was bathed in moonlight diffused through
> those thousands of panes landlords who rented
> to people with children were prone to put in windows

Recalling a poem her mother taught her on this particular night, the persona determines to teach the same poem to her son, to establish with him the relationship she had with her mother. This relationship is re-created for the reader in the simple description of a place remembered, especially in the quality of light Giovanni uses as the central image of the poem.

In the title poem, Giovanni uses homes and houses to represent the movement toward maturity, symbolized by the movement away from the places, homes, of one's childhood toward establishing a home for oneself, or an identity as a mature person. Like Giovanni's poems about childhood, "My House" is characterized by images of warmth and security, emphasizing that in her house the speaker is in complete control:

> i mean it's my house
> and i want to fry pork chops
> and bake sweet potatoes
> and call them yams
> cause i run the kitchen
> and i can stand the heat
>
> . . . .
>
> and my windows might be dirty
> but it's my house
> and if i can't see out sometimes
> they can't see   in either

As Suzanne Juhasz emphasizes, the woman speaker "orders experience and controls it. . . . She controls not only through need and desire, but through strength, ability. . . ."[35] In contrast to the child persona of

"Knoxville, Tennessee," the "i" here has discovered that she is an autonomous being who can shape at least the smaller places of her world to suit her own needs and desires; at the same time, the "i" is willing to take responsibility for her actions, to pay the price for such control.

In this context, the title poem of the volume *My House* takes on a deeper level of meaning. In fact, Erlene Stetson has identified the house as a dominant symbol in poetry by women, especially black women, explaining: "The house represents the historic quest by black women for homes of their own—apart from the house of slavery, the common house of bondage, the house of the patriarchy. The house embodies women's search for place and belonging and for a whole and complete identity. . . . In addition, the house is a symbol for place—heaven, haven, home, the heart, women's estate, the earthly tenement, the hearth—and for region—Africa, the West Indies, America, Asia, the North, and the South."[36] Stetson does not emphasize, as she might, that this use of place as symbol is particularly significant in the tradition of Southern literature to which Nikki Giovanni and a number of other black women poets belong.

Many of Giovanni's poems are set, as I have mentioned, in Africa. For Giovanni, as for black Southerners and other black Americans in the twentieth century, the significance of this place lies mostly in the past—a past with which each individual must come to terms. Like other Southern writers in the period since World War I, Giovanni recognizes that no one can live in the past or relive the past, yet there is no meaningful life in the present or the future without an understanding of, often involving a confrontation with, the past. In a three-poem sequence in *My House,* she creates powerful images of the displacement of a people who in their racial past were forced to leave their homeland involuntarily.

The first poem in the group, "Africa I," describes a plane journey to Africa. During the flight, the speaker dreams of seeing a lion from the plane but is jarred by the statement of a companion that "there are no lions / in this part of africa." Her response is quick: "it's my dream dammit." The poem closes at the journey's end, with the following thoughts:

we landed in accra and the people
clapped and i almost cried wake up
we're home
and something in me said shout
and something else said quietly

your mother may be glad to see you
but she may also remember why
you went away

Seeing Africa as a woman, a mother, as she did in the fantasy poem "Ego-Tripping," Giovanni movingly illustrates how the significance of this place relates to the past of these tourists, visitors, just as the significance of an adult's mother usually lies more in the past than in the present. In one's personal past as well as in one's racial past may exist harsh memories difficult to confront. Yet coming to terms with the past is necessary in order to grow and mature, as an individual or as a people.

"They Clapped," the third poem in this sequence, demonstrates even more explicitly that the dream of Africa and the reality, the past and the present, are not the same. The black American tourists clap because they are so happy to be landing in "the mother land"; then they see the realities of poverty and disease, as well as of their own foreignness. As they leave to return to America, they appear to have come to terms with the past in a way that frees them for their lives now and later. Giovanni uses the metaphor of possession, a subtle allusion to the horrors of slavery in the past, to convey the theme of displacement:

they brought out their cameras and bought out africa's drums
when they finally realized they are strangers all over
and love is only and always about the lover not the beloved
they marveled at the beauty of the people and the richness
of the land knowing they could never possess either

they clapped when they took off
for home despite the dead
dream they saw a free future

So the physical confrontation with this place serves to make these tourists aware of their historical past as past rather than as present or future. They have learned too that, as modern men and women, they are "strangers all over," that in a very important sense they do not belong anywhere except in the place they must create for themselves as individuals. Thus Giovanni reminds the reader that the visitors to Africa are returning home, to America.

Many of the best poems in Giovanni's next volume, *The Women and the Men,* such as "Ego-Tripping" and "Walking Down Park," originally appeared in *Re:Creation*. The new African poems, including "Africa" and "Swaziland," are less successful than the Africa sequence in *My House* because they depend more on abstract diction than concrete images to convey themes. Yet one new symbolic poem, "Night," uses complex metaphorical language to contrast New York City with Africa and the Caribbean. The latter are both portrayed as places where the night is strong, natural, black:

in africa night walks
into day as quickly
as a moth is extinguished
by its desire for flame

the clouds in the caribbean carry
night like a young man
with a proud erection dripping
black dots across the blue sky
the wind a mistress of the sun howls
her displeasure at the involuntary
fertilization

In contrast, the night in New York is seen to be unnaturally white, with humans being unable to adjust to their environment:

but nights are white
in new york
the shrouds of displeasure
mask our fear of facing
ourselves between the lonely
sheets

Again Giovanni contrasts the natural environment of the warm Southern country and continent with the literal and metaphorical cold of the urbanized northeastern United States, dominated by white culture. The images of masking and of death suggest that no one, black or white, can live a meaningful life in a place like New York. However, the negative images in the earlier sections of the poem—death, rape—reveal the generally grim situation for modern man or woman in Africa, in the Caribbean, anywhere.

The volume *Cotton Candy on a Rainy Day* contains mostly poems relying on images of placelessness or homelessness rather than security, or dominated by ideas rather than strong central images. The title poem sets a fairly pessimistic tone for the volume yet hints at what may follow in Nikki Giovanni's career. Characterizing the seventies as a decade of loneliness, Giovanni uses the image of cotton candy poignantly:

But since it is life   it is
  Cotton Candy

on a rainy day
The sweet soft essence
of possibility
Never quite maturing

Though she speaks of a lack of maturity, in this poem Giovanni uses an uppercase "I" to define the speaker, acknowledging perhaps unconsciously a certain kind of maturity that seems to have been missing in earlier poems such as "My House," regardless of their bravado.

At any rate, the speaker is characterized as a lonely, placeless person, yet one who can write a prescription to improve her own condition:

Everything   some say   will change
I need a change
        of pace   face   attitude and life
Though I long for my loneliness
I know I need something
Or someone
Or . . . . . .

Perhaps acknowledging the desire to succumb to loneliness, to the temptations of the solitary life, allowed Giovanni herself to move forward, to change in a way that profoundly affected her poetic subject matter and technique.

This sense of placelessness is perhaps seen most clearly in an urban poem different from those in Giovanni's earlier volumes. "The New Yorkers" focuses on the so-called bag people, "night people" who seem to "evaporate during the light of day," others who are seen during the day but appear to have nowhere to go at night. Of these placeless people, she comments:

How odd to also see the people
of New York City living
in the doorways of public buildings
as if this is an emerging nation
though of course it is

In addition to its commentary on American society in the 1970s, the poem provides a commentary on the persona's shaky self-image, as "an old blind Black woman" says on hearing her voice, "You that Eyetalian poet ain't you? I know yo voice. I seen you on television." Yet the old woman feels the poet's hair and determines that she is truly black; symbolically, her identity is intact.

Among the innovations in *Those Who Ride the Night Winds* is a different sense of place, a sense of space, of openness, as well as a concern with "inner" rather than "outer" space, both striking contrasts with earlier uses of place in Giovanni's work. For example, in "This Is Not for John Lennon (And This Is Not a Poem)," the speaker implores:

> . . . Don't cry for John Lennon cry for ourselves . . . He was an astronaut of inner space . . . He celebrated happiness . . . soothed the lonely . . . braced the weary . . . gave word to the deaf . . . vision to the insensitive . . . sang a long low note when he reached the edge of this universe and saw the Blackness . . .

This view of John Lennon leads to the conclusion that "those who ride the night winds do learn to love the stars . . . even while crying in the darkness. . . . " In other words, only those who travel far enough, metaphorically, to confront the harshness of reality are able to transcend it, as Lennon did.

An extreme example of this philosophy is seen in "Flying Underground." Dedicated to the children of Atlanta who died in the mass murders of the early 1980s, the poem develops the idea that in death these innocent children "can make the earth move . . . flying underground. . . . " Giovanni thus takes the entrapment of the place "underground"—literally, the grave—and transforms it into a sense of freedom and possibility. The reader is reminded of the old slave's cry so often invoked by Martin Luther King, "Free at last," a phrase Giovanni used with effective irony in a poem on his death, published in *Black Judgement*.

The concluding poem in *Those Who Ride the Night Winds,* "A Song for New-Ark," is an appropriate end to an impressive volume. Giovanni characterizes the city of Newark, New Jersey, where she once lived, in predominantly negative terms, stressing, as she did in the earlier poem "Walking Down Park," the destruction of nature to create this urban environment: "I never saw old/jersey . . . or old/ark . . . Old/ark was a forest . . . felled for concrete . . . and asphalt . . . and bridges to Manhattan. . . . " After drawing analogies between city dwellers and the rats that plague them, the poet-persona closes:

> When I write I want to write . . . in rhythm . . . regularizing the moontides . . . to the heart/beats . . . of the twinkling stars . . . sending an S.O.S. . . . to day trippers . . . urging them to turn back . . . toward the Darkness . . . to ride the night winds . . . to tomorrow . . .

She moves from the confinement of a physical, earthly place to the openness and freedom of outer space and places of fantasy.

In addition to this new sense of place, Giovanni displays a new sense of herself as a poet in *Those Who Ride the Night Winds*. In "A Song for New-Ark" and also in "I Am She," Giovanni seems confident of the role she has chosen for herself, secure in her place in society. As she says in the latter poem, "I am she . . . who writes . . . the poems. . . ." Again the ellipses give the sense of openness, of more to come from this poetic talent. While the poems in this volume seem to reflect Giovanni's own feeling that she has reached maturity as a poet, there are still indications of the necessity of coping with the demands of modern life. She acknowledges the presence of loneliness, not as she did through the poems in the volume *Cotton Candy on a Rainy Day,* where loneliness seemed to be a problem for which she could at the time see no solution, but in a way that indicates the strength of her inner resources. In the poem "The Room with the Tapestry Rug," she creates a persona who confronts loneliness by seeking out "the room . . . where all who lived . . . knew her well. . . ." The room holds memories of the past, symbolized by a garment created by a member of her family who was important in her childhood, used in a literal and metaphorical way to keep out the cold.

But Giovanni moves beyond this fairly traditional symbol, refusing to let the room be only a place of confinement and protection from the larger world; it becomes a place where she can also find comfort in the cool air from outside, while luxuriating in the security of her own space:

> If it was cold . . . she would wrap herself . . . in the natted blue sweater . . . knitted by a grandmother . . . so many years ago . . . If warm . . . the windows were opened . . . to allow the wind . . . to partake of their pleasure . . .

The closing paragraph of the poem indicates the resources of the persona beyond her memories of the past: "Her books . . . her secret life . . . in the room with the tapestry rug. . . ." Here she shows not only the need for but the fact of control over the places in her own life.

In the 1970s, such poems as "My House" conveyed an important theme of the development of a strengthening identity as a single woman; in the 1980s, such poems as "The Room with the Tapestry Rug" and "I Am She" illustrate not only the strength but also the depth and range of that identity. It is appropriate that a volume that so strongly exhibits Giovanni's talents as a writer should also attest to the importance of literature and art in her life, an importance reflected as well in her continued involvement in efforts to bring people and the arts together.

These examples from Nikki Giovanni's poetry—and her prose as well—demonstrate that, for her, place is more than an image, more than a surface used to develop a narrative or a theme, just as place functions in the best poetry of the Southern tradition lying behind her work. Further, the changing sense of place in these poems can be seen to reveal Giovanni's developing sense of herself as a woman and as a poet. Suzanne Juhasz, Anna T. Robinson, and Erlene Stetson all emphasize in their recent critical discussions the growing feminist consciousness they find in Giovanni's work. Her use of place is broader than simply a feminist symbol, though, just as her poetry has developed beyond purely racial themes. The relationships of people to places and the ways people have responded to and tried to control places are important themes for Giovanni, as are the ways places sometimes control people. Greatest in thematic significance are the need to belong to a place or in a place and the necessity of moving beyond physical places to spiritual or metaphysical ones.

Looking at Giovanni's poetry in the context of Southern literature expands rather than limits the possibilities for interpretation and analysis. In fact, this approach reveals that within the body of her work lies a solid core of poems that do not rely on political or personal situations for their success. Rather, they develop universal themes, such as coming to terms with the past and with the present so that one may move into the future—again, themes that have been and continue to be of particular significance in Southern poetry. These themes mark her work as a contribution to the canon not just of Southern poetry, of black poetry, of feminist poetry, but also of contemporary American poetry. However, Giovanni's response to any generalization, any categorization, would probably echo the closing line of her poem "Categories," from *My House*. Emphasizing her uniqueness as an individual, she might well proclaim, "i'm bored with categories."

NIKKI GIOVANNI BIBLIOGRAPHY

POETRY

Black Feeling, Black Talk. Introduction by Barbara Crosby. Detroit: Broadside, 1968.
Black Judgement. Detroit: Broadside, 1969.
Re:Creation. Detroit: Broadside, 1970.
Black Feeling, Black Talk/Black Judgement. New York: Morrow, 1970.

Spin a Soft Black Song: Poems for Children. Illustrated by Charles Bible. New York: Hill & Wang, 1971.

My House: Poems. Foreword by Ida Lewis. New York: Morrow, 1972.

Ego-Tripping and Other Poems for Young People. Illustrated by George Ford. New York: Lawrence Hill, 1973.

The Women and the Men. New York: Morrow, 1975.

Cotton Candy on a Rainy Day. Introduction by Paula Giddings. New York: Morrow, 1978.

Vacation Time: Poems for Children. Illustrated by Marisabina Russo. New York: Morrow, 1980.

Those Who Ride the Night Winds. New York: Morrow, 1983.

NONFICTION

Night Comes Softly: Anthology of Black Female Voices. Edited and with afterword by Nikki Giovanni. Newark, N. J.: NikTom, 1970.

Gemini: An Extended Autobiographical Statement on My First Twenty-five Years of Being a Black Poet. Introduction by Barbara Crosby. Indianapolis: Bobbs-Merrill, 1971.

A Dialogue: James Baldwin/Nikki Giovanni. Foreword by Ida Lewis; afterword by Orde Coombs. Philadelphia: Lippincott, 1973.

A Poetic Equation: Conversations between Nikki Giovanni and Margaret Walker. Washington, D.C.: Howard University Press, 1974.

Black, Southern, Womanist:
The Genius of Alice Walker

*

GLORIA WADE-GAYLES

ALICE WALKER grew up in Eatonton, Georgia, a rural town, as one of eight children in a poor sharecropping family. Her formal education took place in a "segregated school that was once the state prison and that had on the second floor, the large circular print of the electric chair that had stood there."[1] Her spiritual nurturing took place in a house of two or three rooms Walker shared with her family and in the black community where "houses [were] set so far back in the woods that at night it was impossible for strangers to find them."[2]

The culture to which she was exposed, and would later celebrate in her art, was not the so-called finest in music, art, and theater. It was the culture of black people attached to the land they worked and loved but did not own. Their music was the gospel, the spirituals, and the blues. Their art was the beauty of handmade quilts, variegated flower gardens, and the faces of family at church gatherings. Their theater was the telling and acting out of stories about black people who, though poor, maintained their humanity and dignity.

Alice Walker does not have the "pedigree" of a literary genius ("A shack with only a dozen or so of books is an unlikely place to find a young Keats,"[3] she was once told), but she is one of America's most gifted and celebrated writers. She began her literary career in 1968 at the age of twenty-one. By 1984, Alice Walker, not yet forty, had published four books of poetry; two collections of short stories; a children's biography of Langston Hughes; a Zora Neale Hurston reader; a collection of essays destined to become a classic; and three novels, one of which won the American Book Award and the coveted Pulitzer prize.

The distinctive voice in Walker's works is the voice of a woman deeply immersed in her blackness, her womanness, and her Southern-ness. It is a clear voice, neither muted nor strident, and always resonant with Walker's belief in redemption. Even when she writes passionately about problems that ravage the land and the lives of people, Alice Walker emphasizes the healing power of love and the possibility of "change: change personal, and change in society."[4]

This message of hope is a gift from the South, which Walker embraces as her spiritual home. In "The Black Writer and the Southern Experience," she writes with pride and gratitude of her " 'underprivileged' background." The Southern experience, she explains, is an "advantageous heritage" for the sensitive black writer, offering "a compassion for the earth, a trust in humanity beyond our knowledge of evil, and an abiding love of justice."[5]

Walker's images, the terrain of her visions, the sound and rhythm of her characters' lives are decidedly Southern. However, it is not as a *Southern* writer that she has earned national recognition. Rather, it is as a black *woman* writer exploring the complexity of black womanhood in white America. Calvin Hernton is correct when he writes that her art belongs "to the new canon of black women's literature in which the feminist perspective governs the aesthetic and the aesthetic . . . informs the vision."[6]

Feminist is only the general category in which Walker's philosophy belongs, as flower is only the general category for the purple petunia Walker loves. It does not reflect the specifics that make her interest in women's reality distinctive—specifics rooted in her blackness, her Southernness, her womanness. Not surprisingly, Walker chooses a different term for her philosophy. She is a womanist who is to feminist as "purple is to lavender." The term comes from the word "womanish," which black people in the South use to describe a girl who insists on asking questions, demanding answers, and speaking in her own voice, or, in other words, being "too grown for her own good." Womanish is the "opp. of 'girlish,' i.e., frivolous, irresponsible, not serious." A womanist, Walker writes, is "responsible. In charge. *Serious.*"[7]

The layered meaning of womanist is in keeping with Walker's refusal to embrace any ideological mold that is narrow and exclusive and therefore out of harmony with her spirituality. It reflects her commitment to balance, the beauty and power of which make her womanist aesthetic distinctive and healing. There is balance in her thought and in all of her art: balance between concern for women's reality and concern for the larger universe to which black women, like all people, are connected. A womanist, therefore, does not see only her reflection in the mirror of love. She "loves herself. Regardless." But she "loves other women" and is "committed to survival and wholeness of entire people, male *and* female."[8]

As a black writer, Alice Walker is "preoccupied with the spiritual survival, the spiritual *whole*" of her people. As a womanist writer, she is "committed to exploring the oppressions, the insanities, the loyalties, and the triumphs of black women."[9] She understands that race, sex, and class are the major axes on which power and influence turn in white America, and in the lives of her characters, the turning produces a painful and complex reality.

Self-love, Walker explains, does not come easy, if at all, for any group that is powerless and brutalized physically and psychologically. This is a controlling thesis in Walker's womanist fiction, and to its development, she brings not only love and compassion for her sisters, but also her belief that change is possible. It is this womanist balance that informs the vision of Walker's first novel, *The Third Life of Grange Copeland* (1970).

The novel is "ostensibly about a man and his son," Walker explains, but "it is the women and how they are treated that colors everything."[10] It begins with a compassionate portrait of Grange Copeland, a poor sharecropper, who, in the 1920s, looks older than his thirty-five years. In the violence of Southern heat, he tills the white man's land but knows no harvest. He is a broken man, ravaged by fear, self-hatred, and the humiliation of being unable to provide for his wife, Margaret, and their young son, Brownfield. "His face and eyes had a dispassionate vacancy and sadness, as if a great fire had been extinguished within him and was just recently missed."[11]

Walker's focus on the misery of Grange Copeland is central to the novel's theme of destructive relationships between broken men and loyal women. For having pulled from us sympathy for Grange, she widens her artistic lens so that we can see the misery that envelops Grange's wife, Margaret. When she leaves in the morning to "pull bait for ready money," she gives her son Brownfield a sugar-tit and hasty kisses. Her "legs were always clean" and "always coated with mud and slime when she returned home"(6).

Margaret is burdened as mother and worker, but she experiences her deepest pain as the wife of a man victimized in the pernicious system of sharecropping. She lives with Grange's brooding silence, drunkenness, and abuse. When he is not abusing her, he is cutting into her soul by preparing openly for weekends with his woman, Josie. Margaret's loneliness is profound: "While Grange was away, she washed and straightened her hair. She dressed and sat, all shining and pretty, in the open door, hoping anxiously for visitors who never came" (12).

She makes no effort to clear a space in their lives for her needs and dreams. She cannot, for Margaret is a totally submissive woman, socialized in a sexist culture to believe there is no way out of suffering. Brownfield, only ten at the time, thought "his mother was like their dog in some ways. She didn't have a thing to say that did not in some way show her submission to his father" (5). When Grange is home, she is obedient and "wifely"; when he is away, Margaret becomes a "hauntress of soft touches, gentle voice and sex without arguments over the constant and compelling pressures of everyday life" (20). The shifts "between submissiveness and wantonness," writes Robbie J. Walker, "neither trait bearing significant potential for enhancing the quality of her life, form the pattern of her coping strategy and represent the extent of her efforts to alter the quality of her existence."[12]

Margaret's response to her reality is, of course, unsuccessful. A sexist culture punishes women for the same sins men commit with impunity. Grange can openly have an affair with Josie, but Margaret, even privately, cannot take on new lovers. In addition to double standards for men and women, Margaret's physical vulnerability as a female makes her search for sex without the pressures of her everyday life a tragic mistake. When she succumbs to the lust of Grange's boss and gives birth to a half-white child, Margaret Copeland commits two unpardonable sins for black women in white America: she violates her vow of fidelity and, worse, she sleeps with the enemy.

Grange deserts her and their legitimate son, Brownfield, for the North he had once refused to consider as refuge from suffering in the South. Sinned against and sinful, unloved and deserted, Margaret kills herself and her bastard child. Walker's poignant and poetic epitaph for Margaret Copeland captures the oppression of black women in the rural South who were slaves of black men who were themselves slaves: "married not into ecstasy, but into dread. Not into freedom, but into bondage; not into perpetual love, but into deepening despair" (176).

Grange's woman, Josie, is also a victim of the sexist culture that causes Margaret's suicide. Pregnant at sixteen, she is disowned by her father and humiliated at a party she gives in an effort to regain his love. She vows never again to be dependent on any man for anything. "Like a phoenix who rises from the ashes with unfurled wings, she soars above male control to become the richest and most powerful black person, male or female, in the community."[13] She becomes a prostitute, and in a small house on Poontang Street, aptly named, she vents her woman's rage. Unfortunately, her liberation from male control does not put her in touch with her personhood. As a prosperous prostitute, she is still confined to a role that requires woman's service to man.

When Brownfield finds her in the rural community while searching for his father, Josie envelops him in unchecked passion, attempting to "eat him up, swallow him down alive" (36). Her interest in Brownfield is similar to the sexist interest men have in women. She desires Brownfield because he is unspoiled, untouched, virginal, and like men who boast that they were the "first," Josie takes pride in teaching Brownfield about the pleasures of the flesh.

The texture of Brownfield's life changes when Josie's niece, Mem, comes to visit during her summer break from college. She is fragrant; Josie carries "the sweet odor of decay." Gentle and innocent, Mem awakens in Brownfield a need for something more spiritual than the relationship he has with Josie and her daughter, Lorene. His awkward attempts to win her love suggests that Josie has not completely ruined him. His marriage to Mem seems to be a first step from the shadow of Grange's empty life.

Mem is fertile, giving birth to three children in three years, and happy. For Brownfield, she is "someone to be loved and spoken to softly, someone never to frighten with his rough, coarse ways" (45). Mem "sang while she cooked breakfast in the morning and sang when getting ready for bed at night. And sang when she nursed her babies, and sang to [Brownfield] when he crawled in weariness and dejection into the warm life-giving circle of her breast" (49).

Hope falls on fallow ground in the rural South. Twenty years later, the pernicious system that claimed Grange Copeland claims his son:

> He thought of suicide and never forgot it, even in Mem's arms. He prayed for help, for a caring President, for a listening Jesus. He prayed for a decent job in Mem's arms. But like all prayers sent up from there, it turned into another mouth to feed, another body to enslave to pay his debts. He felt himself destined to become no more than an overseer, on the white man's plantation, of his own children. (46).

In time, like his father before him, Brownfield becomes a victim of the system and, like his father, vents his rage against a black woman who understands and attempts to soothe his pain. He takes Mem "in his drunkenness," Walker writes, and boasts to his friends of his sexual power and fist power. He beats her wantonly out of rage, self-hatred, and humiliation:

> His crushed pride, his battered ego, made him drag Mem away from school teaching. . . . It was his ignorance that sent her into white homes as a domestic, his need to bring her down to his level!

It was his rage at himself, and his life and his world that made him beat her. . . . His rage could and did blame everything, *everything,* on her. (55)

Once proud of her education, Brownfield now resents it and takes cruel pleasure in knowing that she uses the pages of her book to stuff large rat holes in their shack. She saves to buy a house in the city for the family; he uses the money to buy a pig. She begins to save again; he uses the money to buy a car—for himself, of course. She has no rights that he must observe: "Her role is clearly defined. She is woman. He is lord. She must please him. He is free to please only himself."[14] She is Brownfield's inferior simply because she is a woman and he is a man. The similarity between sexism, which oppresses women, and racism, which oppresses blacks, is startling.

Misery is a running, bleeding sore in Mem's life, but she continues to struggle for a better life for her family. She rents a house in the city and insists that Brownfield obey the rules in *her* house. She understands what the South, the white man, has done to him, but she would have him understand that he should "quit wailing like a seedy jackass" (59). Mem does not dismiss racial oppression in Brownfield's life; it is real and devastating. However, she rejects it as an excuse for his transgressions against the family. This is Mem's message to Brownfield as she holds a loaded gun to his genitals, which indicates that she is seeking liberation from sexual oppression, not simply racial oppression and economic deprivation. Walker writes that Brownfield "did not have the courage to imagine life without the existence of white people as a prop" (4).

Mem's liberation is short-lived. Not understanding evil, she could not have known comfort, cleanliness, and sunshine in the new house could not change Brownfield. Two miscarriages weaken her and render her helpless against Brownfield's cruel plans for her destruction. In one fell swoop, he descends like a vulture on her weakened body and returns her to *his* house, an inadequate shack, where she must abide by *his* rules. On Christmas Day, as she comes home from her job as a domestic, she faces the loaded barrel of Brownfield's gun. Seconds later, she lies "faceless in a pool of blood" (122).

As womanist, Walker asserts that change is not possible in black women's lives unless we recognize the need for change and hold accountable anyone who obstructs change. She does both in her portrait of Brownfield. For some readers, the portrait is too harsh. His cruelty, they say, is implausible: "nobody's [that] mean." But Walker knows real men like him. They exist, she says, and "there is no way [we] are going to avoid them."[15] Certainly there is no way a womanist writer can avoid breaking the silence on black men's sexism.

Readers who criticize Walker's portrait of Brownfield obviously do not see the balance between Brownfield, who chooses brutality, and Grange, who chooses gentleness. Grange in his third life is the hope Walker offers to the reader. During Mem's most difficult days with Brownfield, Grange returns to the small town to do penance for his past sins. He attempts to touch Brownfield with new hands and to teach him about inner strength in the face of white brutality. He tells his son to "hold tight" a place where racism cannot reach. He pleads with him to understand

> the danger of putting all the blame on somebody else. . . . And I'm bound to believe that that's the way the white folks can corrupt you even when you done held up before. 'Cause when they got you thinking that they're to blame for *everything* they have you thinking they's some kind of gods! (200)

Brownfield is beyond reach. Bitter and consumed by self-hatred, he chooses to punish his father rather than assume responsibility for his life and his family. He chooses sorrow over joy, and revenge over responsibility. The tragic result of these choices is the destruction of his family. He murders his wife and drives his daughter Daphne to insanity and his daughter Ornette into prostitution.

Grange makes different choices. He commits his life to the survival and *wholeness* of Brownfield's youngest daughter, Ruth. Symbolically, their relationship begins in 1960, when black people and white people, together, are struggling to change the face of the South. Together, Grange, now in his sixties, and his granddaughter Ruth suggest the possibility of change. Ruth reinforces Grange's new philosophy that black people should not make white folks god: "Nobody's as powerful as we make them out to be. We got our own *souls* don't we?" (223). Grange nurtures Ruth's *womanish* attitude toward life.

Ruth asks questions, demands answers, and speaks with her own voice. Grange says of Ruth, "I never in my life seen a more womanish girl" (200). He wants her to be free of the curse of the generations that claimed Margaret and Mem, and perhaps women before them. In a word, he wants her to be "responsible. In charge. *Serious.*"[16] At the end of the novel, Grange murders his own son and waits heroically for the posse, against which he knows he has no chance for survival. He dies so that Ruth might live *whole* in the light of her own suns.

Alice Walker suceeds in making *The Third Life of Grange Copeland* "a very realistic . . . and absolutely visual" novel. We see a "little of Georgia—the trees, the hills, the dirt, the sky" and we "feel it, . . . feel the pain and the struggle of the family, and the growth of the little girl Ruth."[17] What we see little of is a black community peopled with individuals who are as different as they are alike. Everyone is burdened and victimized in the novel; the darkness never gives way to the sun. And this is as it should be, of course, because *The Third Life of Grange Copeland* was written as "a grave book in which the characters see the world as entirely menacing."[18]

In Love and Trouble: Stories of Black Women (1973), Walker's first collection of short stories, is not as grave a book, and the setting is not as bleak. Collectively, the thirteen stories make up a black community composed of individual black women—"mad, raging, loving, resentful, hateful, strong, ugly, weak, pitiful, and magnificent" black women who "try to live with the loyalty to black men that characterizes all of their lives."[19]

Walker owes their creation to her mother's memory and sensitivity. Over the years, she listened to her mother's stories and "absorbed not only the stories themselves, but the manner in which her mother spoke, something of the urgency that involves the knowledge that her stories—like her life—must be recorded."[20] The stories in *In Love and Trouble,* then, are her mother's stories and the stories of other Southern women from whom Walker received the "creative spark; the seed of the flower [the women] themselves never hoped to see."[21]

In several of the stories, Walker highlights the resilient strength of black women, who, in spite of the exigencies of racism and poverty, keep their humanity and dignity in focus. "Everyday Use," Walker's most anthologized work, is such a story. It examines the values of an adult black woman who had lived her life entirely in a simple, but love-filled, frame house in the rural South, and the new values of a militant daughter who has tasted a larger world. The daughter returns home, only as a visitor, to collect artifacts of black culture. A quilt made by black women and representative of their creativity is not an artifact. In choosing to give the quilt to the daughter who has remained home and doubts her beauty, the mother not only embraces the girl with love but also affirms the beauty and value of black women's culture.

Other stories show black women struggling to survive and stay sane. In "Strong Horse Tea," a black mother chases a mare in a fierce storm to catch urine, hoping the "tea" will cure the child whom the doctor refuses to treat. In "The Welcome Table," an elderly black woman, touched by the Holy Spirit, is thrown bodily from a white church; Southern Christianity is but racism reserved for Sunday. In "The Revenge of Hannah Kemhuff," whose prototype is Walker's own mother, a black woman is denied government food for her starving children because the white woman in charge resents the cast-off clothes Mrs. Kemhuff wears. These stories focus mainly, though not exclusively, on the burdens of racism in the women's lives. Each woman faces the hardships of her life alone. Each woman suffers for someone other than herself.

Like *The Third Life of Grange Copeland,* this collection of short stories strikes a balance between Walker's interest in exploring racism in the South and her interest in exploring male insensitivity in black male-female relationships. Indeed, some of the stories on sexism are harbingers of Walker's later works. "Her Sweet Jerome" is such a story. The central character, a beautician in a small Southern town, takes pride in her marriage to a schoolteacher ten years her junior. The marriage gives her a name, "Mrs. Jerome Franklin Washington," but it deprives her of the status she once had as a woman who made it on her own. Jerome beats her, verbally abuses her, and humiliates her in the presence of his friends. Mrs. Washington's dark shades do not conceal the black and blue marks Jerome gives her in regular beatings, and her bright-colored clothes and orange shoes do not gain his attention or approval. She is devastated when she discovers that Jerome had been involved, not with another woman, but with a group of "intellectuals" who read books that contain words she does not understand. In a fit of confusion and rage, she sets fire to his room and, in her death, becomes all that Jerome had studied but never understood: "Black Rage, Black Fire, Black Anger."[22]

In appearance, interests, and situation, Myrna, the heroine in "Really, Doesn't Crime Pay?," is very different from Mrs. Jerome Franklin Washington. She is married to a black man who provides for her in exchange for her being all that he wants in a woman: someone visibly more white than black, someone feminine, and someone to have his babies. Myrna wants to write stories; her husband suggests that she go shopping or make herself useful in other womanly ways. Frustrated because her husband does not understand or respect the creativity she talks about but does not believe is hers, Myrna becomes involved with another man, but only because he pretends to appreciate the artist in her. He steals her stories and publishes them as his own. Neither man in her life understands who she is or what she desires. She records in a journal, which makes up the entire story, details of her nervous breakdown and abortive plans to murder her husband. "Having tried the madness of murder and failed, Myrna concocts a far more subtle way . . . to secure her freedom": she is the adoring and dutiful wife who says *yes* to everything—"until she had yessed her husband to fatigue."[23]

The problem of "woman's place" in marriage is also the subject of "Roselily," which is written in the "plastic, shaping, almost painting quality of words."[24] It is a quiet story that takes place almost entirely in the character's mind. As the single parent of three children, Roselily is fortunate to be wed to a clean-cut, well-spoken Muslim from the North; he can rescue her from a life of poverty and backwardness in the South. But Roselily experiences no bliss during the marriage ceremony. She knows that, in exchange for security, she will have to make more babies and live with her husband's efforts to "redo her into what he truly wants."[25] The minister reads traditional marriage vows, and Roselily dreams of a life such vows do not promise. She "wants to live for once. But doesn't know quite what it means. Wonders if she has ever done it. If she ever will" (8).

Most of the women in *In Love and Trouble* and those in *The Third Life of Grange Copeland* are self-sacrificing women resigned to the weary centers and rough edges of their lives. They have internalized the narrowly defined "woman's place" and believe that in that "place" there are no alternatives to loneliness, exhaustion, and denial of self. This, Walker suggests, is perhaps the greatest tragedy of their lives: their disbelief in the possibility of a different reality, in the possibility of "change personal and change in society."[26] When we go inside their lives, guided by Walker's compassion and sensitivity, we understand that images of black women as persons of superior strength and endurance, so pervasive in American culture, have distorted the complexity of their reality.

Mary Helen Washington calls women like those in Walker's first two works of fiction "suspended women," who "either kill themselves or . . . are used up by the man, or the children . . . or by . . . whatever pressures against them." In Walker's "evolutionary treatment" of black women, composed of three cycles, we see the women's experiences as "a series of movements from women totally victimized by society and by the men in their lives to the growing developing women whose consciousness allows them to have control over their lives."[27]

Interestingly, the cycles correspond to so-called priorities on the national agenda for change in this country. In the 1960s, the priority was racial liberation. In 1970, if not as early as the late 1960s, racial liberation had to make room for, or yield its space entirely to, sexual liberation. A new movement was born, similar in goals to women's movements as far back as the nineteenth century. In 1973, with the founding of the National Black Feminist Organization and Black Women Organized for Women, hundreds of black women discussed publicly, as they had done privately among themselves, the victimization of black women at the hands of black men. They invoked the spirit of Harriet Tubman, Ida Wells-Barnett, Frances Harper, and other nineteenth-century black women activists and held before the nation the womanist example of Shirley Chisholm, Angela Davis, Fannie Lou Hamer, and other contemporary black women activists. Achieving their goal, the racial *and* sexual liberation of black women, required the courage to speak, write, and even sing about "double jeopardy." Their focus was on black women as powerless and brutalized human beings, as victims.

Walker's first collection of poetry, *Once,* written when she was twenty-one and a senior at Sarah Lawrence College, is a work of the sixties. A slim volume, *Once* demonstrates Walker's ability to "express mystery, evoke beauty and pleasure, paint a picture—and not dissect or analyze in any way," in three or four lines.[28] Images in the volume are of black people in the South and in Africa. Again, balance is present. Walker writes of the evils of racism, but she suggests hope in the picture of a little black girl who waves an American flag "with / the very / *tips* / of her fingers."[29] She captures the beauty and dignity of people in Africa (romanticized by black militants as a near-perfect place called the Motherland), but she does not ignore the ugly face of poverty: "A tall man / Without clothes / Beautiful / Like a statue / Up close / His eyes / Are running / Sores" (20). Singularly absent from this volume is Walker's examination of black women's double jeopardy.

By the mid-1970s and certainly by 1980, the movement, having gained larger numbers, more visibility, and unquestionable strength, entered its second stage. Black women in the movement no longer focused on women as victims. Clearly, it was time to effect change by showing the face of change. To this stage belong women of the third cycle that Mary Helen Washington discusses: they insist on their own space and the right to their own names; they refuse to be victims of any kind.

Walker's poetry reflects changes in the movement and, as well and understandably, changes in her own sexual consciousness. *Revolutionary Petunias and Other Poems,* unlike *Once,* is a work of the 1970s. In this volume, often considered her finest, we see Walker's celebration of the spiritual strength of black people who struggle to maintain their dignity in a region—a nation—that wants them to half-step, if at all, toward their dreams. Petunias, which Walker's mother grew in splendid profusion, can be put "in any kind of soil and they bloom their heads off—exactly, it seemed to me, like black people tend to do."[30]

Revolutionary Petunias belongs to both the civil rights movement and the new movement gaining strength in the seventies. For in the same soil in which petunias bloom, sexism grows like weeds, uncared for, prolific, and unchallenged. "He Said Come" is one of the most poignant poems on sexism published during this period: "He said come / Let me exploit you; / somebody must do it / And wouldn't you / Prefer a brother?"[31]

In her third volume, *Goodnight Willie Lee, I'll See You in the Morning* (1979), Walker's focus is on woman's personhood rather than victimization. For many black women activists, "On Stripping Bark from Myself" is the definitive poetic statement on liberation in the 1970s, just as Sojourner Truth's speech, "Arn't I a Woman?" was the definitive statement on slavery and sexism in the 1800s. Clearly, Walker has raised her own sexual consciousness since she published her first work in 1968. In 1981, she will "not keep silent" because she is a woman. She is "finished with living / for what my believes / for what my brother and father defend / for what my elevates / for what my sister, blushing, denies or rushes embrace." She finds her "own small person / a self / against the world," and she is "happy to fight / all murderers / as I see I must."[32]

The Third Life of Grange Copeland and *In Love and Trouble* were written during the period of the movement and the stage of Walker's consciousness that sensitized readers to the truths of black women's pain. Appropriately, the women in these works belong to the first stage that Mary Helen Washington discusses; they are victims, not liberated persons. By the middle of the seventies, educating readers about black women's victimization was not as urgent, or as needed, as teaching readers the meaning of liberation. In Walker's second novel, *Meridian,* published in 1976, four years before the new decade, a black woman gives birth to self.

At the beginning of the novel, Meridian Hill is a naïve high school student who has sex with her young boyfriend as often as he wants it, "sometimes every single night."[33] Since no one had taught her about woman's biological vulnerability, Meridian's "pregnancy came as a total shock" (53). She drops out of school, marries her lover, and awaits the birth of her child. Her entire life has been changed—and by an experience she did not enjoy.

Meridian's attitude toward sex is important to Walker's challenge of the assumption that the sexual potency of men makes sex a pleasurable experience for women, and that a woman loved well belongs to a man forever. This is the assumption that confuses love with romance and that makes women sex objects and men sex experts. Womanist scholars in the 1970s argued that sexual pleasure for women does not come from technique without tenderness, or rhythm without respect. Meridian finds sex an uninteresting experience, but important because it protects her from her fear of men. Only when she is sexually involved with a man, Walker explains, can Meridian "look out at the male world with something approaching equanimity, even charity; even friendship" (53).

Walker also challenges the assumptions that motherhood is woman's "sacred calling," that all women want to be mothers, and that all women function well in that role. Socialized in a culture that makes motherhood a sexist institution, many women internalize the "joys of motherhood" and discover in the experience of motherhood that "joys" often give way to boredom, frustration, exhaustion, and rage. Mrs. Hill is such a woman. For her, motherhood is like "being buried alive, walled away from one's own life, brick by brick" (41). When she asks with a vacant stare in her eyes, "Have you stolen anything?" (41), Meridian understands that by being born and remaining alive she has stolen her mother's life.

Like Mrs. Hill, Meridian finds motherhood unfulfilling: "So this, she mumbles, . . . is what *slavery* is like. Rebelling, she began to dream each night, just before her baby sent out cries, of ways to *murder him*" (63). Marriage is also unfulfilling. Community people tell Meridian that Eddie is a good man because he does not abuse her in any way—"implying that, as a man, he has the right to do so, and that, as a woman, she has the obligation to adjust her needs to provide for his rights."[34] They do not understand that her need for a different reality does not depend on Eddie's goodness. Convinced that the small town, marriage, and motherhood will never fulfill her, she deserts her family for her own dreams. She leaves to attend college in Atlanta and begins to journey toward the third cycle.

In Atlanta, she falls in love with Truman Held, a young black revolutionary who speaks the rhetoric of the civil rights movement poetically, throwing in a little French for effect. He is not brutal, as Brownfield is, but he is no less sexist. He wants an ideal woman—a virgin—because that is what the culture teaches men have a right to expect on their wedding night. And he wants that virgin to be a strong and supportive woman: "a woman to rest in, as a ship must have a port. As a train must have a shed" (139).

By the time Meridian discovers she is pregnant, Truman Held is involved with a white exchange student. She sees them together, happy and courageously in love, as she travels to an abortionist. Even in her weakest moment, she is subjected to male insensitivity. Like many men who believe they have something to offer women with their sex, he

313

promises to tie Meridian's tubes if she will sleep with him. As Truman and Lynn are together, free-spirited and in love, Meridian's pain flows in buckets of blood.

Meridian leaves Atlanta and settles in a small Mississippi town to recover from blinding headaches, seizures, thinning hair, and strange fainting spells. She struggles with her inability to be—ever—like black women throughout history who sacrificed and suffered so that their children could live. She struggles with the deep pain of a woman used and discarded by a man. And she struggles for an answer to the question militants put to her in the movement: could she kill for the revolution?

In the final chapter of the novel, Meridian emerges from her small shack cleansed of the sickness that had claimed her for years. The headaches, seizures, and fainting spells are gone. So too is the bitterness and pain she felt as a woman used and discarded. She forgives and even pities Truman, but she is emphatic about her new sense of self: "You are free to be whichever way you like, to be with whoever, of whatever color or sex you like—and what you risk in being truly yourself, the way you want to be, is not the loss of me." She adds that he is "*not free* . . . to think she is a fool" (223). She is free of the haunting question, could she kill for the revolution. She decides that that martyrdom is foolish. Her obligation to the struggle for justice is to live and to keep alive the old songs of her people.

Truman will take her place in the small shack, and "Meridian [will] return to the world cleansed of sickness" (226). She has made a commitment to life, to wholeness. Her struggle, Walker writes, is "symbolic . . . of the struggle each of us will have to assume in our own way."[35] Like Meridian, who gives birth to self, we must recognize that the special sun in our lives comes from within and must challenge the darkness in which the essence of our humanity is often hidden.

Walker's second collection of short stories, *You Can't Keep a Good Woman Down* (1981), examines subjects that womanists and feminists in the late seventies were writing about and discussing at conferences and in published works of various kinds: abortion, pornography, sadomasochism, rape, and other "unpalatable" concerns. The stories are as daring in structure as they are in theme. The women too are daring in their insistence on freedom and personhood. Two stories in particular capture the tone and perspective of the collection.

The central character in "How Did I Get Away with Killing One of the Biggest Lawyers in the State?" murders the man who became her lover after he raped her when she was only fourteen. When the man manipulates her into turning against her mother, the woman wakes up.

She cannot undo the damage of the years, but she can put an end to the victimization. Without guilt, she murders him. She commits the perfect crime because no one in the white community would ever believe a black woman would have the courage to murder a white man. With sassy humor, she recounts that on the day of his funeral, she, the murderer, is sitting in his house and eating food his wife had prepared. This story makes us aware, as sociologists did in a number of studies published in the seventies, the existence of women who liberate themselves from victimization by murdering the victimizer. Interestingly, the victim in this case is a white man.

Black women are also driven to abortion in order to save their own lives. Like Meridian and Roselily, the character in "The Abortion" wants other options for her life than motherhood. Pregnant with her second child, she remembers an abortion she had as a college student; it was a "seizing of the direction of her own life." Her desire for a second abortion is no less so: "Another child would kill me."[36] She has no guilt about her decision. Calmly and confident that her decision is right, she speaks to the unborn child: " 'Well, child, it was you or me, Kiddo, and I chose me' " (70).

For some readers, this collection lacks the poetry and honesty of *In Love and Trouble*. It is flawed, writes David Bradley, by didacticism and "unassimilated rhetoric; simplistic politics and a total lack of plot and characterization." Walker ignores "the human power of situations in favor of political symbolism."[37] He cites as examples "Porn," obviously a story about pornography, and "Advancing Luna—and Ida B. Wells," a story about interracial rape.

It might well be that form poses a problem for Bradley and other readers, for womanist literature is more than a way of seeing and thinking. It is also a way of creating art. In the 1960s, writers of the black arts movement made this point about their commitment to blackness. It needed and created new forms and language. We embraced the works of such writers as Don L. Lee, Amiri Baraka, Sonia Sanchez, and others, but we are slow to embrace writers who demonstrate that womanism needs and has created new forms. Many of the stories in *You Can't Keep a Good Woman Down* show "a link between process (the unraveling of thought and feeling) and the way women have perceived the world." Barbara Christian explains that, "in keeping with this theory, Walker often gives us the story as it comes into being, rather than delivering the product, classic and clean. . . . For many of these stories reflect the present, when the process of confusion, resistance to established order, and the discovery of a freeing order is, especially for women, a prerequisite for growth."[38]

You Can't Keep a Good Woman Down is very different from all of Walker's earlier works in that it features women Walker knew many readers would not understand, and certainly not love. Unfortunately, Bradley and other readers mistakenly attribute their discomfort, which they do not acknowledge, to flaws in the collection. The problem with *You Can't Keep a Good Woman Down* might very well lie not in the collection but in ourselves as readers. Many of us are not "ready" for women who are introduced as already whole, and who remain whole. It is as if we want first their tears, and then their personhood.

The Color Purple (1983) begins with the tears of a young black girl named Celie, who learns by the end of the novel how to smile, to walk with confidence, and to speak her name with pride. This is Walker's most brilliant work, fully deserving of the national and international attention it has received. Not surprisingly, its setting is reminiscent of the rural South of Walker's youth. In fact, in order to listen to the characters—to give them voice and flesh in the novel—Walker moved to a place in northern California that resembles the town in Georgia that is the setting of the novel.

That Walker's most celebrated novel returns her to the rural South is no accident. This is as it should be, for it was not Spelman, where she matriculated for two years; Sarah Lawrence, from which she graduated; *Ms.,* where she worked for a number of years; or travel abroad that nurtured Alice Walker, a sharecropper's daughter, into an artistic genius. Her nurturers were black people in Eatonton, especially Walker's mother. When she moves from the rural South to urban cities; from small frame houses in isolated clearings, to colleges with stretches of campus green; from the reality of rural black folks in *The Third Life of Grange Copeland* and *In Love and Trouble,* to the life-styles of new women in *You Can't Keep a Good Woman Down;* from women who believe abortion and murder are sins, to women who commit both deliberately and without guilt, Alice Walker is telling the stories of her generation.

Without question, they are urgent stories that needed to be written. They enlarge our understanding of the black woman's reality, and they push us further into the center of truth and the need for change. They are richly crafted stories—poignant, compelling, powerful, and replete with poetry that is as penetrating to the soul as it is pleasing to the ear. But they are not as rich in spirituality as her mother's stories. *The Color Purple* is immensely rich in spirituality because it was, in part, inspired by Walker's search for her "mother's garden." It belongs to the rural South, which pulls from Walker her most brilliant fiction. It is her gift to the ancestors whose gift to Alice was "the creative spark, the seed of the flower they themselves never hoped to see; or like a sealed letter they could not plainly read."[39]

The Color Purple is an epistolary novel, made up entirely of letters Celie writes to God and to her sister Nettie and, later in the novel, letters Nettie had written to Celie over a period of thirty years. Walker handles the epistolary form with such commanding grace that readers feel they have come upon, by chance, the private letters of a poor black woman named Celie, who was raped at fourteen by her presumed father, who kills the first child she bore him and gives away the other two. To protect himself, he tells Celie: "You better not never tell nobody but God. It'd kill your mammy."[40] Thus begins Celie's refuge in writing letters to God.

When her mother dies, Celie is left defenseless against the man's brutality. Willingly, she gives him her body to protect her sister Nettie. When he tires of Celie, who can no longer bear children, he marries her off to Mr.———(cited hereafter as Mister), who needs a woman, not for companionship, but for the straining job of caring for his four unruly children. First owned by the man she believes to be her father, Celie is now owned by Mister. Her status is similar to that of a slave. In the institution of slavery, black people, regardless of sex or age, were slaves. In the institution of patriarchy, black women, regardless of age, are slaves.

Celie has "no rights, receives no money for her many services and is subjected to regular beatings." As Calvin Hernton writes in "Who's Afraid of Virginia Woolf: The Color Purple as Slave Narrative," Mister "treats her any way he chooses, because the overriding morality (ethics) of patriarchy toward women is that women have no rights that men are bound to respect. In the process, women are infantilized and rendered completely dependent on male paternalism for any kindness they might be accorded."[41]

Walker balances Celie's submissiveness with Sophia's feisty refusal to be controlled by anyone—by whites, regardless of sex, or by men, regardless of race. Mister tells his son Harpo, Sophia's husband, that "wives is like children. You have to let 'em know who got the upper hand. Nothing can do that better than a good sound beating" (42). Celie, who has internalized man's right to beat women, also tells Harpo that Sophia would be a better wife if she received a beating. When Harpo attempts to beat Sophia, it is he who receives the bruises.

From Sophia, Celie should have learned that a marriage stripped of sexist definitions of work brings happiness not only to women, but also to men. Harpo enjoys so-called woman's work, Sophia tells Celie. He "love cooking and cleaning and doing little things 'round the house"

(63), and Sophia loves so-called man's work—hammering, repairing, and working outside. When men and women are persons in a relationship, liberated from narrow definitions of masculine and feminine, they are able to enjoy the pleasure of their union. Unfortunately, Harpo is not strong enough to be his own person. His masculine need for control and his desire for approval from his male peers, especially his father, destroy the happiness he and Sophia enjoy.

In spite of Sophia's example of strength, Celie remains docile and submissive in her marriage to Mister. She does not know how to fight and, having internalized the community's attitude toward women, she does not believe women should fight. Life for Celie is about "staying alive" and suppressing anger and waiting for letters from Nettie, which never come. The tragedy of her situation is that "staying alive" means accepting absolute powerlessness and extreme brutality, living with a "terrible nothing" (47).

Shug Avery helps remove the "terrible nothing" from Celie's life. She teaches Celie how to laugh, how to speak her mind, and how to see herself as a woman deserving of love. Mister's former lover and the woman he yet worships, Shug is worldly, strong, sensuous, and fiercely independent. Calvin Hernton captures Shug's essence when he writes that she is the blues/jazz singer who articulates "the sorrows, brutalities, endurances and love-fleeting moments of women who, like Celie, are shackled down and rendered inarticulate in this woman-hating world."[42]

In Celie's eyes, Shug Avery is the most beautiful woman she has ever seen. When Shug becomes ill and moves in with Celie and Mister, Celie looks forward to spending time with her—bathing her, combing her hair, "fixing" and doing for her. Shug is friend, sister, teacher, preacher, comforter, and guardian angel who protects Celie from Mister's brutality and teaches her a new song of self. In the small club that sits isolated in the rural clearing, Shug dedicates a song to Celie. In a letter to God, Celie writes: "First time somebody made something and name it after me" (75).

Physical love between Shug and Celie develops naturally from their spiritual bonding. Indeed, it is a part of the therapy that makes Celie whole and central to the womanist definition of the total liberation of women. Walker's treatment of their physical relationship challenges the homophobic notion that physical love between two women is a perversion. It does not result from women's hatred of men; Shug loves men and heterosexual lovemaking. It is not an expression of women's confusion about their sexual identity; Shug is very much a *woman,* and Celie, hating men, has no desire to be a man. Rather, it is simply an expression of love between two human beings who happen to be women. When the essentials of love are in place—trust, compassion, understanding, gentleness, and friendship—love between two women, like love between a man and a woman, can be a fulfilling experience. Holding tight to our homophobic belief that women should love only men is tantamount, in the face of Mister's brutality, to choosing sorrow over joy for Celie. Walker writes lyrically of their lovemaking and moves on.

She does not focus on what readers call "lesbianism" in the novel because Shug's spirituality is a greater influence on Celie's life than the women's moments of physical pleasure. Shug is a feeling, caring person connected to the universe. Many of her concerns are Walker's concerns. She cares about the plight of Indians: "People insane. . . . Here they building a dam so they can flood out a Indian tribe that been there since time" (189). She cares about peace: "People fussing and fighting and pointing fingers at other people, and never even looking for no peace" (189).

She cares most profoundly about Celie's lack of self-love. Her most important gift to Celie is not sexual pleasure, but a liberating definition of God. The concept of God as a man is enslaving, not liberating. Walker makes a similar point in an interview conducted in 1973. If God is a person, Walker believes, "he has to look like someone. But if he's *not* a person, if she's not a person, if *it's* not a person. . . . Or, if it is a person, then everybody is it, and that's all right." She has replaced the "oppressive image with . . . everything there is, . . . the desert, the trees . . . the birds, the dirt; . . . And that's all God."[43]

In black folk English, Shug, always the voice of reason and love, tells Celie that God "ain't a picture show. It ain't something you can look at apart from anything else, including yourself." Her explanation that God is in everything and everybody explains the title of the novel. If people see God in everything, Shug tells Celie, they "can't walk by the color purple in a field somewhere and don't notice it." All of us "come into the world with God. But only them that search for it *inside* find it" (italics added, 178). Only Celie, then, not the God to whom she writes, can change her world.

Celie's metamorphosis from an ugly girl who submits to brutality to a beautiful woman who "loves self. Regardless" is gradual. It begins, of course, with Shug's arrival in Celie's life and in the lives of other women in the novel; it continues and culminates in Celie's personhood because of sisterhood. In various ways, the women characters—Celie, Shug, Sophia, and Mary Agnes—defend, protect, fight for, and love one another. "Sister's Choice," the quilt Celie makes, is a symbol of the female bonding that "restores the women [even brutalized Celie] to a sense of completeness and independence."[44]

The Color Purple repulses some readers because the brutality of black men in the novel is heinous. But not all black men in Walker's vision are as despicable as Celie's stepfather and Mister. Always there is balance in Walker's works. Samuel, who marries Nettie, is a very caring man, a missionary in Africa who is committed to the liberation of his people and sensitive to the plight of women. Nettie's letters, which Shug rescues from Mister, say as much. They also relate her experiences with the Olinka tribe, which reinforce a fact womanists know: sexism, or patriarchy, is not endemic to any one nation, any one culture, or any one time in the history of human civilization.

Moreover, Mister, like Grange Copeland and like Celie, undergoes a metamorphosis. He stretches himself to the furthest point of male dominance and brutality only to discover that violence destroys the victimizer as much as it damages the victim. When Celie changes and when the power of female bonding is everywhere evident in the small community, Mister is dethroned. Just as Grange Copeland feels better about himself in his third life, so does Mister feel better about himself as a new person. No longer tied to sexist definitions of men and women, he talks to Celie, shares his emotions, and participates in the so-called womanly art of sewing.

Walker suggests in her portrait of the new Mister, as she suggests in her portrait of the new Grange, that sexual liberation is not "for women only." Everyone wins when everyone is free to be a person. Mister, who has earned the right to his name (Albert), tells Celie: "I'm satisfied this the first time I ever lived on Earth as a natural man. It feel like a new experience" (230). It is significant, very significant, that Mister says "*natural*" man rather than *real* man. The latter carries the ugly sound of macho; the former suggests the presence of God, which, according to Shug, is inside everyone at birth. It is symbolic of Mister's redemption.

Alice Walker embraces the new Mister no less than she embraces the women characters in all stages of their growth into persons. It is this way with Walker's belief in forgiveness and the healing power of love. In both *The Color Purple* and *The Third Life of Grange Copeland,* and to some extent in *Meridian,* redeemed men earn the right to articulate Walker's philosophy. Albert's message of love is Walker's message. He wonders why people are black, why people are men and women, and why people suffer. "So what you think?" Celie asks. He answers: "I think us here to wonder, myself. To wonder. To ast. . . . " And the more he wonders, he says, "*the more I love*" (italics added, 247).

The abject misery and suffering with which the novel begins is balanced by the joyousness with which the novel ends. Celie is reunited with her two children and with her sister Nettie. Family and friends, men and women celebrate their new world, symbolically, on the Fourth of July. When white people are celebrating independence, "black folks are celebrating each other" (249). Celie writes her final letter: "Dear God. Dear stars, dear tree, dear sky, dear peoples, Dear Everything" (249). She has searched for and found God in everything, including herself. She has given birth to self. By the end of the novel, writes Gloria Steinem, "we believe that this poor, nameless patch of land in the American South is really the world—and vice versa," and that the redemption that Walker's characters experience is possible for all of us. "The color purple, an odd miracle of nature, symbolizes the miracle of human possibilities."[45]

Not all readers are as kind as Steinem. Some criticize Walker for staying clear of direct attacks on white Southerners because to do so would rob her, they claim, of a place in the mainstream of American literature. The result of this desire, writes Loyle Hairston, is "no sharp insights, no penetrating ideas that illuminate what the real world is made of, no serious challenges to the status-quo, no wave-making."[46] Trudier Harris, who says that she wrestled with her response to the novel, writes that the novel reads like a "political shopping list of all the IOUs Walker felt that it was time to repay": IOUs to feminists, lesbians, black nationalists, Pan-Africanists, career-minded women, born-again male feminists, and black culture in the use of the blues and the folk idiom.[47]

The peripheral significance of white people is not Walker's desire to claim a space in the mainstream of American literature, as Hairston suggests. Her success, which came very early in her career, makes such a desire unnecessary. She focuses on black people because she is committed to their spiritual whole and survival. To focus on white people would be tantamount to making the mistake that destroyed Brownfield, that is, making white people gods in black reality.

Moreover, Walker makes whites peripheral to her visions because, as womanist, she explores the *inside* reality of black women, and for obvious reasons. It is the inside reality, where women function as wives and mothers, that usually defines "woman's place." What Walker discovers when she goes inside is that black women seek comfort there from the onslaughts of racism and poverty and often discover new and sometimes more excruciating pain.

No one can prove or disprove that politics influenced the womanist vision in *The Color Purple*. Influences do not announce themselves; they seep into our consciousness silently. Even when they are there, we are not sure where they come from, or why. Art, after all, is never written in a vacuum. In various ways, it reflects (not to be confused with mirrors) the world in which it was created and the world that stands at the center of the vision. Feminists, lesbians, black nationalists, career-minded women, etcetera—all are a part of the American culture to which Walker belongs and of which she writes. The larger question, then, is not about influence, but about effectiveness. How well does Walker weave all of the political influences Harris cites into her novel? The success of the work gives us the answer.

Walker's commitment to honesty and truth about her personal life suggests that honesty and truth, as she perceives it, shape her art. In interviews, essays, and speeches, she shares her personal life with an openness rare for celebrated writers, especially young celebrated writers. She could choose to keep her scars and secrets hidden from us—to leave them for a scholar who would go down in literary history as author of the definitive biography of Alice Walker, a sharecropper's daughter who became a literary genius. But Walker chooses openness. The accident that left her blind in one eye at the age of eight; her father's withdrawal; her family's poverty; her mother's belief that white women are, after all, more beautiful than black women; her interracial marriage; her abortion; her contemplation of suicide—few things escape her desire to share herself with us. It is as if, in exchange for our belief in the truths of her artistic visions, she will let us examine her scars and open wide the closet of her most intimate secrets.

She has no need to defend her work, and she does not. She is an artist; she must be free to create! She is a womanist writer; she must weave the threads of black women's lives into her work. This is as it should be, "because no matter what anyone says, it is the black *woman's* words that have the most meaning for [black women], her daughters, because she, like us, has experienced life not only as a black person, but as a woman."[48]

Alice Walker, as womanist, believes in change and redemption, and it is, in part, because of this belief that she can write without consuming rage of black men's victimization of black women. She holds them accountable because she believes they have within them the seeds of their own redemption. To excuse them, then, would be like letting go of hope and that, for Walker, would be like letting go of life itself.

The essential Alice Walker is a woman who remains alive and continues to write because she believes that all of us can change and must change our personal lives and the world in which we live. Always, the center of her art is hope. It is this Alice Walker who will write new short stories and novels that will be penetrating, compelling, brilliantly crafted, and, in their exposure of women's pain, very unsettling. She is capable of leading us out of psychological enslavement, as it relates to women, into liberation: "as in, 'Mama, I'm walking to Canada and I'm taking you and a bunch of other slaves with me.' Reply: 'It wouldn't be the first time.' "[49]

ALICE WALKER BIBLIOGRAPHY

NOVELS

The Third Life of Grange Copeland. New York: Harcourt Brace Jovanovich, 1970.
Meridian. New York: Harcourt Brace Jovanovich, 1976.
The Color Purple. New York: Harcourt Brace Jovanovich, 1983.

SHORT STORY COLLECTIONS

In Love and Trouble: Stories of Black Women. New York: Harcourt Brace Jovanovich, 1973.
You Can't Keep a Good Woman Down. New York: Harcourt Brace Jovanovich, 1981.

POETRY

Once. New York: Harcourt Brace Jovanovich, 1968.
Revolutionary Petunias and Other Poems. New York: Harcourt Brace Jovanovich, 1973.
Goodnight Willie Lee, I'll See You in the Morning. New York: Harcourt Brace Jovanovich, 1979.
Horses Make the Landscape More Beautiful. New York: Harcourt Brace Jovanovich, 1983.

NONFICTION

In Search of Our Mothers' Gardens: Womanist Prose. New York: Harcourt Brace Jovanovich, 1983.

Lee Smith:
The Storyteller's Voice

*

HARRIETTE C. BUCHANAN

"WHAT I'm trying to do all the time is just tell a story."[1] So saying, Lee Smith modestly, or perhaps disingenuously, backs away from the complexity and richness of her narratives about life in the small-town South. Seen in context, that statement sheds light on the intentionality of her art: "I get really involved in the characters and the story, and it's hard for me to talk about whether I have any of what my [English] class calls the DHM, the Deep Hidden Meaning. What I'm trying to do all the time is just tell a story, essentially, and if the other stuff comes in, it just has to sort of creep in, I think."[2] Creep in it does. In her six novels, one volume of short stories, and uncollected stories, Lee Smith not only tells about characters and their stories, she also provides insights into the contemporary South and the realities of life in the face of change that ring true and create themes fraught with "Deep Hidden Meaning."

Often compared with such predecessors as William Faulkner, Carson McCullers, Flannery O'Connor, and Eudora Welty, Lee Smith is attaining her own stature by doing what they did so well, telling stories of her own people and places, stories told with irony and love, humor and compassion. Smith has also been compared favorably with such contemporary Southern writers as Bobbie Ann Mason. All of these writers have, in part, achieved fame because they write about their people, times, and places with warmth, humor, and ironic detachment. Lee Smith's settings are Southern, her interest in and ability for storytelling are Southern, but her characters and stories, because of their realism, even ordinariness, are universal.

Born in 1944, Lee Smith grew up in Grundy, a small mining town in the mountains of western Virginia. Smith began writing when she was a child and continued to write when she went away to school, first at St. Catherine's School, a private Episcopalian school in Richmond, Virginia, and then at Hollins College, which she selected because of its writing program. Like many novice writers, Smith first experimented with exotic characters and settings, thinking that fiction had to be about "something glamorous, something exciting."[3] Only after reading Faulkner, O'Connor, and Welty did she realize that the stuff of everyday life in the South could be the source of good fiction. With this realization, Smith began successfully to mine her personal experience for the characters and places that make her stories compelling.

Smith's first novel, *The Last Day the Dogbushes Bloomed* (1968), grew out of her senior writing project at Hollins and, like many first novels, is the coming-of-age story of a preadolescent child. The talent displayed in this first novel was recognized with a Book-of-the-Month Club Writing Fellowship. Later awards included two O. Henry awards for short fiction and the 1984 North Carolina Award for Literature. In her career, Smith juggles her writing with a teaching career (she is currently a member of the English Department at North Carolina State University) and the rearing of two sons.

The Last Day the Dogbushes Bloomed was followed in 1971 by *Something in the Wind* and in 1973 by *Fancy Strut*. During the eight-year gap between *Fancy Strut* and *Black Mountain Breakdown* (1981), Smith's publications were limited to short stories that appeared in little magazines, such as the *Carolina Quarterly,* and in popular magazines, such as *Redbook* and *Mademoiselle. Black Mountain Breakdown,* the first novel in which Smith makes full use of her Virginia mountain background, was followed in short order by *Cakewalk* (1981), a collection of short stories.

The early novels received scant critical attention, but *Black Mountain Breakdown* and *Cakewalk* were more widely and favorably received. With *Oral History* (1983), Smith's reputation as a prominent contemporary writer was firmly established. Widely and well reviewed, *Oral History* and *Family Linen* (1985) became book club selections and generated television interviews for Smith. *Oral History* and *Family Linen* deserve this attention because they demonstrate a mature novelist in full control of her material.

With this recognition, Smith has felt free to continue the vein of fiction in which she excels: the stories of a wide range of characters, told with careful detail. Attention to detail and to point of view are conscious devices that Smith deliberately manipulates in her work. She has referred to attention to detail as "art you don't normally think of as art."[4] She has also commented about "point of view and the difference it causes in the narrative. . . . different people telling and retelling the same incident."[5] Smith's use of point of view, of the voices with which she tells the story, is always true. Like a singer with perfect pitch, Smith's ear for the nuances and tones of true speech is always convincing.

The first-person narrator of *The Last Day the Dogbushes Bloomed* is Susan Tobey, a self-centered child who in the course of the story is forced to the realization that the world is not as she imagines it. During her momentous ninth summer, Susan and her friends are organized into a club by the visiting Eugene. Eugene and his mentor, the invisible, imaginary Little Arthur, destroy the innocence of the small-town children by introducing them to deliberate, heedless cruelty and to sex. On top of this change, a flood alters the valley in which they live by washing away homes and, more importantly to Susan, the "wading house," which "was not a real house. It was a soft, light green tree, a willow, that grew by the bank of the stream. . . . it was the only wading house in the world, and I was the only one that knew about it. It was a very special place" (12). Susan not only sees the tree as a house, she also sees the creatures that live at its base as "people that . . . were my good friends" (12). The flood washes the bank of the stream and her animal friends are never seen again. Another childhood illusion is gone. Susan's family also changes. Her mother, whom she calls the Queen, goes off with a man whom Susan has dubbed the Baron. The Castle is thus irrevocably changed because the Queen and the Princess, Susan's older sister, have left, and without the Queen's presence, with her shimmery dresses and flowery perfumes, the house is just a house.

The story is conventional, even predictable, but it is redeemed from the ordinary by Smith's unfailing control of Susan's voice and perspective. Susan is unaware of the conflicts within her family, including her mother's adultery, which is revealed obliquely to the reader when Susan throws reference to it in a secondary position to what she sees as the chief event, her personal situation: "I had been busy with eating a banana and listening to the radio and bending my feet, all at the same time, but then the Baron and the Queen came downstairs and when they made me turn off the radio and told me why didn't I go wash my feet, I thought about the club meeting and left" (149–50). Susan's pride at being able to eat a banana, listen to the radio, and bend her feet "all at the same time" overshadows the fact that the Queen and the Baron have been upstairs together. Their nagging about turning off the radio and washing her feet is what impinges on Susan's consciousness.

By the end of the novel, Susan has come to realize that Eugene is to be avoided, that the Queen is never coming back, and that she is no longer afraid of the dark terrors of the night, personified by Little Arthur, who now lives under the dogbushes. The thematic significance of the conventional loss-of-innocence plot is indicated in a passage in which Susan explains the meaning of the term "dogbushes": "The flowers didn't look like dogs or anything. The dogbushes I called dogbushes because one time when I was seven and one month I found a dog under the ones along the middle of the fence" (10). Susan's solipsistic view of the world is destroyed during the course of the story; therefore, her ninth summer will be the last during which the dogbushes will bloom: the next summer she will call the bushes by their more ordinary name, whatever that is.

Title is again a key to theme with *Something in the Wind* (1971), Smith's second novel. Smith quotes the line "There is something in the wind," from Shakespeare's *The Comedy of Errors* (ix). The Shakespearean line is spoken by Antipholus of Ephesus as he and his party are trying, in vain, to gain entrance to his house. Just as Antipholus feels that some outside force in the wind prevents his entering his house, Brooke Kincaid feels that some unnamed force prevents her from finding what she should do with her life.

Several thematic elements echo from Susan Tobey's story to Brooke Kincaid's. Susan's story ended with the loss of childhood fantasy and family structure. Brooke's story begins with the loss of the childhood friend with whom she had identified and to whom she had looked for guidance. At the end of her story, Susan is able to smile, unafraid, at the shadow of Little Arthur. At the end of her story, Brooke laughs, a bit hysterically, at the comedy of errors that she has lived as she tried to develop her life plan.

Brooke formulates the concept of the life plan at the first of the story: "I wrote in my notebook: 'I am the only one who knows that I am different.' I based my life plan on that. . . . The only concrete thing about the life plan was that it involved imitation. I would imitate everybody until everything became second nature . . . and I wouldn't have to bother to imitate any more, I would simply *be*" (25). In imitating her college roommate, Diana Barker, Brooke learns to be a popular, sociable coed. "At first I double-dated with Diana all the time, but then I got the hang of it. The more I acted like Diana, the more often the phone rang for me" (65). She is, however, sometimes not so sure about her qualities as an imitator. She becomes friends with Elizabeth, who "was the only threat I had. Elizabeth never knew what she was doing. She could go into a neat room, any room, and have it completely wrecked by the time she left, without any effort on her part at all. . . . Eventually, Elizabeth and I started spending a lot of time together, which was a bad thing for my life plan" (61–62).

Brooke drifts from being Diana's roommate to being Elizabeth's to moving in with Bentley, a long-haired golf jock. As she follows Brooke's progress, Smith casts an amused eye on college life of the mid-1960s. The locale is Southern, but not uniquely so. Anyone who went to college in the sixties would recognize the places, the happenings, and the people, especially the hapless Brooke. Because Brooke is eighteen rather than nine, the tone of the story she tells is more sophisticated than Susan's. While Brooke has led a sheltered existence before coming to college, she has a literary bent that enables her to describe the things that happen to her with irony, some insight, and a good vocabulary. Brooke's insight enables her to see the folly of people around her, but very little of her own. In the course of the novel, she dissociates herself from the Tri Delts, loses the notebook with the life plan and the copy of Ripley's *Believe It or Not,* to which she has resorted in times of trouble, and finally moves out of Bentley's apartment, after becoming convinced that he is not just pleasantly crazy but genuinely disturbed. By the novel's end, Brooke is in a confused state in which she is not sure whether to laugh or cry. She opts for laughter.

This laughter begins when, remaining in town after school has ended, she volunteers to walk Lady, her landlady's "medium-size, medium-age black dog of no special breed who had a lot of inertia" (234). Wearing sunglasses and half dragging Lady along the street, Brooke is approached by a stranger who insists on helping her across the street in the mistaken belief that she is blind. Brooke protests but is unable to dissuade him. She returns to the apartment disturbed and shaken by the experience: "Then all of a sudden the whole thing, everything, struck me as funny and I started laughing and once I started laughing I couldn't stop. The idea of Lady as a Seeing Eye dog was the funniest part. I rolled on the bed, laughing and laughing" (237). If Brooke survives her life, if she can truly be, rather than imitate, it will be because of the saving grace of laughter.

Something in the Wind is another novel with a conventional plot, a typical first-year-in-college story. Brooke is somewhat detached from what is happening around and to her and so is able to tell her story with a certain amount of irony and humor. The pain of her awareness that her life has no direction is buffered by her inability to feel that any of it means much. Smith's use of the first-person point of view has been flawlessly controlled but has also restricted what she could do in presenting character and plot.

With *Fancy Strut* (1973), Smith branches out by using a third-person voice. This omniscient narrator focuses not on one character whose progress is closely followed but on a whole cast of characters who act various roles in the pageantry and profiteering of the sesquicentennial celebration of Speed, Alabama. This more detached point of view enables Smith to tell the story of Speed with ironic humor. In a series of disjointed frames or segments, the narrator sees the characters as none of them would ever be able to see themselves.

Both the initial and final frames of the novel focus on Miss Iona, the self-appointed "custodian of beauty and truth in Speed, the champion of the pure and good" (4). Miss Iona's means of promoting truth and beauty, purity and goodness, is as the society and ladies' editor of the Speed *Messenger*. The narrator indicates Miss Iona's position in the community and at the same time ironically comments on social convention: "What was the good of having a party if Miss Iona didn't write it up? You might as well not have bothered. What was the good of wearing a silver lamé dress if Miss Iona wrote you up in beige lace? The truth is what you read in the paper" (4). Miss Iona, with frequency, writes not what really happens but what she would have preferred to happen, because it is her mission in life to save the younger generation from its crassness, epitomized, in her view, by the vulgarity of the majorettes who participate in the Susan Arch Findley Memorial Marching Contest.

The Majorettes, who perform the Fancy Strut figure, are not, however, important characters. Their mothers receive the narrator's focus. Mrs. Frances Pitt is the overstuffed, overzealous stage mother. The high point of her life comes when her daughter Theresa wins the Fancy Strut contest over Sharon DuBois, daughter of Frances's cousin and rival of long standing, Sandy. The Pitts and the DuBois, along with the DuBois' next-door neighbors, the Cartwrights, represent working-class Speed. All three of these families have, by dint of hard work or luck or timing, raised themselves from dirt-farm poor to respectable middle class. While they live in new tract housing, their coarse behavior and polyester pantsuits indelibly mark their origins.

The more established upper middle class is represented by the Neighbors family and the Warner family. Manly Neighbors is the owner-editor of the *Messenger*. Manly is exceedingly pleased to be editor of a small-town newspaper; his only problem is the mystery of who could be sending the paper letters threatening the celebration. His wife, Monica, inordinately proud of the new house on which she has lavished attention and money, feels her superiority to the community when she shows the house off: " 'Why, it looks just like a page out of *Good Housekeeping*, honey,' Monica's bridge club had exclaimed in one breath when it was Monica's turn to be hostess. Monica winced, having had *Vogue* in mind" (27). In the novel's course, Monica has a satisfyingly sordid affair with Buck Fire, the professional manager of the pageant. While Manly and Monica are firmly of the upwardly mobile New South, the Warners represent stereotypes from the Old South. Lloyd is the dipsomaniac lawyer, an image he carefully cultivates to disguise the intelligence that would alienate him from the community. A self-consciously Faulknerian character, he sits in his dark, dusty office and observes the celebration with a mixture of amusement and despair. His mother is an Old South crazy lady who has immured herself in her home and whose view of life is expressed by the way in which she refers to her husband's suicide: " 'When Mr. Warner bravely met his end' . . . exactly as if he had died in a war" (223).

Outsiders Buck Fire and Luther Fletcher have come to organize the pageant and, not incidentally, to make a large profit for the White Company. Their dreams of easy money and progressive triumph from the celebration are shattered when the pageant disintegrates as Lloyd attempts suicide during the Civil War scene and as the fire that Bevo Cartwright set consumes the scaffolding.

The novel ends with Miss Iona's indictment of the pageant: "The whole pageant had been a mockery of her heritage and the Southern way of life. It had been diametrically opposed to her own Ideal Pageant. Instead of an exalting theatrical experience, it had been nothing more than a medicine show, a carnival, pandering to the lowest possible tastes. It had deserved to be struck by fire" (328). Unable to endure further the vulgarity of the modern world, Miss Iona slips into a fantasy world in which the peacock on her dressing gown dances his own "fancy strut" (329).

Smith has orchestrated the fancy strut of her characters through the events of the sesquicentennial celebration. As each character goes through his or her own series of personal crises, Smith shows various faces of the New South, from the go-getter eagerness of Bill Higgins, Bob Pitt, and Ron-the-Mouth Skinner, to the stolid complacency of Manly Neighbors, to the bitter cynicism of Lloyd Warner. The women express a similar range, from the restless ambition of Ruthie Cartwright and Sharon DuBois, to the brassy aggression of Frances Pitt, to the bored listlessness of Anne Cartwright and Monica Neighbors, to the withdrawn unreality of Mrs. Warner and Miss Iona. Hanging the complicated maneuvering of these characters on the simple plot device of the sesquicentennial celebration, Smith gives a cross section of the small-town South during the late 1960s. She tells the stories of her characters with irony and humor, but never with scorn. The humor dominates; *Fancy Strut* is above all a funny story.

The tone of Smith's next novel, *Black Mountain Breakdown* (1981), is, despite many funny episodes, tragic. Retaining the third-person perspective, Smith returns to the narrative device of the first two novels by following the growing pains of a single female character. Crystal Spangler, like Susan Tobey and Brooke Kincaid, is roughly disabused of childhood innocence. Crystal's story, in fact, strongly echoes those of Susan and Brooke. Like Susan, the child Crystal prefers a world where phantoms are as real as family. A dreamy, artistic child, Crystal wants only to laugh, sing, and be happy. Like Susan's, her fantasy ends with family dissolution; she abruptly comes to the end of childhood when her father dies. Crystal's sense of loss of direction after her father's death echoes Brooke's. Like Brooke, Crystal vacillates between trying to follow the role of the good girl and rebelling at that role with promiscuous sexual adventures. Brooke first bases her "life plan" on imitation but eventually abandons that plan for laughter. Crystal, also trying on different, imitative roles, never learns to laugh.

Crystal's failure to find the grace of laughter or to act with stoic acceptance, as her mother does, is the source of her tragedy. In talking about this novel, Smith describes one of her motives for writing the story: "to really make a thematic point . . . that if you're entirely a passive person, you're going to get in big trouble. The way so many women, and I think particularly Southern women, are raised is to make themselves fit the image that other people set out for them, and that was Crystal's great tragedy, that she wasn't able to get her own self-definition."[6]

Black Mountain Breakdown is set in rural western Virginia during the 1960s and 1970s. In high school, Crystal participates, with her mother's permission, in beauty pageants and religious revivals and, without her mother's permission, in an affair with the disreputable Mack Stiltner, who eventually leaves her for a career in Nashville as a country singer. Crystal also eventually leaves for college.

After a five-year absence, she returns home to find her mother and the Black Rock community enjoying a new prosperity created by increasing demand and prices for coal. Crystal joins the Junior Women's Club and takes a job teaching English at the junior high school, which she "falls into . . . so easily that it's as if she had never done anything else. It's like there's a part of her which knows how to do it already. . . . She's very busy" (182) and relatively satisfied with her roles as a teacher and member of the community.

This tranquillity is shattered when, on the day of her mother's remarriage, former high school sweetheart Roger Lee Combs reappears in Crystal's life. Roger takes over, assuring her: " 'I know you, sweetheart, I know everything you've been and everything you've done. I've watched you go through all these changes, one right after another. You might *think* you're happy now, Crystal, but you're not' " (199). Crystal falls under Roger's influence. They run away; he divorces his wife and marries Crystal; they begin working on his political campaigns.

Crystal settles into a new pattern as the successful candidate's wife, the darling of the society pages. There is, however, a shadow in this existence. Despite her love for Roger, Crystal shrinks from committing herself to him more fully by having a baby: "Because things are not exactly as Roger thinks, anyway. Things are more precarious. They have edges now. . . . Ever since the beginning—ever since that day when he came up to her mother's house—she has been conscious of the end" (210).

The end is precipitated by a campaign visit to a mental hospital, where the mindless face of a retarded man stirs long-repressed memories of the time she was raped by her father's half-witted brother, Devere, a trauma that Crystal has submerged in her unconscious and that represents the cloud that has apparently prevented Crystal from dealing constructively with her life. Crystal leaves Roger and returns to her mother's house, where she soon retreats into catatonia.

Crystal is cared for by her mother, Lorene, and her childhood friend Agnes McClanahan, women who have persevered and even triumphed over their experience by a devotion to duty and a determination to "deal with problems by rising above them" (21). Both women, though humorless, display a shrewd business acumen and a flair for survival in a world that offers little to independent women. Lacking their strength, Crystal simply withdraws from painful change: "And who knows what will happen in this world? Agnes reflects. . . . Why, Crystal might jump right up from that bed tomorrow and go off and get her Ph.D. . . . Or she might stay right here and atrophy to death. What Agnes really thinks, though, is that Crystal is happy, that she likes to have Agnes hold her hand and brush her hair, as outside her window the seasons come and go and the colors change on the mountain" (227–28). Crystal withdraws, but life goes on in Black Rock. Roger wins his election; Lorene and Odell go on trips; Agnes continues to expand her business interests.

Susan Tobey, Brooke Kincaid, and Crystal Spangler are all idealistic, imaginative girls who are disabused of their dreams by harsh reality. They represent artistic sensitivity crushed by the modern world. But is artistic sensitivity an unadulterated good and commercial progress an unqualified evil? No. Artistic sensitivity can lead to Crystal's paralysis or to Miss Iona's madness; commercial progress can bring the comfortable prosperity that enables Lorene and Agnes to feel satisfied with their lives. Lee Smith tells her stories with ironic humor but also with a balanced vision. She sees both sides of her characters and their stories; she does not make the kinds of opinionated judgments so frequently made by many of her characters.

The irony that shows the difference between Lee Smith's humanism and the narrow, judgmental views of her characters is especially evident in the stories collected in *Cakewalk* (1981). Mrs. Joline B. Newhouse, the narrator of the lead story, "Between the Lines," is such a judgmental character. Smith's handling of these characters is evident as Joline introduces herself by justifying the standard closing for her newspaper column. She had considered "Yours in Christ," but she rejected it because: "I am in Christ but I know for a fact that a lot of them are not. . . . 'Peace be with you,' as I see it, is sufficiently religious without laying all the cards right out on the table in plain view. I like to keep an ace or two up my sleeve. I like to write between the lines" (11). Working in a vein that Miss Iona would have recognized, Joline B. Newhouse's professed aim is to uplift her readers. If that means reporting a wife beating as: "Mrs. Alma Goodnight is enjoying a pleasant recuperation period in the lovely, modern Walker Mountain Community Hospital while she is sorely missed by her loved ones at home" (12), then so be it. The "mere facts" of human interactions are not important to Joline: "Because that is a *mystery,* and I am no detective by a long shot. I am what I am, I know what I know, and I know you've got to give folks something to hang on to, something to keep them going. That is what I have in mind when I say *uplift*" (12–13). Although Joline is pompous and self-righteous in her judgments of the needs of others, she is not an object of ridicule; rather, Smith uses her to present the major theme of the mystery of life. At the end of the story, Joline asks a question that resonates throughout Smith's fiction: "Now where will it all end? I ask you. All this pain and loving, mystery and loss. And it just goes on and on" (25). The sensitivity of this question goes far toward redeeming the self-righteousness of Joline's earlier pronouncements about her fellow citizens in Salt Lick. Mrs. Joline B. Newhouse too is human and deserves compassion.

This is true of the host of other characters who are presented in all their passivity and frailty in *Cakewalk.* "Georgia Rose," who can see the future, spends her life running from it. Helen, in "All the Days of Our Lives," prefers vicariously enjoying the houses and affairs of soap opera characters to taking a promotion at work and opportunities for solid relationships in her own life. Debbi drifts with the drifter who strands her in "Gulfport," dreaming of life as it is lived in magazine spreads. "And it just goes on and on."

Some of the characters, including Florrie in the title story "Cakewalk," manage to break away from passivity and isolation, but whether or not this is a real victory is not clear. At the end of "Artists," Jennifer, who had identified earlier with her artistic, otherworldly grandmother and had jealously guarded the long hair her grandmother admired, finally cuts her hair. "It looked terrific. . . . So I grew up. And I never became an artist, although my career has certainly had its ups and downs, like most careers. Like most lives" (123), like the closest many Lee Smith characters come to self-realization and strong assertion.

Several of the narrative voices of *Oral History* (1983) echo the sense of assertiveness that Jennifer of "Artists" demonstrates. Granny Younger, Ludie Davenport, Ora Mae, and Sally are all assured of who they are and of their places in the community around Hoot Owl Holler. The passive heroine, yearning for some undefined and perhaps undefinable something that will deliver her into a life somehow more or better, is also present in *Oral History*. Interestingly, these passive women do not tell their own stories; rather, it is their stories that the other, stronger women tell. The beautiful and doomed Dory and her restless and talented daughter Pearl are the figures around whom the action of the story swirls. The community believes that these women have been cursed by the first Almarine Cantrell's Red Emmy; the curse is conveyed in the gold earrings owned by Almarine's wife, Pricey Jane, who mysteriously dies of the "dew pizen" (78). The earrings pass to Pricey Jane's daughter Dory, who commits suicide by lying on the railroad track. They then go to Dory's daughter Maggie, who, apparently dying of polio, gives them to her twin sister, Pearl. Maggie recovers, but Pearl, enduring an unhappy marriage, has an affair with a high school boy, after which she mysteriously dies following the premature stillbirth of a baby whose paternity is uncertain. The curse is presumably expiated after Pearl's funeral, when Ora Mae, daughter of Almarine's second wife, Vashti, throws the earrings down a gorge.

More complex and broader in scope than any of Smith's previous works, *Oral History* exhibits Lee Smith's maturity and mastery of her craft. Fully in control of point of view, Smith shifts effortlessly from an omniscient third person to the first-person voices of most of the story's narrators. The novel opens and closes in a present time sequence focusing on Jennifer, Pearl's daughter from the stifling marriage, who has come to record, for her oral history course, the rumored haunted sounds from the family homestead in Hoot Owl Holler. After she has set up her tape recorder, Jennifer writes in her journal, in self-conscious student prose: "One feels that the true benefits of this trip may derive not from what is recorded or not recorded by the tape, . . . but from my new knowledge of my heritage and a new appreciation of these colorful, interesting folk. My *roots*" (19). Jennifer's condescension toward her mountain relatives and the fact that this condescension is misplaced are demonstrated when, closing her journal entry with "I shall descend now, to be with them as they go about their evening chores" (20), she returns to the house to find no one doing "chores." Little Luther and Ora Mae are sitting on the porch, Al is puttering with his van, his children are watching *Magnum* on television. The twentieth century has come to Hoot Owl Holler; the outsider's stereotypes have little to do with reality.

Having established a late-twentieth-century reality, Smith shifts back almost one hundred years to have Granny Younger begin telling the Cantrell family saga, replete with passion, pain and loving, mystery and loss. A traditional granny-woman healer, Granny Younger tells Almarine's story by providing his family background since Civil War times and by picking up the threads of the narrative in 1902, when Almarine returned to Hoot Owl Holler after a five-year absence.

Granny Younger knows how to spin a yarn and how to keep her audience, of whom she is always conscious, on the edges of their seats. She carries the main thread of the narrative but weaves in digressionary fibers and tales, as well as throws out hints of what is to come in the story. Granny Younger's voice keens like a mountain ballad. Directly addressing her audience, she says: "I said I know moren you know and mought be I'll tell you moren you want to hear. I'll tell you a story that's truer than true, and nothing so true is so pretty. It's blood on the moon, as I said. The way I tell a story is the way I want to, and iffen you mislike it, you don't have to hear" (37). But Granny knows that by the time she issues that warning she has her audience firmly in hand; there is not one who does not want to hear.

Like the best regional writers, Smith writes not in the literal dialect that an ethnologist would record, with numerous apostrophes indicating dropped and elided syllables, but in a lyric prose that captures an authentic flavor of the speech of the people who live in the mountains around Hoot Owl Holler. Authentic rhythms, speech patterns, and expressions are recorded; peculiar vocalizations for vowel and consonant sounds are ignored. Like Granny Younger, Smith is aware of her audience and wants them to listen to and understand the human richness of the characters' voices, not to be shut out by eccentric pronunciations indicated by alien print symbols.

Granny Younger tells of Almarine Cantrell's passion for Red Emmy, of the mysterious end of their affair, of his marriage to Pricey Jane, of the birth of their daughter Dory. Along the way, she also tells a lot about folk medicine, witches, and everyday life.

The third-person narrator tells about Pricey Jane, with her beautiful black hair and golden earrings, who yearns secretly for something she cannot name but that she suspects is out there somewhere in the wider world. As Pricey Jane falls ill, the narrator shifts focus to Almarine, who returns home to find his wife and son dying and wildly brings in Granny Younger and the neighbors to try to stay the inevitable. Rose Hibbits, who is not normal, tells part of the story; then the third-person narrator closes the first part of the novel with an account of Pricey Jane's funeral.

The second section of the novel picks up the story in 1923, when Dory has grown to young womanhood. It is Dory's story now, but it is told by the outsider Richard Burlage as he writes in his journal, with a self-consciousness and arrogance that echoes Jennifer's, about what he sees as his "pilgrimage to a simpler era, back—dare I hope it—to the very roots of consciousness and belief" (97), a pilgrimage on which he hopes to find himself. Burlage fails in this quest. While he does go back in time by coming to the Hoot Owl Holler community, he does not find a simpler era. He finds the reality of a close, closed community with its own ways, suspicious of the ways of outsiders. Burlage falls hopelessly in love with Dory, an affair doomed by her family's distrust of him and by his inability to accept what she and her family really are. He finally leaves Hoot Owl Holler, Tug, and Black Rock in disgrace, his affair with Dory having been discovered, and unaware that Dory is pregnant.

When Burlage returns, some nine years later, he has fooled himself into believing that he has matured. He has become a photographer and returns hoping to record on film scenes from a past time. In the time he has been away, he has changed only externally; internally, he still has no real sense of who he is or of who the mountain people are. He can only deal with the surface reality of what can be recorded by his camera. He learns that Dory has married Luther Wade and goes past their house, hoping to see her. He catches a glimpse of her, but the lingering images are those that he has captured on film, the most haunting of these being beautiful twin girls, who he does not know are his daughters.

Richard Burlage, because of the pompous self-consciousness of his prose, is the least attractive of *Oral History*'s narrators. Yet, it is he who holds the stage the longest. In addition to the third-person omniscient narrator, there are eleven different perspectives for telling the Cantrell family's story. Eight of these perspectives are first-person narrators who tell the story as they can see and decode it. These include the important and memorably distinct voices of Granny Younger; Richard Burlage; Jink Cantrell, Dory's half-brother; and Sally, Dory's daughter by Luther Wade, as well as the lesser voices of Rose Hibbits, Little Luther Wade, Mrs. Ludie Davenport, and Ora Mae. Among these first-person voices are woven the sections told in a third-person voice, but focusing on the perspective of one of the characters, including Pricey Jane, Almarine, and Jennifer. Burlage speaks as long as Granny Younger and Sally combined. They, in turn, each speak twice as long as Jink, who speaks more than twice as long as Ora Mae. Why do these characters hold the stage for such precisely varying lengths?

The key to this mystery lies in the heart of the story, Dory. Granny Younger provides the family background and tells about the curse of Red Emmy; her story ends with Dory's birth. Sally tells about Dory's death and about the working out of the curse in the lives of Maggie and Pearl. Granny Younger and Sally are the first and last voices heard within the frame device of Jennifer's story. In the middle falls the long passage in which Burlage grapples with his love for Dory and his inability to reach out and touch and know any more than her body. He is fascinated by the enigmatic smile and golden Botticelli hair, but he never knows or understands the personality behind the smile and hair.

That personality is the central mystery of the novel. Granny Younger has set up the mystery with her tales of witches and curses. Burlage, with his air of outside rationality, tries in vain to penetrate it. Sally, with her frank openness, simply acknowledges it. She describes her mother's position in the rest of the family, using the image of a kaleidoscope they once had: "It had a bright blue spot in the middle of all the patterns, one spot that never moved no matter which way you turned it or how many pretty bright patterns came and went all around. Our family was like that, with Mama at the center, not doing anything particular but not *having* to either, and all the rest of us falling in place around" (238). The kaleidoscope image not only serves Sally as a way to describe her family, but it also serves as a way to describe and organize Lee Smith's narrative design for *Oral History*.

Jennifer, the contemporary outsider, begins and ends the story in her quest for family history. Within this frame fall Granny Younger and Sally and all the others, with Burlage at once the closest and yet the most distant from the heart, the core, the center of the design, Dory. It is Burlage's outsider, foreign status that enables him to get closest to Dory but keeps him farthest away. The other characters, by blood, by marriage, by propinquity, are physically closer, but Dory's elusive personality is absolutely beyond their ken. Burlage has clues about what Dory can be, about the nature of her vague yearnings for some kind of beauty in life that cannot be found in the mountains of western Virginia. He is, however, powerless to break the bonds that tie her to her family and place. Dory is the center, but her reality remains a mystery because her story is told by first-person narrators, not by the omniscient third-person voice that focuses only on peripheral characters.

"No matter who's telling the story, it is always the teller's tale, and you never *finally* know exactly the way it was," says Lee Smith of her work. "I guess I see some sort of central mystery at the center of the past, of any past, that you can't, no matter what a good attempt you make at understanding how it was, you never can quite get it."[7] Smith varies the narrative voices in order to produce several good attempts to get at the center of the Cantrell family past. But because each teller is telling about his or her own perception of or need from Dory, Dory herself remains elusive; the family focus keeps shifting like the pieces in Sally's kaleidoscope. Dory is the center of the family history because she most clearly, yet elusively, represents the family's yearning for something beyond themselves. Sally refers to this in her analysis of the curse that haunts the Cantrell family: "People say they're haunted and they are—every one of them all eat up with wanting something they haven't got" (235). But, of course, this is Sally's oversimplification, her need to deny the catastrophic yearning. Even though she is happily married to Roy, she too was once a lost, unhappy woman, wanting something and not even knowing it. Sally, like the other narrators, tells about Dory and about the other Cantrells' history, but the central mystery is only partially illuminated.

Jennifer's experience in Hoot Owl Holler has not given her a positive picture of her "roots"; rather, it has given her an unwelcome glimpse of the dark mystery. She does not understand Little Luther or Ora Mae or, most of all, "Uncle Al," who is no blood kin of hers. The younger Almarine shows Jennifer both a cruel brutality and a rough good ole boy humor that, along with his threatening warning that she should not return, bewilder her. She leaves in tears, but her bewilderment vanishes as physical distance from her family becomes emotional distance and comfortable stereotype. She now sees them as "primitive people, . . . some sort of early tribe. Crude jokes and animal instincts—it's the other side of the pastoral coin" (284). Unable to understand what she has experienced, Jennifer retreats into the outsider's disregard for the reality of mountain people. The passions that drive the Cantrells are conveniently labeled as attributes of a "primitive people,"

people whom Jennifer can pigeonhole and forget. Lee Smith has en-
sured, however, that the readers, hearing all the narrators' voices and
following the shifting focus of the Cantrells' story, will never forget
the variety of people who inhabit Hoot Owl Holler.

Attempting once again to get at the mystery of the past, Lee Smith
airs the *Family Linen* (1985) of the Bird-Hess family. This time there is
also a conventional mystery involved, the question of whether or not
Sybill Hess really saw her mother murder her father with an ax and
dump his body in the well in the backyard of the family home. As with
Oral History, Smith uses shifting perspectives to work around the central problem. This time, however, the story is told not by an omniscient
or by first-person narrators; the voice is third person, but with a focus
limited to one narrator at a time. The story opens with Sybill Hess's
visit to a hypnotist, who she hopes will be able to cure her recurring
headaches. Under hypnosis, Sybill "sees" the murder. But the hypnotist, Bob, warns her that the vision may be a fear-generated fantasy.
Determined to get to the bottom of the mystery, Sybill returns to her
childhood home in Booker Creek, Virginia.

The narrative then switches to focus on Sybill's younger sister Myrtle. Where Sybill is a prim, uptight old maid, Myrtle is a yuppie housewife who, in college, had been intent primarily on "her 'MRS,' and
she's got it, and that's good enough for her. . . . their three children are
her 'PHD'" (46). Myrtle has returned home from a tryst with her
lover, Gary Vance, the exterminator, to learn that her mother has been
hospitalized with a stroke. Sybill arrives to learn of this traumatic
event, which will frustrate her desire to confront her mother about the
truth of her vision.

The disarray into which the family is plunged by Miss Elizabeth's
stroke is next seen from a somewhat more detached viewpoint, that of
Myrtle's teenage son, Sean. The family's confusion is refracted through
the perspective of Sean's own adolescent confusion, indicated by his reaction to the family furor: "I looked at *Playboy* for a while, all those
foxes, and then I got up and got this stupid stuffed dog, . . . don't ask
me why it's still around . . . and listened to "Thriller" and thought
about Mom and Aunt Sybill yelling. . . . And I could tell from their
voices they were scared" (68).

The family gathers to watch at Miss Elizabeth's bedside, and Lacy,
the youngest daughter, begins telling her version of the events. Lacy
feels she is more Miss Elizabeth's daughter than the others, *"the poetry*
took, *with me"* (69), and cannot see much further than the trauma of
desertion by her husband, Jack. A Ph.D. candidate at the University of
North Carolina at Chapel Hill, Lacy feels distanced from the everyday

lives of her kin in Booker Creek. She scorns the blondness, blandness, and "absolute invincible belief in human perfectibility" (72) that she feels Myrtle and her husband, Don, embody. She identifies with the idealism that she sees symbolized in her mother's house, which sits on the hill that dominates Booker Creek. At the same time, she ponders the "Gothic" (76) involvements of her family, especially her Aunt Nettie's many marriages and unexplained estrangement from her mother.

By this stage in the novel, the reader recognizes that the story is not a simple murder mystery. Sybill's questions for Miss Elizabeth have taken a backseat as other mysteries of the family's past become more prominent. The reader has also begun to realize that the narrative pattern of the novel is not straightforward. It is not even so straightforward as the shifting focuses of *Oral History.* The thirdperson limited perspective is at once less personal and yet more immediate than the combination of first-person and omniscient narrator. By Lacy's section of *Family Linen,* the reader is well and truly caught up in the kaleidoscopically shifting patterns of the different family members' perspectives on the life, illness, and central mystery that is Miss Elizabeth. Just as Dory is the central, fixed spot in the kaleidoscope of *Oral History,* Miss Elizabeth is the center of *Family Linen.* The primary narrators are her children, Sybill, Arthur, Candy, Myrtle, and Lacy. In addition, her sisters, Fay, a crazy recluse whose world consists of television and such papers as the *National Enquirer,* and Nettie, whose estrangement is not explained until late in the novel, and her grandson Sean tell their versions of what is happening. Of these narrators, only Candy, a beautician and proud of it, seems satisfied with her life and herself.

When Miss Elizabeth dies without ever regaining consciousness, it is Candy who retains a sense of equilibrium. Arthur is dismayed that yet another person has died on him, and Sybill is enraged that her mother died before she could learn the truth about her father's death. Candy fixes her mother's hair for the funeral and ponders the mysteries of hair and death. Hair is "the most vital organ of the body by a long shot. . . . It will grow after death. It's one of the great mysteries. Along with death. Candy has always been good with hair. And sometimes she thinks she was born knowing all about death, too" (122).

After Miss Elizabeth's funeral, Don and Myrtle, who have inherited her house, decide to move in and remodel it. One modification they plan is the addition of a swimming pool, requiring the bulldozing of the backyard. Ever practical, Don has decided to serve his own purposes as well as to answer Sybill's mystery. Lacy, meanwhile, searches the house over for her own answer to the mystery, to the "secret here, at the heart of the house" (161). What she finds is a journal Miss Elizabeth had written more than fifty years earlier, before either of her marriages. The journal opens with an elaborate metaphor, illustrating her poetic bent and explaining her feelings about exploring her family history. "I approach the Past as a young maiden, bearing a candle, might approach a deserted mansion deep within the Enchanted woods. . . . The wind . . . is my anxiety manifest. I shield my candle with my trembling hand, and if I reach the mansion, will its paltry light be sufficient to illuminate That which lies therein?" (164). The journal recounts Miss Elizabeth's happy childhood with father, mother, and sisters Fay and Nettie. After her mother's death, the family fortunes begin to slip, sinking finally into bankruptcy with the death of her father and Elizabeth's refusal to sell the family home to try to save the family business, the beginning of her estrangement from Nettie, who had been running the business as their father's health had declined. Clinging to the home as a symbol of the beauty and good that her mother had represented, Elizabeth determines to passively await what will come. What Lacy and the reader have learned about is Elizabeth's pride and determination, but the mystery of her being and of whether or not she could have killed her husband remain.

As Lacy finishes reading Miss Elizabeth's journal, the bulldozer uncovers a body, that of Jewell Rife, Elizabeth's first husband and the father of Sybill and Arthur. Lacy confronts her Aunt Nettie with the evidence of the family rift found in the journal and demands an explanation. Nettie, who has known most of the story for a long time but has not seen any "point hanging dirty linen on the line" (213), now tells her version of the family history, including the sordid details of Elizabeth's marriage to the worthless, philandering Jewell, who had been committing adultery with Elizabeth's sister Fay as well as with other women. Nettie reveals that Fay is Candy's mother and that, in her determination to raise Candy as her own child, Elizabeth drove both Fay and Nettie away.

The kaleidoscope shifts again when Fay is discovered dead in an old car outside the One Stop where she and Nettie and Nettie's stepson, Clinus, another half-wit, live. Nettie now knows: "She must of done it, then, Fay" (271). Nettie thus solves the murder mystery; Jewell was murdered by Fay, who strongly resembled Elizabeth, because he had reneged on his promise to take her when he left for Florida. The story then settles into the essentially happy confusion, as the family continues to squabble over the division of Miss Elizabeth's things, of the arrival of Myrtle's and Don's pregnant daughter, Karen, and her boyfriend, Karl.

The last pages of the novel shift to over a month after the discovery of Jewell's body and Fay's death. Karen's wedding day is celebrated by the entire family, with Candy happily at the center fixing everyone's hair, except Karen's. The house has been remodeled, with the pool and patio completed to be the scene of the wedding and reception, and many of the family problems have been settled. Sybill is over her headaches and is in her element as the director of the wedding; Myrtle has settled into happy domesticity and a new career in real estate, wondering what she ever saw in Gary Vance; Arthur is courting the nurse Mrs. Palucci and beginning a new career as manager of the One Stop; and Lacy has begun work on her dissertation as well as seeing Jack once a week. The novel ends with a section focused on Lacy, the youngest, who is thinking about Clinus's message on the sign at the One Stop: "KAREN AND KARL, TODAY IS THE FIRST DAY OF THE REST OF YOUR LIFE. It is, too. That goes for everybody" (272). On this optimistic note, the kaleidoscope of *Family Linen* ceases to shift and leaves the reader with the image of Miss Elizabeth, her position as the idealistic matriarch of the family still firmly in place. The murder mystery has been solved, but the central mystery of the past remains somewhat murky, because the human perceptions that are our access to it are not fully resolved. Nor, according to Lee Smith, will, or should, they ever be. The exploration and representation of those mysteries, of those human lives, are the artist's endeavor, and she will continue to present them to us as her characters, in their own ways, tell us their stories.

Lee Smith's artistry has fully emerged from her early works to the mature recent works *Oral History* and *Family Linen*. The earlier work shows Smith's development in her flexibility with point of view, which becomes so practiced a device in *Oral History* and *Family Linen* that it at once dominates and disappears. Complexity of plot and character also develop through the course of the earlier works. From the simple plot and elementary character development of *The Last Day the Dogbushes Bloomed,* Smith has worked to the complex plots and intricate character interrelationships of *Oral History* and *Family Linen*. In *Something in the Wind,* character was developed in somewhat more depth and breadth; in *Fancy Strut,* plot was much more complicated; in *Black Mountain Breakdown,* character and plot were presented over a longer time span than previously. Smith's continued experimentation with point of view and plot should enable her power as a storyteller to grow even further in future fictions.

With only a few notable exceptions, the characters with whom Smith primarily deals are women hamstrung by their environments and cultures. Susan Tobey, like many Southern girls, has been, on the one hand, overprotected and sheltered from reality and, on the other hand, denied her parents' time and presence. Raised by a servant whose primary responsibility is the house, Susan understandably grows up without a strong or realistic sense of who she is or where she fits in her family or her community. She is very likely to follow in Brooke Kincaid's footsteps and be completely bewildered once she is removed from a sheltered situation. Both are likely to grow up to be like the Monica Neighbors at the first of *Fancy Strut* and the Myrtle Dotson at the first of *Family Linen,* who define themselves by the external standards presented in magazines and social conventions. Whether or not they will find the limited sense of self-assertion that Monica and Myrtle finally achieve is unclear.

Crystal Spangler is the most helpless of all of Smith's women because her life holds not even the faintest hope of self-realization. Crystal is a victim, however, not only of her environment but of her own passiveness. She allows herself to fall into the beauty queen/politician's wife pattern that is socially desirable. Her affair with Mack Stiltner is not a clear and open rebellion but is more a drifting with the currents of circumstance. While she enjoys teaching, she is unable to resist Roger's determination that she be his. Her only assertion is the retreat to her mother's home and into catatonia.

The central woman in *Oral History,* Dory, is similarly helpless and unable to break out of the bonds of family and place to try to be what she wants. Like Crystal, Dory asserts herself with self-destruction. When her daughter Pearl does attempt to shape her life positively, she fails, perhaps because she has had no role models to show her the way. Pearl's half-sister, Sally, is the only Cantrell woman who is content with a life that she has chosen for herself, but Sally had to go through drifting and an unhappy marriage before she found Roy and her job and a life to enjoy.

Miss Elizabeth, the central woman in *Family Linen,* resembles Dory in that she is limited by her environment and considerations of family, but she seizes more control, for good or for ill, by adopting Candy and marrying Verner Hess and bearing two more children, Myrtle and Lacy. The lost woman of this novel is Fay, whose right to a life, to her child, and to a mind are all denied by birth and family circumstance. The strong women of *Family Linen* are Nettie and Candy, who, from the first, are not afraid to buck social convention and be themselves; only they remain essentially unchanged from the novel's beginning to its end. Sybill, Myrtle, and Lacy all change for the better, emerging as more self-confident and self-directed as a result of the airing of the *Family Linen*.

Smith's stories are about women faced with a world for which they are unprepared. These women are not only unprepared but also have little idea of where to look for guidance, because their families and communities provide so little in the way of honest or genuinely nurturing support. The families are usually broken, with key members either physically or mentally absent. These characters are so frequently lost and spiritually impoverished that they see no solution to their problems. Women's periodicals, soap operas, and television shows offer the only consolation, and what they offer is impersonal and unrealistic. Although their hopes and dreams are unrealistic, Smith's characters sound absolutely real to the reader because their stories have been told in such strong, true voices.

While the stories of these women's lives are mostly tragic, the telling is extremely funny. Of this quality in her writing, Smith has said: "I think I tend to see life fairly tragically. If you do that, you've got two choices: you can either go in the closet and sit in the dark or you can make jokes."[8] Fortunately, Lee Smith is not in a closet sitting in the dark. She is telling her stories with as many jokes as she can muster. Like Sally, she can see the funny ironies in tragic lives. Her sad stories are told with warmth, compassion, and humor. The voices with which she tells her stories are truer than true, and the reader cannot help but want to hear them. The Deep Hidden Meaning creeps in because the stories are so true, and therefore basic patterns and meanings of human existence are there.

Lee Smith knows her characters and in her most recent work has delved more deeply into the specific times and places in which those characters live. Her storytelling is, therefore, gaining depth and breadth. Her characters, while often bizarre, are real, and their voices resound truthfully. Smith's conscious variation in narrative voice and tone not only underscores her vision of the ultimate complexity and unknowableness, the mystery, of human life, but it also forces us to read between the lines and look for answers to the ambiguities present in the shifting focuses of her narrative patterns. Smith, like Mrs. Joline B. Newhouse, asks, "Now where will it all end? I ask you. All this pain and loving, mystery and loss. And it just goes on and on." Fortunately, because the mystery of life does go on and on, Lee Smith will not run out of subject matter for her art. As readers we sit enthralled by her stories, her narrative voices, ready to hear more. Tell us another story, Lee Smith.

Lee Smith Bibliography

NOVELS

The Last Day the Dogbushes Bloomed. New York: Harper & Row, 1968.
Something in the Wind. New York: Harper & Row, 1971.
Fancy Strut. New York: Harper & Row, 1973.
Black Mountain Breakdown. New York: Putnam, 1981.
Oral History. New York: Putnam, 1983.
Family Linen. New York: Putnam, 1985.

SHORT STORY COLLECTION

Cakewalk. New York: Putnam, 1981.

ARTICLES

"In the Beginning . . ." *Writer* 96 (December 1983): 9–11, 43.
"A Stubborn Sense of Place: Writers and Writings on the South." *Harper's* 273
    (August 1986): 38.

INTERVIEWS

Arnold, Edwin T. "An Interview with Lee Smith." *Appalachian Journal* 11
    (Spring 1984): 240–54.
Lodge, Michelle. "Lee Smith." *Publishers Weekly* 228 (20 September 1985):
    110–11.
Sill, Melanie. "In Her Books Lee Smith Goes Home Again." Raleigh, N.C.,
    News and Observer, 21 August 1983 (available in *Newsbank*—Literature—
    September 1983—23:B 13–14).

Notes

*

MARGARET WALKER:
BLACK WOMAN WRITER OF THE SOUTH

1. Charles Rowell, "Poetry, History and Humanism: An Interview with Margaret Walker," *Black World* 25 (1975): 15.
2. Richard Barksdale, "Margaret Walker: Folk Orature," in *Black American Poets between Worlds, 1940–1960,* ed. R. Baxter Miller (Knoxville: University of Tennessee Press, 1986), 106.
3. Rowell, 13.
4. Claudia Tate, *Black Women Writers at Work* (New York: Continuum, 1983), 148.
5. I explore reasons for the dearth of historical fiction by Afro-American writers in my dissertation, "The Search for a Usable Past: Black Historical Fiction" (University of North Carolina, Chapel Hill, 1983). Arna Bontemps's *Black Thunder* (1936), the story of Gabriel Prosser's rebellion, is set during the antebellum period but only narrowly re-creates the folk culture as appropriate background to the activities of Gabriel Prosser.
6. Minrose Gwin, "*Jubilee:* The Black Woman's Celebration of Human Community," in *Conjuring: Black Women's Fiction and Literary Tradition,* ed. Marjorie Pryse and Hortense J. Spillers (Bloomington: Indiana University Press, 1985), 134.
7. See Tillie Olsen, *Silences* (New York: Delacorte, 1978). The book confronts the relationship between gender oppression and the cessation or absence of writing by women.
8. Janet Sternburg, *The Writer on Her Work* (New York: Norton, 1980), 100–101.
9. Blyden Jackson and Louis Rubin, *Black Poetry in America* (Baton Rouge: Louisiana State University Press, 1974), 68.
10. Rowell, 9.
11. Eugenia Collier, "Fields Watered with Blood: Myth and Ritual in the Poetry of Margaret Walker," in *Black Women Writers (1950–1980): A Critical Evaluation,* ed. Mari Evans (Garden City, N.Y.: Anchor/Doubleday, 1984), 503.
12. Barksdale, 110.

MONTANI SEMPER LIBERI: MARY LEE SETTLE
AND THE MYTHS OF APPALACHIA

1. Robert Higgs and Ambrose Manning, *Voices from the Hills: Selected Readings of Southern Appalachia* (New York: Frederick Unger, 1975), xix.
2. See, for example, Jim Wayne Miller, "Appalachian Literature," *Appalachian Journal* 5 (Autumn 1977): 82–91, and his " . . . And Ladies of the Club," *Appalachian Journal* 14 (Fall 1986): 64–69.
3. For a fuller discussion of perceptions of Appalachia, see Henry Shapiro, *Appalachia on Our Mind: The Southern Mountains and Mountaineers in the American Consciousness* (Chapel Hill: University of North Carolina Press, 1978); see also Mary Noailles Murfree, *In the Tennessee Mountains* (Knoxville: University of Tennessee Press, 1970), and Jack Weller, *Yesterday's People: Life in Contemporary Appalachia* (Lexington: University of Kentucky Press, 1965), for examples of local-color writing about Appalachia and a much-criticized sociological study of Appalachian people.
4. David Whisnant, *All That Is Native and Fine: The Politics of Culture in an American Region* (Chapel Hill: University of North Carolina Press, 1983), 13.
5. W. H. Ward, "The Rush to Find an Appalachian Literature," *Appalachian Journal* 6 (Spring 1978): 331.
6. T. S. Eliot, "Tradition and the Individual Talent" (much anthologized).
7. John F. Baker, "CA Interviews the Author [Mary Lee Settle]," *Contemporary Authors* (89–92), ed. Frances Locher (Detroit: Gale Research, 1980), 467.
8. Roger Shattuck, "A Talk with Mary Lee Settle," *New York Times Book Review,* 26 October 1980, 43.
9. Granville Hicks, "Seesawing on the Social Ladder," *Saturday Review,* 5 September 1964, 22.
10. "Briefly Noted," *New Yorker,* 24 November 1986, 149.
11. George Garrett, "Mary Lee Settle," in *Dictionary of Literary Biography,* ed. James E. Kibler, vol. 6 (Detroit: Gale Research, 1980), 281.
12. Ibid., 288.
13. William J. Schafer, "Mary Lee Settle's Beulah Quintet: History Darkly, through a Single-Lens Reflex," *Appalachian Journal* 9 (Autumn 1982): 72–86; Jane Gentry Vance, "Mary Lee Settle's The Beulah Quintet: History Inherited, History Created," *Southern Literary Journal* 17 (Fall 1984): 40–53.
14. Nancy Carol Joyner, "Mary Lee Settle's Connections: Class and Clothes in the Beulah Quintet," *The Southern Quarterly* 22 (Fall 1983): 32–45.
15. Joyce Coyne Dyer, "Mary Lee Settle's *Prisons:* Taproots History," *Southern Literary Journal* 17 (Fall 1984): 26–39; "*The Clam Shell*: Mary Lee Settle on East Coast Gentility," *Appalachian Journal* 13 (Winter 1986): 171–83; "Embracing the Common: Mary Lee Settle in World War II," *Appalachian Journal* 12 (Winter 1985): 127–34.

16. Shattuck, 43.
17. Mary Lee Settle, *The Killing Ground* (New York: Bantam, 1983), 52. Subsequent references will appear parenthetically in the text.
18. Shattuck, 43.
19. Ibid.
20. Mary Lee Settle, *The Scopes Trial: The State of Tennessee v. John Thomas Scopes* (New York: Franklin Watts, 1972), 34. Also quoted in Settle's *Prisons*, 46.
21. Shattuck, 43.
22. Mary Lee Settle, *Prisons* (New York: Ballantine, 1981), 45. Subsequent references will appear parenthetically in the text.
23. Dyer, "Mary Lee Settle's *Prisons*," 29.
24. Mary Lee Settle, *O Beulah Land* (New York: Ballantine, 1981), 68. Subsequent references will appear parenthetically in the text.
25. Mary Lee Settle, *Know Nothing* (New York: Ballantine, 1981), 13. Subsequent references will appear parenthetically in the text.
26. The Know-Nothing party, so called because of its clandestine nature, grew in the 1850s in opposition to the political power of immigrant groups. Also called the American party, it became antislavery and flourished in the border states.
27. Baker, 467.
28. Mary Lee Settle, *The Scapegoat* (New York: Ballantine, 1982), 41. Subsequent references will appear parenthetically in the text.
29. Shattuck, 44.
30. Ibid., 46.
31. David Whisnant, *Modernizing the Mountaineer: People, Power, and Planning in Appalachia* (New York: Burt Franklin, 1980), xii.
32. E. L. Doctorow, "Mother Jones Had Some Advice," *New York Times Book Review*, 26 October 1980, 42.
33. Settle, *The Scopes Trial*, 69.
34. Ibid.
35. Ron Eller, *Miners, Millhands, and Mountaineers: Industrialization of the Appalachian South, 1880–1930* (Knoxville: University of Tennessee Press, 1982), xviii.
36. Schafer, 83.
37. Doctorow, 41.
38. William Peden, "Back to Beulah Land," *Saturday Review*, 5 November 1960, 33.
39. Robert Houston, "Blood Sacrifice," *Nation*, 8 November 1980, 471.
40. Roger Shattuck, introduction to *O Beulah Land* (1956; reprint, New York: Ballantine, 1981), xvi.
41. Peden, 33.
42. Houston, 469.
43. T. S. Eliot, "The Uses of Poetry and the Uses of Criticism" (much anthologized).
44. Shattuck, "A Talk with Mary Lee Settle," 44.

45. Houston, 470.
46. Shattuck, "A Talk with Mary Lee Settle," 43.
47. Shattuck, "Introduction," xvi.
48. Shattuck, "A Talk with Mary Lee Settle," 44.
49. Doctorow, 41.
50. Miller, 82.

ELLEN DOUGLAS

1. Unpublished interview with Susan Williams.
2. Jerry Speir, "Of Novels and the Novelist: An Interview with Ellen Douglas," *University of Mississippi Studies in English,* n.s. 5 (1984–87): 231.
3. Williams interview.
4. Ibid.
5. "Ellen Douglas," in *Mississippi Writers Talking,* ed. John Griffin Jones (Jackson: University Press of Mississippi, 1982), vol. 1, 60–61.
6. Page numbers (cited parenthetically in the text) refer to the book under discussion and the edition listed in the bibliography. Citations from Douglas's latest novel are not paginated because the authors worked from a pre-publication typescript.
7. Williams interview.
8. Ibid.
9. Ibid.
10. Ibid.
11. Ibid.
12. To Panthea Broughton, October 1982.
13. Speir, 244.
14. Though the *Times Literary Supplement* did add the title "Scarlet Rage" to Panthea Broughton's review of that novel, apparently assuming that female Southern writers and/or characters may all be identified with Scarlett O'Hara.
15. Speir, 237.
16. *New York Times,* 16 September 1963, 33.
17. Speir, 234.
18. "Not Going Gentle at All," *New York Times Book Review,* 31 October 1982, 11, 34.

ELIZABETH SPENCER

1. John M. Bradbury, *Renaissance in the South: A Critical History of the Literature, 1920–1960* (Chapel Hill: University of North Carolina Press, 1963), 9–10.
2. Charles T. Bunting, " 'In That Time and at That Place,': The Literary

World of Elizabeth Spencer," *Mississippi Quarterly* 28 (Fall 1975): 438, 440; John Griffin Jones, ed., *Mississippi Writers Talking* (Jackson: University Press of Mississippi, 1982), vol. 1, 111; Elizabeth Spencer, "Emerging as a Writer in Faulkner's Mississippi," in *Faulkner and the Southern Renaissance,* ed. Doreen Fowler and Ann J. Abadie (Jackson: University Press of Mississippi, 1982), 131–33. An excellent discussion of the effect of Faulkner on later writers is Louis D. Rubin, Jr., "The Difficulties of Being a Southern Writer Today: Or, Getting out from Under William Faulkner," *Journal of Southern History* 29 (November 1963): 486–94. See also Frederick J. Hoffman, *The Art of Southern Fiction: A Study of Some Modern Novelists* (1945; reprint, Carbondale: Southern Illinois University Press, 1967), chap. 1, which analyzes the tradition of which Faulkner is the leading figure.

3. Stanley J. Kunitz and Vineta Colby, eds., *Twentieth Century Authors, First Supplement: A Biographical Dictionary of Modern Literature* (New York: H.W. Wilson, 1955), 940.

4. James Vinson, ed., *Contemporary Novelists,* 3d ed. (New York: St. Martin's, 1982), 602.

5. Biographical material is drawn from entries on Elizabeth Spencer in *Twentieth Century Authors, First Supplement,* 940–41; *Contemporary Novelists,* 602; and Robert Bain, Joseph M. Flora, and Louis D. Rubin, Jr., eds., *Southern Writers: A Biographical Dictionary* (Baton Rouge: Louisiana State University Press, 1979), 422–23.

6. *Fire in the Morning* (New York: Dodd, Mead, 1948), 33. Subsequent references to this novel will be indicated in parentheses in the essay.

7. At the beginning of *Fire in the Morning,* Spencer states: "In appearance and personality, Daniel Armstrong bears an identical resemblance to my grandfather John Sidney McCain I (1851–1934); but no parallel in the circumstances of their lives has been attempted."

8. F. Scott Fitzgerald, *The Great Gatsby* (New York: Scribners, 1925), 158.

9. The image of fire looking unreal in the daylight, Spencer later noted, symbolizes the situation created when the Gerrards become a leading family in the town that no longer remembers their past crimes. Elizabeth Pell Broadwell and Ronald Wesley Hoag, "A Conversation with Elizabeth Spencer," *Southern Review* 18 (Winter 1982): 119. The connection between Spencer's novel and *Nightwood* is developed in Peggy Whitman Prenshaw's excellent study *Elizabeth Spencer* (Boston: Twayne, 1985), 28–29.

10. As quoted in the epigraph to *This Crooked Way* (New York: Dodd, Mead, 1952). Subsequent references to this novel will be indicated in parentheses in the essay.

11. For instance, see Harvey Swados, "Faithful Disciple?," a review of *This Crooked Way, Nation* 174 (7 June 1952): 561; Anthony West, review in *New Yorker,* 22 March 1952, 117–18.

12. Broadwell and Hoag, 119. For detailed discussion of the ending of *This Crooked Way,* see Prenshaw, 42–46.

13. Jones, 117.
14. *The Voice at the Back Door* (New York: McGraw-Hill, 1956), 26. Subsequent references to this novel will be indicated in parentheses in the essay.
15. Jones, 116.
16. Ibid., 121.
17. *The Stories of Elizabeth Spencer* (Garden City, N.Y.: Doubleday, 1981), 69. Subsequent references to *The Stories* will be indicated in parentheses in the essay.
18. The other Marilee stories are "Sharon" and "Indian Summer." Spencer has called Marilee "a kind of alter ego": "I feel closer to her than to any other character I've created" (Broadwell and Hoag, 113).
19. "The Cousins," *Southern Review* 21 (Spring 1985): 477.
20. The themes of entrapment and escape are also developed in "Ship Island," "A Kiss at the Door," and "I, Maureen." Prenshaw notes the frequency with which Spencer's heroines are defined by the words *closed, enclosed,* and *confined* (68).
21. Henry James, *The Art of the Novel* (New York: Scribners, 1934), 172 (preface to vol. 12 in the New York Edition).
22. Josephine Haley, "An Interview with Elizabeth Spencer," *Notes on Mississippi Writers* 1 (Fall 1968): 53.
23. Elizabeth Janeway, "For Better and Worse," *New York Times Book Review,* 20 November 1960, 6.
24. George Steiner, "Winter of Discontent," *Yale Review* 50 (Spring 1961): 424.
25. James, 159–60.
26. *The Light in the Piazza* (New York: McGraw-Hill, 1960), 67.
27. Bunting, 448.
28. James, 220 (preface to vol. 15).
29. Henry James, "The Art of Fiction," in *Partial Portraits* (London: Macmillan, 1911), 389.
30. *Knights and Dragons* (New York: McGraw-Hill, 1965), 3. Subsequent references to this novel are indicated in parentheses in the essay.
31. Jones, 113.
32. Bunting, 450.
33. Ibid., 450, 452.
34. Jones, 121.
35. Ibid., 122.
36. Bunting, 445, 446.
37. *No Place for an Angel* (New York: McGraw-Hill, 1967), 273. Subsequent references to this novel will be indicated in parentheses in the essay.
38. *The Snare* (New York: McGraw-Hill, 1972), 207. Subsequent references to this novel will be indicated in parentheses in the essay.
39. The importance of Baudelaire as a literary influence and the pervasive imagery from *Les Fleurs du mal* are documented by Prenshaw, 122–26.
40. Broadwell and Hoag, 128.
41. Not included are "Pilgrimage," *Virginia Quarterly Review* 26 (Summer

1950): 293–404; "A Beautiful Day for the Wedding," *Redbook* 119 (September 1962): 48–49, 98–102; "The Atwater Fiancée," *The Montrealer* 37 (September 1963): 24–26; and "The Name of the Game," *McCall's* 99 (September 1972): 94–95, 112, 114, 117–18.

42. See, for instance, reviews by John Fludas in the *Saturday Review,* February 1981, 64; and Margaret Wimsatt in *America,* 11 July 1981, 19.

43. Broadwell and Hoag, 124–25.

44. *The Salt Line* (Garden City, N. Y.: Doubleday, 1984), 38. Subsequent references to this novel will be indicated in parentheses in the essay.

45. Bunting, 458.

46. Ibid., 450.

47. Foreword to *Marilee: Three Stories by Elizabeth Spencer. A Southern Landscape, Sharon, Indian Summer* (Jackson: University Press of Mississippi, 1981), 6.

JOAN WILLIAMS: THE REBELLIOUS HEART

1. The following abbreviations will be used for page citations from Williams's published works: *TMTE—The Morning and the Evening* (New York: Atheneum, 1961); *OPM—Old Powder Man* (New York: Harcourt, Brace & World, 1966); *TW—The Wintering* (New York: Harcourt Brace Jovanovich, 1971); *CW—County Woman* (Boston: Atlantic/Little, Brown, 1982); *P—Pariah* (Boston: Atlantic/Little, Brown, 1983).

2. Anne Goodwyn Jones, *Tomorrow Is Another Day: The Woman Writer in the South, 1859–1936* (Baton Rouge: Louisiana State University Press, 1981), 39–40.

3. Interview with Judith Bryant Wittenberg, 12 August 1983 (hereafter referred to as "Interview").

4. Joan Williams, " 'You-Are-Thereness' in Fiction," *Writer* 80 (April 1967): 20 (reproduces a paragraph of Williams's from this period, which the professor had saved as an example of vivid writing).

5. Interview. Louise Fitzhugh went on to write and publish a number of children's books.

6. Ibid.

7. Ibid.

8. Details of their meeting and subsequent relationship can be found in Joan Williams, "Twenty Will Not Come Again," *Atlantic Monthly* 245 (May 1980): 58–65, and Joseph Blotner, *Faulkner: A Biography* (New York: Random House, 1974), vol. 2, 1291–93.

9. Joseph Blotner, ed. *Selected Letters of William Faulkner,* (New York: Random House, 1977), 297.

10. Ibid., 336–37.

11. Letter of 14 March 1954, in *Faulkner: A Comprehensive Guide to the Brodsky*

Collection, vol. 2, *The Letters* (Jackson: University Press of Mississippi, 1984), 138.

12. Letter of 4 January, probably 1960, in ibid., 269.
13. Letter of 31 December 1951, quoted in Blotner, *Faulkner,* 1406.
14. Interview.
15. Ibid.
16. Undated letter quoted in Blotner, *Faulkner,* 1730–31.
17. Letter, Joan Williams to Judith Bryant Wittenberg, 29 August 1983.
18. Jones, 45.
19. James M. Ethridge and Barbara Kopala, eds., *Contemporary Authors,* 1st rev., vols. 1–4 (Detroit: Gale Research, 1967), 1006.
20. See Joan Williams, "Remembering," *Ironwood* 17 (1981): 105–10, for a memoir of that summer and of Frank Stanford.
21. Robert Scholes, *New York Times Book Review,* 15 May 1966, 40.
22. Williams, " 'You-Are-Thereness' in Fiction," 72–73.
23. Interview.
24. Oates's review appeared in the *Detroit Free Press,* 15 May 1966; Warren's in *Life,* 20 May 1966.
25. Interview.
26. Letter, Williams to Wittenberg, 31 July 1981.
27. Interview.
28. Ibid.
29. Ibid.
30. *Publishers Weekly* 199 (25 January 1971): 260; *Kirkus Reviews* 39 (1 February 1971): 139.
31. Joan Williams, "In Defense of Caroline Compson," in *Critical Essays on William Faulkner: The Compson Family,* ed. Arthur F. Kinney (Boston: G. K. Hall, 1982), 402–7.
32. Interview.
33. Ibid. For a discussion of some of the other difficulties critics face in evaluating Williams's oeuvre, see Judith Bryant Wittenberg, "The Career of Joan Williams: Problems in Assessment," in *Women Writers of the Contemporary South,* ed. Peggy Whitman Prenshaw (Jackson: University Press of Mississippi, 1984), 273–82.
34. Letter, Williams to Wittenberg, 9 September 1987; telephone conversation, Williams and Wittenberg, 13 December 1987.

MAYA ANGELOU: SELF AND A SONG
OF FREEDOM IN THE SOUTHERN TRADITION

1. See Maya Angelou, "Why I Moved Back to the South," *Ebony* 37 (February 1982): 133–34.
2. Ibid., 130. Describing the paradoxical nature of the South, Angelou writes that "the South is an often bitterly beautiful Black race memory."

3. See chapter bibliography for complete publication information. All excerpts from Angelou's primary works are noted in parentheses immediately following the quotations in the text and are identified by the abbreviations given here: *CB—I Know Why the Caged Bird Sings* (New York: Bantam, 1971); *GT—Gather Together in My Name* (New York: Bantam, 1975); *SS—Singin' and Swingin' and Gettin' Merry Like Christmas* (New York: Bantam, 1977); *HW—The Heart of a Woman* (New York: Bantam, 1982); *TS—All God's Children Need Traveling Shoes* (New York: Random House, 1986); *CD—Just Give Me a Cool Drink of Water 'fore I Diiie*, in *Poems* (New York: Bantam, 1981); *MW—Oh Pray My Wings Are Gonna Fit Me Well*, in *Poems* (New York: Bantam, 1981); *IR—And Still I Rise*, in *Poems* (New York: Bantam, 1981); *SW—Shaker, Why Don't You Sing?* (New York: Random House, 1983); *NS—Now Sheba Sings the Song* (New York: Dutton/Dial, 1987).

4. Sidonie A. Smith, "The Song of a Caged Bird: Maya Angelou's Quest after Self-Acceptance," *Southern Humanities Review* 7 (1973): 365–75. Smith reads *Caged Bird* as a quest for "acceptance, for love, and for the resultant feeling of self-worth." Her comments on "displacement" are limited to Angelou's relationship to the "larger black community" and to her "loss of self-worth."

5. Several central articles on *Caged Bird* focus on its interest as a historical or biographical rendition of certain social phenomena, such as racial discrimination in the rural South or economic conditions in the postdepression years. See Liliane K. Arensberg, "Death as Metaphor of Self in *I Know Why the Caged Bird Sings*," *College Language Association Journal* 20 (December 1976): 273–91; John T. Hiers, "Fatalism in Maya Angelou's *I Know Why the Caged Bird Sings*," *Notes on Contemporary Literature* 6, no. 1 (1976): 5–7; Myra K. McMurray, "Role-Playing as Art in Maya Angelou's *Caged Bird*," *South Atlantic Bulletin* 41, no. 2 (1976): 106–11; and George E. Kent, "Maya Angelou's *I Know Why the Caged Bird Sings* and Black Autobiographical Tradition," *Kansas Quarterly* 7, no. 3 (1976): 72–78.

6. Angelou credits both her grandmother and Bailey "with saving [her] life." See Jeffrey M. Elliot, "Author Maya Angelou Raps," *Sepia* 26 (October 1977): 22.

7. Roger Rosenblatt, "Black Autobiography: Life as the Death Weapon," in *Autobiography: Essays Theoretical and Critical*, ed. James Olney (Princeton, N.J.: Princeton University Press, 1980), 175. Rosenblatt comments on the use of both "physical and psychological disguise" as a means for survival by main characters in black autobiography. Angelou's fantasy can be seen as a survival tactic or a type of "psychological disguise," as she illustrates how necessary her fantasy versions of life were to overcoming disappointments and loss.

8. See also Sidonie A. Smith, "Black Womanhood," in *Where I'm Bound: Patterns of Slavery and Freedom in Black American Autobiography* (Westport, Conn.: Greenwood, 1974), 125.

9. In a recorded interview with Bill Moyers shortly after the publication of

Caged Bird, Angelou echoes her mother's philosophy as she speaks about the necessity of defeat in the form of advice to a child: "You might encounter many defeats but you must never be defeated, ever. It might even be necessary to confront defeat. It might be necessary . . . to get over it, all the way through it, and go on."

10. In several interviews, the author describes the "perfect" life of the 1950s housewife: "I thought it would be magnificent if I could be the June Allyson–type—you know, have a big house, a station wagon, and lots of kids. I would stay home, of course, and do the cooking and the cleaning. My husband would have a good job and bring home the money" (Elliot, 23).

11. G. O. Taylor, "Voices from the Veil: Black American Autobiography," *Georgia Review* 35 (Summer 1981): 341–61. Taylor links the "issues of literal and literary survival" in his study of black American autobiography and recognizes the tendency of the black autobiographer to identify "the personal with the race's general condition."

12. Angelou traces the title of her fourth book in the autobiographical series to a poem by Georgia Douglas Johnson. The poem includes these lines: "The heart of a woman goes forth with the dawn, as a lone bird, soft winging, so restlessly on . . . The heart of a woman falls back in the night and enters some alien cage in its plight, and tries to forget it has dreamed of the stars while it breaks, breaks, breaks on the sheltering bars." See Judith Paterson, "Interview: Maya Angelou," *Vogue* 172 (September 1982): 417.

13. On the distortion of history, Angelou comments, "The races who created those sounds and understood their meanings [of Southern place names] have, for the most part, gone down beneath their own fateful earth and are not to be found, in any true aspect, in the pages of history" (*Ebony* 37 (February 1982): 130).

14. The forceful rhythm and uplifting message characteristic of much of her poetry is often reminiscent of gospel songs and spirituals, which Angelou identifies as "the first poetry I ever knew" (Elliot, 23).

15. In an interview, Angelou explains what it takes for the caged bird to sing: "It's necessary, therefore, to be tough enough to bite the bullet as it is shot into one's mouth, to bite it and stop it before it tears a hole in one's throat. One must learn to care for oneself first, so that one can then dare to care for someone else. That's what it takes to make the caged bird sing" (Elliot, 27).

SHIRLEY ANN GRAU'S WISE FICTIONS

1. Quoted by Paul Schlueter, *Shirley Ann Grau* (Boston: Twayne, 1981), 17. Much of this biographical information comes from Schlueter and from the Mary Rohrberger interview with Grau and her husband, "Conversation with Shirley Ann Grau and James K. Feibleman," *Cimarron Review* 43 (April 1978), 35–45.

2. Schlueter, 18.

3. Ibid., 21.
4. Frederick J. Hoffman, *The Art of Southern Fiction: A Study of Some Modern Novelists* (1945; reprint, Carbondale: Southern Illinois University Press, 1967), 9.
5. Ibid., 6, 7.
6. John Stewart, *The Burden of Time: The Fugitives and Agrarians* (Princeton, N.J.: Princeton University Press, 1965), 96.
7. Hoffman, 11.
8. Ibid., 9.
9. Sandra M. Gilbert and Susan Gubar, *The Madwoman in the Attic: The Woman Writer and the Nineteenth Century Literary Imagination* (New Haven, Conn.: Yale University Press, 1979), 73–74 ff.
10. Ellen Glasgow's own progress from the novel of the male protagonist to stories about achieving women is discussed in my *Ellen Glasgow: Beyond Convention* (Austin: University of Texas, 1982). Both Gilbert and Gubar and Elaine Showalter, *A Literature of Their Own* (Princeton, N.J.: Princeton University Press, 1977), are invaluable on these matters. Another definitive analysis has been Ann Pratt, *Archetypal Patterns in Women's Fiction* (Bloomington: Indiana University Press, 1981).
11. Anne Goodwyn Jones, *Tomorrow Is Another Day: The Woman Writer in the South, 1859–1936* (Baton Rouge: Louisiana State University Press, 1981), 44. And see Anne Firor Scott, *The Southern Lady: From Pedestal to Politics, 1830–1930* (Chicago: University of Chicago Press, 1970).
12. Jones, 43. According to Rosemary Daniell, conditions have changed little, even to the present (*Fatal Flowers: On Sin, Sex, and Suicide in the Deep South;* New York: Holt, Rinehart, and Winston, 1980).
13. Tillie Olsen in *Silences* (New York: Delacorte/Seymour Laurence, 1978) enumerates, and mourns, the countless writers who never met their promise—many of them women, and even more of them women with families.
14. Louise Y. Gossett, *Violence in Recent Southern Fiction* (Durham, N.C.: Duke University Press, 1965), 177–86.
15. As Emily Stipes Watts has so accurately said in *The Poetry of American Women from 1632 to 1945* (Austin: University of Texas Press, 1977), even the subject matter of women's art differs immeasurably from that of men. Women tend to write of relationships, of inner worlds, their bodies and senses, their homes and communities (7).
16. Shirley Ann Grau, *The House on Coliseum Street* (New York: Knopf, 1961), 240. Subsequent references cited hereafter in the text.
17. Shirley Ann Grau, *The Hard Blue Sky* (New York: Knopf, 1958), 410–11.
18. Quoted in Don Lee Keith, "A Visit with Shirley Ann Grau," *Contempora* 2, no. 2 (1972): 14.
19. Shirley Ann Grau, *The Keepers of the House* (New York: Knopf, 1964), 3. Subsequent references cited hereafter in the text.
20. Shirley Ann Grau, *The Condor Passes* (New York: Knopf, 1971), 35.
21. Shirley Ann Grau, *Evidence of Love* (New York: Knopf, 1977), 40. Subsequent references cited hereafter in the text.

22. Shirley Ann Grau, *Nine Women* (New York: Knopf, 1985), 5. Subsequent references cited hereafter in the text.

Doris Betts at Mid-Career: Her Voice and Her Art

1. Jonathan Yardley, "The Librarian and the Highwayman," review of *Heading West* by Doris Betts, *Washington Post,* 29 November 1981, 3–4.
2. Evelyn Eaton, "A Fine Debut," review of *The Gentle Insurrection and Other Stories* by Doris Betts, *Saturday Review* 37 (10 July 1954): 14.
3. George Wolfe, "The Unique Voice: Doris Betts," in *Kite-Flying and Other Irrational Acts,* ed. John Carr (Baton Rouge: Louisiana State University Press, 1972), 169.
4. "The Fingerprint of Style" (unpublished paper), The Autonomous Voice: Encounters with Style in Contemporary Fiction, Tenth Alabama Symposium on English and American Literature, University of Alabama, 13–15 October 1983.
5. Wolfe, 158.
6. Rod Cockshutt, "Q & A with Doris Betts," *Tar Heel: A Magazine of North Carolina* 9 (December 1981): 48.
7. William E. Ray, "Doris Betts on the Art and Teaching of Writing," in *Man in 7 Modes,* ed. William E. Ray (Winston-Salem, N.C.: Southern Humanities Conference, 1977), 40.
8. Biographical material in this paragraph and the following paragraphs was provided by Doris Betts in an interview with Dorothy Scura, 23 October 1983.
9. Wolfe, 153–54.
10. Cockshutt, 46.
11. "The Fingerprint of Style."
12. Scura interview, 23 October 1983.
13. Wolfe, 151.
14. Ray, 43.
15. Wolfe, 171–72.
16. Robert Tallant, "The Sad People," review of *The Gentle Insurrection and Other Stories* by Doris Betts, *New York Times Book Review,* 30 May 1954, 4.
17. Riley Hughes, *Catholic World* 179 (August 1954): 392–93.
18. Benedict Kiely, "The Sky and the River and Man," review of *The Astronomer and Other Stories* by Doris Betts, *New York Times Book Review,* 6 February 1966, 4.
19. *Virginia Quarterly Review* 42 (Spring 1966): xlviii.
20. Michael Mewshaw, "Surrealism and Fantasy, review of *Beasts of the Southern Wild, New York Times Book Review,* 28 October 1973, 40.
21. Wolfe, 162.

22. Quotations in this paragraph are from the 23 October 1983 interview with Dorothy Scura.
23. Evelyn Eaton, "A Recognizable South," review of *Tall Houses in Winter* by Doris Betts, *Saturday Review* 40 (27 April 1957): 28.
24. Borden Deal, "Some Things to Do before Dying," review of *Tall Houses in Winter* by Doris Betts, *New York Times Book Review,* 3 March 1957, F-4.
25. New York *Herald Tribune Book Review,* 3 March 1957, 6.
26. Reviews of *The Scarlet Thread* quoted in this paragraph: C. P. Collier, *Best Sellers* 24 (1 March 1965): 464; J. M. Carter, *Library Journal* 90 (1 February 1965): 664; William Peden, "Myth, Magic, and a Touch of Madness," *Saturday Review* 48 (6 February 1965): 32; John C. Coleman, "*The Scarlet Thread,*" in *Survey of Contemporary Literature,* ed. Frank Magill, rev. ed., vol. 10 (Englewood Cliffs, N.J.: Salem, 1977), 6648.
27. Reviews of *The River to Pickle Beach* cited in this paragraph: Jonathan Yardley, *New York Times Book Review,* 21 May 1972, 12; *Choice* 9 (September 1972): 809; William B. Hill, *Best Sellers* 32 (15 June 1972): 143.
28. John Leonard, "Books of the Times," review of *Heading West* by Doris Betts, *New York Times,* 17 December 1981, C-23.
29. Yardley, "The Librarian and the Highwayman," 3–4.
30. Beth Gutcheon, "Willing Victim," review of *Heading West* by Doris Betts, *New York Times Book Review,* 17 January 1982, 12.
31. Information in this paragraph came from "*Souls Raised From the Dead:* A Novel," unpublished paper by Doris Betts, handed out prior to a reading from the manuscript of the novel, A Doris Betts Weekend Seminar, Chapel Hill, North Carolina, 21–22 November 1986.

The Southern Imagination of Sonia Sanchez

1. Sonia Sanchez, *Sister Son/ji,* in *New Plays from the Black Theatre,* ed. Ed Bullins (New York: Bantam, 1969), 104.
2. Sonia Sanchez, "Reflector Interview: Sonia Sanchez," *Reflector* (literary magazine of English Department, Shippensburg University, Shippensburg, Pennsylvania, 1984), 20.
3. Lateifa Hyman, "Multi-dimensional Struggle," *African Woman* 24 (November/December 1979): 18–19.
4. Haki Madhubuti, "Sonia Sanchez: The Bringer of Memories," *Black Women Writers (1950–1980): A Critical Evaluation,* ed. Mari Evans (Garden City, N.Y.: Anchor/Doubleday, 1984), 422.
5. Sonia Sanchez, *Love Poems* (New York: Third Press, 1973), 35. Also in *I've Been a Woman: New and Selected Poems* (Sausalito, Calif.: Black Scholar Press, 1978), 37.
6. *I've Been a Woman,* 39.
7. Ibid., 30.
8. Margaret Walker Alexander, review of *I've Been a Woman: New and Se-*

lected Poems by Sonia Sanchez, *Black Scholar* 11 (January/February 1980): 92.

9. C. Hugh Holman, *The Immoderate Past: The Southern Writer and History* (Athens: University of Georgia Press, 1977), 1.

10. Sonia Sanchez, *A Blues Book for Blue Black Magical Women* (Detroit: Broadside, 1974), 21.

11. George Kent, "Notes on the 1974 Black Literary Scene," *Phylon* 6 (June 1975): 197.

12. Sanchez, *A Blues Book,* 23.

13. Ralph Ellison and James Allan McFerguson, "Indivisible Man," *Atlantic* 226 (December 1970): 59.

14. Sonia Sanchez, interview with Joanne V. Gabbin, at the poet's home in Philadelphia, 13 December 1983.

15. Sonia Sanchez, *Under a Soprano Sky* (Trenton, N.J.: Africa World Press, 1987), 54–55.

16. Ibid., 55.

17. Sanchez, *A Blues Book,* 26–27.

18. Gabbin interview.

19. Sanchez, *A Blues Book,* 28.

20. Anita Cornwell, "Attuned to the Energy: Sonia Sanchez," *Essence* 10 (July 1979): 10.

21. Richard Wright, *Black Boy: A Record of Childhood and Youth* (New York: Harper & Row, 1966), 133.

22. Ladell Payne, *Black Novelists and the Southern Literary Tradition* (Athens: University of Georgia Press, 1981), 66.

23. Gabbin interview.

24. Sonia Sanchez, *homegirls & handgrenades* (New York: Thunder's Mouth Press, 1984), 55–56.

25. Sanchez, *A Blues Book,* 31–32.

26. Ibid., 23.

27. Robert Farris Thompson, *Flash of the Spirit: African and Afro-American Art and Philosophy* (New York: Random House, 1983), 74.

28. Ibid., 79.

29. Cornwell, 10.

30. Enrico Maria Sante Pablo Neruda, *The Poetics of Prophecy* (Ithaca, N.Y.: Cornell University Press, 1982), 15–16.

31. Cornwell, 10.

32. Ruth Limmer and Louise Bogan, *Journey around My Room: The Autobiography of Louise Bogan* (New York: Viking, 1980), xix.

33. Sanchez, *A Blues Book,* 33.

34. Ibid., 37.

35. Sanchez, *I've Been a Woman,* 50.

36. Ibid., 94.

37. Ibid., 95.

38. Ibid., 95.

39. Kenneth Lincoln, *Native American Renaissance* (Berkeley: University of California Press, 1983), 45.

40. Ibid., 44.

41. Sonia Sanchez, "The Poet as a Creator of Social Values," in *Crisis in Culture: Two Speeches by Sonia Sanchez.* (New York: Black Liberation Press, 1983), 1–2.

42. Ibid., 2.

43. Sanchez, *I've Been a Woman,* 97.

44. Joyce Ann Joyce, "The Development of Sonia Sanchez: A Continuing Journey," *Indian Journal of American Studies* 13 (July 1983): 67.

45. Sanchez, *I've Been a Woman,* 99.

46. Ibid.

47. Ibid., 99–101.

48. Sanchez, *homegirls & handgrenades,* 11.

49. Ibid., 71.

50. Ibid., 73–74.

51. Sanchez, *Under a Soprano Sky,* 96.

GAIL GODWIN AND HER NOVELS

1. Gail Godwin, "Becoming a Writer," in *The Writer on Her Work,* ed. Janet Sternburg (New York: Norton, 1980), 231–33.

2. Godwin, "Becoming," 233.

3. Godwin, "Becoming," 233; Gail Godwin to Anne Cheney, letter, 1 July 1985.

4. Gail Godwin to Anne Cheney, telephone interview (Woodstock, N.Y.), 8 January 1984; letter, 1 July 1985.

5. Mary Vespa, "A Vonnegut Protégée (and John Irving Pal) Warms Bad Winter with a Hot and Ambitious Book," *People,* 8 March 1982, 69.

6. The Episcopal Church, especially then, held that divorce constituted breaking a covenant with God. Therefore, unless the bishop decreed otherwise, a second marriage could result in excommunication.

7. Godwin, "Becoming," 232.

8. Godwin, "Becoming," 232.

9. Nancy Brower, "A Celebration of History," *Asheville Citizen-Times,* 8 January 1984, C-1.

10. Sister Kathleen Winters to Anne Cheney, interview (St. Genevieve's, Asheville, N.C.), 14 January 1984.

11. Winters interview.

12. Norma Merchant to Anne Cheney, interview (Asheville, N.C.), 16 January 1984. Mrs. Lawrence Merchant is a modest woman and would not ascribe any of these admirable traits to herself, but they were self-evident to me.

13. Dr. Margaret (Pat) Merchant Verhulst to Anne Cheney, interview (Ashe-

ville, N.C.), 16 January 1984. All subsequent references are to this date unless otherwise noted.

14. Brower, C-1.
15. Winters interview.
16. Godwin interview.
17. Winters interview.
18. Godwin, "Becoming," 237.
19. Winters interview.
20. Verhulst interview, and previous telephone interview, 13 January 1984.
21. Verhulst interview.
22. Godwin, "Becoming," 237; Godwin letter.
23. Mrs. Colene Bonham, deputy for registrar of deeds of Buncombe County, N.C., found the first date in the Vital Statistics Records, 26 January 1984. Mrs. Mary Ellis, church secretary, found the second date in the Parish Registry of St. Mary's Episcopal Church, Asheville, N.C., 19 January 1984.
24. Verhulst interview.
25. Godwin, "Becoming," 238.
26. Mrs. Joan C. Marshall, layreader, checked the Parish Registry on 14 January 1984, to verify that Kathleen Cole transferred her membership to All Souls Parish, Asheville, N.C., on 11 November 1957.
27. Godwin, "Becoming," 240–42.
28. Godwin letter; Godwin, "Becoming," 242–43.
29. Godwin, "Becoming," 244–45; Vespa, 69.
30. Godwin letter.
31. Vespa, 69; Godwin interview.
32. Vespa, 69.
33. Ibid.
34. Verhulst interview.
35. Laurie L. Brown, "Interviews with Seven Contemporary Writers," *Southern Quarterly* 21, no. 4 (Summer 1983): 5.
36. Joyce Carol Oates, review of *The Perfectionists* by Gail Godwin, *New York Times Book Review,* 7 June 1970, 5.
37. Robert Scholes, review of *The Perfectionists* by Gail Godwin, *Saturday Review,* 8 August 1970, 37–38.
38. Scholes, 38.
39. Marilynn J. Smith, "The Role of the South in the Novels of Gail Godwin," *Critique* 21, no. 3 (Summer 1980): 104.
40. Joyce Renwick, "An Interview with Gail Godwin," *Writer* 96, no. 10 (October 1983): 15.
41. Gail Godwin, "Finding the Right Shape for your Story," *Writer,* September 1975, 11.
42. Oates, 5.
43. Review of *The Perfectionists* by Gail Godwin, *Publishers Weekly,* 9 March 1970, 80.
44. Joyce Carol Oates, "Transparent Creature Caught in Myth," in "Book World," *Washington Post,* 1 October 1972, 10.

45. Anatole Broyard, "The Fiction of Freedom," *New York Times,* 21 September 1972, 45.
46. John Alfred Avant, review of *Glass People* by Gail Godwin, *Library Journal* 97 (August 1972): 2643.
47. Review of *Glass People* by Gail Godwin, *New Yorker,* July 1972, 159.
48. Godwin letter.
49. In her fine article, Marilynn J. Smith astutely points out that Godwin hints at the North Carolina setting in *Glass People* (104).
50. Sara Blackburn, review of *Glass People* by Gail Godwin, *New York Times Book Review,* 15 October 1972, 2.
51. Smith correctly notes that "allusions to Thomas Wolfe, the French Broad River, and the mountains . . . suggest Asheville" (105). Unaccountably, Elaine Feinstein ("Which Words," *New Stateman,* 15 August 1975, 204) believes this setting to be Cleveland, Ohio.
52. Doris Betts, "More Like an Onion Than a Map," *Ms.,* March 1975, 41.
53. Lore Dickstein, review of *The Odd Woman* by Gail Godwin, *New York Times Book Review,* 20 October 1974, 4.
54. Review of *The Odd Woman* by Gail Godwin, *New York Review of Books,* 20 February 1975, 35.
55. Feinstein, 204.
56. Diane F. Sadoff, review of *The Odd Woman* by Gail Godwin, *Antioch Review* 33, no. 2 (Summer 1975): 121.
57. Katha Pollitt, "Her Own Woman," *New York Times Book Review,* 21 May 1978, 10.
58. Janet Malcolm, review of *The Odd Woman* by Gail Godwin, *New Yorker,* 18 November 1974, 234.
59. Victoria Glendinning, "Book Learning," *Times Literary Supplement,* 4 July 1975, 732.
60. Larry McMurtry, "Laughs Are Few in Iowa City," in "Book World," *Washington Post,* 21 October 1974, 5.
61. Godwin, "Becoming," 241–42.
62. Godwin telephone interview; Verhulst telephone interview.
63. Smith, 105.
64. John A. Avant, review of *The Odd Woman* by Gail Godwin, *New Republic,* 25 January 1975, 27.
65. Ibid., 26.
66. Review of *The Odd Woman* by Gail Godwin, *Library Journal* 99 (1 November 1974): 2871.
67. Susan Shreve, "Figures of Clay," in "Book World," *Washington Post,* 21 May 1978, E-6.
68. Frances Taliaferro, review of *Violet Clay* by Gail Godwin, *Harper's,* July 1978, 88.
69. John Fludas, review of *Violet Clay* by Gail Godwin, *Saturday Review,* 10 June 1978, 39.
70. Review of *Violet Clay* by Gail Godwin, *Publishers Weekly,* 27 March 1978, 65.

71. Zahir Jamal, "Pressed Men," *New Stateman*, 18 August 1978, 220.
72. Shreve, E-6; Fludas, 39; Zane Kotker, "Holding Pattern," *National Review*, 15 September 1978, 1154.
73. Lorna Sage, review of *Violet Clay* by Gail Godwin, *Times Literary Supplement*, 15 September 1979, 1011.
74. John Leonard, review of *Violet Clay* by Gail Godwin, *New York Times*, 18 May 1978, C-21.
75. Fludas, 39.
76. Smith, 106–7.
77. Godwin's stepfather, Frank Cole, was in the 101st Airborne, but he never went to Europe.
78. Frank Cole entertained Gail's friends at parties in this fashion.
79. Godwin herself believes in dreams and the power of the subconscious. A dream provided the impetus for "Mr. Bedford." See Margaret M. Verhulst, "From Dreams Come Novels: Gail Godwin," *Arts Journal* 7, no. 9 (June 1982): 13, 15.
80. Fludas, 39.
81. Godwin interview.
82. John F. Baker, "Gail Godwin," *Publishers Weekly*, 15 January 1982, 10.
83. Anne Tyler, "All in the Family," *New Republic*, 17 January 1982, 40.
84. Jonathan Yardley, "Gail Godwin: A Novelist at the Height of Her Powers," in "Book World," *Washington Post*, 31 December 1981, 3.
85. Josephine Hendin, "Renovated Lives," *New York Times Book Review*, 10 January 1982, 40.
86. Edmund Fuller, "A Sensitive Novel about Modern Mores," *Wall Street Journal*, 11 January 1982, 26.
87. Laura Geringer, review of *A Mother and Two Daughters* by Gail Godwin, *Saturday Review*, January 1982, 64.
88. Jennifer Uglow, "Out of the Bin, into the Pressure Cooker," *Times Literary Supplement*, 5 March 1982, 246.
89. Arlene Croce, review of *A Mother and Two Daughters* by Gail Godwin, *New Yorker*, 18 January 1982, 129.
90. Tyler, 40; Yardley, 3; Fuller, 26; Uglow, 246; Pat Verhulst, "Forbidden Thoughts & Convincing Nightmares: Gail Godwin's Asheville Novel," *Arts Journal* 7, no. 7 (April 1982): 10.
91. Verhulst, "Forbidden Thoughts," 10.
92. Uglow, 246.
93. Brigette Weeks, "Gail Godwin's Third Novel: The 'Odd Woman' Wises Up," *Ms.*, January 1982, 39.
94. Many people in Asheville believe that this character is based on Leonora Hunt.
95. Yardley, 3.
96. Sybil S. Steinberg, "PW Forecasts," *Publishers Weekly*, 4 December 1981, 41.
97. Yardley, 3.
98. Weeks, 41.

99. Paul Gray, "Deliberate Speed, Stunning Effect," *Time,* 11 February 1985, 87.

100. William H. Pritchard, "Maiden Voyage," *New Republic,* 25 February 1985, 32.

101. Christopher Lehmann-Haupt, review of *The Finishing School* by Gail Godwin, *New York Times,* 24 January 1985, C-23.

102. Frances Taliaferro, " 'Dream Daughter' Grows Up," *New York Times Book Review,* 27 January 1985, 7.

103. Charles Mongahan, "Strong Women and Their Wimpy Men," *Wall Street Journal,* 13 February 1985, 28.

104. Brigette Weeks, "The Treacherous Path of Betrayal," *Ms.,* February 1985, 76.

105. Ibid.

106. Gray, 87; Pritchard, 31; Lehmann-Haupt, C-23.

107. Taliaferro, 7.

108. Gray, 87.

109. Gail Godwin to Jane Pauley, television interview, *Today* (New York, N.Y.), 15 February 1985.

110. Pritchard, 31.

111. Pritchard, 32.

112. Beverly Lowry, "Back Home in Carolina," *New York Times Book Review,* 11 October 1987, 28.

113. Jonathan Yardley, "Gail Godwin: Reflection and Renewal," in "Book World," *Washington Post,* 13 September 1987, 3.

114. Paul Gray, "Polite Forms of Aggression," *Time,* 5 October 1987, 82.

115. Alan Cheuse, review of *A Southern Family* by Gail Godwin, on "All Things Considered," National Public Radio (Washington, D.C.), 27 November 1987.

116. Linda Tylor, "The Scapegoat's Demise," *Times Literary Supplement,* 20–26 November 1987, 1274.

117. Gail Godwin to Jane Pauley, television interview, *Today* (New York, N.Y.), 13 October 1987.

118. Laurie Graeber, "Sticking to the Insoluble," *New York Times Book Review,* 11 October 1987, 28.

119. Susan Bell, "A Talk with Gail Godwin," *Book-of-the-Month Club News,* January 1988, 5.

120. Lowry, 28.

Sylvia Wilkinson:
Passages through a Tarheel Childhood

1. Fred Chappell, "Unpeaceable Kingdoms: The Novels of Sylvia Wilkinson," *Hollins Critic* 8 (April 1961): 1.

2. Sylvia Wilkinson, "Growing Up in America: The South," *Mademoiselle* 68 (April 1969): 300–302.

3. Sylvia Wilkinson, "Three Teachers," in *An Apple for My Teacher* (Chapel Hill, N.C.: Algonquin, 1987), 132–38.

4. Wilma Dykeman, "Taking Life as It Comes," *New York Times Book Review,* 14 August 1966, 26.

5. Review of *Moss on the North Side* by Sylvia Wilkinson, *Booklist,* 1 September 1966, 35.

6. "Land Girl," review of *Moss on the North Side* by Sylvia Wilkinson, *Times Literary Supplement,* 27 July 1967, 659.

7. Dykeman, 26.

8. Review of *Moss on the North Side* by Sylvia Wilkinson, *Best Sellers,* 15 August 1966, 183.

9. Roberta Farr, "Young Women and Fiction," *American Scholar* 36 (Autumn 1967): 680.

10. Review of *A Killing Frost* by Sylvia Wilkinson, *Publishers Weekly,* 3 July 1967, 58.

11. James W. Clark, review of *Cale* by Sylvia Wilkinson, *Carolina Quarterly* 23 (Winter 1971): 73.

12. Review of *Cale* by Sylvia Wilkinson, *Virginia Quarterly Review* 47 (Winter 1971): R-8.

13. Louis D. Rubin, Jr., "Foreword: A New Edition of *Cale,*" *Cale,* 2d ed. (Chapel Hill, N.C.: Algonquin, 1985), x–xi.

14. Review of *Bone of My Bones* by Sylvia Wilkinson, *Publishers Weekly,* 11 December 1981, 50.

15. David Quammen, "The *Bildungsroman* That Didn't Build," Review of *Bone of My Bones* by Sylvia Wilkinson, *New York Times Book Review,* 21 February 1982, 13.

16. Jane Gentry Vance, "Fat Like Mama, Mean Like Daddy: The Fiction of Sylvia Wilkinson," *Southern Literary Journal* 15 (1982): 36.

17. Jonathan Yardley, "Her Aching 'Bones': On Being Young and Female in the Old South," Review of *Bone of My Bones* by Sylvia Wilkinson, *Washington Post,* 10 February 1982, C-9.

ANNE TYLER

1. John Updike, "On Such a Beautiful Green Little Planet," review of *Dinner at the Homesick Restaurant* by Anne Tyler, *New Yorker,* 5 April 1982, 194.

2. Benjamin DeMott, "Funny, Wise, and True," review of *Dinner at the Homesick Restaurant* by Anne Tyler, *New York Times Book Review,* 14 March 1982, 1.

3. Anne Tyler, "Because I Want More Than One Life," *Washington Post,* 15 August 1976, G-7.

4. DeMott, 14.
5. Vivian Gornick, "Anne Tyler's Arrested Development," review of *Dinner at the Homesick Restaurant* by Anne Tyler, *Village Voice,* 30 March 1982, 40–41.
6. Sarah English, "Anne Tyler," in *Dictionary of Literary Biography Yearbook: 1982,* ed. Richard Ziegfield (Detroit: Gale Research, 1983), 194.
7. John Updike, "Family Ways," review of *Searching for Caleb* by Anne Tyler, *New Yorker,* 29 March 1976, 112.
8. Anne Tyler, "Still Just Writing," in *The Writer on Her Work,* ed. Janet Sternburg (New York: Norton, 1980), 15.
9. Roger Sale, review of *Earthly Possessions* by Anne Tyler, *New York Review of Books,* 26 May 1977, 39.

Nikki Giovanni: Place and Sense of Place in Her Poetry

1. Unless otherwise indicated, autobiographical material in this essay is taken from Nikki Giovanni, *Gemini: An Extended Autobiographical Statement on My First Twenty-Five Years of Being a Black Poet* (Indianapolis: Bobbs-Merrill, 1971). Biographical facts come from standard reference works in black literature or from works cited in these notes.
2. Don L. Lee, *Dynamite Voices I: Black Poets of the 1960s* (Detroit: Broadside, 1971), 72–73.
3. Peter Bailey, "Nikki Giovanni: 'I am Black, Female, Polite . . . ,'" *Ebony,* February 1972, 56.
4. Sheila Weller, "To Be a Poet," *Mademoiselle,* December 1969, 159–60.
5. Ruth Rambo McClain, review of *Re:Creation* by Nikki Giovanni, *Black World* 20 (February 1971): 63–64.
6. "The Undaunted Pursuit of Fury," *Time,* 6 April 1970, 100.
7. Martha Duffy, "Hustler and Fabulist," *Time,* 17 January 1972, 63–64.
8. Gwen Mazer, "Lifestyle: Nikki Giovanni," *Harper's Bazaar,* July 1972, 50.
9. Bailey, 49.
10. Ida Lewis, foreword to *My House* by Nikki Giovanni (New York: Morrow, 1972), ix, x, xv.
11. Alex Batman, "Nikki Giovanni," in *Dictionary of Literary Biography,* vol. 5, *American Poets since World War II, Part I: A–K,* ed. Donald J. Greiner (Detroit: Gale Research, 1980), 289.
12. Kalamu ya Salaam, review of *My House* and "Like a Ripple on a Pond" by Nikki Giovanni, *Black World* 23 (July 1974): 70.
13. "The '60s: Over and Out: An Epitaph by 7 Young Survivors," *Mademoiselle,* May 1973, 228.
14. Nikki Giovanni, " 'I learned early that you don't *have* a happy Christ-

mas. . . . You make a happy Christmas,' " *Mademoiselle,* December 1973, 116.

15. Mazer, 50.

16. Jay S. Paul, "Nikki Giovanni," in *Contemporary Poets,* 3d ed., ed. James Vinson (New York: St. Martin's, 1980), 558.

17. Jeanne Noble, *Beautiful, Also, Are the Souls of My Black Sisters: A History of the Black Woman in America* (Englewood Cliffs, N.J.: Prentice Hall, 1978), 197–98.

18. "She Takes Her Poetry to the People," *Africa Woman,* no. 15 (May/June 1978): 25.

19. Paula Giddings, "A Woman of the Seventies," introduction to *Cotton Candy on a Rainy Day* by Nikki Giovanni (New York: Morrow, 1978), 19, 15.

20. Batman, 289.

21. Giddings, 16.

22. Anna T. Robinson, *Nikki Giovanni: From Revolution to Revelation* (Columbus: State Library of Ohio, 1979), 23.

23. Stephanie J. Stokes, " 'My House': Nikki Giovanni," *Essence,* August 1981, 86.

24. Claudia Tate, "Nikki Giovanni" (interview), in *Black Women Writers at Work* (New York: Continuum, 1983), 75.

25. Mozella G. Mitchell, "Nikki Giovanni," in *Dictionary of Literary Biography,* vol. 41, *Afro-American Poets since 1955,* ed. Trudier Harris and Thadious M. Davis (Detroit: Gale Research, 1985), 150.

26. Tate, 67.

27. Quoted in M. Cordell Thompson, "Nikki Giovanni: Black Rebel with Power in Poetry," *Jet,* 25 May 1972, 20.

28. Louis D. Rubin, Jr., "Southern Literature: The Historical Image," in *South: Modern Southern Literature in Its Cultural Setting,* ed. Louis D. Rubin, Jr., and Robert D. Jacobs (Garden City, N.Y.: Doubleday, 1961), 46.

29. George Schuyler, "What the Negro Thinks of the South" (1945), in *Black American Literature: Essays, Poetry, Fiction, Drama,* ed. Darwin Turner (Columbus, Ohio: Charles E. Merrill, 1970), 88.

30. Robert B. Heilman, "The Southern Temper," in *South,* 48–59.

31. Frederick J. Hoffman, "The Sense of Place," in *South,* 60–75.

32. Giovanni, " 'I learned early . . . ,' " 116.

33. Roger Whitlow, *Black American Literature: A Critical History* (Chicago: Nelson Hall, 1973), 179.

34. R. Roderick Palmer, "The Poetry of Three Revolutionists: Don L. Lee, Sonia Sanchez, and Nikki Giovanni," *College Language Association Journal* 15 (September 1971): 36.

35. Suzanne Juhasz, *Naked and Fiery Forms: Modern American Poetry by Women, a New Tradition* (New York: Harper & Row, 1976), 172.

36. Erlene Stetson, introduction to *Black Sister: Poetry by Black American Women, 1746–1980* (Bloomington: Indiana University Press, 1981), xxii.

BLACK, SOUTHERN, WOMANIST:
THE GENIUS OF ALICE WALKER

1. Alice Walker, "Beyond the Peacock: The Reconstruction of Flannery O'Connor," in *In Search of Our Mothers' Gardens: Womanist Prose,* ed. Alice Walker (New York: Harcourt Brace Jovanovich, 1983), 44.
2. Alice Walker, "The Black Writer and the Southern Experience," in *In Search of Our Mothers' Gardens,* 18.
3. Ibid. Walker explains that she has no desire to be a poet writing for the queen of England. She wants to write for her people.
4. Alice Walker, "From an Interview," in *In Search of Our Mothers' Gardens,* 252.
5. Walker, "The Black Writer," 21.
6. Calvin Hernton, "The Black Woman and the Sexual Mountain," *Black American Literature Forum* 18 (Winter 1984): 141.
7. Walker, *In Search of Our Mothers' Gardens,* xi.
8. Ibid., xi–xii.
9. Walker, "From an Interview," 250.
10. Ibid.
11. Alice Walker, *The Third Life of Grange Copeland* (New York: Harcourt Brace Jovanovich, 1970), 13. Subsequent references to this work will appear in the body of the paper.
12. Robbie J. Walker, "The Women in Alice Walker's Novels," *College Language Association Journal* 30 (June 1987): 408.
13. Gloria Wade-Gayles, *No Crystal Stair: Visions of Race and Sex in Black Women's Fiction, 1946 to 1976* (New York: Pilgrim, 1984), 130.
14. Ibid., 134.
15. Claudia Tate, ed., *Black Women Writers at Work* (New York: Continuum, 1983), 178.
16. Walker, *In Search of Our Mothers' Gardens,* xi.
17. Tate, 176.
18. Walker, "From an Interview," 263.
19. Ibid., 251.
20. Alice Walker, "In Search of Our Mothers' Gardens," in *In Search of Our Mothers' Gardens,* 240.
21. Ibid.
22. Alice Walker, "Her Sweet Jerome," in *In Love and Trouble: Stories of Black Women* (New York: Harcourt Brace Jovanovich, 1973), 50.
23. Barbara Christian, "The Country Women of Alice Walker: A Study of Female Protagonists in *In Love and Trouble,*" in *Black Feminist Criticism: Perspectives on Black Women Writers,* ed. Barbara Christian (New York: Pergamon, 1985), 38.
24. Walker, "From an Interview," 263.
25. Walker, "Roselily," in *In Love and Trouble,* 6. Subsequent references to this work will appear in the body of the paper.

26. Walker, "From an Interview," 252.
27. Mary Helen Washington, "An Essay on Alice Walker," in *Sturdy Black Bridges: Visions of Black Women in Literature* (Garden City, N.Y.: Doubleday, 1979), 137.
28. Walker, "From an Interview," 252.
29. Alice Walker, *Once* (New York: Harcourt Brace Jovanovich, 1968), 36. Subsequent references to this work will appear in the body of the paper.
30. Walker, "From an Interview," 267–68.
31. Alice Walker, *Revolutionary Petunias and Other Poems* (New York: Harcourt Brace Jovanovich, 1973), 50. Subsequent references to this work will appear in the body of the text.
32. Alice Walker, *Goodnight Willie Lee, I'll See You in the Morning* (New York: Harcourt Brace Jovanovich, 1979), 23–24.
33. Alice Walker, *Meridian* (New York: Harcourt Brace Jovanovich, 1976), 41. Subsequent references to this text will be given in the body of the paper.
34. Wade-Gayles, 203.
35. Tate, 180.
36. Alice Walker, *You Can't Keep a Good Woman Down* (New York: Harcourt Brace Jovanovich, 1981), 29. Subsequent references to this work will appear in the body of the paper.
37. David Bradley, "Novelist Alice Walker: Telling the Black Woman's Story," *New York Times Magazine,* 8 January 1984, sec. 6.
38. Barbara Christian, "The Black Woman Artist as Wayward," in *Black Women Writers (1950–1980): A Critical Evaluation,* ed. Mari Evans (Garden City, N.Y.: Anchor/Doubleday, 1984), 468.
39. Walker, "In Search of Our Mothers' Gardens," 240.
40. Alice Walker, *The Color Purple* (New York: Harcourt Brace Jovanovich, 1983), 11. Subsequent references to this work will appear in the body of the paper.
41. Cavin Hernton, *The Sexual Mountain and Black Women Writers: Adventures in Sex, Literature and Real Life* (Garden City, N.Y.: Anchor/Doubleday, 1987), 13.
42. Ibid., 19.
43. Tate, 179.
44. Mae Henderson, "*The Color Purple:* Revisions and Redefinitions," *Sage: A Scholarly Journal on Black Women* 2 (Spring 1985), 17.
45. Gloria Steinem, "A Profile of Alice Walker," *Ms.* 10 (June 1982), 90.
46. Loyle Hairston, "Alice in the Mainstream: An Essay Review," *Freedomways* 24 (Winter 1984), 189.
47. Trudier Harris, "On *The Color Purple,* Stereotypes, and Silence," *Black American Literature Forum* 18 (Winter 1984), 160.
48. Alice Walker, "A Letter to the Editor of *Ms.,*" in *In Search of Our Mothers' Gardens,* 275.
49. Walker, *In Search of Our Mothers' Gardens,* xi.

LEE SMITH: THE STORYTELLER'S VOICE

1. Edwin T. Arnold, "An Interview with Lee Smith," *Appalachian Journal* 11 (Spring 1984): 248.
2. Ibid.
3. Ibid., 243.
4. Michelle Lodge, "Lee Smith" *Publishers Weekly* 228 (20 September 1985): 110.
5. Ibid.
6. Arnold, 244–45.
7. Ibid., 246.
8. Ibid., 252.

Bibliography

*

Alexander, Margaret Walker. Review of *I've Been a Woman: New and Selected Poems* by Sonia Sanchez. *Black Scholar* 11 (January/February 1980): 92–93.

Allen, Dexter. "History in the Service of Popular Art." *Commonweal,* 31 August 1956, 545–47.

Anderson, Hilton. "Elizabeth Spencer's Tale of a Mermaid." *Mississippi Folklore Register* 12 (Spring 1978): 32–34.

———. "Elizabeth Spencer's Two Italian Novellas." *Notes on Mississippi Writers* 13 (1981): 18–35.

Arensberg, Liliane K. "Death as Metaphor of Self in *I Know Why the Caged Bird Sings.*" *College Language Association Journal* 20 (December 1976): 273–91.

Arnold, Edwin T. "Talking and Knowing: The Richness of Voices." Review of *Oral History* by Lee Smith. *Washington Book Review* 3 (Fall 1983): 13, 20.

———. "An Interview with Lee Smith." *Appalachian Journal* 11 (Spring 1984): 240–254.

Bailey, Peter. "Nikki Giovanni: 'I Am Black, Female, Polite . . . ,' " *Ebony,* February 1972, 49–56.

Baker, Carlos. "Two American Marriages." Review of *No Place for an Angel* by Elizabeth Spencer. *New York Times Book Review,* 22 October 1967, 8.

Barksdale, Richard. "Margaret Walker: Folk Orature." In *Black American Poets between Worlds, 1940–1960,* ed. R. Baxter Miller, 104–17. Knoxville: University of Tennessee Press, 1986.

Batman, Alex. "Nikki Giovanni." In *Dictionary of Literary Biography.* Vol. 5, *American Poets since World War II, Part I: A–K,* ed. Donald J. Greiner. Detroit: Gale Research, 1980.

Bell, Millicent. "Tobacco Road Updated." Review of *The Tin Can Tree* by Anne Tyler. *New York Times Book Review,* 21 November 1965, 77.

Berland, Alwyn. "The Fiction of Shirley Ann Grau." *Critique* 6, no. 1 (1963): 78–84.

Betts, Doris. "More Like an Onion Than a Map." *Ms.,* March 1975, 41–42.

———. "The Fiction of Anne Tyler." *Southern Quarterly* 31 (Summer 1983): 23–37.

Blackford, Staige D. "Women at War." *Sewanee Review* 90 (Spring 1982): 305–13.

Bloom, Lynn Z. "Heritages: Dimensions of Mother-Daughter Relationships in Women's Autobiographies." In *The Lost Tradition: Mothers and Daugh-*

ters in Literature, ed. Cathy N. Davidson and E. M. Broner, 291–303. New York: Ungar, 1980.

Boucher, Anthony. "Heirs of the Trial-Breakers." *New York Times Book Review,* 24 May 1964, 39.

Bouton, Katherine. Review of *Earthly Possessions* by Anne Tyler. *Ms.,* 6 August 1977, 35–36.

Bradley, David. "Novelist Alice Walker: Telling the Black Woman's Story." *New York Times Magazine,* 8 January 1984, sec. 6.

Brinnin, John Malcolm. "Black and White in Redneck Country." In "Book World," *Washington Post,* 15 May 1983, 10.

Brooks, Mary Ellen. "Anne Tyler." *American Novelists since World War II, Second Series. Dictionary of Literary Biography* 6 (1980): 336–45.

Broughton, Pat Panthea Reid. "Scarlet Rage." Review of *A Lifetime Burning* by Ellen Douglas. *Times Literary Supplement,* 22 July 1983, 791.

Brower, Nancy. "A Celebration of History." *Asheville Citizen-Times,* 8 January 1984, C-1.

Brown, Jerry E. "Southern Fiction Writer Miraculously Arrives." Review of *Cakewalk* and *Black Mountain Breakdown* by Lee Smith. *Birmingham News,* 10 January 1982 (available in *Newsbank*—Literature—February 1982—64:B 4).

Brown, Laurie L. "Interviews with Seven Contemporary Writers." *Southern Quarterly* 21, no. 4 (Summer 1983): 3–22. Reprinted in *Women Writers of the Contemporary South,* ed. Peggy Whitman Prenshaw. Jackson: University Press of Mississippi, 1984.

Brown, Rosellen. "Trapped in the Mines." *The Republic,* 27 December 1980, 37–39.

Broyard, Anatole. "The Fiction of Freedom." *New York Times,* 21 September 1972, 45.

———. "Tyler, Tracy, and Wakefield." Review of *Earthly Possessions* by Anne Tyler. *New York Times Book Review,* 8 May 1977, 12.

Burger, Nash K. "Elizabeth Spencer's Three Mississippi Novels." *South Atlantic Quarterly* 63 (Summer 1964): 351–62.

Busch, Frederick. "Voices of Hoot Owl Holler." Review of *Oral History* by Lee Smith. *New York Times Book Review,* 10 July 1983, 15.

Callahan, John. "The Higher Ground of Alice Walker." *The New Republic,* 14 September 1974, 21–22.

Carter, J. M. Review of *The Scarlet Thread* by Doris Betts. *Library Journal* 90 (1 February 1965): 664.

Chappell, Fred. "Unpeaceable Kingdoms: The Novels of Sylvia Wilkinson." *Hollins Critic* 8 (April 1961): 1–10.

Cheatwood, Kiarri Teule-Hekima. Review of *We Be Word Sorcerers* by Sonia Sanchez. *Black World* 24 (August 1975): 51–52T.

Cheney, Anne. "The Well Mannered Rebels: Gail Godwin and Jesse Hill Ford." *Proceedings of the GRENA Conference.* Aix en Provence, France. Fall 1987, 19–32.

———. "A Hut and Three Houses: Gail Godwin, Carl Jung, and *The Finishing School.*" *Southern Literary Journal* 22, No. 2 (Spring 1989), 64–71.

Cheuse, Alan. Review of *A Southern Family* by Gail Godwin. On "All Things Considered," National Public Radio. Washington, D.C., 27 November 1987.

Christian, Barbara. "Alice Walker: The Black Woman Artist as Wayward." In *Black Women Writers (1950–1980): A Critical Evaluation,* ed. Mari Evans, 457–77. (Garden City, N.Y.: Anchor/Doubleday, 1984.

Clark, James W. Review of *Cale* by Sylvia Wilkinson. *Carolina Quarterly* 23 (Winter 1971): 73.

Clark, Sebastian. "Sonia Sanchez and Her Work." *Black World* 20 (June 1971): 44–48, 96–98.

Cockshutt, Rod. "Q & A with Doris Betts." *Tar Heel: A Magazine of North Carolina* 9 (December 1981): 44–49.

Cole, Hunter McKelva. "Windsor in Spencer and Welty: A Real and an Imaginary Landscape." *Notes on Mississippi Writers* 7 (Spring 1974): 2–11.

Coleman, John C. "*The Scarlet Thread.*" In *Survey of Contemporary Literature,* ed. Frank Magill. Englewood Cliffs, N.J.: Salem, 1977.

Coles, Robert. "Mood and Revelation in the South." *New Republic* 150 (18 April 1964): 17–19.

———. "To Try Men's Souls." *New Yorker* 27 (February 1971): 104–6.

Collier, C. P. Review of *The Scarlet Thread* by Doris Betts. *Best Sellers* 24 (1 March 1965): 464.

Collier, Eugenia. "Fields Watered with Blood: Myth and Ritual in the Poetry of Margaret Walker." In *Black Women Writers (1950–1980): A Critical Evaluation,* ed. Mari Evans, 449–510. Garden City, N.Y.: Anchor/Doubleday, 1984.

Cornwell, Anita. "Attuned to the Energy: Sonia Sanchez." *Essence* 10 (July 1979): 10–11.

Cudjoe, Selwyn R. "Maya Angelou and the Autobiographical Statement." In *Black Women Writers (1950–1980): A Critical Evaluation,* ed. Mari Evans, 6–24. Garden City, N.Y.: Anchor/Doubleday, 1984.

Deal, Borden. "Some Things to Do before Dying." Review of *Tall Houses in Winter* by Doris Betts. *New York Times Book Review,* 3 March 1957, F-4.

Dean, Michael F. "Ellen Douglas's Small Towns: Fictional Anchors." *Southern Quarterly* 11, no. 1 (Fall 1980): 161–71.

Delbanco, Nicholas. Review of *Earthly Possessions* by Anne Tyler. *New Republic,* 28 May 1977, 35–36.

Demetrakopaulos, Stephanie A. "The Metaphysics of Matrilinearism in Women's Autobiography." In *Women's Autobiography: Essays in Criticism,* ed. Estelle C. Jelinek, 180–205. Bloomington: Indiana University Press, 1980.

DeMott, Benjamin. "Funny, Wise, and True." Review of *Dinner at the Homesick Restaurant* by Anne Tyler. *New York Times Book Review,* 14 March 1982, 1, 14.

Disch, Thomas M. "The Great Imposter." Review of *Morgan's Passing* by Anne Tyler. In "Book World," *Washington Post,* 15 March 1980, 5.

Doctorow, E. L. "Mother Jones Had Some Advice." *New York Times Book Review,* 26 October 1980, 1, 40–42.

Donaghue, Denis. "Life Sentence." *New York Review of Books,* 17 (2 December 1971): 28–30.

Doyle, Paul A. "Anne Tyler." In *Contemporary Novelists,* ed. James Vinson, 648–49. 3d ed. New York: St. Martin's, 1982.

Dyer, Joyce Coyne. "Mary Lee Settle's *Prisons:* Taproots History." *Southern Literary Journal* 17 (Fall 1984): 26–39.

———. "Embracing the Common: Mary Lee Settle in World War II." *Appalachian Journal* 12 (Winter 1985): 127–34.

———. "*The Clam Shell:* Mary Lee Settle on East Coast Gentility." *Appalachian Journal* 13 (Winter 1986): 171–83.

Dykeman, Wilma. "Taking Life as It Comes." Review of *Moss on the North Side* by Sylvia Wilkinson. *New York Times Book Review,* 14 August 1966, 26.

Eaton, Evelyn. "A Fine Debut." Review of *The Gentle Insurrection* by Doris Betts. *Saturday Review* 37 (10 July 1954): 14.

———. "A Recognizable South." Review of *Tall Houses in Winter* by Doris Betts. *Saturday Review* 40 (27 April 1957): 28.

Egejura, Phanuel, and Robert Elliot Fox. "An Interview with Margaret Walker." *Callaloo* 2 (1979): 29–35.

Ehle, John. "Home-Style Mayhem." Review of *Family Linen* by Lee Smith. *New York Times Book Review,* 6 October 1985, 15.

English, Sarah. "Anne Tyler." In *Dictionary of Literary Biography Yearbook: 1982,* ed. Richard Ziegfield, 187–94. Detroit: Gale Research, 1983.

Erickson, Peter. " 'Cast Out Alone / to Heal / and Recreate Ourselves': Family Based Identity in the Work of Alice Walker." *College Language Association Journal* 23 (September 1979): 71–94.

Evanier, David. "Song of Baltimore." Review of *Morgan's Passing* by Anne Tyler. *National Review,* 8 August 1980, 972–73.

Evans, Elizabeth. "Negro Characters in the Fiction of Doris Betts." *Critique: Studies in Modern Fiction* 17 (1975): 59–76.

———. "Another Mule in the Yard: Doris Betts' Durable Humor." *Notes on Contemporary Literature* 11 (March 1981): 5–6.

Evans, Mari, ed. *Black Women Writers (1950–1980): A Critical Evaluation.* Garden City, N.Y.: Anchor/Doubleday, 1984.

Evoy, Karen. "Marilee: 'A Permanent Landscape of the Heart.' " *Mississippi Quarterly* 36 (Fall 1983): 569–78.

Farr, Roberta. "Young Women and Fiction." Review of *A Killing Frost* by Sylvia Wilkinson. *American Scholar* 36 (Autumn 1967): 676–80.

Ferguson, Mary Anne. "Doris Betts." *American Women Writers,* ed. Lina Maniero. New York: Ungar, 1979.

Firestone, Bruce M. Review of *Shadow of the Mountain* by Sylvia Wilkinson. *Library Journal,* 15 April 1977, 951.

Fowler, Carolyn. "Solid at the Core." *Freedomways* 14 (First Quarter 1974): 56–62.

Froula, Christine. "The Daughter's Seduction: Sexual Violence and Literary History." *Signs* 11, no. 4 (1986): 621–44.

Fuller, Edmund. "Allegheny Upheaval." *New York Times Book Review,* 3 April 1955, 5.

————. "Feuding Mountain Clans and a Poignant Family Comedy." Review of *Dinner at the Homesick Restaurant* by Anne Tyler. *Wall Street Journal,* 20 April 1982, 30.

Ganim, Carole. "Herself: Woman and Place in Appalachian Literature." *Appalachian Journal* 13 (Spring 1986): 258–74. Discussion of Lee Smith on pp. 271–73.

Gant, L. Review of *We a BadddDDD People* by Sonia Sanchez. *Black World* 2 (April 1971): 84–87.

Gardiner, Elaine, and Catherine Rainwater. "A Bibliography of Writings by Anne Tyler." In *Contemporary American Women Writers: Narrative Strategies,* ed. Catherine Rainwater and William J. Scheick, 142–52. Lexington: University Press of Kentucky, 1985.

Gardiner, Judith K. " 'A Sorrowful Woman': Gail Godwin's Feminist Parable." *Studies in Short Fiction* 12 (Summer 1975): 286–90.

Garrett, George. "Mary Lee Settle's Beulah Land Trilogy." In *Rediscoveries,* ed. David Madden, 171–78. New York: Crown, 1971.

————. "Fables and Fabliaux of Our Times." *Sewanee Review* 85, no. 1 (1977): 104–10.

————. "An Invitation to the Dance: A Few Words on the Art of Mary Lee Settle." *Blue Ridge Review* 1 (1978): 18–24.

Gaston, Karen C. "Beauty and the Beast in Gail Godwin's Glass People." *Critique* 21, no. 2 (1980): 94–102.

Gibson, Donald B., ed. *Modern Black Poets: A Collection of Critical Essays.* Englewood Cliffs, N.J.: Prentice Hall, 1973.

Giddings, Paula. " 'A Shoulder Hunched against a Sharp Concern': Some Themes in the Poetry of Margaret Walker." *Black World* 21 (1971): 20–25.

Gilbert, Sandra. "A Platoon of Poets." *Poetry* 128 (August 1976): 290–99.

Giovanni, Nikki. Review of *We A BadddDDD People* by Sonia Sanchez. *Black World* 2 (September 1971): 88–89.

Godwin, Gail. Review of *Celestial Navigation* by Anne Tyler. *New York Times Book Review,* 28 April 1974, 34–35.

Gornick, Vivian. "Anne Tyler's Arrested Development." Review of *Dinner at the Homesick Restaurant* by Anne Tyler. *Village Voice,* 30 March 1982, 40–41.

Gossett, Louise Y. *Violence in Recent Southern Fiction.* Durham, N.C.: Duke University Press, 1965.

Gottlieb, Annie. "Three Hapless Heroines." Review of *Black Mountain Breakdown* by Lee Smith. *New York Times Book Review,* 29 March 1981, 14–15.

Graeber, Laurie. "Sticking to the Insoluble." *New York Times Book Review,* 11 October 1987, 28.

Graham, John. "Sylvia Wilkinson." Interview in *The Writer's Voice: Conversations with Contemporary Writers,* ed. George Garrett. New York: Morrow, 1973.

Grau, Joseph A., and Paul Schlueter. *Shirley Ann Grau: An Annotated Bibliography*. New York: Garland, 1981.

Gray, Paul. "The Rich Are Different." Review of *Morgan's Passing* by Anne Tyler. *Time*, 17 March 1980, 91.

———. "Deliberate Speed, Stunning Effect." *Time*, 11 February 1985, 87.

———. "Polite Forms of Aggression." *Time*, 5 October 1987, 82.

Grissom, Margaret S. "Shirley Ann Grau: A Checklist." *Bulletin of Bibliography* 28 (July–September 1971): 76–78.

Gutcheon, Beth. "Willing Victim." Review of *Heading West* by Doris Betts. *New York Times Book Review*, 17 January 1982, 12.

Gwin, Minrose. "*Jubilee:* The Black Woman's Celebration of Human Community." In *Conjuring: Black Women's Fiction and Literary Tradition*, ed. Marjorie Pryse and Hortense J. Spillers, 132–49. Bloomington: Indiana University Press, 1985.

Hairston, Loyle. "Alice in the Mainstream: An Essay Review," *Freedomways* 24 (Winter 1984): 183–90.

Hanscom, Marion. Review of *Family Linen* by Lee Smith. *Library Journal* 110 (August 1985): 119.

Harris, Trudier. "Folklore in the Fiction of Alice Walker." *Black American Literature Forum* 2 (Spring 1971): 170–77.

Harrison, Paul C. *The Drama of Nommo: Black Theatre in the African Continuum*. New York: Grove 1972.

Henderson, Stephen Evangelist. *Understanding the New Black Poetry: Black Speech and Black Music as Poetic References*. New York: William Morrow, 1973.

Hernton, Calvin. *The Sexual Mountain and Black Women Writers: Adventures in Sex, Literature and Real Life*. Garden City, N.Y.: Anchor/Doubleday, 1987.

Hicks, Granville. "Seesawing on the Social Ladder." *Saturday Review*, 5 September 1964, 21–22.

———. "Lives Like Assorted Pastries." Review of *No Place for an Angel* by Elizabeth Spencer. *Saturday Review*, 21 October 1967, 29–30.

Hiers, John T. "Fatalism in Maya Angelou's *I Know Why the Caged Bird Sings*." *Notes on Contemporary Literature* 6, no. 1 (1976): 5–7.

Hill, William B. Review of *The River to Pickle Beach* by Doris Betts. *Best Sellers* 32 (15 June 1972): 143.

Hoffman, Eva. "When the Fog Never Lifts." Review of *Morgan's Passing* by Anne Tyler. *Saturday Review*, 15 March 1980, 38–39.

Hoffman, Frederick J. *The Art of Southern Fiction: A Study of Some Modern Novelists*. 1945. Reprint. Carbondale: Southern Illinois University Press, 1967.

Holman, David Marion. "Faith and the Unanswerable Questions: The Fiction of Doris Betts." *Southern Literary Journal* 15 (Fall 1982): 15–22.

Hooks, Bell. *Ain't I a Woman? Black Women and Feminism*. Boston: South End, 1981.

Houston, Robert. "Blood Sacrifice." *Nation*, 8 November 1980, 469–71.

Hughes, Riley. Review of *The Gentle Insurrection* by Doris Betts. *Catholic World* 179 (August 1954): 392–93.

Hull, Gloria. "Black Women Poets from Wheatley to Walker." *Negro American Literature Forum* 9 (1975): 91–96.

Hyman, Lateifa. "Multi-dimensional Struggle." *African Woman* 24 (November/December 1979): 18–19.

Jackson, Angela. Review of *A Blues Book for a Blue Black Magical Woman* by Sonia Sanchez. *Black World* 24 (March 1975): 88–90.

Jackson, Blyden, and Louis Rubin. *Black Poetry in America*. Baton Rouge: Louisiana State University Press, 1974.

Jamal, Zahir. "Pressed Men." *New Statesman,* 18 August 1978, 219–20.

Jefferson, Margo. "Two for the Road." Review of *Earthly Possessions* by Anne Tyler. *Newsweek,* 2 May 1977, 75–76.

Johnson, Diane. "Southern Comfort." Review of *The Accidental Tourist* by Anne Tyler. *New York Review of Books,* 7 November 1985, 15.

Jones, A. Wesley. *"Beasts of the Southern Wild and Other Stories."* In *Survey of Contemporary Literature,* ed. Frank N. Magill. Englewood Cliffs, N.J.: Salem, 1977.

Jones, Anne Goodwyn. *Tomorrow Is Another Day: The Woman Writer in the South, 1859–1936*. Baton Rouge: Louisiana State University Press, 1981.

———. "The World of Lee Smith." *Southern Quarterly* 22, no. 1 (Fall 1983): 115–39.

Jones, John Griffin, ed. *Mississippi Writers Talking*. 2 vols. Jackson: University Press of Mississippi, 1983.

Jones, Madison. "The Snare." *New York Times Book Review,* 17 December 1972, 6.

Joyce, Joyce Ann. "The Development of Sonia Sanchez: A Continuing Journey." *Indian Journal of American Studies* 13 (July 1983): 37–71.

Joyner, Nancy Carol. "Mary Lee Settle's Connections: Class and Clothes in the Beulah Quintet." *The Southern Quarterly* 22 (Fall 1983): 32–45.

Juhasz, Suzanne. *Naked and Fiery Forms: Modern American Poetry by Women, a New Tradition*. New York: Harper & Row, 1976.

Karl, Frederick R. *American Fictions 1940–1980: A Comprehensive History and Critical Evaluation*. New York: Harper & Row, 1983.

Kaufman, Joanne. "Lee Smith: Her People Will Do *Anything*." Review of *Family Linen*. *Wall Street Journal,* 17 October 1985, 26.

Keith, Don Lee. "A Visit with Shirley Ann Grau." *Contempora* 2, no. 2 (1972): 10–14.

Kent, George E. "Struggle for the Image: Selected Books by or About Blacks during 1971." *Phylon* 33 (1972): 304–23.

———. "Maya Angelou's *I Know Why the Caged Bird Sings* and Black Autobiographical Tradition." *Kansas Quarterly* 7, no. 3 (1976): 72–78.

Kersh, Gerald. "A Closing of Old Wounds." Review of *A Killing Frost* by Sylvia Wilkinson. *Saturday Review,* 7 October 1967, 44.

Kiely, Benedict. "The Sky and the River and the Man." Review of *The Astrono-*

mer and Other Stories by Doris Betts. *New York Times Book Review,* 6 February 1966, 4, 8.

Kline, Betsy. "Scaling a Mountain of Emotional Trauma." Review of *Black Mountain Breakdown* by Lee Smith. *Kansas City Star,* 1 February 1981 (available in *Newsbank*—Literature—July 1980–June 1981—79:D 4–5).

Kinsman, Clarke D., ed. "Doris (Waugh) Betts." In *Contemporary Authors.* Detroit: Gale Research, 1975.

Klotman, Phyllis Rauch. " 'Oh Freedom': Women and History in Margaret Walker's *Jubilee.*" *Black American Literature Forum* 11 (1977): 139–45.

"Land Girl." Review of *Moss on the North Side* by Sylvia Wilkinson. *Times Literary Supplement,* 27 July 1967, 659.

Latham, Aaron. "The End of the Beulah Quintet." *New York Times Book Review,* 11 July 1982, 1, 20–21.

Lee, Don L. *Dynamic Voices I: Black Poets of the 1960s.* Detroit: Broadside, 1971.

Lehmann-Haupt, Christopher. "A Small Pebble with a Big Splash." Review of *The Tin Can Tree* by Anne Tyler. *New York Times,* 23 December 1965, L-25.

Leonard, John. "Books of the Times." Review of *Heading West* by Doris Betts. *New York Times,* 17 December 1981, C-23.

Levin, Martin. Review of *A Killing Frost* by Sylvia Wilkinson. *New York Times Book Review,* 12 November 1967, 68.

———. "New and Novel." Review of *Fancy Strut* by Lee Smith. *New York Times Book Review,* 7 October 1973, 47.

Lodge, Michelle. "Lee Smith." *Publishers Weekly* 228 (20 September 1985): 110–11.

Long, John Allan. "New Southern Novel." Review of *If Morning Ever Comes* by Anne Tyler. *Christian Science Monitor,* 21 January 1965, 9.

Lorsche, Susan E. "Gail Godwin's *The Odd Woman:* Literature and the Retreat from Life." *Critique* 20 (Winter 1978): 21–32.

Lowes, Saundra. "Something about This Holler Seems Primordially Familiar." Review of *Oral History* by Lee Smith. *St. Louis Globe-Democrat,* 3–4 September 1983 (available in *Newsbank*—Literature—September 1983—23:C 3).

Lowry, Beverly. "Back Home in Carolina." *New York Times Book Review,* 11 October 1987, 1, 28.

Luneau, Teresa. "Add Lee Smith to Southern Literary Roll." Review of *Oral History.* Little Rock *Arkansas Gazette,* 21 August 1983 (available in *Newsbank*—Literature—September 1983—23:C 1).

McDaniel, Maude. "Don't Ax Why." Review of *Family Linen* by Lee Smith. *Washington Post,* 23 September 1985, C-2.

McDowell, Deborah. "The Self in Bloom: Alice Walker's *Meridian.*" *College Language Association Journal* 24 (March 1981): 272–75.

MacKethan, Lucinda H. "Artists and Beauticians: Balance in Lee Smith's Fiction." *Southern Literary Journal* 15, no. 1 (Fall 1982): 3–14.

McMurray, Myra K. "Role-Playing as Art in Maya Angelou's *Caged Bird.*" *South Atlantic Bulletin* 41, no. 2 (1976): 106–11.

McMurtry, Larry. "Laughs Are Few in Iowa City." In "Book World," *Washington Post,* 21 October 1974, 5.

———. "Life Is a Foreign Country." Review of *The Accidental Tourist* by Anne Tyler. *New York Times Book Review,* 8 September 1985, 1, 36.

Madhubuti, Haki. "Sonia Sanchez: The Bringer of Memories." *Black Women Writers (1950–1980): A Critical Evaluation,* ed. Mari Evans, 419–31. Garden City, N.Y.: Anchor/Doubleday, 1984.

Madden, David. "The Astronomer and Other Stories." In *Survey of Contemporary Literature,* ed. Frank N. Magill, 418–23. Englewood Cliffs, N.J.: Salem, 1977.

Major, Clarence. *The Dark and the Feeling: Black Writers and Their Work.* New York: Third Press, 1974.

Malkoff, Karl. *Crowell's Handbook of Contemporary American Poetry,* 276–77. New York: Thomas J. Crowell, 1973.

Mangione, Jerry. *The Dream and the Deal: The Federal Writer's Project, 1935–1943.* Boston: Little, Brown, 1972.

Manning, Carol S. "Ellen Douglas: Moralist and Realist." *Southern Quarterly* 21, no. 4 (Summer 1943): 116–34.

Mathewson, Joseph. "Taking the Anne Tyler Tour." Review of *The Accidental Tourist* by Anne Tyler. *Horizon,* September 1985, 14.

Mazer, Gwen. "Lifestyle: Nikki Giovanni." *Harper's Bazaar,* July 1972, 50–51.

Mewshaw, Michael. "Surrealism and Fantasy." Review of *Beasts of the Southern Wild and Other Stories* by Doris Betts. *New York Times Book Review,* 28 October 1973, 40–41.

Michaels, Marguerite. "Anne Tyler, Writer 8:05 to 3:30." *New York Times Book Review,* 8 May 1977, 13, 42–43.

Mickelson, Anne Z. *Reaching Out: Sensitivity and Order in Recent American Fiction by Women,* 68–86. Metuchen, N.J.: Scarecrow, 1979.

Miller, R. Baxter. "The 'Etched Flame' of Margaret Walker: Biblical and Literary Re-creation in Southern History." *Tennessee Studies in Literature* 26 (1981): 157–72.

Mitchell, Mozella G. "Nikki Giovanni." In *Dictionary of Literary Biography,* vol. 41, *Afro-American Poets since 1955,* ed. Trudier Harris and Thadious M. Davis. Detroit: Gale Research, 1985.

Mizener, Arthur. "Shadow and Sun." Review of *Knights and Dragons* by Elizabeth Spencer. *New York Times Book Review,* 11 July 1965, 5.

Mojtabai, A. G. "A State of Continual Crisis." Review of *Morgan's Passing* by Anne Tyler. *New York Times Book Review,* 23 March 1980, 14, 33.

Nesanovich, Stella. "The Individual in the Family: A Critical Introduction to the Novels of Anne Tyler." Ph.D. dissertation, Louisiana State University, 1979.

Neubauer, Carol E. "Displacement and Autobiographical Style in Maya Angelou's *The Heart of a Woman.*" *Black American Literature Forum* 17, no. 3 (Fall 1983): 123–29.

Noble, Donald. "The Future of Southern Writing." *A History of Southern Literature,* ed. Louis D. Rubin, Jr. Baton Rouge: Louisiana State University Press, 1986.

Noble, Jeanne. *Beautiful, Also, Are the Souls of My Black Sisters: A History of the Black Woman in America.* Englewood Cliffs, N.J.: Prentice Hall, 1978.

Oates, Joyce Carol. Review of *The Perfectionists* by Gail Godwin. *New York Times Book Review,* 7 June 1970, 5, 51.

———. "Transparent Creature Caught in Myth." In "Book World," *Washington Post,* 1 October 1972, 8, 10.

———. Review of *Dream Children* by Gail Godwin. *Fiction International* 6–7 (1976): 147–48.

O'Hara, J. D. "What Rogue Elephants Know." *Nation* 20 (May 1978): 605–6.

O'Neale, Sondra. "Reconstruction of the Composite Self: New Images of Black Women in Maya Angelou's Continuing Autobiography." In *Black Women Writers (1950–1980): A Critical Evaluation,* ed. Mari Evans, 25–36. Garden City, N.Y.: Anchor/Doubleday, 1984.

Palmer, R. Roderick. "The Poetry of Three Revolutionists: Don L. Lee, Sonia Sanchez, and Nikki Giovanni." *College Language Association Journal* 15 (September 1971): 25–36.

Park, Clara Claiborne. "A Personal Road." *Hudson Review* 34 (Winter 1981–82): 601–5.

Parker-Smith, Bettye. "Alice Walker's Women: In Search of Some Peace of Mind." In *Black Women Writers (1950–1980): A Critical Evaluation,* ed. Mari Evans, 478–93. Garden City, N.Y.: Anchor/Doubleday, 1984.

Paul, Jay S. "Nikki Giovanni." In *Contemporary Poets,* ed. James Vinson. 3d ed. New York: St. Martin's, 1980.

Pearson, Ann. "Shirley Ann Grau: Nature Is the Vision." *Critique* 17, no. 2 (1975): 47–58.

Peden, William. "Back to Beulah Land." *Saturday Review,* 5 November 1960, 33.

———. "Myth, Magic, and a Touch of Madness." Review of *The Scarlet Thread* by Doris Betts. *Saturday Review* 48 (6 February 1965): 32.

Perez Minik, Domingo. "Shirley Ann Grau y los Atridas de Madison City." *Insula* 21, no. 236–37 (1966): 27.

Pipes, Charles D. Review of *A Killing Frost* by Sylvia Wilkinson. *Literary Journal,* August 1967, 2813.

Pollitt, Katha. Review of *Searching for Caleb* by Anne Tyler. *New York Times Book Review,* 18 January 1976, 22.

———. "Southern Stories." Review of *Cakewalk* by Lee Smith. *New York Times Book Review,* 22 November 1981, 14, 24.

Powell, Bertha J. "The Black Experience in Margaret Walker's *Jubilee* and Lorraine Hansberry's *The Drinking Gourd.*" *College Language Association Journal* 21 (1977): 304–11.

Prenshaw, Peggy Whitman. "Elizabeth Spencer." *The History of Southern Literature,* ed. Louis D. Rubin, Jr., 497–500. Baton Rouge: Louisiana State University Press, 1985.

————. *Elizabeth Spencer.* Boston: Twayne, 1985.

Prenshaw, Peggy Whitman, ed. *Women Writers of the Contemporary South.* Jackson: University Press of Mississippi, 1984.

Prescott, Peter S. "Mr. Chameleon." Review of *Morgan's Passing* by Anne Tyler. *Newsweek,* 24 March 1980, 82–85.

————. "Watching Life Go By." Review of *The Accidental Tourist* by Anne Tyler. *Newsweek,* 9 September 1985, 92.

Price, Reynolds. "The Art of American Short Stories." Review of *The Stories of Elizabeth Spencer. New York Times Book Review,* 1 March 1981, 1.

Pritchard, William H. "Maiden Voyage." *The New Republic,* 25 February 1985, 31–32.

Pugh, David G. "*The Voice at the Back Door:* Elizabeth Spencer Looks into Mississippi." In *The Fifties: Fiction, Poetry, and Drama,* ed. Warren French, 103–10. Deland, Fla.: Everett/Edwards, 1970.

Quammen, David. "The *Bildungsroman* That Didn't Build." Review of *Bone of My Bones* by Sylvia Wilkinson. *New York Times Book Review,* 21 February 1982, 13.

Ramsey, Priscilla R. "Transcendence: The Poetry of Maya Angelou." *Current Bibliography on African Affairs* 17, no. 2 (1984–85): 139–53.

Ray, William E. "Doris Betts on the Art and Teaching of Writing." *Man in 7 Modes,* ed. William E. Ray, 40–50. Winston-Salem, N.C.: Southern Humanities Conference, 1977.

Reed, J. D. "Postfeminism: Playing for Keeps." *Time,* 10 January 1983, 46–47.

Reeves, William J. "The Significance of Audience in Black Poetry." *Negro American Literature Forum* 9 (Spring 1975): 30–32.

Renwick, Joyce. "An Interview with Gail Godwin." *Writer* 96, no. 10 (October 1983): 15–17.

Review of *Moss on the North Side* by Sylvia Wilkinson. *Best Sellers,* 15 August 1966, 183.

Review of *Moss on the North Side* by Sylvia Wilkinson. *Booklist,* 1 September 1966, 35.

Review of *A Killing Frost* by Sylvia Wilkinson. *Publishers Weekly,* 3 July 1967, 58–59.

Review of *Cale* by Sylvia Wilkinson. *Virginia Quarterly Review* 47 (Winter 1971): R-8.

Review of *Bone of My Bones* by Sylvia Wilkinson. *Publishers Weekly,* 11 December 1981, 50.

Rhodes, Carolyn. "Gail Godwin and the Ideal of Southern Womanhood." *Women Writers of the Contemporary South,* ed. Peggy Whitman Prenshaw, 55–66. Jackson: University Press of Mississippi, 1984.

Robertson, Mary F. "Anne Tyler: Medusa Points and Contact Points." In *Contemporary American Women Writers: Narrative Strategies,* ed. Catherine Rainwater and William J. Scheick, 119–42. Lexington: University Press of Kentucky, 1985.

Robinson, Anna T. *Nikki Giovanni: From Revolution to Revelation.* Columbus: State Library of Ohio, 1979.

Rohrberger, Mary. " 'So Distinct a Shade': Shirley Ann Grau's Evidence of Love." *Southern Review* 14 (January 1978): 195–98.

———. "Conversation with Shirley Ann Grau and James K. Feibleman." *Cimarron Review* 43 (April 1978): 35–45.

———. "Shirley Ann Grau and the Short Story." In *Women Writers of the Contemporary South,* ed. Peggy Whitman Prenshaw, 83–101. Jackson: University Press of Mississippi, 1984.

Ross, Jean W. "Doris Betts." In *Dictionary of Literary Biography Yearbook: 1982,* ed. Richard Ziegfield. Detroit: Gale Research, 1983.

Ross, Michele. "Barefootin' through Hoot Owl Holler." Review of *Oral History* by Lee Smith. *Atlanta Journal,* 5 June 1983 (available in *Newsbank*—Literature—July 1983—6:B 9).

Rowell, Charles. "Poetry, History and Humanism: An Interview with Margaret Walker." *Black World* 25 (1975): 4–17.

Rubin, Louis D., Jr., and Robert Jacobs, eds. *South: Modern Southern Literature in Its Cultural Setting.* Garden City, N.Y.: Doubleday, 1961.

Sale, Roger. Review of *Earthly Possessions* by Anne Tyler. *New York Review of Books,* 26 May 1977, 39.

Salkey, Andrew. Review of *I've Been a Woman: New and Selected Poems* by Sonia Sanchez. *Black World* 24 (March 1975): 88–90.

Schafer, William J. "Mary Lee Settle's Beulah Quintet: History Darkly, through a Single-Lens Reflex." *Appalachian Journal* 9 (Autumn 1982): 77–86.

Schlueter, Paul. *Shirley Ann Grau.* Boston: Twayne, 1981.

Schmidt, Jan Zlotnik. "The Other: A Study of the Persona in Several Contemporary Women's Autobiographies." *CEA Critic* 43, no. 1 (1980–81): 24–31.

Scoles, Robert. Review of *The Perfectionists* by Gail Godwin. *Saturday Review,* 8 August 1970, 37–38.

Schwartz, Lynn. Review of *Searching for Caleb* by Anne Tyler. *Saturday Review,* 6 March 1976, 28.

Scruggs-Rodgers, Emma. Review of *A Sound Investment* by Sonia Sanchez. *Sepia* 30 (December 1981): 78.

Scura, Dorothy M. "Doris Betts' Nancy Finch: A Heroine for the 1980s." *Southern Quarterly* 22 (Fall 1983): 3–12.

———. "Doris Betts." *Fifty Southern Writers after 1900,* ed. Joseph M. Flora and Robert Bain, 53–63. Westport, Conn.: Greenwood, 1987.

Shattuck, Roger. "A Talk with Mary Lee Settle." *New York Times Book Review,* 26 October 1980, 43–46.

"She Takes Her Poetry to the People," *Africa Woman,* 15 (May/June 1978): 24–25.

Sheppard, R. Z. "Eat and Run." Review of *Dinner at the Homesick Restaurant* by Anne Tyler. *Time,* 5 April 1982, 77–78.

————. "Innocent with an Explanation." Review of *The Accidental Tourist* by Anne Tyler. *Time,* 16 September 1985, 78.

Skelton, Billy. "G'ville Author Ellen Douglas Writes, Reads Consistently." *Clarion-Ledger-Jackson Daily News,* 20 April 1969, A-3.

Skow, John. "This Old House." Review of *Family Linen* by Lee Smith. *Time,* 18 November 1985, 104.

Smith, Barbara. "The Souls of Black Women." *Ms.* 2 (February 1974): 42.

Smith, Marilynn J. "The Role of the South in the Novels of Gail Godwin." *Critique* 21, no. 3 (Summer 1980): 103–10.

Smith, Sidonie A. "The Song of a Caged Bird: Maya Angelou's Quest after Self-Acceptance." *Southern Humanities Review* 7 (1973): 365–75.

Spears, James E. "Black Folk Elements in Margaret Walker's *Jubilee.*" *Mississippi Folklore Register* 14 (1980): 13–19.

Starke, Catherine Juanita. *Black Portraiture in American Fiction: Stock Characters, Archetypes, and Individuals.* New York: Basic Books, 1971.

Steier, Rod. "Lee Smith's Art Reflects Life." Review of *Cakewalk. Hartford Courant,* 15 November 1981 (available in *Newsbank*—Literature—November/December 1981—35:F 11).

Steinem, Gloria. "A Profile of Alice Walker." *Ms.* 10 (June 1982): 35.

Stepto, Robert. "The Phenomenal Woman and the Severed Daughter." *Parnassus: Poetry in Review* 8, no. 1 (1979): 312–20.

Sternburg, Janet. *The Writer on Her Work.* New York: Norton, 1980.

Stetson, Erlene, ed. *Black Sister: Poetry by Black American Women, 1746–1980.* Bloomington: Indiana University Press, 1981.

Stockwell, Joe. *Ellen Douglas.* Jackson: Mississippi Library Commission, 1977.

Stokes, Stephanie J. " 'My House': Nikki Giovanni." *Essence,* August 1981, 84–88.

Stuckey, Sterling. "Through the Prism of Folklore: The Black Ethos in Slavery." *Massachusetts Review* 9 (1968): 417–37.

Sullivan, Walter. "Gifts, Prophecies, and Prestidigitations: Fictional Frameworks, Fictional Modes." Review of *Searching for Caleb* by Anne Tyler. *Sewanee Review* (Winter 1977): 116–22.

Taliaferro, Frances. Review of *Violet Clay* by Gail Godwin. *Harper's,* July 1978, 88.

————. Review of *Oral History* by Lee Smith. *Harper's* 267 (July 1983): 74–75.

————. " 'Dream Daughter' Grows Up." *New York Times Book Review,* 27 January 1985, 7.

Tallant, Robert. "The Sad People." Review of *The Gentle Insurrection* by Doris Betts. *New York Times Book Review,* 30 May 1954, 4.

Taormina, C. A. "On Time with Mary Lee Settle." *Blue Ridge Review* 1 (1978): 8–17.

Tate, Claudia. *Black Women Writers at Work.* New York: Continuum, 1983.

Taylor, Linda. "The Scapegoat's Demise." *Times Literary Supplement,* 20–26 November 1987, 1274.

Thompson, M. Cordell. "Nikki Giovanni: Black Rebel with Power in Poetry." *Jet*, 25 May 1972, 18–24.

Thompson, Robert F. *Flash of the Spirit: African and Afro-American Art and Philosophy*. New York: Random House, 1983.

Traylor, Eleanor W. "Music as Theme: The Blues Mode in the Works of Margaret Walker." In *Black Women Writers (1950–1980): A Critical Evaluation*, ed. Mari Evans, 499–510. Garden City, N.Y.: Anchor/Doubleday, 1984.

———. " 'Bolder Measures Crashing Through': Margaret Walker's Poem of the Century." *Callaloo* 10, no. 4 (1988): 570–95.

Turner, Darwin, ed. *Black American Literature: Essays, Poetry, Fiction, Drama*. Columbus, Ohio: Charles E. Merrill, 1970.

Tyler, Anne. "Mining a Rich Vein." In "Book World," *Washington Post*, 28 September 1980, 1, 13.

Uglow, Jennifer. "Out of the Bin, into the Pressure Cooker." *Times Literary Supplement*, 5 March 1982, 246.

Updike, John. "Family Ways." Review of *Searching for Caleb* by Anne Tyler. *New Yorker*, 29 March 1976, 110–12.

———. "Loosened Roots." Review of *Earthly Possessions* by Anne Tyler. *New Yorker*, 6 June 1977, 130–34.

———. "Imagining Things." Review of *Morgan's Passing* by Anne Tyler. *New Yorker*, 23 June 1980, 97–101.

———. "On Such a Beautiful Green Little Planet." Review of *Dinner at the Homesick Restaurant* by Anne Tyler. *New Yorker*, 5 April 1982, 189–97.

———. "Leaving Home." Review of *The Accidental Tourist* by Anne Tyler. *New Yorker*, 28 October 1985, 130–34.

Vance, Jane Gentry. "An Interview with Sylvia Wilkinson." *The Kentucky Review* 2 (1981): 75–88.

———. "Fat Like Mama, Mean Like Daddy: The Fiction of Sylvia Wilkinson." *Southern Literary Journal* 15 (1982): 22–36.

———. "Sylvia Wilkinson." *Critical Survey of Long Fiction*, ed. Frank N. Magill, 2889–96. Englewood Cliffs, N.J.: Salem, 1983.

———. "Mary Lee Settle's The Beulah Quintet: History Inherited, History Created." *Southern Literary Journal* 17 (Fall 1984): 40–53.

Verhulst, Margaret M. "From Dreams Come Novels: Gail Godwin." *Art Journal* 7, no. 9 (June 1982): 13–16.

Vespa, Mary. "A Vonnegut Protégée (and John Irving Pal) Warms Bad Winter with a Hot and Ambitious Book." *People*, 8 March 1982, 69–70.

Wade-Gayles, Gloria. *No Crystal Stair: Visions of Race and Sex in Black Women's Fiction, 1946–1976*. New York: Pilgrim, 1984.

Walker, Barbara. "Sonia Sanchez Creates Poetry for the Stage." *Black Creation* 5 (Fall 1973): 12–13.

Washington, Mary Helen. "Black Women Image Markers." *Black World* 23, no. 10 (August 1974): 10–18.

Watkins, Floyd C. *The Death of Art: Black and White in the Recent Southern*

Novel, Mercer University Lamar Memorial Lectures, no. 13. Athens: University of Georgia Press, 1970.

Weeks, Brigitte. "Gail Godwin's Third Novel: The 'Odd Woman' Wises Up." *Ms.,* January 1982, 39, 41.

———. "The Treacherous Path of Betrayal." *Ms.,* February 1985, 75–76.

Weeks, Carl Solana. "Gail Godwin." In *Dictionary of Literary Biography: American Novelists since World War II.* 2d series, vol. 6, 105–8. Detroit: Gale Research, 1980.

Weller, Sheila. "To Be a Poet." *Mademoiselle,* December 1969, 126–27, 159–62.

Whitlow, Roger. *Black American Literature: A Critical History.* Chicago: Nelson Hall, 1973.

Whittington, Mary Jane. "Ellen Douglas: An Apostle of Light." *Jackson Magazine,* June 1978, 19.

———. "Gail Godwin: A Novelist at the Height of Her Powers." In "Book World," *Washington Post,* 31 December 1981, 3.

———. "Women Write the Best Books, and Men Are Losing Their Grip on Literature." *Washington Post,* 16 May 1983, B-1.

———. Gail Godwin: Reflection and Renewal. In "Book World," *Washington Post,* 13 September 1987, 3.

Williams, David. "The Poetry of Sonia Sanchez." *Black Women Writers (1950–1980): A Critical Evaluation,* ed. Mari Evans, 433–48. Garden City, N.Y.: Anchor/Doubleday, 1984.

Williams, Deborah. Review of *A Blues Book for the Blue Black Magical Women* by Sonia Sanchez. *Library Journal* 99 (August 1974): 1960.

Wolcott, James. "Some Fun!" Review of *Morgan's Passing* by Anne Tyler. *New York Review of Books,* 3 April 1980, 34–35.

———. "Strange New World." Review of *Dinner at the Homesick Restaurant* by Anne Tyler. *Esquire,* April 1982, 123–24.

Wolfe, George. "The Unique Voice: Doris Betts," in *Kite-Flying and Other Irrational Acts,* ed. John Carr. Baton Rouge: Louisiana State University Press, 1972.

Yardley, Jonathan. Review of *The River to Pickle Beach* by Doris Betts. *New York Times Book Review,* 21 May 1972, 12.

———. "An Essay on Alice Walker." In *Sturdy Black Bridges: Visions of Black Women in Literature,* ed. Roseann Bell et al., 133–49. Garden City, N.Y.: Doubleday, 1979.

———. "A Jaunty Novel of the South." Review of *Black Mountain Breakdown* by Lee Smith. *Washington Star,* 18 January 1981 (available in *Newsbank—Literature*—July 1980–June 1981–64:C 8).

———. "The Librarian and the Highwayman." Review of *Heading West* by Doris Betts. *Washington Post,* 29 November 1981, 3–4.

———. "Her Aching 'Bones': On Being Young and Female in the Old South." Review of *Bone of My Bones* by Sylvia Wilkinson. *Washington Post,* 10 February 1982, C-1, C-9.

Contributors

*

DORIS BETTS received the Medal of Merit for the Short Story from the American Academy of Arts & Letters in 1989. She holds the alumni distinguished professorship in the English department at the University of North Carolina at Chapel Hill. She is the author of four novels and three collections of short stories.

PANTHEA REID BROUGHTON is professor of English at Louisiana State University. She is author of *William Faulkner: The Abstract and the Actual* and editor of *Stratagems for Being: The Art of Walker Percy*. For four years, she wrote the Faulkner chapter for *American Literary Scholarship*. Her review of Ellen Douglas's *A Lifetime Burning* appeared in the *Times Literary Supplement* in 1983. She is currently at work on a book on Virginia Woolf.

HARRIETTE C. BUCHANAN is a member of the Department of Interdisciplinary Studies at Appalachian State University. She has published articles on Southern women in *American Women Writers*, the *Dictionary of Literary Biography: American Poets, 1880–1945*, and *Publications of the Missouri Philological Association*, as well as articles on composition practice. She is currently continuing work on Lee Smith and on John Ehle, another Appalachian writer.

ANNE CHENEY is an associate professor of English at Virginia Polytechnic Institute and State University. She has published *Millay in Greenwich Village* (Alabama, 1975) and *Lorraine Hansberry* (Twayne, 1984). She has completed *The Liberation of Jesse Hill Ford: Selected Letters* and is editing *Imagination in the South* for Bowling Green, an outgrowth of her American Culture Association work. She teaches Southern literature and business writing.

MARTHA COOK is a member of the Department of English at Longwood College in Virginia. She has published essays on a variety of topics in Southern literature, ranging from the Fugitive poets to Flannery O'Connor. In 1987, she taught a course in modern Southern literature as a Fulbright lecturer at the University of Waikato in New Zealand. She served as coeditor of the journal *Resources for American Literary Study* from 1980 to 1986.

JOANNE VEAL GABBIN is professor of English and director of the Honors Program at James Madison University. She is the author of *Sterling A. Brown: Building the Black Aesthetic Tradition* and has published articles on Sterling A.

Brown, Askia M. Toure, Raymond G. Dandridge in the *Dictionary of Literary Biography*.

SUSAN GILBERT is professor of English at Meredith College in Raleigh, North Carolina. She is the author of articles on contemporary women writers Joan Didion, Anne Tyler, and Ruth Prawer Jhabvala.

TONETTE BOND INGE is president of the Delphi International Group, a Washington, D.C.–based organization engaged in international exchange, training, and business development. Her scholarly works include *Ellen Glasgow: A Reference Guide* (G. K. Hall) and articles and essays on Ellen Glasgow and Kate Chopin.

ELSA NETTELS is professor of English at the College of William and Mary. She is the author of *James and Conrad* and *Language, Race, and Social Class in Howells's America*, as well as of a number of articles about American and British fiction. She is currently working on a study of ideas about language and gender in nineteenth-century American literature.

CAROL E. NEUBAUER is a member of the Department of English and Foreign Languages at Bradley University. She has published numerous articles on Maya Angelou and other contemporary minority writers in such scholarly journals as *Black American Literature Forum, The Journal of Modern African Studies, MELUS, World Literature Written in English,* and *The Massachusetts Review.* Currently, she is working on a study of recent Chinese women writers, based on research conducted during her year as a Fulbright scholar in the People's Republic of China.

JOYCE PETTIS is a member of the Department of English at North Carolina State University. She has contributed articles to the *Dictionary of Literary Biography* on poets Margaret Walker and Eugene Redmond and has written book reviews for several publications, among them *Belles Lettres: A Review of Books by Women* and *Signs.* She is criticism editor of *Obsidian II: A Review of Black Literature,* and she is at work on a critical study of Paule Marshall and an edited collection of essays on ethnic women writers.

DOROTHY M. SCURA is head of the English Department at the University of Tennessee at Knoxville. She has published and annotated bibliography of secondary sources, *Henry James, 1960–1974: A Reference Guide,* as well as articles on Southern women writers, among them, Ellen Glasgow and Doris Betts.

JEAN HASKELL SPEER is director of the Appalachian Studies Program at Virginia Polytechnic Institute and State University, Blacksburg. She has published *The Appalachian Photographs of Earl Palmer* (University Press of Kentucky) and numerous articles on cultural performances and cultural politics in Appalachia.

GLORIA WADE-GAYLES is currently associate professor of English at Spelman College. She is author of *No Crystal Stair: Visions of Race and Sex in Black Wom-*

en's Novels, 1946–1976. Other works include numerous poems; a personal narrative; and scholarly articles on the civil rights movements, black women novelists, and nineteenth-century black women journalists. Recipient of a Mellon Research Grant, she is presently engaged in writing a critical study of the fiction of Alice Walker.

LINDA WAGNER-MARTIN holds the Hanes Chair in English and Comparative Literature at the University of North Carolina, Chapel Hill. For many years, she taught at Michigan State, where she edited *The Centennial Review*. Recent books include *Sylvia Plath: A Biography; Ellen Glasgow: Beyond Convention;* and *Anne Sexton: Critical Views*. She has published widely on American modernist writers Ernest Hemingway, William Carlos Williams, John Dos Passos, Joyce Carol Oates, William Faulkner, Denise Levertov, and others.

SUSAN MILLAR WILLIAMS is a member of the English Department at the College of Charleston. She has published several articles and reviews on Southern women writers, most recently in *The Southern Review* and *Tulsa Studies in Women's Literature*. She is currently at work on a biography of Julia Peterkin.

JUDITH BRYANT WITTENBERG is associate professor of English at Simmons College. She has published essays on William Faulkner, Thomas Hardy, and Ellen Glasgow and is the author of *Faulkner: The Transfiguration of Biography*.

ANN M. WOODLIEF is an associate professor of English at Virginia Commonwealth University. She has published articles on Emerson, Thoreau, and science in American popular culture, as well as *In River Time: The Way of the James*.

Index